Modern Manhood and the
Boy Scouts of America

Modern Manhood and the Boy Scouts of America

Citizenship, Race, and the Environment, 1910–1930

Benjamin René Jordan

The University of North Carolina Press *Chapel Hill*

Set in Espinosa Nova and Alegreya Sans by Westchester Publishing Services
Manufactured in the United States of America

The University of North Carolina Press has been a member of the Green Press Initiative
since 2003.

Cover illustrations Front: Boy Scout at the White House, Washington, D.C. (1925);
courtesy of the Library of Congress, Prints and Photographs Division (LC-H234-A-9609).
Back: Parade of 1,500 Boy Scouts in Washington, D.C., at start of Forest Protection
Week (1924); courtesy of the Library of Congress, Prints and Photographs Division
(LC-H234-A-8218).

Library of Congress Cataloging-in-Publication Data
Jordan, Benjamin René, author.
Modern manhood and the Boy Scouts of America : citizenship, race, and the
environment, 1910–1930 / Benjamin René Jordan.
pages cm
Includes bibliographical references and index.
ISBN 978-1-4696-2765-6 (pbk : alk. paper)—ISBN 978-1-4696-2766-3 (ebook)
1. Boy Scouts of America—History. 2. Masculinity—United States—History. I. Title.
HS3313.J67 2016
369.4301'9—dc23
2015033879

Portions of chapter 4 were published as "'Conservation of Boyhood': Boy Scouting's
Modest Manliness and Natural Resource Conservation, 1910–1930." *Environmental History*
(Oct. 2010): 612–42. Used by permission.

For my loving and patient wife, Heather,
and our delightful Jack, Caroline, and Jules

Contents

Figures

Acknowledgments

Considering and articulating the people, places, and experiences that supported the development of this book has been a surprising and meaningful exercise. Growing up in a Jordan family that valued and helped other people enjoy and be able to access books formed the foundation for my love of reading and learning. With my mother, Donna, as a public school reading teacher and my father, René, as a public librarian, my siblings and I embraced books as an essential and joyful part of everyday life. Seth and Matt have maintained the family's official link to university and public libraries, but it is a rare occasion to speak with Chad or my sisters, Carol and Jill, without someone bringing up the latest book he or she has read or is trying to find. The constant presence of books in my childhood, combined with the love and support of my large family, contributed greatly to the desire to add my own book to the library shelf and the lifelong journey of knowledge and perspective that it represents.

College and early work experiences and friendships have been key influences on my intellectual path toward this book. Bard College drew me as an undergraduate with its elegant and accurate slogan, A Place to Think. Its liberal arts distribution requirements and a first and fascinating college history class on the Age of Exploration with Professor Fernando Gonzalez de Leon shifted my allegiance from science to the endlessly fascinating realm of history. The role modeling of my adviser, Mark Lytle, and thesis committee members Genady Shkliarevsky and James Chace helped me realize that I wanted to spend my life teaching people about their past and other cultures. Bard friendships with Rami Cohen, Liz Weiner, Billy Yeskel, Bucky Purdom, and Roger Scotland prompted me to see the college setting and professorial role as ideal means to achieve those goals. In terms of my interest in adolescent and environmental education, years of counseling at Camp Marymount in Fairview, Tennessee, with the inspiring leadership of my brother Matt and friends Brian and Kevin Wyatt, Peter and Beau Smith, Mike Lewis, Frankie Harris, Pat McKenzie, and Pat Shelton first led me to analyze the different ways in which Americans have shaped the character and civic development of young people through the outdoors. Our year of working with James Linkogle, Mike and Amina King, and residential students from over thirty countries at the American International School at Salzburg, Austria, helped me reflect on and critically study the culture in which I was raised. Superb graduate faculty at the University of California, San Diego, including Danny Vickers, Michael Bernstein, Yen Espiritu, Frank Biess, and Rebecca Klatch, broadened my understanding of and approach to history. I especially want to thank my co-advisers, Becky Nicolaides and Rachel Klein, and gender history mentor Rebecca Plant for their wisdom, diligence, and patience as I learned how to think like and be an academic historian. Fellow students Lauren Cole, David Miller, Volker Janssen, Nicholas Rosenthal, Andrew Strathman, Matt Johnson, and Sarah Sanders made the rigors of graduate study invigorating and memorable.

Regarding the period during which I was researching and developing this particular manuscript, Steven Price and the rest of the staff at the extensive Boy Scouts of America National Archive and Museum in Texas; librarians at the nearby Irving Public Library and the University of Tennessee, Knoxville; Christian Brothers University Inter-Library Loan specialist Melissa Verble; and archivists at the Library of Congress and National Archives and Records Administration in Washington, D.C., deserve special praise. I appreciated the encouragement of mentors like Jeff Bowman during my first year of teaching at Kenyon College and Melissa Wilcox in my year as the Johnston Visiting Professor of Gender Studies and Environmental Humanities at Whitman College. The friendship of Christian Brothers University History and Political Science Department colleagues Neal Palmer, Karl Leib, and Marius Carriere; collaboration with fellow Living Learning Community contributors Tracie Burke, Jeff Gross, José Davila, James Allen, Alton Wade, Tim Doyle, and Wilson Phillips; and support of leaders such as Paul Haught and Frank Buscher have made the last six years of teaching in Memphis a rewarding and enjoyable endeavor. Students in my history and interdisciplinary courses have pushed me to better synthesize environmental, gender, and youth dynamics in America's past. Co-panelists and audiences at the American Society for Environmental History and the Society for the History of Childhood and Youth conferences provoked important questions and insights about my research. Noell Wilson, Tammy Proctor, and René and Harriet Jordan have spent many hours reading drafts of this manuscript and offering invaluable critiques and suggestions about both its historical context and my writing style and clarity. The editorial team at the University of North Carolina Press, led by Mark Simpson-Vos, and the sage wisdom and thorough feedback of two anonymous readers greatly sharpened and contextualized my original manuscript. Copyeditor Jamie Thaman, proofreader Barbara Johnson, indexer Robert Swanson, and a timely Professional Development Grant from Christian Brothers University's School of the Arts were immensely helpful in the book's final stages of production. Last but certainly not least, the gracious and enduring support of my wife, Heather; her family members Ken, Nancy, and Adam Cross; and my wonderful children, Jack, Caroline, and Jules, inspired me to finish this manuscript process and share what I have learned with fellow historians and students of interdisciplinary studies, the general public, and Scouting's devoted legions.

Modern Manhood and the
Boy Scouts of America

Introduction

Ax-Men and Typewriter-Men:
The BSA's Full-Orbed Manhood

At first glance, the two halves of the sketch and caption in Figure I.1 might suggest that these two male archetypes present contrasting and incompatible ways of life. The Ax-Man, embodying a preindustrial hand tool, possesses individualistic outdoor skills, such as pioneering, camping, and cooking in the woods. He appears physically fit, confident, and on the move. The Typewriter-Man, taking the form of a modern office machine, specializes in cooperative organization, finance, publicity, and written plans. He looks bloated and passive by comparison. The figures represent work roles and masculine ideals from two different eras in American history: the Ax-Man's pioneering self-reliance conducive to the nineteenth century's self-made family farms and small businesses, and the Typewriter-Man's bureaucratic methods needed for the early twentieth century's large-scale corporations and government agencies. The new century's urbanization and industrialization offered the potential of a more lavish and wonder-filled existence but seemed to threaten the individualistic and self-made qualities that had been fostered by the nineteenth century's emerging capitalist system and expanding western frontier. How to simultaneously hold on to some semblance of traditional American manhood, adapt it to a modern society and workforce, and defeat or co-opt disruptions to their authority thus became a pivotal task for native-born white men in this period.[1]

The two figures shaking hands in this 1926 sketch from the *Scout Executive*, the Boy Scouts of America's magazine for Local Council administrators, captured the partnership between traditional and modern skills and values that formed the basis of the organization's popularity and its new vision of dominant manhood and civic leadership. The accompanying article happily noted that students of the first monthlong national training school for new Local Council Executives, held the previous year, believed that Scouting could and should achieve equilibrium between these two ideals in order to train young men for a changing American society. The author stated that the Typewriter-Men and their modern

Figure I.1 The bureaucrat and the outdoorsman coming to an agreement. "Typewriter vs. Ax," *Scout Executive*, February 1926, 15. (Courtesy of Boy Scouts of America National Scouting Museum Archival Collection)

office milieu emphasized centralized authority, standardized procedures, and scientific analysis. The Ax-Men stressed that individual spontaneity, outdoorsmanship, and working at play were keys to maturing males' success in Scouting and in life. The Ax-Men—represented by charismatic outdoorsmen like Indian-lore advocate and Chief Scout Ernest Thompson Seton, and pioneer-lore enthusiast and National Scout Commissioner Dan Beard—held initial sway when the organization began in 1910 but failed to encompass the balanced masculine model necessary to garner broad public support. The data-driven Typewriter-Men—such as the majority of the Executive Board and the new Executive Secretary it appointed in 1911, James West—made increasing inroads and soon achieved an effective consensus with the Ax-Men and the traditional masculine heritage they represented. This book's primary argument is that the Boy Scouts of America (BSA) articulated and widely promulgated a new male norm that used a structured engagement with nature to meld select Victorian character virtues, such as modest self-control and a diligent work ethic, with the scientific efficiency, corporate loyalty, and expert management skills that white males needed to maintain control of an increasingly urban and corporate-industrial society.

The Scout debate on the ideal model of manhood and authority for modern American men had peaked by the mid-1910s. Arthur Astor Carey (the first director of the BSA's Sea Scout branch for boys over fifteen as well as the great-grandson of powerful western fur merchant John Jacob Astor) presented the BSA national office with a petition signed by some volunteer Scoutmaster troop leaders, teachers, and other concerned men that the organization's increasing bureaucracy and zeal for commercial fund-raising came at the expense of moral training for boys and self-government by local leaders. In a *New York Times* article in December 1915, Seton criticized the Executive Board for allowing a lawyer with no knowledge of boys or the blue sky (West) to take over the BSA. At the same time, it became difficult in the Progressive Era to dismiss the BSA's dramatic membership growth and renowned bureaucratic efficiency, which West and the other Typewriter-Men had helped achieve. West and his supporters made modest gestures toward the antidemocratic criticisms, expelled Seton and his Indian role model (with some help from Beard), and continued to standardize the BSA's administrative machinery. Most Scout literature and programming increasingly emphasized scientific efficiency, expert management, and corporate-like loyalty over martial training and Indian primitivism. However, the volunteer Scoutmaster's ideal of unselfish, democratic service and the appeal of pioneering Ax-Men such as Beard remained essential for energizing the emerging movement. As the sketch in Figure I.1 suggests, the BSA retained a measured dose of outdoorsmanship and masculine heritage to aid the efforts of white boys and men from the cities and towns to adapt to a modernizing society while preserving elements of American men's unique identity.[2]

Boy Scouting's public stature, rapid growth, longevity, and focus on teaching a daily life model of adult behavior and identity to which a widening range of American boys and men ascribed make it an optimal site for studying mainstream manhood in the early twentieth century. The Boy Scouts became one of the largest voluntary organizations in American and world history, serving over 4 million American boys and nearly 1 million American men between 1910 and 1930. In 2008, 185 of the 192 countries of the world operated Boy Scout organizations and tallied over 28 million registered members. One historian estimated that over 300 million boys worldwide had been Scouts by 2002. However, the appeal and influence of Scout manhood extended far beyond its formal membership totals. By the 1930s, some publishing authorities calculated the Boy Scout handbook to be the second best selling English language book in history, behind only the Bible. The BSA drew a remarkable breadth of popular and government support from across the economic, ethnic, and political spectrum for its modern manhood and practical citizenship teachings. Advocates ranging from such elites as the Rockefeller family and Theodore Roosevelt to reformers as varied as Jacob Riis and Eugene Debs expressed their appreciation for Scouting's values. Upper-class, professional, lower middle-class, and working-class men and boys throughout the country joined the organization. Government officials from small town mayors to presidents of the United States accepted honorary BSA positions, gave speeches on the importance of the organization, and orchestrated public Scout ceremonies—some with audiences in the tens of thousands. In 1916, Congress granted the BSA the second-ever federal charter, which Scout leaders used to elicit gifts of money, camping and conservation land, office buildings, training, and transportation from government agencies and private donors across the country. Moreover, the federal charter guaranteed the BSA a monopoly on the term "Scout," which enabled it to eliminate competing boys' organizations and collect royalties from hundreds of corporations making products with the word "Scout" in their names. This book examines the common denominators of Scout character, citizenship, and outdoorsmanship in the 1910s and 1920s that appealed to a wide spectrum of boys and men across the nation as they attempted to adapt to a changing society. In the process, this book tells three intertwined stories: the contested development and teaching of the BSA's popular new masculine and civic ideal through a productive engagement with the outdoors, how boys and volunteer members responded to this core program, and Scout manhood's refinement by applying it to allocate status and privileges to different groups of American males.[3]

Modernization and Scout Manhood

In the early twentieth century, the increasingly corporate-industrial nature of the American economy, children's changing roles in society, the loosening of traditional authority, bids for autonomy by females and racial minorities fostered by the growing cities, and the displacement of partisan and patronage politics by expert-managed government prompted the reconfiguration of white manhood. This particular social environment created a fertile ground for the development of American Boy Scouting, which served as a key arena not only for reformulating men's norms and identities but also for teaching them to boys. The BSA triumphed over competing outdoor youth organizations and emerged as a powerful cultural and political force in the 1910s by offering what its leaders termed a "full-orbed manhood" that simultaneously paid homage to traditional masculine values, reasserted white men's authority, and better prepared both boys and men to maintain their power and privileges in a changing society. Child development experts and education reformers in this era criticized the inability of traditional schooling and privatized family homes to teach boys to engage in corporate-industrial work and practical democratic leadership. Boy Scouting and its nature-based programming offered members an apprenticeship in such modern values and skills to replace the experiences many teenage boys in previous generations had gained through junior career training. BSA troop leaders and other adult supporters became, in turn, (Scout)masters of modern manhood and citizenship.

The independent yeoman homesteader, master craftsman, and free-wheeling small entrepreneur had been fitting norms of white American masculinity and civic leadership in the nineteenth century, when there were still underdeveloped areas on the western frontier and in the country's emerging industrial-capitalist economy. By the early twentieth century, however, corporate industrialization had undercut work satisfaction and the status promised by Victorians' ideal of self-made manhood by transforming holistic production into monotonous, specialized tasks. Large corporate factories and machines increasingly displaced small-scale food and goods production and the corresponding opportunity for a young man to earn the economic and political independence that possessing his own small farm, business, or craft shop entailed. In the 1910s, Frederick Taylor's principles of scientific management and Henry Ford's moving assembly line helped consolidate this transformation from handicraft to automated mass production and finished dislodging the apprenticeship system in which many boys of previous generations had learned men's work skills and community engagement. Advanced industrialization and corporatization created a more stratified workforce into which most young men had to learn to fit themselves without losing status or their sense of personal identity.

Over the course of the 1910s and 1920s, the growing size of cities and some assertions of autonomy by racial minorities, females, and teenagers were disrupting traditional small town and rural bonds and had begun to chip away at native-born, white middle-class and elite men's community leadership. Rapid urbanization—the counterpart to advanced industrialization—seemed to widen the distance between individuals and various social groups. Light-skinned southern and eastern European immigrants and African Americans from the rural South flocked to the burgeoning cities. European immigrants settled in neighborhood enclaves and built their own churches, private schools, and political organizations. Racial segregation forced and enabled African American migrants to establish independent professions, businesses, churches, and cultural forms, such as the jazz and literature of the Harlem Renaissance. The "new woman" began to seep into male spheres outside the home, such as professional work, higher education, and politics. More women pursued college degrees and laid the groundwork for emerging social-work careers in settlement centers like Chicago's Hull House. Building on their efforts to achieve such moral reforms as abolition and temperance, some women's volunteer clubs pushed successfully for a national suffrage amendment in 1920. Following the example of single working-class women, young middle-class and elite flappers would assert women's right to men's leisure spaces and practices in the 1920s. As more teenagers attended high school and then college, the 1920s also witnessed the rise of an independent, coed youth subculture that exacerbated worries about their maturation in a rapidly urbanizing and industrializing society. Aided by automobiles and the expansion of public leisure spaces, older teenagers formulated their own system of status, dress, and custom as they spent more time with their peer group than with their parents. American social critics often expressed concerns about the "new youth," the "new woman," the "new Negro," and "new immigrants" as intertwined modern problems.

America's early twentieth-century political system placed growing emphasis on expert management and efficient analysis. Reformers worked to "clean up" late nineteenth-century politics' pervasive partisanship and expand civil service measures to replace patronage with appointment of government posts by merit-based, standardized exams. Expert committees and city managers increasingly decided on and carried out government policies. New Progressive Era laws, such as the public referendum, recall, initiative, and direct election of senators, assumed the good modern citizen was more knowledgeable, active, and impartial in public affairs.

Together these broad economic, social, and political changes prompted a rearticulation of mainstream manhood in the 1910s and 1920s. Some men did enjoy temporary escapes in leisure forms like rugged sports, western films, and fraternal orders, such as the Freemasons and Odd Fellows, but these pursuits primarily provided outlets from corporate-industrial work and urban living rather than values for maintaining dominance over a modernizing economy and society. Other men pursued a remasculinization of key institutions—such as the church, home, and political sphere—that had been increasingly "feminized" by the late 1800s. While some politicians had ramped up calls for martial training and aggressive expansion in the 1890s, Cubans' resistance to American occupation and the shift toward data-driven, expert-managed government by the early twentieth century made strident militarism appear increasingly outdated if not counterproductive to some Americans. Muscular Christians tried to infuse church practices and the image of Jesus with manly vigor and martial imagery, but it remained difficult to overcome the pervasive presence of women and children in church congregations and the seeming mismatch between spiritual endeavors and the growing American emphasis on scientific expertise and corporate priorities. Some critics issued calls for a new fatherhood movement to reclaim the home; however, its increasing separation from modern work and political governance left many men with little time for or interest in challenging women's primacy in rearing young children and housekeeping.

Of the many early twentieth-century efforts to rearticulate masculine traits and behaviors for a modernizing American society, solving what the era's commentators and theorists called the adolescent "boy problem" garnered one of the broadest ranges of popular and political support. Reformers commonly assumed that most girls would be contained at home with domestic duties and homemaker training under a mother's supervision. However, middle-class and elite men worried that their sons might be feminized by the transformed home, school, and church now dominated by women. Overprotective mothers and female teachers supposedly turned boys into mollycoddles and Little Lord Fauntleroys who were well-mannered but incapable of independent work or men's civic leadership. Schoolboys could escape feminization during their growing leisure time; however, the lack of proper adult supervision made them susceptible to the city's "foreign" elements, heterosocial youth culture, and mass entertainment. Early twentieth-century reformers and child development experts argued that adolescent boys were vulnerable to corruptive influences but were also malleable enough to be saved and guided along the proper path. Companionship with worthy men in structured teaching environments could balance the time boys spent under feminine influences while reinforcing new masculine and civic standards among male leaders and supporters. Such efforts, which became collectively known as "boys' work," offered inexpensive, long-term responses to the effects of modernity on both boys and men.[4]

The first type of solution to the early twentieth-century boy problem took legislative and judicial forms and focused on nonwhite and immigrant working-class boys. Many native-born, white middle-class and elite reformers believed that such boys were innately flawed or that bad parenting and the urban tenement environment led them into juvenile delinquency. Reformers hoped that compulsory schooling (legislated in all states by 1918) and child labor laws would protect such boys from these influences. Labor laws passed in many states decreased the number of children working in factories, mines, and street trades while not significantly interfering with children's rural farm work or teenagers' part-time work in the service industry. Such laws affected middle- and upper-class children less because most of them already attended school for longer periods and did not work full time. New juvenile courts, first established in 1899 in Chicago and spreading to most states by 1925, promised to catch those that fell through the legislative cracks by treating them as children in need of better guidance instead of prosecuting them in adult courts and sending them to adult jails. Juvenile courts, blaming delinquency in part on disrupted adolescent development and poor environment, emphasized moral suasion to correct wayward youth and prevent them from falling into a lifetime of criminality. Judges focused on understanding delinquents' underlying motives for negative behaviors, scrutinizing their parents, and using probationary methods and short-term juvenile confinement.[5]

The child study movement, directed by leading American psychologist Granville Stanley Hall, popularized the theories of adolescence and racial recapitulation as a means of coming to terms with the effects of modernization and providing a scientific solution for its perceived threats to middle- and upper-class white boyhood. The decline of apprenticeship in the wake of advanced industrialization and child labor laws, combined with the rise of compulsory school attendance and other segregated spaces for socializing children, had helped create a new dependent life stage for American boys in their early teens. However, in his influential 1904 book titled *Adolescence: Its Psychology and Its Relations to Physiology, Anthropology, Sociology, Sex, Crime, Religion and Education*, Hall characterized what he termed the adolescent life stage of early puberty as an essential but tumultuous period of change in a child's biological-racial development. He theorized that children recapitulated the racial, character, and political development stages of primitive societies as they aged. Hall argued that inferior races and younger boys were selfish, individualistic, impulsive, intolerant, and chaotic. Advanced races and older boys who successfully recapitulated became altruistic, cooperative, self-controlled, tolerant, and organized. He stated that heredity was the primary force behind a child's development until about age twelve, at which time social and environmental influences came to the fore. According to Hall, adolescent boys in their young teens were particularly susceptible to either good or bad moral influences, so this stage was the key time to draw out good character or it would be lost forever. He argued that boys' primitive phase prompted them to engage in mischief and pranks, so adolescent dependence should be lengthened to allow such natural proclivities to run their course. A corrupt environment or unsavory companions would strand an adolescent boy in childlike selfishness and cruelty, leading him into juvenile delinquency and lifelong criminality. The child study movement advocated that small groups of select adolescent boys should be socialized in isolated natural environments under the leadership of worthy men in order to protect them from harmful urban influences and guide them along the proper developmental path to leading manhood and social responsibility.[6]

Adult-led, voluntary youth organizations drew on Hall's ideas and related theories to support a noncompulsory, recreation-based solution to the boy problem. Starting in the late nineteenth century, the Young Men's Christian Association (YMCA), the Boys' Club, and the Big Brother Movement had attempted to get working-class immigrant boys off the streets and to Americanize them via supervised gymnasiums, playgrounds, libraries, and meetings. YMCA and Fresh Air Fund summer camps isolated poor children from their immigrant parents and street life by placing them under the care of trained youth workers for extended periods of time. In the first decade of the twentieth century, national organizations such as the Woodcraft Indians, the Sons of Daniel Boone, and, especially, the Boy Scouts of America helped expand efforts to protect middle-class and elite boys and develop their positive traits by socializing them outdoors. Boys' work of the early twentieth century downplayed religious conversion and created character-building programs intended to appeal across class and ethnic lines. The Woodcraft Indians and the Sons of Daniel Boone offered independent groups of boys the chance to learn self-reliance by reliving the primitive life of Indians and pioneers, but they provided little in terms of adult male leadership or training for modern living. The Boy Scouts of America quickly emerged as the dominant voluntary organization in the youth and camping field by using adult leadership of regulated troops to teach modern manhood and practical civic leadership.[7]

The teaching methods and physical settings of voluntary youth programs such as the Boy Scouts fit neatly with progressive educators' critiques of rote memorization, stationary desks, and rigid discipline in traditional schools. Child development experts like Hall and John Dewey insisted that children's education should be based on their instinctive interests and need for active involvement in the community. Reformers advocated placing more emphasis on children's guided team play, civic cooperation through group projects, flexible learning environments, and pursuit of individual interests. However, many public schools either ignored these new theories or only partially adopted them through expansion of vocational and physical education. On the other hand, when a BSA national commission surveyed 288 teachers, principals, and college professors from around the nation in 1928, 85 percent replied that Scouting had significantly benefited the development and practice of educational theory. Positive responses cited examples that Scouting helped emphasize learning by doing, provided a new method of vocational guidance through practical play, aroused students' natural curiosities, fostered greater sympathy between pupil and teacher, cultivated appropriate peer-group loyalties, and developed the whole capacity of the boy.[8]

Boy Scouting's instructional methods and vision of modern manhood and practical citizenship enjoyed a broad and expanding spectrum of educational, popular, and political support in the 1910s and 1920s. BSA national leaders promised a universal character and civic training program for boys that would ease growing class and cultural tensions. American Scout officials used nature-based milieus to teach boys and men skills to address daily life concerns, like the modernization of work, successfully navigating urban living, and changing social relations. Boy Scouting merged select Victorian virtues, such as self-reliance and modesty, with the scientific efficiency, expert management, and hierarchical loyalty needed for corporate-industrial work and progressive political leadership. Boy Scouting's balanced, modern manhood also helped white urban and town males maintain superior status relative to females, nonwhite minorities, and rural boys. BSA leaders carefully regulated—but did gradually open—African Americans' and Native Americans' access to Scouting membership and leadership posts. Since many early national administrators argued that the Scout character traits required for civic and social leadership were inherently and exclusively masculine qualities, they tried to eliminate the American Girl Scout organization, established in 1913. Scout administrators and supporters, however, heavily qualified or rejected outright hypermasculine values, such as aggression, unfettered competition, primitivism, instinctive spontaneity, violent sports, and bodybuilding. While BSA sources of the 1920s exhibited a slight drift toward developing a businessman's "pleasing personality," the organization continued to emphasize self-control and a productive work ethic as keys to young men's success in work and in life. BSA leaders insisted that being completely other-directed and focused on superficial consumption was too feminine and dependent to serve as the primary standard of leading manhood and citizenship.

This book uses the BSA as a lens for complicating two key patterns in historians' and gender studies researchers' characterization of dominant American manhood in the early twentieth century. First, most studies of the late nineteenth and early twentieth century have argued that masculinity was in crisis—greatly imperiled by broad forces such as corporate industrialization, urbanization, the closing of the western frontier, rapid immigration, and the feminization of society. Many of these works have defined white manhood in this era as an identity-driven performance that had to be constantly and anxiously exhibited to oneself and to other white men. The emphasis on masculinity as a burdensome, unsatisfying self-performance in recurrent crisis sometimes clouds white middle-class and elite men's successful and enduring use of gender ideology to control the means of power and wealth. This book argues that Boy Scouts of America administrators and supporters effectively adapted Victorian manhood to modernization; the mature organization's masculine and civic norms expressed and ensured its many adherents' superiority and confidence rather than their anxiety.[9]

The BSA's emphasis on full-orbed manhood and practical citizenship contrasts with a second common argument: that most white American men responded to the crises of modernization by rejecting Victorian manhood outright in favor of what has been termed a modern "masculinity" or "passionate manhood." Based in part on colonial and Early Republic masculine ideals of the independent yeoman and master craftsman, Victorians' self-made manhood that represented the dominant American gender standard of the nineteenth century had emphasized such values as a strong work ethic, thrift, punctuality, modesty, self-control, moral rectitude, willpower, and entrepreneurial ambition. According to the prevailing historiographical interpretation, white middle-class and elite men increasingly prized primitive virility, aggressive physicality, sexual prowess, instinctive spontaneity, and defiant individualism by the early twentieth century. Many historians and gender studies researchers have stated that the early BSA exemplified this modern manhood; however, they have mischaracterized Scouting by assuming that Seton's Indian role model or Beard's pioneer hero best represented the mature organization's teachings. This book demonstrates that a striking economic, political, religious, and ethnic range of supporters coalesced on the BSA's new masculine and civic norm that integrated select Victorian virtues with scientific analysis, corporate-style management, and efficient group cooperation.[10]

This book analyzes the national scope and core tenants of Boy Scouts of America gender teachings and practices, covering the organization's origins and expansion in the 1910s as well as its maturation and membership diversification in the 1920s, which solidified its leaders' vision of modern manhood and hierarchical citizenship. Historians have argued that primitivist frontier imagery and overt militarism played central roles in early Boy Scouting in other countries, but most prominent BSA leaders and published teaching materials downplayed such themes in favor of boys learning modern skills and values. Despite occasional exceptions—such as local camping honor societies and race policies, discussed in later chapters—the overall trend toward consistency of local Scout practices across the nation and among different socioeconomic groups helps demonstrate the widespread, mainstream nature of the BSA's masculine and civic norms. Several academic histories of American Girl Scouting and international Boy Scouting and Girl Guiding have found noticeable differences in practices based on local context. Scouting and Guiding in British Africa, for example, demonstrated marked variations in race policies as well as troop sponsorship and points of teaching emphasis—in large part depending on the portion of whites present and the stringency of the race line. Early Canadian Boy Scout practice varied by region, such as the emphasis on literacy and Canadianization in the Prairie Provinces, but also paralleled British Boy Scouting in becoming more structured and professional after World War I. Girl Scout and Guide historians have identified similar patterns of local variation in practices along with increasing leader training and organized camping in the late 1910s and 1920s. The BSA exhibited the trend toward regularization of local practices earlier and more completely than did the American Girl Scouts or international Scout and Guide organizations. Scout officials in other countries critiqued the BSA for its unusual dependence on bureaucracy and standardized programming that sometimes undercut volunteers' charisma and Scoutmasters' initiative. Even British Scout founder Robert Baden-Powell quietly came to criticize "West's Big Office" and his "typewriters and figures" for coming at the expense of American boys and their interests.[11]

This book's two halves explore the early BSA's use of the outdoors to teach modern manhood and practical citizenship; boy and volunteer members' reactions to these values; and the selective incorporation of racial minority, immigrant working-class, and rural farm boys. The four chapters of part 1 examine Boy Scouting's reformulation of American manhood through the program's four core elements in the 1910s and 1920s: the balance between charismatic volunteerism and bureaucratic professionalism that allowed it to best competing boys' organizations, the modern work ethic and social behaviors possessed by men of good character, the nonpartisan but participating responsibilities and corresponding privileges of leading citizens, and a scientific engagement with nature as the prime teaching ground for learning these masculine and civic skills. These chapters also use five large-scale surveys, local Scout council histories, and personal memoirs to examine a cross-section of boy and adult reflections on the character and civic virtues Scouting taught and the value of regular troop meetings and outdoor experiences to members' development and adult lives. Part 2 argues that BSA officials honed their ideology and teaching of modern manhood and leading citizenship through creating differential membership policies and masculine teaching norms for subordinate groups of boys, simultaneously helping white urban males quell or co-opt challenges to their cultural and political power. Chapter 5 illustrates that by assuaging the concerns of labor union leaders and making special recruitment concessions to Polish nationalists and Catholic and Jewish clergy, the BSA administration—made up predominantly of white Anglo-Saxon Protestants—advocated broadening dominant white manhood in the 1910s to allow cooperative working-class males and non-Protestant, southern and eastern European urban immigrants to join the American mainstream. Chapter 6 demonstrates that BSA national leaders partly predicated their modern manhood and practical civic leadership norms on the marginalization of rural males of all ethnicities because they were deemed incapable or unprepared for the scientific, efficient life ways of twentieth-century society. Chapter 7 argues that while some BSA local councils excluded or restricted African American boys' access to Scouting in the 1910s and early 1920s, BSA national officials used a significant grant from the Rockefeller Foundation to successfully encourage southeastern councils to increase the number of African American troops beginning in the late 1920s. An epilogue briefly explores the effects of the Great Depression on Scouting, the growth of troops at Native American boarding schools, the continued debate on the role of "white nationality groups" in the organization, and how this history of early Scouting may shed new light on current BSA membership policies. Collectively, the book's chapters demonstrate how and why the BSA spread quickly and cut across barriers of race, class, religion, and place to create a powerful, mainstream model of modern manhood to which a broad range of boys and men did and continue to aspire.

Part I Adapting Dominant Manhood to Modern America

1

The BSA's Triumph

Balancing Traditional and Modern
Manhood and Authority

At the BSA's first large public event—a September 1910 dinner at New York City's posh Waldorf Astoria Hotel—over two hundred of the country's elite gathered to welcome British Boy Scout founder General Robert Baden-Powell and to receive his official blessing for the American branch. John D. Rockefeller Jr., psychologist G. Stanley Hall, and muckraking editor Jacob Riis agreed with the other philanthropic representatives, bankers, reformers, educators, clergy, and youth organization leaders at the banquet that Boy Scouting offered a highly effective solution to a broad array of boys' and men's concerns resulting from the modernization of society. What has most intrigued historians and gender studies researchers alike about the event is that following BSA Chief Scout Ernest Thompson Seton's introduction of Baden-Powell as the "Father of Scouting," the general diplomatically responded that there were many who deserved credit for originating the Scouting idea—and that he was but one of its uncles. He was alluding to the influence of Seton's Woodcraft Indians and Beard's Sons of Daniel Boone on outdoor programs for boys, but Baden-Powell's organization was notably different. Moreover, in focusing on Baden-Powell's statement and the question of which of these three men was the true originator of the Boy Scout ideal, most researchers have tended to overlook other remarks made at the banquet about the importance of peacetime civic responsibilities and corporate values in the emerging BSA. The expansion of supervisory oversight and bureaucratic processes partly explains the BSA's victory over competing youth organizations such as Beard's and Seton's. The balance between traditional and modern men's authority and values that the BSA's corporate-style administration and teachings helped achieve made an even larger contribution to the organization's rapid growth and popular support. Its efficient bureaucratization aided a tilt from the American heritage of individualistic volunteer men toward twentieth-century society's professional standards and expert management and governance. BSA administrators soon modernized Baden-Powell's character and civic teachings to the point that it can sometimes be more revealing to contrast BSA manhood against that of the British Boy Scouts and, especially, the Woodcraft Indians and Sons of Daniel Boone rather than lump them together, as does the "three uncles" concept.[1]

Despite the military-like uniforms, the association of the term "Scout" with forward military units, and General Baden-Powell's having originated Boy Scouting in London, most BSA officials and local practices would soon come to stress civilian duties and corporate values over primitive virility and military aggression. One of the banquet's most impressive moments came when a letter was read aloud from former president Theodore Roosevelt accepting the honorary vice presidency of the BSA, in which he emphasized that Scouting should primarily teach boys to be good citizens and men for times of peace rather than war. In addition to Baden-Powell having declined that day to review troops from publisher William Randolph Hearst's rival and more militarist American Boy Scout organization, his speech stressed that proper Scouting taught British boys civic service, Life Saving, and doing a Good Turn to others daily. Baden-Powell stated that while British Scouting needed to "put back some of the wild man in the city boys," the BSA should instead teach a balanced program of chivalry, discipline, and helpfulness to American boys, who already had enough of the pioneer spirit in them. Finally, he commented that the BSA's organizers had exhibited more foresight in planning a corporate-like organization than had the movement he led in England. An article in the *New York Times* summed up the speech: "With true American genius, too, he went on, they had organized a combine, a trust, and then had got Col. Theodore Roosevelt to be Vice President of it. 'Upon this trust you can depend.'" While he seemed to be paying the BSA a compliment and may have aimed the remark at the many captains of industry, banking, and commerce present in the Waldorf Astoria's banquet room that evening, the early BSA had already steered away from British Scouting's values and begun to shift toward a corporate makeup and governance.[2]

Focusing on Baden-Powell's remark that he shared credit with Beard and Seton for developing Boy Scouting also obscures the man who would help resolve these core tensions as the lead BSA administrator from 1911 to 1943: child welfare specialist and lawyer James West. While realizing that Beard and Seton were becoming disgruntled with the new direction the organization and its masculine teachings were taking, the Executive Board hired West as the new Executive Secretary to replace the staff on loan from the Young Men's Christian Association and moved the BSA out of its original YMCA home to larger, separate headquarters on Fifth Avenue in January 1911. On the surface, West's hiring seemed to point the organization toward an even greater focus on underprivileged, immigrant urban youth than the YMCA leaders provided. As a crippled orphan who put himself through law school, West embodied a prime example of how poor urban children could be redeemed by education and effort paired with a proactive social welfare system. A key authority on prominent Progressive reform institutions for poor urban youth like the Playground Movement, the juvenile court system, and the National Child Rescue League, West had recently organized the seminal White House Conference on Dependent Children in 1909, which helped shift parentless children's placement from orphanages to foster homes. The BSA, however, did not become another destitute boys' organization. American Scouting increasingly focused on the needs of white middle- and working-class town and urban boys at the expense of rural farm and destitute boys. West helped guide the transformation of the BSA into a centralized bureaucracy that hedged Seton's and Beard's self-reliant primitivism and Baden-Powell's military tone with modern virtues like scientific efficiency, expert management, and loyalty to corporate hierarchy. BSA administrators, partly due to their desire to cleanse the organization from any debt to Seton and his writings, curtailed use of his Indian model in national Scout publications and conferences after 1910. Some local leaders continued to deploy Indian lore in camp rituals and Scout fraternal societies like the Order of the Arrow, but it was clearly not the dominant ideal in the BSA through the 1920s. The change of West's title from Executive Secretary to Chief Scout Executive exemplified his triumph over the ousted Chief Scout Seton and symbolized the BSA's merger of traditional and modern masculine values.[3]

The balance the BSA achieved between self-reliant volunteerism and its emerging administrative apparatus helps account for the organization's widespread popularity and rapid growth. This chapter illustrates how and why the BSA's masculine and civic ideology, leadership structure, and membership focus shifted markedly after the September 1910 Waldorf Astoria banquet. As the BSA emphasized more corporate methods and modern masculine skills, it soon distanced itself from its Woodcraft Indian, Sons of Daniel Boone, British Boy Scout, and YMCA heritage. Moving the BSA beyond the narrow confines of aggressive militarism, primitive pioneer and Indian lore, and denominational leadership to lay claim to providing a universal model of modern American manhood and leading citizenship necessitated such changes. Only then did it triumph over other youth and Scout organizations and garner its broadest popular and governmental support. In the process of exploring these shifts, this chapter explains how the early BSA operated, of what and whom it consisted, and its key advocates. It examines two intertwined masculine and civic debates the BSA helped resolve: charismatic volunteerism versus professional management, and the balance of power between central and local authority. These debates connected with the broader shift from men's self-made individualism of the nineteenth century toward their corporate-like, cooperative hierarchy of the twentieth century.[4]

The BSA's Victory over Competing Scout and Youth Organizations

The BSA's modern manhood and balanced authority responded better to the needs of early twentieth-century American males and differed significantly from the focus on primitive virility in less successful boys' organizations as well as from Boy Scouting's British military origins. Given Baden-Powell's Waldorf Astoria banquet comment that Scouting was partly inspired by Seton and Beard and the fact that these two charismatic men joined the leadership of the BSA, many historians have assumed that the BSA promoted individualism and primitive virility like the Woodcraft Indians and the Sons of Daniel Boone. Other historians read militarism into Baden-Powell's reputation as the British South African "Hero of Mafeking" during the Anglo-Boer War, the Boy Scouts' military-like uniform and name, and the possibility that William Smith's Boys' Brigade youth organization was a model for Boy Scouting. Baden-Powell did borrow selectively from all three organizations in forming British Boy Scouting, but it is essential to understand that Smith's, Seton's, and Beard's organizations failed to attract significant memberships or popular support in America because their masculine ideals and their administrative apparatuses could not help men and boys trying to adapt to a modernizing society and workforce. If Seton or Beard had truly succeeded in fashioning the BSA according to his vision, then the organization would never have flourished to the same degree and history would likely have long since forgotten about it. Moreover, as Baden-Powell himself insisted at the banquet, the BSA became a unique adaptation distinct from his original British Scouting. The BSA soon distanced itself from British Scouting and beat out or absorbed a dozen or more competing Boy Scout organizations in the United States, most of which had quite different interpretations of men's authority and what constituted proper character and civic training for adolescent boys.[5]

Despite having a head start on Scouting, the Boys' Brigade, Woodcraft Indians, and Sons of Daniel Boone never enjoyed a broad range of support or large membership in America because their heroes and masculine skills were too nostalgic and narrow in scope to be useful for daily living in a modern society. In 1883, Scotland's William Smith started the Boys' Brigade using martial regalia and drill to interest boys in church lessons and temperance. Through a series of 1902 articles in the *Ladies Home Journal* and then a full-scale handbook, Seton initiated the decentralized American Woodcraft Indians movement focused on idealized primitive Indian crafts and boys' self-government. Beard's Sons of Daniel Boone organization, developed via ideas from his late nineteenth-century *American Boy's Handy Book* and his 1905 writings for *Recreation Magazine*, heroized the rugged, individualistic outdoor skills of frontier pioneers.

Baden-Powell effectively incorporated elements of each of these existing organizations into his own unique program, which soon proved more attractive to boys and men throughout the British Empire. His 1899 training manual for soldiers, *Aids to Scouting*, contained some of the rudimentary forms and goals of the Boy Scout organization he would develop. The adult manual provided instructions on how patrols of eight soldiers, under the supervision of a trained officer, could learn the outdoor and military skills needed to succeed in the British Empire's scout army. Rejecting the traditional infantry drill employed by the regular army and Smith's Boys' Brigade, Baden-Powell argued that scouting developed self-reliance by encouraging each soldier to take initiative based on his own observations and deductions. To adapt the book for boys, he added stories, games, a moral code, and a system of ranks and topical merit badge honors. Baden-Powell incorporated some of the soldierly dress and ritual of Smith's Boys' Brigade, but he balanced the Brigade's adult authority and strict obedience by dividing the Scout troop into patrols of eight boys. Under the leadership of an elected boy, the British Scout Patrol learned to think and act independently of the troop's adult Scoutmaster. Seton's and Beard's organizational structures, however, were even looser and did not rely on paid staff or even require boy units to have an adult leader. It is likely that neither American organization surpassed twenty thousand active members at any point, and even that is hard to pinpoint, since Seton and Beard did not invest much time or interest in maintaining precise membership rosters or statistics (an idea that BSA administrators would soon come to abhor). Still, Seton's Woodcraft Indians appeared to provide much of the skeletal form and method of Boy Scouting, including the system of ranks and merit awards as well as the notion of a boys' oath and set of organizational laws. Baden-Powell's Boy Scout handbook gestured briefly to "primitive" races, like Seton's Native American heroes and Australian aborigines, but he clearly focused on developing the character attributes of men from the supposedly advanced white races. Baden-Powell also adopted some of the peaceful handicraft and outdoor pioneering emphasis of the Sons of Daniel Boone.[6]

With the 1908 publication of Baden-Powell's Boy Scout handbook and a weekly paper facilitated by the savvy promotional support of publisher Sir Arthur Pearson, the British organization quickly outpaced previous boys' programs and spread rapidly throughout the world. Baden-Powell's small staff could hardly keep up with the flood of requests for membership and more information. One hundred and ten thousand British boys had joined by September 1909, eclipsing membership figures for the other three youth organizations combined. Army officers, educators, and missionaries helped extend Scouting throughout Britain's vast empire. As the handbook and news of the organization reached other countries, boys and youth workers began their own troops and associations. Official national Scout organizations quickly formed in at least twenty-six countries, including such disparate nations as France, Russia, Turkey, Argentina, South Africa, and Japan. People across the world recognized the Scout uniform and the manly character and leading citizenship it represented. However, Scouting in America would soon become much more centralized, modern, and adult led—to the point that it drew criticisms from Scout officials in other countries and from Baden-Powell himself.[7]

In 1908, boys, girls, and interested adults across the United States began forming their own Scout troops based on Baden-Powell's handbook. Despite the prior existence of church-based youth organizations, such as the Boys' Brigade and the Knights of King Arthur, church leaders and Young Men's Christian Association officials helped start or support many of these early Boy Scout troops. A few American units applied for charters from the British office, while others established independent troops or their own Scout associations. Some patrols of boys or girls simply read the handbook and interpreted it for themselves, without the help of adult leaders. This was unsurprising, since Baden-Powell's original handbook encouraged youth to start patrols on their own initiative and suggested that Scouting could also benefit girls.[8]

It took two failed incarnations in its first year before the BSA settled on the modern masculine character, civic teachings, and centralized bureaucratic management that would help it defeat Scouting competitors and become the largest voluntary youth organization in the country's history. Before the Waldorf Astoria banquet in September 1910, the BSA appeared as if it might end up teaching Baden-Powell's militarism or primitive virility and youth self-government via Seton's Indian or a medieval knight role model to rural boys or urban working-class boys. Rural publishing magnate William D. Boyce started and incorporated the BSA in February 1910. Boyce initially planned to use Boy Scouting as a form of welfare capitalism to instill a good work and civic ethic in his army of newsboys in rural districts across the Midwest and to help increase his subscriptions and profits. He hired a former clergyman to promote a decentralized, loosely run BSA along the lines of the British program, but his efforts did not produce tangible results. Boyce soon found himself in a Scout organizing and publicity race against publisher William Randolph Hearst's American Boy Scouts, which emphasized strict military drill and rifle practice. Meanwhile, YMCA officials had started a number of their own Scout troops and used Baden-Powell's methods at some of the four hundred existing YMCA summer camps. Edgar M. Robinson, the head of the YMCA's international Boys' Work division, had been consulting with his friend Ernest Thompson Seton on designing a Scout program with a Native American theme for the urban YMCA. Upon hearing about Boyce's new BSA corporation, they instead decided to team up with him. Boyce was relieved when Robinson approached him in May 1910 to join forces and take the BSA under the wing of the much larger and longer-established Boys' Work and summer camp division. Robinson leaned toward using Seton's Indian hero, while John Alexander (his main BSA assistant brought over from the YMCA) championed a chivalric medieval knight—similar to that of the Knights of King Arthur church organization—as the best role model for adolescent American boys.[9]

Robinson and Alexander opened a one-room BSA headquarters in the YMCA's New York City office, but requests for information and support quickly overwhelmed the small staff. Alexander reportedly lost track of troops, and a number of Scoutmasters resigned. Pioneer lore enthusiast Dan Beard (who had a modest national following as an outdoors writer and an illustrator for such works as Mark Twain's *A Connecticut Yankee in King Arthur's Court*) came aboard, but he and Seton quickly locked horns. Boyce's promised financial support for the organization soon disappeared. The fledgling BSA staff and administrators spent several months trying to recruit additional allies but tellingly failed in their first effort to win a federal charter from the U.S. Congress. Neither rural and working-class boys nor nostalgic Indian and knight role models remained the focus of the rapidly evolving BSA.[10]

The September 1910 Waldorf Astoria banquet, capped by Theodore Roosevelt's letter of support and Baden-Powell's blessing, marked a significant turning point in the BSA's fortunes. Administrators began recruiting a broader base of support and leadership, but only by making marked changes in its program, masculine ideology, and target membership. Over two hundred prominent men at the banquet pledged the support of the thirty-seven institutions they represented. Influential American politicians, reformers, clergy, educators, and child development theorists soon lined up behind the shifting BSA. Leading businessmen and politicians provided essential public marketing and money, which helped enable the BSA to establish a virtual monopoly on American Scouting. Some of the country's wealthiest families (such as the Rockefellers, the Vanderbilts, the Carnegies, and the Sages) made large financial contributions, especially during the BSA's formative period. The substantial and ongoing public relations support and privileges that government and military officials at all levels gave to the BSA—highlighted by the 1916 federal charter from Congress and the U.S. presidents serving actively as honorary BSA presidents—would be another key factor in its success.[11]

As it evolved, the BSA corporation absorbed or eliminated independent Scout troops and a slew of narrowly focused, rival American Scout associations that had formed between 1908 and 1912: Peace Scouts of California; Salvation Army Scouts; Polish National Alliance Scouts; Rhode Island Boy Scouts; Colonel Peter Bomus's Boys' Brigade-like Boy Scouts of the United States; Adjutant-General William Verbeck's National Scouts of America, which focused on promoting highway safety; media magnate William Randolph Hearst's militaristic American Boy Scouts; and the frontier-inspired Leatherstocking Scouts and Jack Crawford Scouts. All used Baden-Powell's handbook as a jumping-off point, but they disagreed on which masculine and civic values a proper Scout organization should emphasize and how it should be run. While some of the smaller Scout organizations limited membership to a particular area or to one social or religious group, the BSA promised an inclusive national organization that would ameliorate class and cultural rifts in America's modernizing society. A second difference among the groups involved attitudes toward teaching military or pacifist principles. Organizations like Verbeck's and Hearst's highlighted militaristic nationalism, while the Peace Scouts of California emphasized internationalism and pacifism. BSA officials navigated a more broadly agreeable middle road between these extreme positions, claiming to be patriotic but neither military nor antimilitary. The proper balance of power between national headquarters, local administrators, troop leaders, and boy members formed a key point of disagreement among the American Scout groups. The BSA became the most centralized and standardized of the organizations, but volunteer local officials and Scoutmasters worked to maintain some of their own authority and freedom of action. Several Scout associations merged into the BSA at a June 1910 organizational meeting. Some independent groups, such as the American Boy Scouts and the rural-based Lone Scouts of America, resented and resisted—for a while—the BSA's efforts to monopolize American Scouting. In the end, the BSA's integration of traditional and modern manhood, balanced administrative apparatus, broad support, and 1916 federal charter allowed it to dominate Scouting to the point that few people now know of its early rivals.[12]

BSA national administrators sought not only to absorb all competing Boy Scout organizations but also to eliminate the separate Girl Scouts organization that coalesced in 1913 under the leadership of Juliette Low. Baden-Powell had worked with his sister, Agnes, to develop a Girl Guides branch in 1910 that retained British Boy Scouting's imperialist flavor but replaced some of the militarism and political leadership emphasis with learning women's home and child duties. This compromise disappointed some girls, who had joined the Boy Scout organization as early as 1908, but still offended some conservative critics for being too masculine and martial. The Girl Guiding concept spread quickly through the British Empire and to other nations, such as Chile and Poland, while other countries came to follow the American Girl Scouting model. Juliette Low worked in 1911 with Baden-Powell to run Girl Guide units in Great Britain and then in the United States, but by 1913, her Savannah girls encouraged her to change the American program's name to the Girl

Scouts and adopt a new khaki uniform resembling that of the boys. Lowe and other Girl Scout leaders asserted that girls could take on men's political and career responsibilities through Scouting's outdoor training and military-like forms while still retaining the traditional duties of housewives and mothers. BSA administrators attempted for over two decades to force the Girl Scouts to give up the Scout name and either adopt the British name Girl Guides or, better yet, merge into the more conservative Camp Fire Girls organization, which emphasized domesticity and primitive Indian lore. Both Girl Scout supporters and their critics in the BSA recognized that the term "Scout" laid claim to equal status and citizenship for girls and women. Some early local BSA officials and boy members tolerated or even helped support Girl Scouting, but detractors argued that girls' participation in Scouting would turn them into tomboys or flappers and thereby disrupt their natural development as mothers. Moreover, Girl Scouting would interfere with boys' character growth by feminizing Scouting, and even undermine social and political order. The existence of the Girl Scouts also raised concerns about the BSA's federal copyright to the term "Scout" for licensing and organizing purposes. The fact that Boy and Girl Scout or Guide organizations developed and worked together closely in other nations (such as Great Britain's elaborate family and companionate marriage metaphor, which Robert Baden-Powell and his "helpmeet" wife and Girl Guide director Olave embodied), and that some countries even allowed women to lead Boy Scout troops, made the battles between BSA and Girl Scout national administrators even more striking. American Girl Scouts' broad range of service efforts during World War I; the ratification of the women's suffrage amendment in 1920 without an attending emergence of a distinct women's voting bloc; Juliette Low's death in 1926; the prominent leadership role President Herbert Hoover's wife, Lou Henry, came to play in Girl Scouting; and the Girl Scouts' surpassing of the older Camp Fire Girls organization in membership in the late 1920s helped gradually dissipate most BSA officials' attacks against Girl Scouting.[13]

While the BSA's third incarnation distinguished the organization from the British Boy Scouts and American Girl Scouts and enabled it to defeat competing Boy Scout organizations in the United States, the Waldorf Astoria banquet and the shift in values and methods represented by James West's arrival in January 1911 blossomed into two intertwined, pivotal discussions over which masculine teachings and administrative methods the BSA should emphasize. The first debate pitted charismatic volunteer Scoutmasters and local officials against the professionalizing paid staff and their efforts to centralize and bureaucratize the BSA.

Democratic Volunteers and Corporate Professionals

The balance that leaders developed in the BSA's evolving organizational structure between men's traditional volunteerism, charismatic initiative, individualism, and democratic practice on the one hand and newer values such as paid professionalism, scientific efficiency, corporate standardization, and expert management on the other hand played a key role in its adaptation of traditional American manhood and citizenship to a modernizing society. BSA national administrators argued that different social groups and business interests were appropriately represented by the volunteer Scoutmasters who led troops and the volunteer Local Council board members, and that the national Scout council was democratically composed of a representative from each Local Council and at-large volunteers concerned with American society as a whole. However, some volunteer national and local officials, such as Seton and Beard, criticized the power that paid BSA Executives and office bureaucrats came to hold and expressed concern that professional Scouters' dependence on salaries made them incapable of independent judgment. Professional Scouters such as West responded that regularizing council office staffs through consistent budgeting and increased training would enable the organization to improve and standardize methods of teaching modern manhood and leading citizenship to the growing number of boy members. Friction between democratic volunteerism and corporate professionalism surfaced at both the local and the national levels— particularly in policy debates over Local Council leadership, membership fees, and national budget pledge quotas.[14]

Voluntary service for the good of the community and nation, a marker of dominant American citizenship since the colonial period, helped Scoutmasters and other BSA volunteers claim status through the venerable tradition of independent but civic-minded men. It also supported officials' claims that the BSA was a classless, democratic *movement* rather than just an organization or a corporation. Scoutmaster application data and sociological research demonstrated that early Boy Scouting appealed to a broad class and occupational spectrum of leaders, who took great pride in volunteering to serve as Local Council members, Scoutmasters,

Troop Committeemen, and merit badge instructors. Throughout the 1910s and 1920s, over 99 percent of adults who participated in the BSA remained unpaid volunteers, which made the organization cost efficient to run (particularly at the troop level). Scouting's focus on citizenship training and patriotism—combined with the semipublic status granted to the BSA by the federal charter and by government officials' vocal support of Scouting at every level—made volunteers feel as if they were serving the nation itself. President Woodrow Wilson made this connection more explicit near the end of World War I, when he urged American men to volunteer to be Scoutmasters to replace those troop leaders who had become soldiers, since "anything that is done or given to increase the war efficiency of the Boy Scouts of America will be a real contribution to the nation and will help win the war." BSA national leaders even tried to convince the U.S. Army that Scoutmasters should be officially exempted from military service. Their proposal failed, but it is striking that they envisioned the two as equal national service contributions.[15]

While the appeal of volunteering for a movement was indeed a strong component of Scouting, New York City's Bureau of Municipal Research (which evaluated government agencies and businesses and provided suggestions to improve their administrative and economic efficiencies) ranked the BSA as the second most efficient corporation in the United States—behind only Sears, Roebuck and Company. In a 1914 evaluation, the Bureau of Municipal Research praised the structure and effective methods of the growing BSA national office, which consisted of seventy staff and twelve departments: "The procedure of each department has been definitized along simple but effective lines, and the work of the several units has been properly correlated. Rules and regulations have been promulgated covering every important detail of clerical and office routine. As a result, a high degree of institutional and individual efficiency has been secured. The vast volume of incoming and outgoing correspondence is handled with the maximum dispatch; accounts are kept in a scientific way . . . orders for materials sent direct from producer are handled by headquarters with equal promptitude. . . . The publicity work seems to be efficiently conducted." Most BSA office staff members, especially as their training and pay increased, valued and were required to practice corporate methods like expert management, scientific analysis, and efficient and standardized procedures. Although 99 percent of BSA adults were volunteers, Scout officials from other countries criticized the BSA for its unusual dependence on paid staff and the stifling effects of this bureaucracy. National and local BSA administrators wanted a measure of control over local volunteers and troop Scoutmasters to protect the organization's reputation and to ensure a degree of uniformity in practices. The growing number of pages of statistical data regarding cost effectiveness and bureaucratic and numeric growth in the organization's annual reports to the U.S. Congress represented one vivid expression of this administrative mind-set. Other countries' Scout and Guide organizations slowly professionalized by the 1920s, but this administrative process seemed to conflict with the masculine values those groups taught, such as British Boy Scouting's programming emphasis on escaping corporate-industrial work. However, the early bureaucratization and professionalization of the BSA fit neatly with—and was actually essential for—the teaching values of modern work and expert-managed government that most of its leaders quickly came to emphasize.[16]

The increasingly bureaucratic background and training of the typical Local Scout Council director mirrored these trends. Local Councils in the early 1910s tended to put outdoorsmen, teachers, youth workers, and popular troop Scoutmasters in charge of the offices, because their direct experience working with boys and the outdoors was seen as the best type of training to lead a Local Council. A prominent local man volunteering his time as "Commissioner" and providing his own temporary office space offered a point of pride for early Local Councils. The 1914 Scoutmaster's handbook stipulated that any paid Local Council Executive reported to the volunteer Commissioner, who was his superior, unless the Local Council voted to combine the two positions. The BSA national office, though, soon came to differentiate between "Second Class" Local Councils, led by volunteer Commissioners, and "First Class" Local Councils, directed by paid and increasingly trained Executives. The national Field Staff and Regional Councils worked diligently to convince local Scout supporters to raise money to establish permanent council offices and hire paid Executives (often men with business backgrounds or bureaucratic Scout training) to run them. Two hundred sixty-three Second Class Councils overshadowed 47 First Class Councils in 1915. By 1929, the national office triumphantly announced that 633 First Class Councils countered only 8 Second Class Councils. Since the national office could not force Local Councils to make this change, the trend reflected local leaders' and supporters' increasing preference for Local Councils with trained, paid Executives. Literature and training sessions for the Scoutmasters who led boy troops had doubled for Local Council directors in the 1910s, but in the following decade, the national office created a separate handbook, magazine, training conference, and certification school for Executives. The Executives' handbook, first published in 1921, mirrored Frederick Taylor's scientific management and new corporate human resource techniques in arguing that most councils now viewed their Executive as a "general manager" or a "human engineer." BSA sources insisted that Executives attract and train other men by consent, tact, and moderation instead of by domination or dictation. BSA literature in the 1920s stated that the ideal Scout Executive scientifically managed council planning, record keeping, and staffing—much like bureaucrats in modern corporations and government agencies. However, the ideal Executive's character bore a strong resemblance to the modern manhood that the BSA came to teach troop and boy leaders after 1911.[17]

Examining the development of the BSA's overarching organizational structure demonstrates the effective balance it helped modern men achieve between democratic volunteerism and corporate professionalism. By the 1920s, the BSA's administration consisted of four major pairs: the National Council and office; the thirteen Regional Councils and offices; more than four hundred Local Councils and offices; and the boy troops, with their institutional sponsors and volunteer Scoutmasters and Troop Committeemen. While initially more influential, the volunteer National, Regional, and Local Councils came to focus on public relations while decreasing their policy decision-making. A small percentage of paid professionals increasingly staffed and ran the national, regional, and local offices. National office administrators in New York City directed the general flow of Scouting through its official publications and policies while local office Executives came to oversee most aspects of daily practice. The Local Council and the trained office staff served as bulwarks against wayward volunteer Scoutmasters who might incorrectly interpret or implement the organization's masculine and civic teachings. Some troop leaders formed local Scoutmasters' Associations, but they were not supposed to serve on the Local Councils. Professional Executives, weary of the alternative power base these associations represented, wanted to lead more training sessions for Scoutmasters—and some even tried to circumvent troop leaders' authority by requiring reports from boys' Patrol Leaders or Troop Scribes. Volunteer Scoutmasters, however, did provide the key direct instruction to troops of roughly twenty or thirty boys. Committees of three volunteer men advised each troop and helped it negotiate relations with its institutional sponsor and the community. A large number of parents and other adult volunteers provided additional help with local office, camp, and troop meeting duties. Overall, volunteers exercised more influence at the local and troop levels, since they formed the vast majority of active participants, had the most direct contact with boy members, and delivered much of the core program.[18]

While on the surface a balance between volunteerism and professionalism characterized Scouting at the national level, in reality the expert managers and office bureaucrats came to hold the upper hand there. BSA leaders consistently cited the National Council as evidence of the movement's democratic governance, but as an external 1927 study of the organization and occasional faint grumblings from the Scout field suggested, the National Council was more of an inspirational body than a real power player in policy decisions. The National Council consisted of national office administrators, a representative from each of the several hundred Local Councils, and a varying number of appointed "at large" volunteers from the interested public. Members voted at annual meetings on changes to the Boy Scout national constitution or particular program points to emphasize the following year, but select national office administrators and advisers usually crafted these proposals in advance. Electing the BSA's officers and its Executive Board of about twenty or thirty men constituted the National Council's key power. The Executive Board met more frequently to monitor the national office's budget and to make recommendations about the general activities and scope of the organization. Youth workers and educators had a sizable presence on the first BSA national Executive Board; many had been included in order to absorb competing youth organizations or to gain pledges of support from their institutions. By 1917, however, businessmen, bankers, and philanthropic officials with less experience working with boys had replaced some of them.[19]

Like many other professionally managed enterprises in this era, a nominal committee directed the BSA at the national level, but a small group of experts ran the organization day to day in the name of efficiency and the greater good. The national office, and James West in particular, served as the primary force in BSA national policy and ideology from 1911 to the early 1940s. West often corresponded and met with a volunteer subcommittee of the Executive Board, consisting of BSA Treasurer George Dupont Pratt of the Rockefeller Philanthropies and Lee Hanmer of the Russell Sage Foundation (who was later replaced by manufacturer John Sherman Hoyt). Pratt's and Hanmer's influence on the BSA points to the larger parallels between the bureaucratization of Scouting and the establishment and professionalization of philanthropies, some of which were funded by the same elite families that supported the BSA. This trio appeared to have made some key decisions for the organization or drafted policies on which the broader Executive Board or National Council later voted. The three men rarely discussed this chain of command in public; they usually credited decisions to the National Council or its Executive Board to promote the sense that the organization was democratically governed. The national office divided its administrative work into departments, including Editorial, Education, Field, Supply, Finance, and Camping—the trained and paid heads of which reported to West. The national office guided local practice via published literature, policy changes, promotional efforts, council and troop registration, and a growing number of training sessions and Field Staff inspection visits.[20]

The national office's efforts to expand bureaucracy and to professionalize local administrators and train volunteers through increasing member fees and Local Council pledge quotas encapsulated the eventual compromise between volunteer men's and professional men's authority and status within the organization. Expenditures by BSA national headquarters climbed from $97,000 in 1912 to $1,800,000 in 1920, and then to $2,300,000 in 1929. The portion of national office income spent on the Field Department, though, increased from 4 percent in 1914 to 43 percent by 1926—reflecting headquarters' growing emphasis on providing training and inspection for local Scout practice. In 1912, the national office derived only 1 percent of its budget from registration fees, and the role of the Local Councils had not been formalized in the administrative apparatus. In an effort to move away from the volatility and charity status associated with the BSA's dependence on donations from elite philanthropists, national administrators soon required boys, troops, and councils to formally register; raised annual fees; and attempted national fund-raising drives in the 1910s. These changes improved precision regarding membership registration and analysis of statistical data but failed to meet expanding costs. Local Councils also complained that they had difficulty soliciting local residents for their own budgets, as residents had already been tapped by national fund-raising drives. To resolve these complaints and to regularize its income, the national office instituted the quota plan in 1920, which required Local Councils to pledge a certain amount of money each year to national headquarters' operations. In exchange, the national office agreed to stop soliciting donations in nation-

wide campaigns. Some local officials initially resented the rising registration fees and voluntary pledge quotas, and the increasing national
office oversight they financed. After a couple difficult years, during which
some Local Councils did not pay their full quotas, the system gelled. By
1926, 65 percent of the national office's normal operating expenses de-
rived from annual registration fees and Local Council quotas. This shift
in funding, however, helped local officials maintain some authority over
their movement, since they became the main source of money for the
national office's operation budget and staff paychecks. Despite rising
budgets and bureaucratic machinery, the vast majority of Scout men remained volunteers who retained a fair amount of discretion and flexibility in decision making about local practices. The increasingly paid and
professionalizing administrators and bureaucrats could thus claim to
support Scouting's volunteer majority, who in turn served the nation by
developing tomorrow's leaders. Overall, the 1910s and 1920s witnessed a
balancing of power between charismatic volunteer men and professional
bureaucratic men in the BSA's governance and funding. A key part of
Scout manhood's emerging volunteer-professional alliance and the BSA's
dramatic growth, however, hinged on a parallel debate on local versus
national men's authority in the organization.[21]

The Balancing of Men's Power between
National Administrators and Local Officials

Maintaining control over a modernizing society required white Americans to reconfigure lines of authority among bigger groups of men in an
increasingly segmented national hierarchy; thus, BSA officials gradually
achieved equilibrium between standardized central authority and individual local control. The replacement of free membership and untracked
troops with a strict registration system, increasing fees, more frequent
training of adult volunteers and professional staff, and a growing list of
required bureaucratic forms marked the maturation of the BSA from a
loose movement to a corporate-like organization. The creation of informal Scout committees by local officials and supporters starting in 1911
demonstrated the grassroots base of the BSA movement; however, James
West and other national administrators viewed these intermediate power
centers as a potential threat to standardized practices and centralized control over local Scouting. The formalization of Local Council offices and
increasing training and inspection of volunteer Scoutmasters through the

National Field Department and the new Regional Council offices represented a compromise in authority between national and local men's leadership. New national requirements that each troop have an institutional sponsor and three supervising volunteer Committeemen created both greater support and more oversight for the individual Scoutmaster and his troop. These reorganized lines of authority mirrored the balancing of self-reliant, charismatic volunteerism with professionalism and corporate efficiency in the BSA's masculine and civic teachings; both efforts accelerated the organization's expanding membership and public support.[22]

The contested and evolving troop and council registration and fee system formed a key foundation of the national office's plan to convince local Scout officials to carefully monitor their practices to make them more uniform across the country and aid in data collection and scientific planning. In the BSA's first three years, loose record keeping made it difficult to keep track of membership and maintain influence over local leaders and their teaching methods. Rampant boy, troop, and Scoutmaster turnover made the BSA appear wasteful and ineffective according to the Progressive Era's standards of organization and efficiency. The expanding national office formalized a Local Council and troop registration system in 1913 that allowed it to require a modest amount of supervision and support for each troop, control official recognition status, and tax members. By managing the certification of Local Councils and troops, the BSA national office could also encourage compliance in such areas as membership policies and maintaining high standards in Scout rank and merit badge exams. James West worked to limit the boundaries of each Local Council to one municipality in order to curb its power. Prominent men who successfully applied to the national office for a council charter gained the authority to represent the BSA in their area and screen annual charter applications for individual Scoutmasters and their troops—as well as to oversee Scout practices and training in that area. Headquarters suggested that the Local Council include prominent men in the area, such as businessmen, bankers, educators, clergy, civic leaders, and a representative from each troop-sponsoring institution. However, national leaders deemed it unwise to put either Scoutmasters or women (who served as volunteers and, increasingly, as Scout office secretaries but who were not official members) on the Local Council. The revised annual troop charter application called for a Scoutmaster, a local sponsoring institution, and three volunteer community Committeemen to supervise a troop. Headquarters also instituted a fee for each Local Council and troop that wanted to register, which some members initially resisted. Failure to meet these requirements, though, meant not being granted the troop charter needed to buy official uniforms and attend council camps, competitions, and public rallies.[23]

Figure 1.1 from the new magazine for Local Council Executives conveys how the new registration and fee process was just one part of the mounting array of forms and statistical reports that headquarters required troop leaders and local office staff to submit to the national office. The forms' emphasis on data collection, certification, meeting agendas, and standardized planning brought more of a corporate, bureaucratic flavor to local Scout practices. However, the BSA national office had relatively few means in the 1910s to directly control local practices, so administrators still had to give Local Councils and their volunteer Scoutmasters and Troop Committeemen a fair degree of latitude.[24]

The expansion of the national Field Department and the development of thirteen Regional Councils by the 1920s added a more immediate level of supervision over Local Council men but also gave each region a stronger collective voice in national policies. Twelve of the Regional Councils divided the continental United States; the thirteenth encompassed American colonial territories and U.S. citizens abroad. The Regional Council acted as a liaison for information and concerns between national headquarters and Local Council offices. The Regional Councils studied local Scout conditions and problems and helped enforce the Local Council pledge quotas toward the operation of the national Field Department. After the wave of converting cities' existing informal Scout committees into official and permanent Local Councils in the 1910s, the national Field Department and the Regional Councils played a stronger role in organizing and staffing new Local Councils in the 1920s.[25]

BSA national administrators' desire to curtail Local Council transience and autonomy paralleled their concern about individual Scoutmasters running troops in rural and small town areas without the benefit of council supervision and support. In an attempt to bring all Scoutmasters under the council system and to complete Scout coverage of the entire country, BSA national headquarters promoted Area Councils in the 1920s to supervise sparsely populated rural regions. A 1927 study found that 60 percent of new local Boy Scout councils were created in the following manner. The national office sent in a regional Executive to speak to business, political, educational, church, and community leaders in neighboring

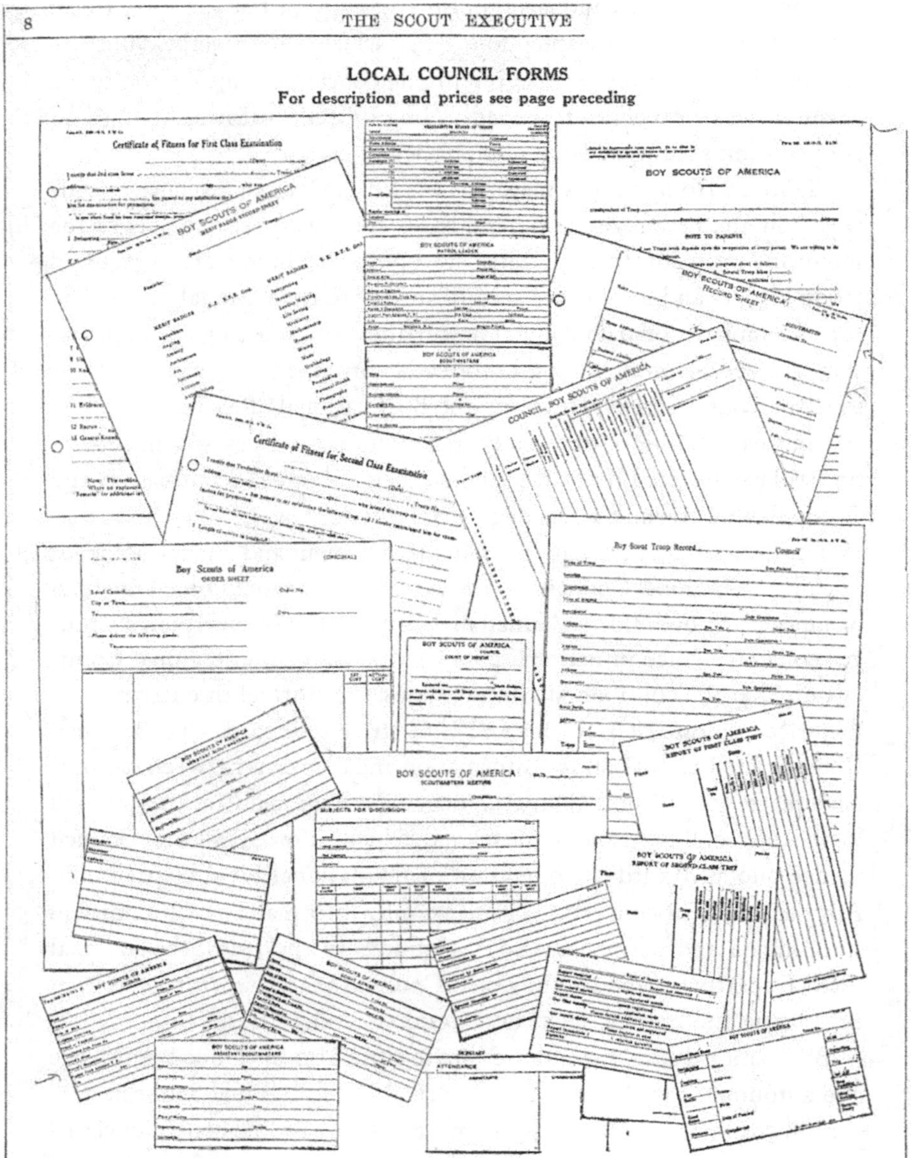
8 THE SCOUT EXECUTIVE

LOCAL COUNCIL FORMS

For description and prices see page preceding

Figure 1.1 The visual growth of bureaucracy in BSA local offices. "Local Council Forms," *Scout Executive*, November 1920, 8. (Courtesy of Boy Scouts of America National Scouting Museum Archival Collection)

target towns. The speaker stoked up enthusiasm and promises of financial support. The national office then sent in a certified Local Council Executive freshly minted from the new national Scout training school. The number of Scouts not under a council peaked in 1919 at 175,125, accounting for nearly 38 percent of total Scouts at the end of the year. With the expansion of Area Councils, only 14,000 Scouts (less than 2 percent of the total) remained without council supervision by 1929.[26]

The fact that the BSA discouraged individual boy applicants and—unlike the Woodcraft Indians and Sons of Daniel Boone organizations—shifted to refusing troops without thorough adult supervision and institutional backing reinforced the notion that hierarchical loyalty to a chain of command was an essential component of BSA character and civic training. The increasingly professional Local Council Executives shared authority over volunteer Scoutmasters and boy members with the institutional troop sponsors and their volunteer Troop Committeemen. BSA national administrators hoped to achieve a modest degree of outside supervision and support for each Scoutmaster by adding the requirement that each troop be sponsored by a local institution, such as a church, school, civic club, or business. Local Council offices decided which Scoutmaster and sponsoring institution applicants would be approved. Sponsors often furnished troops with a free meeting space, Troop Committeemen, a Scoutmaster, merit badge experts, and some measure of financial support. The sponsor provided public legitimacy and continuity to the troop, while hosting a troop enabled the parent institution to provide a service to the community and helped it attract and retain members or customers. In order to gain wider institutional support and greater membership, BSA national leaders decided to allow each sponsor the right to restrict its troop's membership as it saw fit. BSA administrators boasted that Scout troops were miniature "melting pots," which helped democratize and Americanize their members; but in reality, many troops tended to be socioeconomically segregated according to their institutional sponsor. Although the BSA was technically open to all boys at the national level, Local Councils and troop-sponsoring institutions did not have to—and did not—accept everyone.[27]

To understand the early BSA's cultural significance and power to influence mainstream American gender and civic norms, one must envision not a stand-alone organization but a vast spectrum of respected institutions and prominent individuals volunteering their time and resources to help teach Scout values to men and boys whom they hoped would adopt modern manhood and practical civic leadership as lifelong principles. The wide array of church, school, and civic organizations as well as businesses and government agencies that sponsored troops confirmed the broad appeal and application of Boy Scout masculine and civic norms. These institutions' ongoing investment in sponsoring troops suggests not only that they felt teaching modern manhood and civic leadership was important but also that they were incapable of teaching boys such values themselves without the aid of Scouting. Churches have dominated troop sponsorship throughout the organization's history, being responsible for roughly half of the units each year. Middle-class men's organizations, such as the Elks, the Masons, Lions and Rotary Clubs, and the American Legion—which supported Boy Scouting as both a service to the community and fertile ground for future membership recruitment—increased their sponsorship of troops from 4 percent of the BSA's total in 1916 to 18 percent in 1930. Schools, primarily public ones and their Parent Teacher Associations, sponsored a fairly consistent 10 percent of Scout troops during the 1910s and 1920s. However, this figure underestimates schools' support of Boy Scouting, since many provided essential meeting space and volunteer leaders for other institutions' troops. The schools' utilization of Scouting allowed them to "outsource" the Progressive Era's growing expectation to provide experiential, civic, and nature education without having to make their teachers change their core methods or the curriculum. While educators and critics fought over coeducation, religious fundamentalism versus science, and how to teach democracy in schools, many seemed to agree that Scouting provided essential and effective training to prepare boys for a modernizing society. Institutions such as industrial plants, government agencies, police departments, libraries, playgrounds, and community centers together sponsored another 5 or so percent of troops during this era. Groups of interested male citizens with no designated institutional affiliation sponsored most of the remaining as "community troops," suggesting that a consortium of prominent men was itself considered to be a solid source of ongoing support for early Scout troops.[28]

Boy Scout national administrators attempted to solidify troop sponsorship, stem the high rate of turnover among Scoutmasters, and gain some control over wayward troop leaders by adopting the Troop Committee requirement in 1914. The Troop Committee plan may have been an elaboration of the initial requirement that each Scoutmaster applicant provide three personal references. The national office hoped that these volunteer committees of three leading local men, through frequent troop inspections and the power to select and dismiss the Scoutmaster, would guarantee that the Scout program was being properly interpreted to its boy members. Troop Committeemen tended to be of higher economic and cultural status than the Scoutmasters they supervised, replicating the expanding gradation of authority in early twentieth-century American corporations and government. The committee supervised troop business matters and ensured that it had adequate financial support and access to camping facilities. Committeemen arranged a troop meeting place and acted as liaisons between the troop, its sponsor, parents, and the broader community. The level of Troop Committee activity seemed to vary, but the requirement succeeded in involving leading community men in Scouting who might not have had time to be troop leaders. For a Scoutmaster, successfully teaching boys modern manhood and civic leadership to the satisfaction of his Troop Committee supervisors offered potential opportunities for better jobs and social status. As one climbed the early BSA's organizational hierarchy, the class makeup became more elite. Local Council Executives were more likely to be middle-class professionals and businessmen than were Scoutmasters. Local Troop Committeemen and Local and National Council members tended to be from the upper middle class and, especially, the elite. The national Executive Board roster read increasingly like a who's who of Wall Street bankers, big business owners, politicians, and philanthropists.[29]

Balancing power between national and local men enabled BSA administrators to credibly boast that the organization was both an efficient national corporation and a cross-class, locally based movement that preserved American men's democratic and volunteer traditions. By increasing adult training, inspection visits, and administrative oversight, national and regional officials helped guide the BSA's heavily volunteer leadership to a balance with corporate-bureaucratic virtues like scientific efficiency, expert management, and loyalty to hierarchical authority. Volunteer Scoutmasters, Troop Committeemen, and Local Council members came to share power over local Scout practices with paid, trained Executives at the national, regional, and local offices. The BSA's ability to effectively expand the gradation of men's authority and combine democratic volunteerism with bureaucratic professionalism enabled the organization to draw support from the public and a broadening spectrum of modern institutions.

The Patterns of BSA Membership Growth

Achieving a balance between Victorian and modern manhood and authority also helped the BSA attract and manage its growing number of members. BSA national leaders' claim to offer a universal training program open to all American boys contributed significantly to the organization's popularity and government support. Administrators argued that allowing all boys to wear the same uniform and learn the same masculine and civic values made Scouting a force for easing class and cultural conflict in American society. However, the limitations to recruiting racial minority and rural boys illustrated the hierarchical nature of the BSA's modern manhood and leading citizenship. The remainder of this chapter lays out the contours of BSA membership growth from 1910 to 1930 in terms of total numbers, regional spread, community type, age, and socioeconomic groups to demonstrate the broad appeal of Scout teachings.

Total boy and man membership statistics highlighted the wide promulgation of the BSA's training in modern manhood and leading citizenship. The number of active boy members topped 100,000 in 1913. Membership boomed in the second half of the decade, attracting 481,084 boys and 86,737 men during 1918. By 1920, the United States had more Scouts than the rest of the world combined. With help from President Harding's membership "round-up" in 1923, enrollment reached 929,769 boys and 180,000 men in 1927. The BSA's total boy membership to date topped 1,000,000 in 1919 and reached 4,277,833 by 1930. An even more tangible means for expressing the organization's popularity is the rising percentage of available American boys it recruited. In 1911, the ratio of registered Scouts to available boys between the ages of twelve and seventeen was 1 to 112. This ratio quickly improved to 1 active Scout for every 14 boys in 1918, and reached 1 active Scout for every 8 boys by 1927. Of 26,000,000 available boys between 1910 and 1930, 1 boy out of every 6 had been registered as a Scout at some point. The BSA also became more adult focused over time. The percentage of members that were adults (paid male staff, Scoutmasters, Troop Committeemen, council members, and other volunteers) doubled from 1 adult for every 10 boys in the organization's first three years to 1 adult for every 5 boys by 1922.

Five hundred thousand men had been members to date by 1924, and close to 1 million by 1930.[30]

The BSA appealed to and recruited a widening range of boys, but the most common early Scout was between twelve and fifteen years old, from a small to medium-sized town, white, and middle class. National administrators insisted that no females could be members or leaders, and that boys had to be at least twelve and adult troop leaders twenty-one years of age. Scouting best recruited boys in their early adolescence, the stage at which many experts argued that their character development was most at risk and also most malleable to correction. Although the BSA was open to older boys and encouraged members to stay, most boys quit (and new boys failed to join) after age fifteen—partly due to their increasing attraction and access to girls, mass leisure, and paid work. BSA national leaders excluded the throngs of boys younger than twelve who wanted to join the organization, since they believed preadolescents were incapable of advanced masculine character and civic training. Administrators reluctantly developed a separate Cub branch for these boys in 1930, but it taught Native American primitivism and home-based loyalty to these "less evolved" younger boys.[31]

Scouting's modern manhood had become a pervasive national phenomenon by 1928. During the BSA's first five years, the number of troops grew most rapidly in urban-industrial New England, New York, New Jersey, and the Great Lakes states. Between 1915 and 1930, Scout density (calculated as the number of Scouts per ten thousand residents) in the Pacific Northwest and the Rocky Mountain states increased dramatically. Mormon leaders latched onto Scouting as a way to further their civic and spiritual training of boys while allying themselves with Americanism; as a result, Utah and Idaho soon came to lead the BSA in enrollment rates. The BSA recruited the lowest percentage of boys from 1910 to 1930 in the Southeast—particularly Deep South states like Mississippi and South Carolina. The high percentage of African American and rural residents— two groups whom some early BSA officials believed to lack the prerequisite masculine character capacity and environmental influences to lead a modernizing society—contributed to this trend.[32]

After an initial phase of big city growth, Boy Scouting recruited best in small towns with between one and five thousand residents. The 1925 BSA Annual Report noted that small towns (which likely included some areas that would today be classified as suburbs) sponsored 19.2 percent of Scout troops, although they held only 8.6 percent of the U.S. population.

According to historian David Macleod, these communities had the sufficient population density, social cohesiveness, and white Anglo-Saxon Protestant makeup to best support Scouting. Above the five thousand residents mark, the rate of Scout recruitment in the 1920s dropped as the size of the city increased. For example, cities between twenty-five thousand and one hundred thousand residents supported 14.9 percent of Scout troops compared to 9.8 percent of the American population in 1925. Cities over 1 million residents supported only 6.4 percent of Scout troops relative to their 9.6 percent of the U.S. population. Racial heterogeneity, the wide availability of alternative leisure activities, and BSA administrators' relative unwillingness to make changes in uniform prices or troop meeting schedules to better suit working-class boys' needs somewhat undercut Scout recruitment in highly urbanized areas. Rural farm regions were least receptive to BSA recruitment efforts, in part because their population was not dense enough to sustain the viable troops and permanent Local Councils that national administrators saw as vital to good Scouting. The 1920 U.S. census found that 34 percent of boys between twelve and eighteen years of age lived in "open country" areas with less than twenty-five residents, but the 1925 BSA Annual Report noted that only 0.2 percent of Scout troops were located in such areas.[33]

It is difficult to precisely pinpoint Scout recruitment rates among non–white Anglo-Saxon Protestants and different economic classes before 1925 because the BSA did not ask for such information from applicants. The troop-sponsoring institution requirement and the Scoutmaster's application questions on race and occupation did help Local Councils screen "undesirable" boys and give some general membership indicators. A 1927 study of the organization by consultant Mark M. Jones provided this summary of trends in non–white Anglo-Saxon Protestant recruitment: "In the states where there is a substantial negro or foreign-born white population . . . troop Scouting is weak. . . . [In states where Scouting is strongest] the percentage of the total population represented by the foreign-born white and negro population is very low." However, as the second half of this book examines, the BSA made important concessions to attract non-Protestant and non-English-speaking white European immigrants. Moreover, administrators would embark on successful outreach programs to recruit African American and Native American boys in the late 1920s. BSA national leaders did not seek or keep consistent statistics on the class makeup of boy members, partly because of their desire to assuage class tensions in American society. Sociological studies from the period and several histories of the BSA, though, suggest that the early organization recruited best from the middle classes but reasonably well from the skilled working class and up. Boys from elite and skilled working-class families appeared to have joined in proportions roughly equal to their percentage of the American population. Boys from semiskilled, unskilled, and destitute families remained quite underrepresented in American Scouting. This pattern resembled that of the early British Boy Scouts organization, but the British Girl Guides seemed to have somewhat more success among the working classes by partnering with existing girls' clubs and community institutions. However, the costs of different British Scout and Guide uniform and hat qualities often reaffirmed class distinctions among members, while American Boy Scouts had only one "classless" standard uniform.[34]

THE BSA'S MODERN MANHOOD and leading citizenship teachings influenced a growing portion and spectrum of American boys and men between 1910 and 1930. BSA officials brokered effective compromises between national and local authorities and between volunteers and professionals by balancing American men's tradition of democratic self-reliance with modern virtues, such as bureaucratic efficiency and expert management. Parents, educators, and experts on youth issues believed Scouting's troop method and firm Scoutmaster leadership would guide boys in the precarious developmental stage of adolescence. Gaining the support of elite businessmen, progressive reformers, and government officials constituted another key factor in the organization's phenomenal success. The BSA triumphed over competing Scout and youth organizations by offering an effective life apprenticeship for daily living in an urbanizing society and corporate-industrial economy. The next task, then, is to pinpoint the work skills and social relationship values that attracted adherents by examining the Oath and Laws, core programming, and concept of good character that undergirded the BSA's vision of modern manhood.

2

Scout Character

*Men's Skills for Corporate-Industrial Work
and Urban Society*

America's increasingly corporate-industrial economy and rapid urban and technological growth held the potential to revolutionize society and standards of living in the early 1900s, but the values and skills needed to control this new way of life no longer matched Victorians' self-made manhood, which had permeated American gender relations since the 1820s. Owning a successful family farm or artisan shop—a lingering stronghold of manhood in colonial America and the Early Republic— demonstrated a man's independence through becoming his own boss and not being dependent on or beholden to anyone. Many Americans believed that the ability to make political decisions and vote democratically hinged on this economic independence and its prerequisite good character. By the 1830s, the industrial and commercial revolutions strengthened the idea that a man could also demonstrate character through working his way up to owning an independent business. With this emphasis on the individual achieving business or farm ownership by his own hard work and thrift, self-made manhood could be earned through effort and will. A man's self-made character established both his independence and the dependent status of females and nonwhite men, whose access to property and business ownership was often restricted by law and custom. This economic and civic hierarchy also set the tone for social relationships and cultural deference. However, by 1910 rapid urbanization and the decline of free fertile farmland—combined with the shift toward a corporate-led economy fueled by mass production—made self-made manhood elusive for most men and increasingly far-fetched for boys. Many nineteenth-century teenage boys had earned masculine status by demonstrating adult work skills and social behaviors in job apprenticeships and community interactions, but the decline of apprenticeships and the rise of compulsory schooling and segregated socialization spheres for children meant that early twentieth-century boys had to be artificially taught character and civic virtues. Boy Scouting's new configuration of character values and skills for modern work and urban social relations produced a powerful and popular response to these changes.

Scouting's modern character training—within a close-knit troop of peers guided by a worthy man in the outdoors—combined with the opportunity to learn civic leadership through engagement with community adults, allowed the BSA to best its youth organization rivals and achieve dominant cultural and political status. Scout character retained Victorian men's modesty and self-control while replacing their standard of being self-made via farm or business ownership with the scientific efficiency, expert management, and loyalty to corporate hierarchy required to adapt to a modernizing workforce and urban society. Early BSA publications suggested that Scouts who developed this modern character demonstrated their superiority over females as well as nonwhite, tradition-minded immigrant, and "backward" rural males. Responding to the growing focus on business in 1920s American society and politics, Scout administrators and authors placed a bit more emphasis on such attributes as a pleasing personality and salesmanship in some published explanations of Scout character values. However, resurgence in this period of self-reliant Scout heroes, such as the noble Indian and Charles Lindbergh, and the continued emphasis on outdoorsmanship and resourcefulness set limits to the organization's business tone.

This chapter argues that American Scout leaders intentionally and successfully transformed Baden-Powell's original British Boy Scout Oath and nine-part Law, program, and teaching methods into the BSA's core character ideology of modern manhood. Not only did members begin their training and each troop meeting by reciting the twelve Scout Laws and Oath, but also BSA officials and teaching materials consistently tied Scout activities and tests to these fundamental values. The twelve American Laws and other closely associated Scout character virtues can be grouped into solutions to two of middle- and upper-class white Anglo-Saxon Protestant men's principal concerns: the changing nature of work, and social challenges to their authority by the "new woman," "new Negro," and new immigrants from southern and eastern Europe. Of the two, work values occupied more of BSA leaders' attention and programming efforts. Modern corporations needed employees to work together seamlessly on segmented, routine tasks in order to compete against rivals. At the same time, the specialization of function popularized by Frederick Taylor and Henry Ford required a hierarchy of workers. While maintaining the character heritage of self-reliance through outdoorsmanship and individual rank and merit badge standards, half of the BSA's twelve Laws and portions of the Americanized Scout Oath helped teach members a fitting new work ethic for the twentieth century's large-scale industries and management by expertise. A Scout who obeyed the Laws of working cheerfully and spending thriftily asserted status through learning to make his own living while enjoying working for others at whatever job his environment and inherent abilities enabled him to do. The American Scout Laws on being trustworthy, obedient, and loyal to established authority and standards hedged men's traditional independence while carefully avoiding the taint of servility. The BSA taught boys to use self-control to harness extreme independence and combine traditional competition with modern cooperation for an increasingly interdependent society and workforce. Personal thrift and the American Oath to keep himself physically strong and mentally awake required a good Scout to develop a well-rounded body to better endure modern work and urban life's constant pace. The second group of Scout Laws and activities helped resolve leading men's concerns about changing social relations and lines of authority. Scout Laws on helpfulness, courtesy, and kindness promoted white men's supposedly unique ability to provide service to the nation and to groups classified as dependents. Scout Laws and program activities for being thrifty, clean, and morally straight helped distinguish Scouts from females, nonwhite males, and working-class toughs, who were sometimes portrayed in early BSA literature as careless and selfish. The new American Law on reverence, though, encouraged members to be tolerant and accepting of those from other religious faiths. Together, these Scout character values and skills provided adolescent boy members a practical apprenticeship in modern work and urban living.[1]

The New Scout Work Ethic

BSA programming and publications frequently elaborated on and carefully hedged the First, Second, and Seventh Scout Laws on being trustworthy, loyal, and obedient because they conflicted with American men's traditional individualism but were essential character attributes for modern work. Historians of British Scouting have argued that its leaders used these three Laws to maintain England's class hierarchy and ensure loyalty to established authority figures. White American men, however, took great pride in their traditional independence and held faith that the opportunity for each individual to make his own destiny still distinguished the country from European society's artificial, fixed class hierarchy. At the same time, more American men in the twentieth century worked for large companies, lived in growing cities, and were governed by expert-led bureaucracies. BSA explanations of these three Laws thus placed more emphasis on modern values like efficiency, expert management, and group cooperation.[2]

While the term "trustworthy" might be defined simply as not lying or cheating, Sea Scout champion Arthur Astor Carey offered a typical example of BSA officials' modernization of British Scout values when he argued in 1915 that a trustworthy Scout also had to demonstrate punctuality, persistence, and efficiency, because these were the same virtues required in modern business. Being trustworthy had been an expectation of respectable Anglo-American men in the Victorian era, but the increasing scale and autonomy of modern business and cities made it even more essential for success. BSA officials put Scouts on their honor to efficiently and diligently carry out any and all given tasks in troop meetings, camp sessions, pageants, and stories. Being trustworthy was the only Boy Scout Law that carried specific threat of punishment if not performed. A boy might be instructed to turn in his Scout badge if he violated the trustworthy Law, signifying his expulsion from the troop. Baden-Powell's original Scout handbook went so far as to compare this loss of honor to the death of one's manhood; the boy who had to turn in his badge after breaking this Law would "never be allowed to wear it again—he loses his life."[3]

BSA training modernized the Seventh Law, a Scout is obedient, by encouraging corporate-bureaucratic methods like disciplining boys by personality, comradeship, evenhandedness, and constant activities rather than military discipline and repressive measures. Baden-Powell specified that a British boy should "obey orders of his patrol leader or scout master without question. Even if he gets an order he does not like he must do as soldiers and sailors do, he must carry it out all the same *because it is his duty.*" However, the status of the soldier (who had served as an effective archetype of manhood and citizenship from the American Revolution through the Spanish-American War) had slipped in the wake of American isolationism and the backlash against military occupation of overseas colonies. The soldier was too aggressive, blindly obedient, and controversial to serve as a complete and compelling model of American manhood by the early twentieth century—particularly during times of peace. The Boys' Brigade and other youth cadet organizations that emphasized soldiering had, after all, achieved only limited American memberships. The 1911 BSA handbook deleted Baden-Powell's military discipline reference and instead instructed a boy to obey "his parents, scout master, patrol leader and all other duly constituted authorities." Arthur Carey argued that an American Scout's obedience was essential in large-scale businesses and industries, since all cooperative endeavors required that participants act as a unit "under the direction of one guiding mind" to achieve maximum efficiency. The first American Scoutmaster's handbook in 1912 suggested, "Let authority be felt through personality, directorship and closer and stronger common interest presented through comradeship and fellow feeling for a larger life." BSA national leaders discouraged harsh discipline and outright military drill, but they instructed local officials to turn community service and outdoor skills into fun Scout drills to teach boys the efficient, cooperative obedience needed for corporate-industrial work and urban living. Scoutmasters across the country "drilled" troops on tasks as varied as calisthenics, First Aid, and setting up camp or wilderness watch towers. Overflowing public crowds of thousands and even tens of thousands flocked to watch boys drill and compete on such skills at Scout rallies across the nation, which also served as important fund-raisers and community gatherings.[4]

The combination of American men's traditional independence with the imperatives of corporate-industrial work prompted BSA administrators to place emphasis on corporate organizational loyalty over British Scouting's absolute military loyalty. The original British version of the Second Scout Law instructed a boy to be "loyal to the King, and to his officers, and to his country, and to his employers. He must stick to them through thick and thin against anyone who is their enemy, or who even talks badly of them." Early British Scout literature emphasized the fixed nature of class status and that each boy should learn to be satisfied with his lot in life. Based on his work on American urban playground reform and immigration law, Joseph Lee expressed working-class men's concern with Baden-Powell's interpretation of loyalty: "I think the scout ought to be loyal to his employers, but the [Second Law] as drawn now implies that he must not belong to a trade union or be loyal to that. These cases of conflicting loyalties are among those in which our people need much education." Harping on class distinctions also contradicted the belief that America was a land of opportunity, free of Europe's fixed class divisions. Thus, BSA editors deleted the explicit command to be loyal to employers and military officers and also refused to take sides in labor disputes. The 1911 BSA version read, "He is loyal to all to whom loyalty is due: his scout leader, his home, and parents and country." Figure 2.1 from the first local

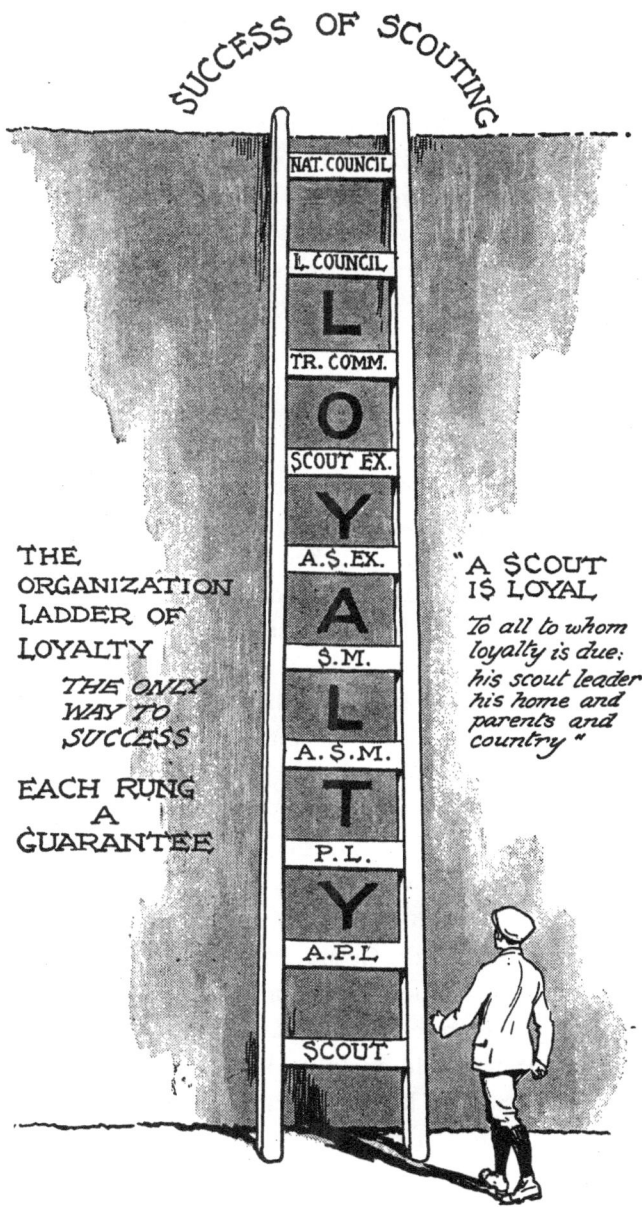

Figure 2.1 Rungs to Scouting success. "The Organization Ladder of Loyalty," William Hurt, *Community Boy Leadership* (1922), 352. (Courtesy of Boy Scouts of America National Scouting Museum Archival Collection)

Scout council Executive's handbook in 1922 exemplified American officials' insistence that loyalty to the organizational system was essential for an individual's success and advancement in Scouting and modern life. This loyalty ladder differed not only from Baden-Powell's original emphasis on military loyalty but also from nineteenth-century American self-made manhood's highlighting of competitive self-reliance and independent initiative for a young man's work and life success. The early twentieth century's large corporate factories and offices required workers to build a fraternity of peers while willingly obeying engineers' and management's overall instructions.[5]

The Efficient Scout Works Cheerfully and Spends Thriftily

BSA officials helped reinvigorate the Protestant work ethic by revising the Eighth and Ninth British Laws on being cheerful and thrifty to teach boys to enjoy both working for others and modern consumption for their character-building qualities. Increasing product availability, discretionary income, and the fantasy of self-fulfillment happily peddled by advertisers and salespeople had heightened Americans' focus on conspicuous consumption and leisure in the early twentieth century, but a realistic model of daily living for most men still required primary emphasis on a diligent work ethic and careful spending. Small-scale, nineteenth-century craftsmen's workshops and farms had integrated downtime and sociable leisure into the day's routine, while Taylorism and Fordism tried to maximize mass production by separating leisure from work and setting a rapid pace via machines and tight organization guided by the factory whistle. Corporate-industrial work depended on employees' consistent, efficient effort on segmented tasks in large-scale settings. Scouting, therefore, tried to make work into a troop game, and leisure into a character-building duty. Many BSA sources and activities stressed the importance of boys working hard and cheerfully at group activities and standardized tasks. BSA officials modernized thrift—a long-standing American man's virtue—to include both time-clock efficiency at work and productive leisure and consumption. Some BSA sources' and elite supporters' explanations of these two Laws embraced a social Darwinist conception of society, in which modern capitalism's unequal distribution of wealth was a natural result of differences in men's characters and their corresponding work ethics.[6]

BSA leaders argued that Scouting, life, and work were grand games to which boys and men should cheerfully give consistent effort. The overall Scout rank and badge program formed a merit-based certification process that encouraged boys to develop the steady and cheerful consistency that modern society's corporate-industrial work and urban living required. The Eighth Law, a Scout is cheerful, insisted not only that Scouts follow orders promptly but also that they show how much they enjoy work: a good Scout "smiles whenever he can. His obedience to orders is prompt and cheery. He never shirks nor grumbles at hardships." Scouting made tasks like learning First Aid and setting up camp fun by turning them into group games or friendly competitions. The Scout Cave column advised *Boys' Life* readers in 1920 that shirkers grumbled and tried to avoid work, while the happiest people were those who worked the most. Colin Livingstone, the prominent banker who served as the President of the BSA from 1910 to 1925, declared in 1928 that a Scout's smile "is a sign of self conquest" that puts him on the "upward road to success." Cheerful work required self-control and internal motivation to complete standardized tasks, instead of relying on external discipline and reward.[7]

The early BSA juxtaposed cheerful, thrifty, and efficient Scouts with hobos and shiftless workers who acted selfishly, ignored their responsibilities, and depended on charity from others. American Scout supporters claimed that the fickle character of inferior men and their unwillingness to work hard caused labor unrest and poverty, while the ability to develop cheerfulness and the prized quality of "stick-to-itiveness" would immunize Scouts from future unemployment and work-related complaints. A 1915 study by Norman Richardson and Ormond Loomis, *The Boy Scout Movement Applied by the Church*, argued that America needed Scouting because a "boy who constantly shifts about from one kind of work to another soon finds himself out of work and among the vacillating mass of poorly paid, little-respected laborers, who are responsible for a large part of society's discontent." Such remarks, though, downplayed the early twentieth century's persistent problems of structural and seasonal unemployment and how American employers benefited from a reserve labor pool that could be used to scab strikers or union advocates. The 1912 Scoutmaster handbook stated that boys unwilling to strive for or incapable of making rapid advancement in rank and merit badge work were not fit to be Scouts: "It will be your business to watch out for natural laggers and shirkers, and to so instill the idea of progression in the minds of the majority of your Scouts as to cause a general movement forward through the force of public opinion." The author suggested that if all else failed to "arouse the shirkers to move onward," the Scoutmaster should appoint a committee to force them to progress or expel them, since "shirkers of the persistent sort are not wanted, and the sooner the organization is rid of them to make room for 'climbers,' the better it will be for all concerned." BSA handbooks and training sessions for adult leaders constantly emphasized that the ultimate purpose of Scouting was rank and badge advancement. Scoutmasters and council leaders were often judged on their boys' demonstrated progress in Scout test taking.[8]

BSA leaders conceived of thrift as a broad indicator of a boy's work ethic, innate character, consumption habits, and ability to serve society rather than depend on others. The Ninth American Law, a Scout is thrifty, stated that a member "does not wantonly destroy property. He works faithfully, wastes nothing, and makes the best use of his opportunities. He saves his money so that he may pay his own way, be generous to those in need, and helpful to worthy objects." BSA supporters hoped that all boys would learn thrift but believed that the results and rewards of that effort were determined by one's innate character and environment. An early BSA pamphlet on thrift by Charles W. Eliot, the longtime president of Harvard University, argued that Scout training enabled boys to make the most of their unequal opportunities: "Heredity and environment combine to make impossible equality of opportunity for children. Nevertheless every child in a free country should be enabled to seize on and make good use of every opportunity which its nature and its surroundings permit it to utilize.... That is the freedom which the thrifty boy scout ought to enjoy." A handwritten note on the BSA national archive's copy of the pamphlet reported that it was not that popular. This may have been because its message conflicted too directly with the traditional belief that America provided unlimited opportunity for any man willing to work hard and save. Tellingly, though, the note stated that the pamphlet was helpful in recruiting the support of America's elite for Scouting. For example, John D. Rockefeller Jr. (the son of the great oil magnate) hoped to capitalize on the thrift training offered by Scouting. In an article he wrote for *Boys' Life* in 1921, he explained that there were right and wrong ways to be thrifty: "How the world needs those who will do their best! That do not seek to see how little work they can do in a day, but how much service they can render. Not restriction in the output of industry, but thrift in conserving the rewards of industry is their motto." A laborer might have argued that limiting his work output served his peers by helping to maintain a reasonable pace of work. Rockefeller hoped to close this loophole by using Boy Scouting to train loyal, efficient employees and to deflate labor union efforts to maintain workers' control over the speed and methods of production.[9]

BSA leaders offered one of their most effective pitches for parental and public support by arguing that adolescent boys' unsupervised and unstructured leisure time might ruin their work ethic and future job prospects by bringing them under the destructive influence of bad boys, street life, and passive mass entertainment. American Scout training conferences and publications stressed that every minute of troop meetings, camps, and hikes should be filled with character-building activities that time-thrifty Scouts cheerfully pursued. Recommended and actual troop meeting programs in BSA literature scheduled activities in five- or ten-minute intervals and suggested an orderly procession through the steps, such as recitation of the Pledge of Allegiance and Scout Oath and Laws; reports about Good Turns they had performed; discussion of a key Scout Law; the Scoutmaster or an expert guest teaching the boys a particular Scout skill to practice for a rank or merit badge exam; and then a form of group exercise, such as tumbling or Capture the Flag. Special troop activities might include a day hike or swimming practice, which helped boys develop a well-rounded body and prepare to pass other rank tests. Daily and weekly schedules for Scout camping were also highly structured. Schedules of troop meeting and camp programs from across the country published in newspapers and council histories reveal that most local leaders followed these time-discipline suggestions and a similar system of Scout character-building activities.[10]

Corporate advertisers played to the BSA's obsession with work thrift and efficiency as well as the organization's integration of work and play. The watch advertisement in Figure 2.2 from the 1919 Boy Scout handbook stressed the time management associated with modern industrial production and mass transportation. The second hand and the radioactive glow-in-the-dark feature encouraged constant monitoring of one's use of time. Both the Boy Scouts and the adult workers in the picture seem magnetically drawn to the giant clock. Although Scouting was an outdoor program, the advertisement suggested that the end goal was helping prepare boys for success in modern work and urban society. A wristwatch

Figure 2.2 A Scout's purposes for monitoring his time. Ingersoll Radiolite Watch Advertisement, BSA, *Handbook for Boys* (1919), 475. (Courtesy of Boy Scouts of America National Scouting Museum Archival Collection)

advertisement in the 1927 handbook from the same company depicted a Scoutmaster reading instructions to a group of attentive Boy Scouts on a hiking trip outdoors. The caption insisted that a Scout must have a watch that "doesn't need to be coddled and petted" and that "keeps time under all conditions of usage," since he received his orders on a time basis. In the 1927 drawing, the Scoutmaster merged into the watchband, implying that his primary function was to discipline boys to the time efficiency required by modern factory and office work. Scouting brought an ethos of industrial efficiency and strict time management into nature itself.[11]

BSA officials sought to reconcile the traditional American focus on thrift with the growing twentieth-century emphasis on consumption. American Scout explanations of thrift taught boys to balance saving with efficient spending. Earning Second and First Class ranks required saving money in a bank account, but a 1929 *Boys' Life* article argued, "Thrift is the middle ground between the spendthrift and the miser. The one spends extravagantly, the other hoards extravagantly." The author declared that careful spending was more difficult than just saving. A common example of this was the instruction to save money from working so that one could spend it on a uniform and Scout equipment and activities that would provide long-term character and career dividends. American Scout literature also instructed thrifty boys to provide assistance to the worthy poor, but to not give handouts to shirkers and beggars who refused to work and save.[12]

BSA values and program activities concerning being cheerful and thrifty represented a middle ground on men's production and consumption values appropriate for the modern American economy and workforce. Scouting reintegrated work and leisure. Taylor and Ford taught employees to work productively in order to have time and money for leisure afterward, but American Scouting sought to make work fun and to make constructive leisure a responsibility for adolescent boys and men. This focus on modern work values and character-building consumption habits distinguished the BSA from British Boy Scouting and Girl Guiding, organizations that historians have linked to modernity primarily through their members' participation by the 1920s in recreational leisure forms such as movies and dances. The cheerful and thrifty Laws facilitated BSA administrators' effort to refit the Protestant work ethic for an increasingly hierarchical and corporate system of mass production. Working cheerfully and thriftily while spending wisely allowed a boy to make the most of his life chances, but it could not fundamentally alter one's inborn capabilities or environment. BSA literature—backed by adolescence and racial recapitulation theories—suggested that corporate capitalism's work roles and rewards were distributed according to permanent differences in character, justifying the better positions and wealth that white men tended to enjoy. However, child development experts and Scout officials believed that innate work qualities needed to be honed through bodily exercise to develop fully.[13]

The Well-Rounded Body:
"The Key Stone in the Arch of the Scout Oath"

BSA leaders argued that the well-rounded body called for in the Scout Oath was intimately connected with the ability to work and consume cheerfully and thriftily: "The Ninth Law refers not only to money. It also refers to your strength, your powers, your time." Violent sports like football and boxing placed an increasing premium on raw strength and physical aggression in this era, but BSA administrators joined health advocates and physical educators in juxtaposing a balanced program of men's exercise, moderation in diet, and conservation of bodily energies and fluids against the detrimental effects of professional sports, excessive exercise, and bodybuilding. American Scout leaders emphasized that the right combination of modern living and outdoorsmanship helped (and required) a boy to maintain a balanced physique and overall health. BSA sources, like those in early British and colonial Indian Scouting, insisted that a well-rounded body was central to building a successful work ethic and character.[14]

BSA officials' consistent advocacy of all-around fitness for career success and their frequent criticisms of "bulging muscles" and "the proportions of our professional strong men" provided evidence of the emphasis modern American society and corporate-industrial work placed on balanced male bodies over virility, brute strength, and primitivism. The 1929 Scout merit badge pamphlet on *Physical Development* declared that building bulging muscles was "really harmful" and "absurd." The pamphlet was one of many early BSA sources that argued a balanced physique was needed to perform the specialized jobs of modern American industry. The author warned boys against aiming for "huge biceps and great knots of muscle. I do mean that he should be supple and enduring ... [in order to] stand the strain of business and also, if necessary, stand the occasional overstrain without bad effects." He suggested that the proper male body was efficient like a machine instead of exaggerated in proportions: "The real essential is the engine, the part under the hood—lungs, heart and internal organs. The engine should be kept oiled if it is to run smoothly and climb the hill, and the right kind of exercise is the lubricant." Gone were the days of celebrating American men's sheer willpower and aggression in business and social life.[15]

American Scout literature argued that competitive sports fostered overly specialized athletes with imbalanced bodies and poor character as well as huge crowds of idle men suffering from "spectatoritis"—symptoms of which included passiveness, gambling, and associating with "unclean" crowds. According to Scout teachings, professional sports left the majority of the population unfit for the responsibilities of modern work and American citizenship. In one of the few points of agreement on ideal manhood between Seton and BSA administrators after 1911, he and Baden-Powell likened American sport audiences to the ancient Roman crowds watching vast circuses and gladiator competitions while the empire fell into disarray. As muckraking reformer and BSA supporter Jacob Riis argued in a 1913 article in the *Outlook* (which the Mormon's Young Men's Improvement Association happily reprinted the following year in its *Improvement Era* journal), Scouting "gives every boy a chance to be in the game. The trouble with baseball and football is that they do not do that. . . . Nine or eleven boys take a hand in them, a hundred or a thousand sit and shout. They have no other part in it. Granted that there are many nines and elevens. Still there are many more whom the game really robs of a boy's most precious quality—initiative; it pauperizes the boys, physically and mentally, by making them take their fun at second hand. . . . If some of the fierce competitive spirit is lost [by Scouting rather than by playing football or baseball] that has run riot in the past, the standards are not." Professional sports, after all, did nothing to remedy the ominous fact that nearly 30 percent of American army registrants failed their physical exam during World War I. BSA leaders believed that every citizen needed to be physically fit in order to perform his duties during both war and peace, so they insisted that local officials refrain from promoting aggressive sport competitions. While a few early local American Scout officials occasionally ran track meets or baseball leagues, most troop and council leaders favored Scout games, calisthenics, hiking, and swimming for physical exercise.[16]

Arthur Astor Carey joined many early BSA leaders in arguing that Scouting's varied exercises and balanced physical development were very different from and superior to collegiate or professional athletic training, since the latter contributed to nervous strain and injured the heart by overexertion. Scouting instead offered each boy the chance to earn individual awards based on set physical standards of merit. Scout's Pace (traversing one mile in twelve minutes by alternating walking and jogging), swimming fifty yards for Life Saving, and hiking fourteen miles— all relatively attainable goals by able-bodied boys with good general fitness—were the only physical tests required to earn advanced Scout ranks. Setting-up drill—an early form of nonintensive group calisthenics for cardiovascular health and general fitness—provided a core feature of many BSA camps, meetings, and rallies across the country in the 1910s and 1920s. Most camp programs listed it as the first order of business each morning. These skills allowed boys to be self-reliant while hiking and camping, and to help people in emergencies. Such activities emphasized the functional regularity and endurance required by modern corporate work and urban living rather than the bursts of frantic speed and extreme strength needed for professional and violent sports.[17]

BSA administrators thus asserted that the best locale for developing the ideal male body was the outdoors rather than the football field, boxing arena, or gymnasium. The 1910 Boy Scout handbook declared, "We have sought out those pursuits which develop the finest character, the finest physique, and which may be followed out of doors, which, in a word, *make for manhood.*" BSA administrators soon jettisoned the primitive Indian hero Seton emphasized, but they adapted his notion of the well-rounded physique Scouts developed outdoors to modern career advancement and practical civic leadership. The Boy Scout handbook in use from 1914 to 1927 argued that the program "aims to touch [a Scout] physically—in the campcraft and woodcraft of the outdoor life in order that he may have strength in after days to give the best he has to the city and community in which he lives, as well as to the nation of which he is a part." Frequent Scout swimming, hiking, camping, calisthenics, and group games helped provide this general conditioning and balanced health to both boy members and Scoutmasters. The 1928 Boy Scout handbook concluded that developing a well-rounded body—"the key stone in the arch of the Scout Oath"—to keep physically strong, mentally awake, and morally straight in turn made it easier for Scouts to hike and camp.[18]

BSA leaders, like many boys' workers and child development experts at the time, believed that developing a man's well-rounded physique and modern character hinged on a boy conserving his bodily fluids and energies. American Scout authors reflected the era's notion of the "spermatic economy" and its confusion between semen, testosterone, and energy. Dr. George Fisher, who worked for the YMCA's Physical Department and later became James West's second-in-command at the BSA national office, wrote one of the few discussions on sexuality or rather masturbation in early Scout literature: "In the body of every boy, who has reached his teens, the Creator of the universe has sown a very important fluid. This fluid is the most wonderful material in the physical world." Fisher's 1911 essay explained that this "sex fluid" deepened a boy's voice and strengthened his muscles, brain, and nerves. He warned readers, "Any habit which a boy has that causes this fluid to be discharged from the body tends to weaken his strength, to make him less able to resist disease, and often unfortunately fastens upon him habits which later in life he cannot break." Fisher instructed boys to conserve this power and fluid by obeying the American Scout Oath to be pure in thought and clean in habit, since "to yield means to sacrifice strength and power and manliness." Much like wasted natural resources, the sex fluid could not be remade or serve future generations if dissipated on selfish endeavors. He explained that the sex fluid, if conserved by self-control, helped a boy develop physically while enlarging his ideas and making him nobler.[19]

In one of the few handbook sections that appeared unchanged in subsequent versions in the 1910s and 1920s, Fisher's chapter on "Health and Endurance" for the 1911 Boy Scout handbook encapsulated the BSA's balanced fitness and health ideal for modern work and urban living. Fisher diagrammed daily setting-up exercises to maintain erect posture and healthy organ function. He praised walking and suggested, "Slow running across country is great; it lacks strain and yet affords splendid stimulation to heart and lungs." Fisher discouraged weight lifting, long sprints, and distance racing: "A boy should be careful not to overdo.... Severe training for athletics should be avoided. All training should be in moderation." Fisher instructed boys to chew food slowly and thoroughly before swallowing and not to overeat or "eat too much of a mixed nature." He denounced stimulants such as coffee and tea as well as depressants like alcohol and tobacco. He suggested that boys have two times each day for "going to stool," even if they felt no desire to do so. This theme of bodily moderation and balanced health ran throughout American Scout literature and programming. BSA leaders argued that the balanced physical development that aided career success was key to self-control and modern character.[20]

From Self-Made to Self-Supporting

BSA administrators delinked self-reliance from the compulsion to achieve the nineteenth century's self-made business or farm ownership by carefully delineating the self-supporting Scout who worked loyally for others but managed himself as well as subordinate employees. Instead of jettisoning the Protestant work ethic completely in favor of a life focused on leisure and consumption, American Scout leaders instructed members to use the Victorian virtue of self-control to reign in self-made manhood's excess individualism and increase their work efficiency. In addition to revising Baden-Powell's original British Oath, American Scout literature and activities placed the values of self-reliance and self-control safely within the cooperative parameters of the adult-led Scout troop and its prescribed civic tasks and modern character-building goals.

Explanations of BSA Laws placed a little more emphasis on business values like developing a pleasing personality during the 1920s, but this shift represented a refinement of American Scouters' vision of manhood rather than a new ideal.

BSA administrators updated self-reliance and self-control in their revision of the British Boy Scout Oath. Baden-Powell's original Oath required Scouts to be loyal to God and king, help others at all times, and obey the Scout Laws. In 1911, the BSA changed "king" to "country" and added the promise, "To keep myself physically strong, mentally awake and morally straight." A likely source for the change was G. Stanley Hall, the leading proponent of the child development theories of racial recapitulation and adolescence. In response to a solicitation for advice from a special BSA committee charged with Americanizing the British Scout Laws and Oath, Hall suggested adding a new Law on purity, "something to the effect that the scout should keep himself clean in body and mind, that he should respect other boys' sisters as he does his own. . . . Some phrase touching on eugenics, not by name and very lightly and remotely, ought to be included." Hall later merged these ideas into his proposed addition to the Scout Oath, "involving doing duty to one's self, such as to keep myself well, true, pure or something of that sort. . . . This is often the best kind of discipline to do duty to other people." Hall's notion of keeping oneself implied that boys who naturally possessed self-control and self-reliance should protect that essence from outside moral contagion (like a white boy's vow of character chastity) rather than the idea that any person could be taught such virtues. The final version of the American Oath made no specific mention of eugenics, but it closely resembled Hall's recommendations. The rewording of the Oath held significant implications, in that officials considered a violation of the Oath to be a major moral and character infraction for a Scout.[21]

Emphasis on self-reliance, sometimes referred to as resourcefulness, threaded through much of the early BSA's programming and ideology. Learning to be self-reliant in the woods (but always within the company of the troop and its adult leader) comprised a key early Scout goal and activity. Outside of thrift and First Aid, most of the Second and First Class rank tests that preoccupied much of boys' Scouting time evaluated standardized camping and hiking skills. Woodcraft focused on outdoor techniques, like scientific animal and plant identification and tracking. Campcraft taught boys to make shelters, cook outdoors, and maintain modern standards of hygiene. Officials described the individually earned merit badges, which covered an increasingly broad range of subjects, as aids to self-reliance. The term "merit badge" suggested that consistent effort and acquired knowledge and skills rather than noble birth or political party connection determined the distribution of life's rewards. The vocational merit badges encouraged boys to learn stick-to-itiveness and find a steady career. By not taking dead-end jobs, Scouts could avoid being dependent on charity or the state.[22]

BSA officials differentiated the self-reliant Boy Scout and the modern corporate-industrial employee he was trained to become from the nineteenth century's dominant masculine ideal of the self-made homesteader, artisan, or businessman—all of whom were defined by ownership of independent farms or businesses. An increasing number of Americans, especially the skilled working class and middle class who made up the majority of BSA membership, worked for large corporations or the government by the early twentieth century. British and American Scout leaders thus asserted the dignity and character-building effects of males working together, faithfully and productively, for businesses and agencies owned or directed by other men. Baden-Powell argued that career training could help Scouts become "self-supporting," a term that helped separate self-reliance from self-made manhood's requirement to become one's own boss. National Scout Commissioner Dan Beard and other BSA national leaders emphasized that every boy needed to at least learn to work for a living so that he would not have to beg, steal, or depend on handouts. Beard argued, "Ready made clothing, food and shelter do not grow wild on trees on public land to be plucked by lazy people—*And* all these things are the product of labor and only made by labor." BSA officials insisted that good Scouts work to earn their own uniforms and fees instead of relying on parents or charity—a skill that would carry over into respectable manhood.[23]

The careful distinction Scout leaders made between working under the direction of others and becoming slavish automatons redirected self-control from its Victorian associations with spiritual well-being and self-employment to a modern, task-oriented focus. Administrators exhorted boy members to develop self-control and self-reliance so that they could work semi-independently on set tasks instead of having to rely on constant instructions and discipline from others. BSA leaders drew on Hall's theories of racial recapitulation and adolescence to argue that less mature boys were controlled by selfish and primitive instincts and therefore had to follow a superior man's firm lead, while evolved adolescent boys developed a balance between self-control and self-reliance that they consciously directed toward managing group endeavors and facilitating the greater good. A 1914 article in *Good Housekeeping* by prominent children's fiction author and nature conservationist Thornton W. Burgess, titled "Making Men of Them," insisted that good Scouts were guided by self-conscience rather than blind obedience to authority: "He is not merely a Scout when under the eye of his scout master. He is a Scout all the time under the tenfold more watchful eye of his own conscience." A 1915 *Boys' Life* article encouraged boys to avoid temper tantrums, loud speech, excessive eating, alcohol, and tobacco because "A SCOUT practices self-control, for he knows that men who master problems in the world must first master themselves."[24]

Over the course of the 1920s, BSA national administrators achieved an effective balance between self-reliance and being other-directed. The booming economy and business craze of the mid-1920s filtered over slightly into BSA programming. Masculine values once directed at paid Local Council Executives seeped a little into training and literature for volunteer Scoutmasters, Patrol Leaders, and regular boy members in the 1920s. For example, priorities related to business became a bit more visible in explanations of Scout Laws, such as being trustworthy and obedient. A 1930 *Boys' Life* article on honesty emphasized that modern business required it: "In business, in all forms of partnership, it's the same way; successful operation depends on mutual trust and confidence, mutual honesty." The virtue extended to consumption: "Every day merchandise worth thousands of dollars is delivered on credit, because the dealer knows that the purchaser will make payment when his bill is rendered." A 1928 *Boys' Life* article by John D. Rockefeller Jr. on "Character and Business" argued that although a boy needed to obey the law, he should respect those who try by legitimate means to repeal laws contrary to the public interest, which "unnecessarily hamper and restrict business and do not serve the common good." Rockefeller also suggested that a boy could no longer be completely self-reliant: "No man can live unto himself alone, our lives are too interdependent." BSA literature from the 1910s had told Scouts they were morally obligated to be courteous toward dependents, such as women and invalids, but a chapter in the 1928 Boy Scout handbook on "The Manners of a Scout" stressed that boys should also act modest and courteous because it brought them advantages in business contacts and job hunting.[25]

The continued emphasis in BSA programming on self-reliance and the slight resurgence of individualistic Scout heroes such as the craftsman, explorer, and noble Indian in the second half of the 1920s provided a counterweight to the business and other-directed drift. BSA literature increasingly argued that a boy's conscience was a better judge of his character than were others. The 1928 Boy Scout handbook instructed boys trying to earn advanced ranks to judge themselves on whether they had done their best to meet the obligations of the Scout Oath and Law. Previous handbooks had required a boy's Scoutmaster, teacher, parents, and minister to assess him on this final and most important test for Second and First Class rank advancement. To a modest degree, the BSA's increasing use of the Patrol Method promoted boy leaders' autonomy and independent thinking. In the second half of the 1920s, Boy Scouts across the country competed to earn invitations to join celebrated explorers on Arctic expeditions, an African safari, and an Alaskan bear hunt. Scout groups greeted Charles Lindbergh at every stop on the popular tour celebrating his solo, trans-Atlantic airplane flight. Such efforts glamorized individual bravery and self-reliance—masculine qualities that served as balances to the corporate, bureaucratic mind-set. However, these voyages also highlighted the welding of heroic manhood and individual effort with modern expertise, such as Byrd's scientific expedition to the Arctic and technological innovation in Lindbergh's airplane flight.[26]

As the 1928 cover illustration from the *Business* merit badge pamphlet in Figure 2.3 suggests, late 1920s BSA manhood represented more of a refinement of the organization's 1910s values than a completely new vision. Since almost half of the fourteen steps to "Honorable Success" in business mirrored BSA Laws, the sketch invited a comparison between the two sets of values. The artist inscribed "cleanliness," "obedience," "politeness," "mental alertness," "honesty," and "courage" almost directly from the Scout Laws and Oath. "Punctuality" formed a key component of being trustworthy and loyal. Order, though not an official Law, comprised a regular method and goal of Scout programming. BSA sources frequently stressed "self-reliance." "Energy" contributed to a Scout's cheerful work, physical endurance, and balanced exercise. Explanations of the Scout Law on thrift emphasized making the best use of one's life opportunities. "Responsibility" and "square dealing" could be seen as linked to the Laws on being trustworthy and honest. In many ways, the

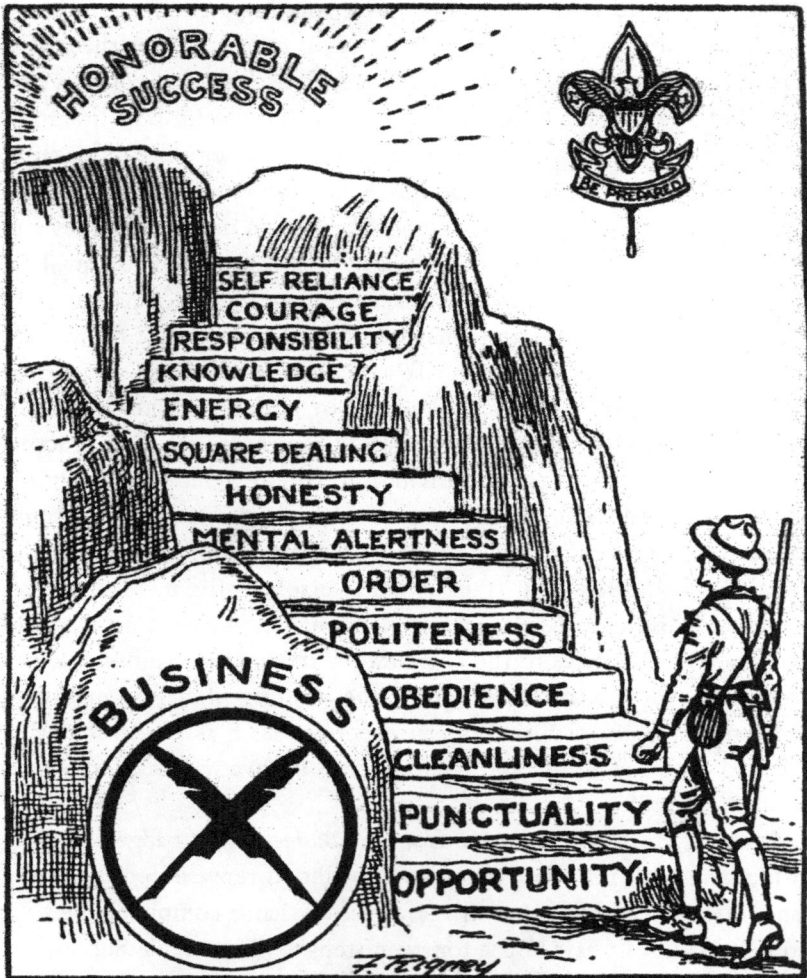

Figure 2.3 Climbing the steps up the business mountain trail. Frank Rigney, "Honorable Success," *Business* (merit badge pamphlet) (1928): cover. (Courtesy of Boy Scouts of America National Scouting Museum Archival Collection)

business model simply clarified or helped modernize traditional BSA values. The absence of the Scout Laws on being helpful, friendly, kind, and reverent on the stairs to business success was noticeable. These Laws could be linked to altruism, equality, and spirituality—life approaches that had little place in modern business. However, this overt business imagery constituted just one of the many cover sketches on Scout merit badge pamphlet titles then being distributed. In fact, combining individual competition with cooperation and group needs proved to be a more consistent refrain in BSA literature and activities.[27]

"The Corporation of Spirit as Well as Effort": Balancing Competition and Cooperation

The BSA's modern character teachings and core programming balanced Victorian men's competitive individualism with the group cooperation and service to the broader community required for a corporate workforce and an increasingly interdependent urban society. As President Coolidge expressed in a speech to the American Scout delegation to the 1924 World Scout Jamboree in Denmark, Scouting taught boys to shed the old individualistic tendencies and adjust to modern, cooperative life and its division of labor. Unregulated competition and the aggressive self-made man represented useful models on the western frontier and in the emerging industrial capitalist system of the nineteenth century, but corporate owners by the early twentieth century believed that unbridled competition was harmful to business. The captains of industry had merged independent businesses into vast corporations and enlisted politicians' help in regulating the economy to smooth out the volatile boom and bust cycles. Even the era's famed trust busting—which on the surface protected the self-made small business endeavor—often seemed to work in favor of large, efficient corporations. Moving-assembly-line production and the new management style in factories and offices encouraged consistent cooperation. At the same time, the specialization of function popularized by Taylor and Ford required a clear hierarchy of knowledge, workers, and management levels. Each corporation expected its employees to work together in order to help the business defeat others in the industry but supposedly allowed workers to compete against one another in a friendly fashion for better positions and pay. Twentieth-century corporate workers advanced by exhibiting efficiency in a group and task-oriented framework and successfully encouraging consistent effort from others. High school and college students' growing independent subculture and clubs of the 1920s similarly blended competition, hierarchy, and group cooperation to prepare its adherents for future success. BSA programming taught Scouts and their adult leaders to maintain this proper balance between competition and cooperation and to sort others into modern corporate work's hierarchy of roles and rewards.[28]

BSA leaders often praised Scouting for being noncompetitive in the sense that each boy earned his own ranks and merit badges based on set standards of achievement, and they primarily taught boys the skills needed to earn individual awards through cooperating within the patrol and troop. James Wilder, Sea Scouting's second director, argued at the 1922 BSA Executives National Training Conference that organized, cooperative selflessness was replacing individualism as the primary trait men needed to succeed in modern American society: "Scouting on the sea, the Scout Law applied in a confined and crowded company of men! Now the days have gone by when Uncle Dan Boone stood on the top of a mountain with his foot on a dead Indian and a coon skin hat. That was the pioneer—a fine idea, but we are moving on and we are getting crowded and we must learn how to live in a crowded community. Now I can see the [Sea Scout] ship as one of the greatest chances in the world to teach modern conscience." Numerous BSA publications and leader training sessions stressed that the troop unit and group activities formed the key mechanisms for teaching boys modern cooperation. This emphasis on interdependence helps explain why so many prominent Americans and institutions supported Boy Scouting. The insistence on congenial cooperation extended equally to male officials in the organization. Discussion session leaders at Boy Scout administrator conferences and Scoutmaster training sessions often asked those participants who objected or disagreed to change their votes to that of the majority to ensure a consensus. For example, at the first National Training School for Executives in 1925, the leader of a strategy session on how to start a theoretical new Local Council asked the following of the few participants who voted against being ready to discuss model plans: "Will the 'no's' kindly make their vote unanimous, so that we have a feeling of co-operation all the way through?" When the dissenters did not reply, the leader said, "Thank you." Such gestures also applied in BSA leaders' discussions about policy changes to sublimate disagreement among members. The session report or minutes then reflected that the decision was unanimous.[29]

Officials recognized that *controlled* competition helped attract members and spur boys to advance through the program. BSA literature instructed Scoutmasters to pit boys, patrols, and troops against each other in friendly efficiency contests. Troop leaders regularly used competition at weekly meetings, camps, and council rallies to prod boys to learn skills. While a particular boy or troop might best the field, even the losers could still earn their own merit and rank badges by displaying the required skill competencies. The 1929 Scoutmaster handbook argued, "The relations between the patrols should be characterized by approximately equal division of cooperation and competition. It is important for the unity and strength of the troop that the patrol cooperate readily and effectively. It is essential to the development of patrol morale that there be between the patrols *continued friendly competition*."[30]

Victorian men tended to see character as an internal, holistic quality, but Scouting and its progress-tracking methods broke character development into segmented tasks, which could be evaluated by set proficiency standards and analyzed quantitatively. BSA literature suggested that troops put a progress grid up on their meeting room walls to chart each boy's and patrol's success in exams and rank achievement: "Each Scout knows right where he stands, and what is better he knows that others are watching his record too. He can also see the progress of other Scouts and he knows that what they do and have done he can do." The chart encouraged boys to compete against each other while cooperating with their patrol against other units. Some Local Councils used more elaborate Scout and troop efficiency contests, referred to as the "credit system," to track uniforms, dues, community service, hiking and camping trips, heroic acts, school grades, and attendance at troop meetings and church. The 1914 Scoutmaster handbook even suggested introducing efficiency percentages for Scout skills, "such a system as [is] used in baseball records of league standings, batting averages, etc."[31]

BSA administrators depended on controlled, friendly competition to spur members through the program but warned troop leaders against fostering excessive ambition or haughtiness in boys. Dr. H. W. Hurt, the psychologist and BSA Research Executive who helped author the new 1928 Boy Scout handbook and was at the time designing the Cub branch for boys under twelve, argued at a 1929 Scoutmasters' conference that the organization needed a rank and badge advancement scheme because "growth is the Law of life" and boys needed goals to inspire character development. He suggested, though, that Scoutmasters ward off the inevitable "small-pox epidemic of badge hunting" by limiting the number of badges an overly eager boy could earn in a month or having him help the other boys with their badge work. In a speech the BSA's national Director of Education gave at the same conference, a section subtitled "Stabilizing Ambition" argued that the Scoutmaster could provide stability in a boy's life by helping him channel his ambition toward a worthwhile vocation and life objective. Whereas individual ambition, willpower, and aggressiveness formed prized and essential virtues for self-made men in the 1800s, with its more open economy and frontier, ambition and competition without a constructive, finite goal and awareness of the overall group's needs risked upsetting American Scout training for an increasingly interdependent urban society and its corporate-industrial economy.[32]

The BSA taught its most promising boy members to sort other people into the hierarchy of roles required by modern work. As the 1912 Scout-master handbook explained, "The *object* is to get the boys to *work together*. The spirit of competition and the individual desire to excel must give place to a *division of responsibility* and the *corporation of spirit as well as effort*. . . . The boys will unconsciously learn to size up and measure the other fellows with whom they are working. The ability to know, to awaken, and finally to use to the best advantage another fellow's skill is the secret of the success of many of our greatest men in the business world. It is the Scout Master's opportunity to start his boys toward a successful career along these lines." The author stated that controlled competition for positions of authority resulted in the willing cooperation and loyalty of subordinate boys to those worthy of being leaders. Managing a modern workforce required knowing how to work with and influence others.[33]

BSA character and its modernized work ethic drew on social Darwinism as well as scientific management. Scouting's emphasis on loyalty, cheerful and efficient work, and cooperation for the greater good helped balance nineteenth-century masculine virtues like self-reliance, self-control, and competition. BSA leaders characterized Scout advancement tests and efficiency contests as a modern-day version of the struggle for the survival of the fittest. As the 1912 Scoutmaster handbook argued, "Every test is in its nature a *selection* in which the efficient survive and enjoy the greater privileges, while the inefficient either drop out or remain in the lower ranks. The desire to survive and to live an efficient life is the spur of our modern commercial age." The author argued that the Scout who advanced in rank demonstrated his fitness for higher positions in the future: "Life is made up of many standards and stations of merit. Good positions select good men, and high honors await the boys of to-day who are worthy to become the representative men of tomorrow." Indeed, the prized Eagle Scout rank served as a broadly accepted standard of good character and a solid work ethic, which applicants eagerly included on job résumés and college admission letters. Learning the proper way to interact with other social groups formed a key complement to Scouting's new work ethic as well as a success guide for an increasingly interdependent nation.[34]

The Scout Laws of Society

The remaining six BSA Laws, the rest of the Scout Oath, and related character teaching activities helped white middle-class and elite men reassert their social dominance in a diversifying urban society. The decline of apprenticeship and the growth of segregated childhood spaces such as schools and playgrounds that quarantined boys from the broader community made Scout lessons for relating properly to adults and other social groups essential. This project intertwined with teaching select boys to guide those with inferior character into subordinate economic roles. Historians of the American idea of success have emphasized that social responsibility declined in self-made men's novels and advice manuals by the late nineteenth century. The vast majority of American Scout publications, however, worked to revive the principle that learning to serve others in the community demonstrated superior character and was a core duty of modern men. BSA leaders explained that the Scout Laws on being courteous and helpful should be practiced on those weaker in character. BSA administrators stated that the Fourth Scout Law on being friendly to others and a brother to every other Scout should be limited to those who possessed worthy character. American Scout officials also added three important new Laws to the original British nine. The Laws on bravery and cleanliness suggested that a Scout should set an example of moral rectitude for others while avoiding intimate interactions with inferior groups who might be moral contagions. A new BSA Law on being reverent stressed tolerance for those belonging to mainstream faiths and the importance of religious belief for developing modern manhood and democratic citizenship. Collectively, these Laws of society trained members to successfully navigate America's growing cities and manage their diversifying populations.

A Scout's helpfulness and courtesy symbolized his strength and preparedness relative to those groups depicted in BSA literature as inferior and less deserving of leadership positions. Officials stated that these duties particularly applied to a Scout's relationships with women, children, the elderly, and other "weak and helpless" people. The Third Law, a

Scout is helpful, instructed boys to "be prepared at any time to save life, help injured persons, and share the home duties. He must *do at least one good turn to somebody every day.*" Some Americans at the time viewed selflessness and kindness as feminine traits, so BSA supporters worked to persuade boy members that being helpful to others was manly. In a 1919 article in the *Outlook* titled "A New Moral Force," Ashley Piper argued, "The Scouting ideal of goodness is not negative, 'sissified,' smug, dour-visaged, of the 'holier than thou' variety. On the contrary, it is positive, virile, modest, healthy, happy. . . . Like a knight, he is sworn to 'reverence his conscience as his king,' to be *helpful to all people at all times.* What more can we ask of, or for, our future citizens?" BSA literature constantly admonished boys to "do a Good Turn daily" to a person in need, which became the organization's slogan. Common Good Turns, such as delivering holiday food baskets to poor mothers, providing directions to lost people, and helping children and ladies across the street, reinforced the notion that Scouts possessed superior character and bodies.[35]

BSA explanations of the Law on being helpful stated that young Scouts would be called on in emergencies to help the injured or save the lives of those who lacked the strength, expertise, and composure to care for themselves. For example, a 1928 *New York Times* headline, "Boy Scout Dives into Bay and Saves Woman While Men Stand Helplessly on the Sea Wall," suggested how a Scout's training proved his superiority to both the victim and unprepared male onlookers. The Scout had to struggle with the drowning woman and finally "subdued her" in order to save her. Annual reports recounted hundreds of such tales of Scouts earning medals of heroism for Life Saving. Training in outdoorsmanship and Life Saving also helped Scouts locate missing persons before government search and rescue units were widely available. A 1914 article reported that Scouts found a missing man after two days of police futility: the man was "exhausted from his wandering. . . . The police force stated at the end of the search that the lads were better adapted to the work than men, as they covered more territory and they did their work more thoroughly than the average man would." The disciplined Scouts showed up the bewildered man and the inefficient police with their preparedness.[36]

BSA leaders often compared the Fifth Law—to be courteous—to a medieval knight's chivalry; both suggested strong men helping weak people. American Scout literature distinguished chivalric courtesy from a woman's mere politeness. A 1926 *Boys' Life* article contrasted a woman's "soft" answer that "turneth away wrath" against a good man's "far more advanced ability of reaching the heart and stirring the kindliness of both friend and foe, which sincere courtesy has never failed to do." Anyone could be polite, but courtesy to a dependent upheld a social hierarchy dominated by self-reliant males. Scout and national media coverage suggested that helpful and courteous acts could also be performed along the axes of racial, class, and bodily differences. Early BSA magazines and reports frequently specified when the recipient of a Good Turn was non-white, poor, or disabled. A *Boys' Life* article praising Scouts for helping African American women and children left destitute by a 1926 hurricane concluded, "I think that Scouting is a good means of engendering race chivalry." One *New York Times* article, titled "Help Aged Negro," praised Spokane, Washington, Scouts for planting a garden for an "ex-slave" that same year. More than sixty years after Emancipation, the former slave still seemed dependent on charity from white males. The BSA's 1924 Annual Report to Congress provided a visual cascade of the gendered, racial, class, and physical ability dimensions to courteous Good Turns reported by Scouts that year. A two-page list of selected Good Turns highlighted the following: eleven acts of kindness to ladies, seven to the elderly, eight to children, two to impoverished people, ten to sick or disabled people, and three to African Americans, including "Indorsed a check for a negro who could not write" and "Carried negro man to his work, 1 mile, in automobile."[37]

The seemingly innocuous Fourth Law, "a Scout is friendly," actually became one of the most contentious in early American Scouting. Baden-Powell instructed British boys, "A Scout is a friend to all, and a brother to every other Scout, no matter to what social class the other belongs. . . . A Scout must never be a SNOB. A snob is one who looks down upon another because he is poorer, or who is poor and resents another because he is rich." As they did with the reference to being loyal to one's employer, BSA editors removed the concluding portion of the Law referring to social classes. American Scout leaders argued that their new version reflected the more democratic nature of the organization and American society: "Note undemocratic phrase in English Law No. 4 to which we happily have nothing to correspond." Early BSA officials did not mean that social classes did not or should not exist but rather that American society was and should be free of Europe's "artificial" social divisions.[38]

BSA lessons on friendliness insisted that discrepancies in wealth were a result of—and insignificant when compared to—real differences in innate character. Arthur Astor Carey warned Scouts in 1916 to avoid being "tied down by what is called 'class prejudice' and give too much importance to the mere circumstances of life, such as wealth or poverty, luxury or hardship.... Life itself is distinct from these and far more important." He claimed that the disadvantages of being rich far outweighed the advantages, so the poor should not despise the rich. (As the grandson of John Jacob Astor, the richest American in the mid-nineteenth century, Carey's words might have rung a little hollow to poor boys.) He instructed boys to adjust the manner in which they were friendly to match the recipient's character. American Scouts had to be friendly to all but were supposed to reserve true friendship for those with similar beliefs and behavior. For example, Carey warned that being friendly to a drowning drunk might require a Scout to "strike him senseless" in order to save his life.[39]

BSA national leaders had to tread carefully regarding the implication of racial equality in the Fourth Law's stipulation that a Scout had to be a brother to every other Scout. Prior to 1924, early BSA national leaders condoned many Local Councils' decisions to avoid the issue by excluding or segregating nonwhite boys and men. Since Scouts were seen to possess superior character and training to non-Scouts, excluding nonwhites from membership confined them to the category of dependents to whom Scouts gave helpful and courteous service rather than allowing them the egalitarian respect required by the friendly Law. Some councils that enrolled nonwhites denied them the opportunity to wear the official uniform. This policy sidestepped the Fourth Law's requirement that a Scout who saw another *uniformed* Scout had to be friendly to him, which would have signified their equality and brotherhood. Scout officials in other countries, such as the British Empire, employed similar techniques.

In consultation with hundreds of leading educators, clergy, businessmen, politicians, and child development experts, BSA administrators added new Laws on being brave, clean, and reverent to complete the Americanization of the nine British Laws in 1911. While these virtues may have carried some individual and internal connotations, BSA sources often stressed that these values helped Scouts navigate a diversifying, urbanizing society. Being brave, clean, and reverent distinguished a good Scout from the masses and demonstrated his ability to lead a modern nation.

The instruction in the Tenth Law on bravery that Scouts "stand up for the right against the coaxings of friends or the jeers or threats of enemies" hinted at fighting for social justice. However, unlike Dan Beard's Sons of

Daniel Boone, most explanations of bravery in BSA national publications through the mid-1920s failed to include suggestions for actively combating racial discrimination. BSA administrators instead highlighted that Scout ancestors—including knights, pioneers, and Pilgrims—had demonstrated bravery by subduing aggressive thugs and savages. BSA literature recounted the knights' fight against law-breaking brigands and irreverent infidels to protect women, children, and social order. Some American Scout publications and pageants praised brave Pilgrims and pioneers for conquering the savage Indians who threatened their wives and children while carving civilized settlements out of the howling wilderness.[40]

BSA stories and published images also suggested that modern-day Scouts could demonstrate this "Racial Inheritance" and "manly heritage" of bravery by standing up against working-class street toughs (typically a code word for Irish or southern and eastern European immigrants in this era). Pageants, local practices, and published sketches occasionally replicated this narrative of a Scout showing bravery in the face of working-class toughs. Some Scout troops performed public skits along this line, implying that the source of working-class immigrant boys' problems and poverty was their aggressive character—diverting attention from nativist discrimination and the structural inequalities of corporate capitalism. A few local leaders reported that Scouts had to endure taunting from working-class boys for their uniforms and parading. However, as chapter 5 will explore, BSA national administrators moved quickly to incorporate working-class and light-skinned immigrants into Scouting and the American mainstream.[41]

The Eleventh BSA Law on cleanliness claimed that it was a moral choice and a potential moral contagion more than a material condition. Like the thrift Law, the cleanliness Law reflected the era's belief that bodily, mental, and moral health were intertwined. Explanations of the cleanliness Law suggested that it stood as a bulwark against the heterosocial, mass-leisure-based youth culture that was increasingly attracting middle-class boys and girls. The Eleventh Law explained that a good Scout "keeps clean in body and thought, stands for clean speech, clean sport, clean habits, and travels with a clean crowd." A 1919 article on the cleanliness Law insisted that a man "may be clean in his thoughts in spite of squalid surroundings, but a mentally clean man would never deliberately choose such an environment. The man who considers perspiration and inspiration synonymous is a back number. The day of dirt is over. The modern business man stands for cleanliness because he knows the salutary effect on his employes [*sic*], he knows that plenty of fresh air and sanitary surroundings not only add to the tone of the place but also add to the profits. . . . A good scout can't be habitually dirty, it is an impossibility." Given the dirty conditions of urban tenement dwellings and factory work as well as the disease and moral dangers that some native-born white Americans associated with nonwhites and new immigrants, the Scout Law on cleanliness implied that boy members should maintain their distance from such contaminating influences. Explanations of the cleanliness Law sometimes contained veiled references to not masturbating. A 1930 pamphlet warned, "There are boys who check nature's work with them by unclean habits. Just as a growing tree loses its sap and its strength if you cut into its bark with your axe, the growing boy loses his strength if he misuses his own body." BSA leaders argued that constructive outdoor activities among worthy peers led by an able Scoutmaster distracted boys from mental contamination and moral filth.[42]

Baden-Powell and his original British Scout program somewhat downplayed the importance of religious belief, but BSA national officials added a Twelfth Law on reverence because they felt it was essential for a modern boy's character and civic development. American Scout administrators argued that the particular ways in which boy members should be reverent demonstrated their ability to be political and business leaders. A 1929 Scoutmasters' training course suggested that rather than Scouts just attending church as individuals, "why not occasionally have [the uniformed troop] gather in the vestibule of the church and march down the aisle to the stirring notes of some march, present the church flag and the Flag of the United States with color guards while the congregation joins in singing one verse of 'America.'" Boy Scouts also showed reverent leadership by mowing church lawns, distributing church literature, serving as ushers, and helping handicapped members attend services.[43]

The BSA Laws on bravery and cleanliness encouraged members to distinguish between people of different socioeconomic groups, but the Law on reverence generally facilitated inclusiveness, at least among churchgoers. Hoping to appeal to a wide spectrum of Americans, BSA national publications offered very little in terms of direct religious instruction outside of encouraging Scouts to attend the church of their choosing and requiring them to "respect the convictions of others in matters of custom and religion." In an era in which discrimination and violence against Jews, Catholics, and other non-Protestants was still common, the reverence Law taught boy members a cosmopolitan tolerance for those belonging to other faiths. The BSA provided a range of religious services at large camps as well as speakers from diverse faiths at conferences and meetings. American Scout officials succeeded in their efforts to elicit statements of support from national leaders of the major church denominations; moreover, churches were the largest type of sponsor of Scout troops in the 1910s and 1920s.[44]

These Scout Laws of society helped the organization's primarily white members develop the modern manhood necessary to reassert their superiority to those groups depicted in BSA sources as having inferior character and underdeveloped civic capacity. Courtesy, helpfulness, and Good Turns carried a tone of condescension toward those dependent on service from Scouts. Being brave, clean, and reverent demonstrated Scouts' advanced character and worthiness to lead society while hinting at the immoral contagion of unfit groups. The BSA's three new Laws provided members essential life guidance in an era in which America's burgeoning cities, diversifying society, and heterosocial youth culture seemed in need of checking. Some American Scout national and local leaders balked at the egalitarian implications of the Law on being friendly; most tended to stress them less than hierarchical Laws like courtesy and helpfulness. While early BSA publications, policies, and administrators' statements provide a clear sense of its leaders' vision of a modern work ethic and proper social relations, how did boy members, troop leaders, and other adults experience and respond to these character ideals?

"Scouting as a Way of Life" for Boys and Adult Members

Surveys and memoirs of Boy Scouts, parents, Scoutmasters, and community adults confirmed that many members and observers believed that the BSA effectively taught its vision of balanced character and modern work to boys in the 1910s and 1920s. Out of 158 parents of San Francisco Boy Scouts surveyed in 1924, for example, 154 replied that Scouting was definitely a positive character influence on their sons. None of the respondents reported that it was a negative character influence. In the additional free-write response section, ninety-two of the parents listed specific favorable character attributes that Scouting had helped develop. Common answers included being considerate, self-reliant, obedient, responsible, and "much better in every way," as well as "will be better man because of Scouting." In 1928, a much larger and nationwide survey of 1,609 community educators, businessmen, ministers, professionals, and other leading citizens who were not BSA members or Scout parents tallied 1,398 answers (87 percent) that Scouting was a "Positive Good" on boys' overall character development. Only twenty-two of the community adults reported it as being harmful to some boys' character. Collectively, these surveys and boy and adult members' later reflections described Scouting's character Laws, Oath, and program activities as a key gateway to men's status and preparation for both success in modern work and a more moral and constructive life.[45]

Belonging to Scouting and undergoing its respected character training marked a pivotal life moment and the first stage of adulthood for many early members. When a BSA national commission surveyed over two thousand boys of mixed ranks and ages in 1928 and asked what they felt were the most important Scout activities for developing their character, the Investiture ceremony that represented their formal entrance into the program ranked second among twelve options. Given its relatively short duration, the surveyed Scouts ranking Investiture so high may seem surprising. In early twentieth-century American society, however, most adolescent boys had lost the coming-of-age rituals and life steps that many teenage boys in previous generations had enjoyed: career apprenticeship, working for enough hours and wages to make a needed contribution to the family's income, plowing a farm field, regularly mixing with other members of the community, or being one of the few boys in town to graduate high school. Scouting, on the other hand, provided each boy a voluntary choice to become part of a selective male organization that taught them adult character and work values, instilled modern social skills, and provided opportunities for independent adventure and community engagement. As a thirteen-year-old Second Class Scout survey respondent explained, "My entrance into Scouting and the ceremony made me feel like living up to the Scout Oath and Law forever afterward. . . . I worked hard to pass my tests and the ceremony of investiture was very inspiring. I always remember that evening when I was taken into Scouting as a red letter day in my life." For many boys, becoming a Scout marked the first publicly recognized and adult-approved step toward becoming not only a man but also a leading citizen, who could earn status and respect from adults beginning at the age of twelve. A fifteen-year-old First Class Scout succinctly explained, "When I entered the Scout world I felt as though I was no longer a 'kid'; I felt as though I had a certain goal to work for." Indeed, in the eyes of the era's presidents of the United States, captains of industry, town mayors, social reformers, professionals, leading educators, and parents, a Boy Scout *was* no longer just a kid.[46]

Just joining the Scouts was a key motivator for some early boy members to begin living a more constructive life: "It changes your morals so as to follow higher ideals. It stops your foolish antics forever." A thirteen-year-old Second Class Scout recalled, "About two weeks after I had joined the Boy Scouts my teacher was scolding me for something I didn't do, so I got fresh and sassed her back. That night when I was saying my prayers and repeating the Scout Oath and Law, I don't know what it was, but I couldn't get past the fifth Law [to be courteous]. I tossed all night and I finally decided to beg my teacher's pardon. If you ever had a boy or were a boy you would know how hard it was for me to do this. The next day I begged my teacher's pardon in front of the class. This inspired me to do better things, and to live up to the Scout Oath and Law." The first striking thing about this new Scout's story is that repeating the Scout Oath and Law was a part of his nighttime prayers, so the values conveyed at Investiture and at the opening of most troops' regular weekly meetings already held special meaning for him. Second, he had internalized the promise to obey the Scout Oath and Law, so the discrepancy between his old schoolboy habits and his new Scout values kept him up that night. Finally, he self-modified and corrected his habit of back-talking a teacher—by admitting his wrongdoing publicly and in front of his school peers—after only two weeks of being a Scout. This boy was not alone in merging the Scout Oath and Law into his behavior choices. Other surveyed Scouts explained how pledging the Oath and Law helped stop them from running with a crooked gang, stealing money, cheating on school tests, and shooting off fireworks against a mother's wishes.

In response to questions about which of the twelve Laws Scouting most consistently taught to boy members, a trio of late 1920s national surveys of Boy Scouts, Scoutmasters, and community adults who were not members of the BSA all ranked trustworthiness first. Indeed, the belief that Scouts were trained to be more trustworthy than the average boy formed a key reason for early Scouts' public status and privileges. Helpful and obedient, two Laws closely related to being trustworthy, came in next on average between the three groups. Surveyed boys and community adults highlighted being helpful more, while Scoutmasters stressed that Scouting taught obedience. Loyal, courteous, and friendly formed the second tier of Scout Laws emphasized or experienced when the three surveys were averaged. Boys stressed that Scouting taught being friendly, while community adults highlighted courtesy among these three. According to the surveys, clean, reverent, and brave formed the third tier of Scout Laws emphasized. Troop leaders placed cleanliness noticeably higher than did the community adults and especially the boys, suggesting that physical and moral cleanliness was more of an adult concern. Scoutmasters also ranked reverent higher than did the other two groups, while community adults believed Scouting taught bravery more than did the boys or Scoutmasters. On average, being cheerful, kind, and thrifty formed the bottom tier of Laws Scouting emphasized or boys experienced. Boys, however, encountered being cheerful more often than adults and Scoutmasters thought.[47]

Community adults expressed that Scouting taught modern character, work, and leadership values much more than it did outdated nineteenth-century virtues or primitive, aggressive, and martial values. One question in the 1928 survey of 1,609 non-BSA community leaders from across the country allowed each respondent to free-write his own list of traits (good or bad) he had seen Scouting develop in actual boys in his town. The community leaders listed most of the twelve official Scout Laws among their top seventeen answers, along with related character values such as initiative, resourcefulness, self-reliance, reliability, leadership, cooperation, and unselfishness. Community adults named outdated masculine virtues such as ambition (twenty-eighth), independence (forty-third) and competition (fifty-eighth) noticeably less. Even more striking in survey responses was the near absence of primitive, martial values such as rashness, audacity, boisterousness, militarism, aggressiveness, and being domineering.[48]

Memoirs and interviews done later in the life of early Boy Scouts and troop leaders frequently highlighted that the boys internalized the Laws, Oath, and other Scout character teachings as both young members and as guides for their adult lives. Verner Kelly, a Texas Boy Scout in the late 1920s who was awarded his Eagle rank in 1931, stated in an interview done nearly seventy years later that as a boy member he "took the Scout motto and laws seriously. I felt they were sensible guides and still do. I was proud to be a Boy Scout. So proud, as a matter of fact, that when at age 14 I accompanied my aunt, my brother and my sister on a summer auto trip to California, I insisted on wearing my Scout uniform all the way out and back. I was a Star Scout at the time and even wore my Merit Badge Sash on some occasions." Kelly served for many years on the BSA's Coastal Empire Council in Savannah, Georgia, and regularly supported Scouting activities and budget drives as an adult. In an interview decades after being a New Jersey Boy Scout from 1911 to 1915, Howard Utter recalled the heavy and lasting influence of the Oath and Laws on boy members when they were embodied and taught by a worthy Scoutmaster: "We would have our regular meeting which often included a recital by each boy of good turns done during the week (errands run for Mother didn't count) and usually a short but extremely powerful and impressive talk by Mr. Gray on some point of the Scout Law or Oath. He had a wonderful ability in giving what was really a short sermon, but not preaching, and every Scout was intent and must carry some of that teaching still." American troop leaders commonly employed this technique of giving a brief but emphatic interpretation of a Scout Law during troop meetings, or invited an influential community leader to do so.[49]

Many men who first got involved in the BSA as adult volunteers seemed to absorb the larger life lessons of Scout character development as well as did those who joined as boys. These men worked to impart these values to boys both inside and outside Scouting. Newton Geiss—longtime educator and Lone Scout and Boy Scout troop leader—wrote a companion book to his memoirs, *Youth—the Hope of the World*, in which he characterized Boy Scouting as the best single way to teach boys proper character and to make the world a better place. The book took the form of a life advice manual for boys, Scout leaders, and educators, but many of its chapters focused on Scout methods, because Geiss believed that most schools, churches, and homes failed to teach American boys life's most important lessons: "I am thinking of Scouting as a *Way of Life*. Scouting is kindness in the home, honesty in business, courtesy in society, fairness in work, pity and concern for the unfortunate (the boy on the other side of the track; the boy from a broken home), resistance toward evil, help for the weak, forgiveness for the penitent, love for one another, and above all else, reverence and love for God (the twelfth point of the Scout Law). This I call—real Scouting. My Eagle Scouts have adopted this philosophy as a part of their teaching program. They help the boys in the lower echelon." Waldo Shaver, who started in the organization as a boy member in 1911 and worked in a variety of troop leader and administrative positions for more than forty years, recalled in his memoir the moral rectitude and confidence of new local Scout professionals who gathered at their 1926 national training conference: "They really believed that they could build a strong America through the promotion of a character building and citizenship training program for boys. . . .

In their notebooks were the most amazing ideas and sketches for camp buildings, trails, training courses and Scouting games. . . . The early executives were the salt of the earth. The pioneer executives were united in their moral philosophy . . . they tried to set an example for boys. There was no smoking or use of liquor at any Scouting function. I recall that at the Hot Springs conference an executive was sent home and out of the Movement because of his drinking."[50]

Leadership by an upstanding, involved Scoutmaster held the key to a successful experience for many boys. A number of Scouts responding to the 1928 survey by a BSA national commission stressed that they wanted to be like their Scoutmasters and live up to their example. As a fifteen-year-old Eagle Scout explained, good Scoutmasters offered a lifelong role model: "The greatest factor in making me a good Scout is the personal contact with good, clean men; living examples of the right way to live." This influence extended far beyond Scout troop meetings or even hikes and camps: "My Scoutmaster knows much about the ways of the world and I have obtained very good advice from him." On the other hand, an overly assertive or negligent troop leader could discourage or disappoint a Scout. A seventeen-year-old Eagle Scout expressed his concern about "the association with some Scoutmasters who expected too much from a boy and accused him of some things he couldn't help doing wrong. He got disgusted with it because of the Scoutmaster's bawling outs now and then got angry and purposely did wrong things and disobeyed." A sixteen-year-old First Class Scout put the matter urgently, "I did not live up to the Scout Oath and Law in my Troop because my Scoutmaster was unworthy of his position and I showed great disrespect for him due to my opinion of him. Scoutmasters who are not real men in most every way do more harm than anything else in Scouting."[51]

The 2,022 Boy Scouts of mixed ranks surveyed in 1928 highlighted the passing of rank and badge tests as the single-most important part of the program in terms of building Scout character and encouraging them to live up to the Oath and Laws. Many of these boys emphasized how rank and badge advancement taught them an honest, diligent work ethic and helped them find future career paths. Several Scouts responded that the process of studying for and passing Scout tests "makes [a Scout] thorough in his workmanship," as one respondent noted, "Before I go to an examiner I make sure that I am prepared and fulfilled every requirement. If I didn't do this it would be going against the code of Scouting, and I consider it a sin to do so." A decorated Eagle Scout from Minnesota surveyed in 1929 stated, "The spirit and the results of hard work probably mean the most. Many tasks have been hard, but when they are completed mean achievement. It is the knack of 'sticking to' a thing and completely working it." A fifteen-year-old Life Scout noted in the 1928 survey that the testing process "helps me to find out what I want to be when I grow up and helps you in later life," while a sixteen-year-old Second Class Scout found that the relationships established with particular merit badge examiners offered practical job benefits: "To be quick and vigilant in passing tests means closer contact with business officials enabling better chances for a good career." Since American apprenticeships dried up for early twentieth-century teenagers and many schoolteachers were women, participating in Scouting and interacting with professionals and business leaders during test passing and community service activities offered key opportunities for boys to improve their job references and future employment chances.[52]

Memoirs of early Boy Scouts and troop leaders emphasized the program's balance between learning competition and cooperation, an essential skill for corporate-industrial work and urban living. Longtime Lone and Boy Scout leader Newton Geiss praised Scouting's ability to build cooperative relationships and interdependence in his 1970 memoir: "Camping is the heart of the Scouting program. There is something about camping that is far more valuable than the skills acquired, and that is the *ability to live with other people*. . . . The program of *relationships* embraces everything *we are* into the very *fabric* we weave and everything *we do* in the Daniel Boone [BSA local] Council. We must regard relationships as a cooperative affair for *mutual understanding* and *effective teamwork*." In a 1995 autobiography highlighting his many experiences as an early Minnesota Boy Scout and Scouting professional, Arvid Edwards explained that competing for and earning his Eagle Scout rank was a key life event for both him and his father, a veteran Scoutmaster, since "Scouting had become a way of life for him . . . and me." From his second year as a member, Edwards admired highly decorated Eagle Scouts like Horace Manesau, who had sixty-six merit badges, even though "envious Scouts called him a 'merit badge hog.'" As Edwards explained, "Every boy who joins the Boy Scouts and takes the program seriously sets his sights on becoming an Eagle Scout. It's a long, tough road for most Scouts and receiving that Eagle Badge is truly a mountaintop experience." Fifty-year Scouting veteran James Henderson's recollection of the careful and useful balance between competition and cooperation he learned as a young member in the late 1920s represented a more typical response. In the weekly gatherings of all the troops in San Angelo, Texas, "We had inter-troop games and contests. We all kept up with what each troop was doing, and it helped to make you try a little harder on your advancement. . . . Each troop and patrol developed a very competitive spirit, but all meeting on the same night, I think there was a good, warm feeling of brotherhood among all the troops in our Scouting community."[53]

Adult volunteers and boy members alike characterized the work values taught in Scouting and its weekly troop meetings in terms of modern industry and business. Eagle Scout and later Scout Commissioner Merritt Lamb explained in his 1916 book of Scout poems and essays, "The growing boy is a locomotive with steam up. Turn that steam through proper channels and it will do a tremendous task; let that steam blow off into the air and it is gone forever; keep it corked up and you had better move. The locomotive was made to run, to do something. So was the boy. . . . Scouting furnishes a vent for the boy's steam. It does more than that. It provides a track on which this boy-locomotive may run easily and safely—with safety first. And the track it provides does not run aimlessly about and lead to nowhere. It is an airline to Character, Manhood, Citizenship and success. These are the four stations on the up-hill grade of achievement. . . . Turn your boy out the wrong door and pay no attention to the throttle and the brake and he may take the path of least resistance down the rails through Blind Alley and Cigarette Street, across Whiskey River into the Marsh of Last Hope." The 2,022 Scouts surveyed in 1928 expressed appreciation in their narrative responses for Scout troop meetings' diligent work, proper order, and businesslike atmosphere. A fourteen-year-old Second Class Scout highlighted a boy's sense of belonging to the broader organization and its vision: "The orderly way in which Troop meetings and business have been carried on has impressed a desire to become a bigger cog in the wheel of Scouting." A thirteen-year-old Second Class Scout declared, "Nothing is more business-like than a troop meeting. It shows a boy the need for cooperation in all matters." Moreover, several Scouts noted that the troop meeting allowed boys to take leadership roles and learn how to positively influence other Scouts.[54]

In their memoirs, both boy and adult members linked their career success as adults with the character values Scouting imbued. William Harrison Fetridge, reflecting on the life path that led him to be the longtime president of Dartnell Corporation, wrote the following about Scouting in the late 1910s: "[It] absolutely enveloped me at 11 and was to be my major interest for five of six boyhood years. Baden-Powell, Dan Beard and James West became my boyhood heroes and today, some six decades later, still win my warm admiration.... My interest, respect and dedication to this great youth movement have remained at fever pitch ever since." Fetridge's memoir stated that his involvement with Scouting and his connection with other BSA supporters helped him get a high-ranking job offer with the Diamond T truck manufacturing company in Chicago in 1959. One week later, his Scouting friend and Diamond T president Zenon Hansen was involved in a major auto accident. During Fetridge's visit to his friend at the hospital, a stranger approached him outside the door and asked if the injured man had been a Scoutmaster in Iowa decades earlier. When Fetridge replied that he had, the man explained, "Then he's the man who was my Scoutmaster.... Twenty-five years ago he gave me the encouragement and the standards that have served me all my life.... I've become quite a success here in Kansas City and I want him to know that my house and my pocketbook are his for I want in some measure to repay all that he did for me."[55]

THE EARLY BSA'S LAWS, Oath, and corresponding character values and activities thus drew widespread support from participants as well as the general public for articulating a new work ethic and character model that better enabled members to manage a modernizing economy and diversifying society. American Scout emphasis on self-control and being helpful and courteous to others prevented self-reliance from devolving into the nineteenth century's rampant individualism, a quality that conflicted with urban society's increasing interdependence. Being trustworthy, obedient, and loyal encouraged Scouts to harness their self-reliance for the good of the nation and modern industry. Scout Laws pertaining to social relations prompted boy members to sort others into a hierarchy of character. Scouts would then adjust their bearing based on where each person fit into this social scheme. Scout helpfulness and courtesy to dependents served as a twentieth-century form of knightly chivalry. The BSA drifted slightly toward business values in the 1920s, but the program's overall character emphases remained consistent from 1911 to the Great Depression. The Scout character Laws and activities for modern work and social dominance connected intimately with the second of BSA manhood's three core elements: practical citizenship and service leadership training.

3

Practical Citizenship

The BSA's new director, James West, knew that a lively endorsement from Theodore Roosevelt about the value of Boy Scout citizenship training would culminate the "Americanizing" of the British handbook and program that West had helped set in motion. In his 1911 correspondence to Roosevelt, West repeatedly clarified the importance of creating a new citizenship framework for young men, to be distributed in a rewritten handbook that would replace the BSA's original 1910 version, which represented an awkward amalgamation of Seton's Woodcraft Indian and Baden-Powell's original British Scouting programs. Seton had insisted that children should think critically about each government policy before deciding whether or not to support it, and that the best civic training was for boys to embrace the primitive Indian's simple tribal life, so as to learn how to make and enforce their own laws. His citizenship model resembled an idealized version of colonial New England or early American Republic civic virtues, but it conflicted heavily with the Progressive Era's shift to bureaucratic governance by scientific experts and statistical analysis. Baden-Powell's civic teachings primarily emphasized that it was a Scout's duty to be loyal to the king, be prepared to defend the empire from military invasion, and obey orders without question. What a regular citizen should proactively do in times of peace on a daily basis, particularly in a modern democratic society, remained unclear. Chief Scout Citizen Roosevelt—building on the sentiments he had expressed five months earlier in the letter read at the BSA's Waldorf Astoria banquet and incorporating points from father of the modern juvenile court system Judge Ben Lindsey, forester and conservation author O. W. Price, and American Civic Federation president J. Horace McFarland—responded in July 1911 with a resounding five-page affirmation on Boy Scouting's unique ability to mold the nation's adolescent boys into exemplary citizens and strong men, which West proudly reproduced in a new chapter on "Patriotism and Citizenship" for the Americanized 1911 handbook. Both Roosevelt and the men who came to dominate BSA administrative posts and lead the organization to new heights believed that Scout training was best able to prepare adolescent boys to perform the widening range of modern civic responsibilities that went far beyond voting, paying taxes, or even military service. Roosevelt's essay for the 1911 BSA handbook revision emphasized four intertwined areas essential for building both good men and leading citizens: learning practical civic rights and responsibilities, developing men's work values for a modern economy, building appropriate relationships with other social groups, and constructively managing nature.[1]

Roosevelt's essay argued that boys learning modern work values simultaneously helped them get good jobs and prepared them for active citizenship in an evolving democracy. He stressed that in addition to learning such ideals as honesty, fair play, and square dealing, boys should earn their own livelihood. Stable jobs allowed young men to support a family while contributing to national growth and social stability. This represented a shift from the early Republican and Victorian insistence that American citizens had to own their own farms or businesses to truly be able to vote independently. By the early twentieth century, making a self-supporting living in the corporate-industrial economy while being an active, knowledgeable participant in community and national affairs could earn a man political status and rights.

The former president insisted that learning how to interact appropriately with social equals, inferiors, and enemies formed another essential component of a good civic education. Such values helped replace late nineteenth-century self-made manhood's outdated emphasis on competitive individualism with the cooperative interdependence required by America's urbanizing society and the increasing involvement of government in daily affairs. Roosevelt, echoing the era's child development experts, stated that boys could only train to be good citizens by associating with other respectable boys and men. This implied that coeducational public schools, churches, and privatized middle-class families were not conducive to boys learning essential civic leadership skills. Roosevelt's essay argued that Scouts should stand stoutly against the nation's enemies and "show courage in confronting fearlessly one set of enemies, and in controlling and mastering the others." He suggested that boys could protect vulnerable children by safeguarding the city playgrounds from gangs of toughs and vandals. Roosevelt insisted that a good Scout be gentle and considerate to all, especially to those weaker, like his mom and sister.

Finally, Roosevelt emphasized that boy citizens should learn to protect parks, birds, trees, and flowers. Rather than waxing nostalgically about or blazing up the dwindling western frontier like their individualistic pioneer ancestors, Roosevelt and the BSA taught boys that modern men protected species and landscapes that held the highest value for Americans as a whole. In order for Scouts to learn to engage constructively with nature and scientifically manage resources for the good of the nation, boys should develop a sound, healthy body (rather than bulging, disproportionate muscles) to help them be efficient and make quick decisions.

Roosevelt and other BSA leaders recognized that civic education for adolescent boys was a key concern, since the decline of work apprenticeship and the corresponding development of segregated children's education and socialization spaces by the 1910s had made it harder for teenaged Americans to learn proper civic and political behaviors. In the 1700s and 1800s, many boys had absorbed community engagement and adult roles through career apprenticeships, often as young teenagers living with or working for another family to learn a trade. Even children as young as six had contributed to work and community affairs when production had centered on the household farm, artisan shop, and small business. Child labor laws and compulsory schooling, though, formed part of the larger process that historian Viviana Zelizer characterized as the "sacralization of childhood" that removed children from the public, adult world of material production and politics in the late nineteenth and early twentieth century. The decline of full-family and community turnout for partisan political rallies and the growth of managed government by experts and committees cut off another route by which boys had once learned political values. Assigning textbook-based memorization and giving children freedom to democratically run their own miniature societies offered two options for teaching modern boys political skills and community engagement. Many schools and playground associations attempted to ramp up textbook teaching of civics and patriotic history, but memorizing abstract principles and historical trivia offered little opportunity to practice real civic engagement. Due to the fear of juvenile delinquency and the independent youth culture as well as the increasing emphasis on managed expertise in America's political and economic systems, relatively few educators or youth organizers tried the latter method. One can see remnants of this concept in high school and college student government associations, but those efforts were confined to the school context and often heavily constrained by adult authority.[2]

Roosevelt's connection of good citizenship with training in modern manhood paralleled the BSA's five key civic concepts, which this chapter explores: citizencraft, nonpartisanship, service leadership and the daily Good Turn, being neither pro- nor antimilitary, and being responsible enough to be put in charge of material resources as adults. For Roosevelt and most BSA officials, leading male citizens had to develop scientific efficiency so that they could expertly manage America's urban-industrial economy and complex government. The Scout citizen supported government policies that took the whole society's needs and long-term stability into account rather than pursuing individual, short-term gains. Good Boy Scouts learned to regularly serve others through the daily Good Turn and emergency aid, especially those groups deemed dependent. Leading Scouts and citizens stayed knowledgeable and actively involved in political affairs, and contributed to the community and the nation's greater good every day, rather than just passively paying taxes and waiting to see if they were called up for military service during a war. The BSA's civic teachings, together with Scout character training's corporate-industrial work ethic and guidelines for social group interaction, thus provided boy members with a well-rounded apprenticeship for success as leading men in a modernizing American society and democracy.

Citizencraft: Active Engagement and Nonpartisan Merit

By the early twentieth century, Progressive Era reform laws and increasing emphasis on expert-led government created the need for a new standard of men's citizenship. American politics in the late 1800s had revolved around individuals' loyalty to a political party and the patronage appointments and material favors it bestowed in return. Historians of the American idea of success have argued that the traditional moral duty for self-made Victorian men to be involved in the political process and to help improve society declined in the wake of the Gilded Age's secularism and materialism. By the early 1900s, though, American government had shifted toward an expert-management model, paralleling the growing emphasis on corporate and scientific leadership in the modern economy. In theory, "unbiased" government officials appointed trained, certified experts and formed committees to scientifically study society's needs and effect data-driven solutions. Although incompletely implemented, the 1873 Pendleton Civil Service Reform Act replaced many patronage appointments with education requirements and standardized merit exams. Progressive American political reforms such as the initiative, referendum, recall, and Australian secret ballot placed greater emphasis on the individual citizen being better informed and more involved in the political process than in the Gilded Age. BSA leaders and supporters argued that training in modern manhood and Scout citizencraft would better prepare boys to lead America's changing government and society than would relying solely on the schools or junior military training.[3]

The evolving citizencraft chapters in the revisions of the Boy Scout handbook insisted that a core civic duty for modern men was to serve the broader community in practical, ongoing ways rather than in episodic bursts, like fighting in the occasional war or turning out annually to vote for the same political party. In addition to emphasizing the opportunities America's democratic system offered its citizens for self-improvement and a benign interpretation of the nation's history and expansion, the 1911 Boy Scout handbook's new "Patriotism and Citizenship" chapter stated that Boy Scouts should demonstrate "practical citizenship" by doing a Good Turn daily, constantly improving the communities in which they lived, regularly obeying the laws, helping policemen, and always being prepared to save others in emergencies. The 1919 BSA handbook revision's "Citizenship" section clarified, "Good citizenship means to the boy scout not merely the doing of things which he ought to do when he becomes a man, such as voting, keeping the law, and paying his taxes, but the looking for opportunities to do good turns by safeguarding the interests of the community and by giving of himself in unselfish service to the town or city, and even the nation, of which he is a part. It means that he will seek public office when the public office needs him. It means that he will stand for the equal opportunity and justice which the Declaration of Independence and the Constitution guarantees. It means that in every duty of life he may be on the right side and loyal to the best interests of the State and Nation." In his new chapter on "Citizencraft" for the 1928 Boy Scout handbook revision, psychologist H. William Hurt articulated the essential qualities the Scout Oath developed that helped build boys into participating daily citizens. American Boy Scouts took an Oath vowing to be "physically strong" (which Hurt defined as cleanliness, regularity, moderation, maintenance, and activity), "mentally awake" (concentration, experience, building habits through action, and learning from others' experiences), and "morally straight" (truthfulness, honor, justice, fairness, duty, courtesy, brotherhood, love, and goodwill to all). Hurt's emphasis on the word "craft" suggested that modern citizenship was a skill that one learned through training and experience and demonstrated in an ongoing fashion, rather than by exercising a passive, permanent status.[4]

The 1929 Scoutmaster's handbook best articulated the second nexus of modern men's practical citizenship: nonpartisanship, nonsectarianism, cooperation, and advancement by merit. The author emphasized that Scouting in troops brings boys "under conditions of association and co-operation which make for democracy." "Cooperation" and "association" had become key watchwords of America's progressive, expert-managed government and corporate-industrial workforce. The handbook insisted, "Just as the Scout movement is in itself broadly democratic in character representing all kinds of boys, from nearly every conceivable kind of home and church and community; being non-partisan and non-sectarian, though clearly religious; making merit the sole test of progress and offering opportunity to one and all alike—so the national organization through which it works is also democratic and widely representative." The handbook reinforced the nonpartisan stance that administrators had articulated in the context of the 1916 presidential election. That year, the BSA Executive Board had issued a "Boy Scout Movement is non-political" resolution, declaring, "The ideals, uniforms, badges, flags, and other insignia, and the name, 'Boy Scouts of America,' and other phraseology peculiarly descriptive of the program and organization of our Movement must at all times be held sacred and inviolate from commercial, racial, religious, political, militaristic, partisan or other factional partiality." BSA national leaders successfully encouraged most members and Local Councils to emphasize broad civic responsibilities over particular party loyalties or militarism in their Scout activities.[5]

The growing links between the BSA and men's civic associations, such as the Rotary Club, point to the role of these organizations in shaping a new standard of modern men's citizenship based on "classless," nonpartisan, and service values. At the 1917 International Association of Rotary Clubs annual meeting, a new Committee on Boys' Work voted that the Rotary Club should focus its support on Boy Scouting, since both organizations emphasized the spirit of service to others. Attendees at the preceding Thirteenth District annual conference in Sacramento had recommended that all Rotary Clubs sponsor Scouting *exclusively* because "we believe that there is a very close parallel between the movement of the Boy Scouts and the movement of Rotarians. The object of the Boy Scouts is to make junior Rotarians. The object of the Rotarians is to make good citizens, and the boy scout graduates into a Rotarian in a very facile manner." BSA leaders from across the country bombarded the program committee chairman for the 1918 International Association of Rotary Clubs meeting with requests to give preference to Boy Scouting in all the Committee on Boys' Work discussions. A Rotary delegate from Pennsylvania singled out the BSA's nonsectarian, nonpolitical stance and its federal charter for praise. A Nebraska delegate suggested that the BSA was the only boys' organization that might ease the "continually growing abyss between capital and labor" because it mixed poor and rich boys and encouraged them to respect each other. A West Virginia delegate added that Rotarians' support of Scouting could benefit boys of all classes because the Scouts would provide service to working-class boys' organizations. The BSA's Samuel Moffett gave an invited speech at the conference that echoed these arguments. To promote these modern civic virtues, Rotary and other middle-class men's organizations sponsored an increasing number of Scout troops, led membership drives, and helped purchase Scout campsites and office buildings in the 1920s.[6]

As demonstrated in a problem-solving session at the first National Training School for Scout Executives in 1925, being nonpartisan meant actively engaging in broad civic activities rather than abstaining from politics altogether. The ensuing discussion confirmed that it was inappropriate for a local leader to allow his uniformed Scouts to participate in a particular political party's program to distribute partisan literature or march in any one party's parade. BSA national administrators consistently discouraged local units from publicly supporting any specific party. However, according to the leaders of this discussion, Local Council Executives should encourage or even require Scouts to participate in such nonpartisan events as an Armistice Day celebration hosted by "a committee representing all patriotic and educational movements of the community, appointed by the Mayor." Uniformed Scouts across the country regularly marched in or provided guides and First Aid booths for citywide parades and festivals. One Local Council history explained that by the 1920s, "in practically every civic and patriotic movement where boys could be of service—there the Scouts would be." Kansas City Scouts, for example, helped control crowds and protect President Calvin Coolidge when he came to dedicate the Liberty Memorial on Armistice Day in 1926. The BSA's frequent voter registration drives showcased another important nonpartisan Scout act of direct political engagement. A 1924 *Scout Executive Bulletin* praised the training Scouts received by getting out the vote in their communities, which helped them learn to be participating citizens before becoming of voting age.[7]

The *Civics* merit badge pamphlet, the apex of the BSA's most advanced rank of Eagle Scout, emphasized a working knowledge of the modern political system and how Scouts could apply that to their daily lives as developing men. A portion of the pamphlet taught general principles of civics and voting practices, the relationship between different branches of government, and legal citizenship rights and responsibilities. The 1930 edition of the *Civics* pamphlet asserted that urban society's increasing interdependence required clear thinking and intelligent voting, replacing the spoils system with the "superior" method of civil service reform and city manager and commission government, and each boy knowing his local politicians and city government system. The pamphlet made extensive use of the BSA requirement that a Scout not only memorize the textbook knowledge for each merit badge test but also be able to demonstrate to the examiner practical application of those concepts in his daily life and how they fulfilled the Scout Laws and Oath. The author suggested that thrift, balanced health, character development, job training skills, Good Turns, earning good grades at school, practicing Life Saving, and other forms of local civic leadership helped boys earn the Civics merit badge and also set them up for successful adult lives and careers.[8]

Leading educators, child development theorists, youth workers, clergy, and even the U.S. Congress agreed that Scout training offered an essential supplement to the schools by developing participating citizenship in adolescent boys for an interdependent, modern society. As Dean James Russell of Columbia University's Teachers College explained in a 1919 interview with BSA national office staff on the relationship of Boy Scouting to new educational theories on experiential and applied learning, "Citizenship cannot be taught wholly from texts, or instilled by lectures. There must be active participation to beget a true conception of civic ideals or practices. The schools are not equipped to furnish this participation to the extent needed for the training of dependable citizens. . . . It is for these reasons, therefore, that I declare the Boy Scout Movement to be the most significant educational contribution of our time. . . . It has marvelous potency for converting the restless, irresponsible, self-centered boy into the straightforward, dependable, helpful young citizen." Dr. Albert Shields of Columbia University's Teachers College led a discussion on the meaning and duties of American citizenship at the 1922 BSA Executives Training Conference in North Carolina, in which he emphasized that industrialization, immigration, and labor unionism had amplified and made much more complex the problem of citizenship. He argued that Scouting helped boys recognize and develop skills for being interdependent with others and adjusting to the growing reach of government in modern American life. Shields even suggested that a new advanced rank of Scout Citizen be developed to highlight the program's ultimate goal of training civic-minded men.[9]

Full-Orbed Citizenship: Service Leadership and Good Turns

The BSA's membership and political status mushroomed in part because the organization offered a tangible method for teaching modern civic skills and values to boys who might otherwise drift into isolated individualism or cynicism: practical citizenship in the forms of service leadership and the daily Good Turn. Dr. George J. Fisher, a prominent proponent of physical education who worked with both the YMCA and the American military before joining the BSA leadership, argued that because most young men in modern America no longer received practical civic education or training, they "stumble into citizenship," assuming that it begins at age twenty-one. Fisher explained that many young men were mistakenly led to believe that citizenship primarily required voting and was more about their rights without the requisite civic duties: "No wonder Democracy is a failure in the cities. To have an effective democracy we must seriously train youth in the principles of democracy. A boy cannot live his boy life entirely separate from any sense of responsibility to society and then be expected as a man to live a full-orbed citizenship. . . . His man experience is dependent upon his boy experience. . . . Full-orbed manhood is based upon full-orbed boyhood." Fisher argued that serving the public in the company of the uniformed Scout troop provided practical civic experiences that tied modern boys to the nation. The 1928 Boy Scout handbook added that service prepared boy members to lead not only the government but also other major institutions: "The challenging need of America is leadership—people who have ability and reliability enough to carry responsibility in business, in government, in church, everywhere. Leadership can only be learned by leading. Scouting offers the opportunity to get this experience. Use it by making an earnest, though modest, effort to SERVE through giving leadership to such activities and work and 'Good Turns' as your own leaders deem wise. To HELP rather than merely to LEAD, is the ideal." Starting with the Americanized 1911 BSA handbook's special section on "Practical Citizenship," each subsequent manual for boys, Scoutmasters, and Executives—as well as the organization's magazines, leader training sessions, and public statements—emphasized Boy Scouts learning civic values and leadership through doing public service. Annual reports, local Scout histories, and newspaper and troop accounts provide numerous examples and statistics of Scouts' acts of service, as well as the civic leadership status and skills these activities garnered for them.[10]

American editions of the Scoutmaster's handbook in the 1910s and 1920s argued that a key benefit of Scouting's daily Good Turn was that it helped boys surrender their immature selfishness and individualism to develop a modern citizen's cooperative spirit, which would in turn prompt the community to serve its boys by willingly providing resources for their leadership training. The 1912 Scoutmaster's handbook, which relied heavily on child development psychologists' theories of adolescence and racial recapitulation, explained that the Good Turn helped channel adolescent boys' emerging group instinct into public service: "A higher appeal for social preference and desire to win favor and friends through the daily good turn can now be made. The response will be a natural approach to good citizenship. The boy must learn to surrender some of his individual desires to the will of the group. He must serve others and learn to regard the good of all as superior to individual choice. The boy will recapitulate the steps of earlier race groupings and like the tribe, he joins the band for a common interest and a common good.... The social self should be nourished by a nearer approach to, and a closer working basis with others." The 1914 Scoutmaster's handbook revision added that Scout service work's emphasis on developing the social self provided essential leadership training: "This ability to cooperate with others in doing the little things will enable a Scout later on to assume his position one day as a leader.... The ultimate aim of every Scout should be leadership." However, BSA officials intended Scout service work to flow in both directions. As the 1929 Scoutmaster's handbook explained, "Scouting is not merely training boys to serve a community, it is also training a community to serve boys."[11]

According to the *Scout Executive*, BSA officials formed special Civic Service Committees at the local and state levels to help promote and coordinate Scout Good Turns and emergency mobilization: "Scouts are in training to be future heads of homes, leaders in business, government, educational, and scientific progress. They aim to enter manhood better prepared for citizenship by virtue of their Scouting Experience. It is essential that scouts have education contacts with civic interests, and in no way can they obtain that contact better than through civic Good Turns." The author instructed the local Scout Civic Service Committees to map out area institutions for rapid mobilization, such as fire and police stations, hospitals, and municipal offices. He advised officials to make ongoing partnerships with government bureaus, businesses, men's fraternal and civic organizations, media outlets, and other key community institutions for Boy Scouts to do regular service as well as emergency relief work. BSA publications and national media sources that frequently extolled Scouts' public services grouped them into general categories that demonstrated the wide scope of BSA civic training and involvement: Americanization and Citizenship Training, Animals, Churches, the Community, Fire Department, Police Department, Conventions, serving "the unfortunates" of the community, Forestry, Schools, and the Home. Scout public service took four major forms, each of which reinforced different aspects of the BSA's modern citizenship: individual acts of kindness for a Scout's or Troop's daily Good Turn; ongoing arrangements for specially trained troops to aid government officials, such as policemen and firemen; national annual Scout service drives; and disaster relief.[12]

That the Scout's daily Good Turn represented a core pillar of not only leading citizenship but also the BSA's overall vision of modern manhood formed a common litany of officials and supporters. Authors and speakers often paired a Scout's Good Turn with a specific masculine value from the BSA's Oath or Laws, such as giving material items to the poor as demonstrating thrift and courtesy. Providing assistance to women or racial minorities constituted knightly or race chivalry. Standing up among one's schoolmates for clean speech showed a Scout's bravery. Scouts acting as guides at large public events—such as parades, fairs, patriotic celebrations with such organizations as the Grand Army of the Republic and the American Legion, and Chamber of Commerce and Rotary Club conventions—were frequent types of troop and Local Council daily Good Turns. The Scouts soon expanded their duties of "convention service" to include First Aid stations, traffic regulation, messenger services, and meeting incoming trains to welcome visitors and guide them to their hotels and meeting rooms. Big city cleanup projects emerged as another

SCOUTS FIGHTING A FOREST FIRE NEAR GREAT FALLS, MONT
(The boys' shoes were burned on the hot ground)

Figure 3.1 Serving the public through conserving the outdoors. "Scouts Fighting a Forest Fire," *American Review of Reviews*, December 1916, 645.

favorite Scout council Good Turn project, which sometimes took the form of "uplifting" racial minorities with modern aesthetics and hygiene concepts. A 1914 article in the *Craftsman*, for example, praised Scouts for collecting garbage and making maps of health risks for city officials: they "take the health officers around and help them clean up the city, thereby not only learning a lesson themselves in civic sanitation and management, but stimulating in even the most indifferent members of the population a desire of hygiene and beauty. On one occasion the New York branch of the boy Scouts had a 'clean-up' campaign, and boys from certain troops went to the Ghetto and other East-side [new immigrant] sections. They were so energetic in clearing away refuse and debris from backyards, roofs and fire escapes that the people themselves became interested and gave most enthusiastic aid." Learning to lead or help groups deemed as inferior in Good Turns such as this taught Scouts modern management skills and demonstrated their potential for civic leadership.[13]

Even more striking than these council-level special events or individual Good Turns, whole troops of Boy Scouts across the country underwent formal service apprenticeships with firefighters, policemen, park rangers, railroad workers, and foresters. The images and accompanying accounts of designated, permanent patrols of Scout firefighters and traffic police published throughout the 1910s and 1920s—such as that in Figure 3.1, showing Boy Scouts using branches and shovels to extinguish a forest fire in Montana as their shoes melted to the ground—demonstrated that the boy members actually did these tasks rather than just being nominal helpers. Some of these arrangements could be very extensive. In 1925, the Brooklyn Police Department designated a sergeant from each of its twenty-seven districts to serve as a special liaison between the department and local Boy Scout troops, to be overseen by a special police adviser in a committee cooperating with the city's Safety Bureau. The sergeants, who received special training on Scouting methods, visited each troop at least monthly to lead a special program or observe their meetings. The sergeants helped recruit Scoutmasters or became Scoutmasters themselves. The Scouts, in return, reported dangerous or unhealthy conditions and criminal activities in their neighborhoods to their assigned sergeant, which sometimes led to arrests. Special Scout troops formed partnerships with city fire departments; some of these troops even served as regular volunteer units, attending training sessions for adult firefighters. Scouts often worked with police departments as traffic guides at large events and public buildings, forming some of the early school Safety Patrols as crossing and parking guards. The New York Police Department even prepared a manual to help Scouts learn their duties as police aids. Since urban adolescent boys were no longer allowed to work in many job fields and had to attend school instead, these service outlets offered important job skills and references for future employment. Moreover, contributing to the community in this substantial way helped Boy Scouts position themselves as future political leaders better than other teenagers could.[14]

In their roles as official police, fire, and National Guard aids, Boy Scouts often operated under an implied authority, granted to them by government officials and the general public. The Baltimore Area Council Scout Commissioner wrote to the national office in 1916 asking for past examples of police giving Scoutmasters authority to make arrests in the BSA's duties as police aids. James West replied that in his judgment, police should not actually give arrest authority to Scouts and their troop leaders, but perhaps "implied authority has been granted." For example, the Macon, Georgia, mayor enlisted the local Boy Scouts in 1921 as an "auxiliary police department" to help straighten out delinquent boys who vandalized property or killed birds wantonly: "We want them to grow up into good men, setting the same kind of mark you boys are reaching for." The mayor suggested that the Scout auxiliary police work through role modeling and the power of persuasion, but "if you run across a boy you can't do anything with let me know his name, and I'll see if we can't help you to get him in line." When the public (including adults) violated a Boy Scout's orders, local officials and even courts backed the Scout's judgment and authority. A motorist in Texas disregarded a Boy Scout traffic officer's signal in 1926, so a judge promptly fined the arraigned man ten dollars—a tidy sum at the time.[15]

Two of the many annual BSA national service drives that united Boy Scouts across the country on a common project demonstrated the wide range of adult responsibilities and practical, modern citizenship skills Scouts learned: leading safe and patriotic city festivities and encouraging voter turnout. These drives also highlighted the active support from municipal, federal, business, and mass media representatives that service leadership garnered for the BSA and its boy members. The first national Scout Good Turn project promoted citywide "Safe and Sane" Fourth of July celebrations to replace the presumably dangerous, drunken fireworks celebrations and ethnically divided festivals. A 1914 *Scouting* magazine article on Baltimore Boy Scouts reported on what to today's ears would sound like an impossible feat for twelve- to fifteen-year-old boys to achieve—in terms of both adolescents' capabilities and the types of adult responsibilities American society would allow boys to have. The Baltimore Boy Scouts and their leaders had exclusive management of the city's main two-day patriotic celebration. The first day the Boy Scouts hosted ten thousand people around campfires and flag ceremonies at the athletic ground near Patterson Park. They camped out in order to be ready for the twenty thousand people who would come out the next afternoon. The boys did guard and escort duty, helped feed the crowd, and led the schoolchildren in games (these services seemed to distinguish the adult-like Scouts as young as twelve from the "children"). In the evening, the tired Scouts made one hundred baskets out of the leftover food and gave them to poor families. The Scouts then policed the night's fireworks, which were attended by ninety thousand people. Their many duties included helping reunite lost children with their families and providing First Aid to many festivalgoers: "One case of unconsciousness was so severe that the Scouts summoned two doctors, both of whom found it unnecessary to supplement the treatment which the boys had already given." The article reported that even though the Boy Scouts had done as much "Safe and Sane" Fourth of July work as they had the previous year, when it had been the national Scout service drive focus, less was said about it in newspaper accounts: "This, however, is not because the Scouts were less active, but rather because people are beginning to expect the

Scouts to do things and are beginning to accept their services as a matter of course." BSA administrators joined with leading civic organizations and philanthropies such as the Russell Sage Foundation to provide suggestions to other Scouts and councils on how to lead a full "Safe and Sane" Fourth of July program in their own communities, which many did.[16]

The 1924 BSA annual service drive prompted a massive Get-Out-the-Vote campaign that allowed adolescent Boy Scouts to serve and lead the nation before they were old enough to vote or run for office. After the mid- to late nineteenth-century decline in voter enthusiasm, resulting in part from the displacement of avid partisanship and patronage favors by civic service reform and the increasing influence of nonelected government bureaucrats, Boy Scouts took a prominent role in reinvigorating adults' political engagement. A *Scouting* article that year, "How Scouts Will Promote Registration and Voting as Training in Citizenship," was accompanied by endorsements by all three presidential candidates as well as a sketch of Uncle Sam working with a Boy Scout to raise the percentage of citizens voting back to its pre-1900 levels. The author instructed the 532,000 American Scouts to work with the 150,000 adult Scout officials and committee members to cover their territory thoroughly, block by block, inducing parents and neighbors to vote and hang up signs at their homes and businesses, and encouraging voter registration and turnout to reduce the number of "vote slackers." The National Association of Manufacturers and *Collier's* magazine used Boy Scouts to distribute millions of copies of their get-out-the-vote pledge cards, signs, posters, and stickers. Boy Scouts in Pasadena worked with prominent local citizens to create lists of unregistered voters to pursue. Scouts blew whistles and rang church bells to remind people to vote. Boy members relieved police officers on traffic duty at the polls and around town so that they could go vote. "Everything that was done by the Boy Scout Organization was on a strictly nonpartisan basis, as a patriotic service to their country and for its citizenship training values to boys, in accord with the Scout executive's definition of the kind of citizen scouting expects scouts to be, namely, a PARTICIPATING CITIZEN." President Coolidge, his cabinet members, state governors, military officials, and big business and civic organization leaders from across the country published letters of praise for this nationwide Scout service drive—which some experts credited with helping raise the national percentage of participating voters from 49 percent in 1920 to 54 percent in 1924.[17]

Throughout the 1910s and 1920s, Boy Scouts across the country also demonstrated their leadership skills by working side by side with National Guardsmen, the Red Cross, the military, firemen, policemen, hospitals, radio stations, transportation companies, and local politicians and health officials to provide essential and timely relief in catastrophic floods, earthquakes, fires, epidemics, and mine and factory explosions. The Red Cross found the Scouts' emergency relief services to be so helpful and eager that they formalized arrangements to write all the First Aid and Life Saving literature for the BSA, and often came to camps and conferences to train and certify Scouts and their adult leaders. Ex-Scouts also frequently volunteered for or were recruited to provide disaster relief service as adults.[18]

In an era with less developed roads and air service and an inadequate adult relief force, communities across the nation called out trained local Boy Scouts to immediately begin and carry out disaster relief services. As a report on a 1926 Florida hurricane noted, "Scout couriers were on duty within an hour of the call for help" for emergency messengers—and they quickly jumped into gathering twenty carloads of donated clothing, amusing babies to help stranded mothers, dispensing food supplies, securing homes for refugees, cleaning the streets, setting up tent shelters, aiding steamship freight deliveries, guarding property in wrecked buildings, managing First Aid stations, assisting the chief of police, re-roofing a drug store building to help save the essential medical supplies it contained, and even assisting doctors during emergency surgery. Thousands of Scouts turned out to aid in one of American history's greatest natural disasters, the 1927 Mississippi River flood that left half a million people without homes. Scouts spread across fourteen hundred miles worked alongside National Guardsmen and health officials for days, often without sleep. A Boy Scout, for example, took charge of a detail of ten adult Mexican refugees to plan and lay out an emergency tent city in Canton. Using Scout camping equipment, two Eagle Scouts managed a refugee camp kitchen and directed the feeding of over one thousand displaced people for days. A Scout in Jackson, Mississippi, noticed that a refugee boat containing an African American mother and infant had begun to sink, but "the negroes in the front boat seemed powerless" to help. The Scout dove overboard, swam underneath the sinking boat, and pushed it up with his head to keep it afloat until more relief boats arrived to rescue the party. Providing emergency relief to dislocated peoples and "less prepared" women, children, and nonwhites helped reinforce Boy Scouts' civic superiority.[19]

In 1916, the U.S. House of Representatives' Committee on the Judiciary highlighted Scouts' national Good Turns and public services, particularly during disasters, as a key reason why Congress should grant the BSA the nation's second-ever federal charter, after the one given to the Red Cross: "During the past two years, boy scouts have demonstrated the value of the education and training they received as an auxiliary force in the maintenance of public order and in the administration of first-aid and practical assistance in times of great public emergencies. Their services on the occasion of the Ohio floods, at the Gettysburg reunion, in the inaugural ceremonies of President Wilson, and at the recent memorable reunion of the Grand Army of the Republic in Washington attracted Nation-wide attention and received general commendation, particularly from the American national Red Cross and the officials of the Federal and State Governments. The importance and magnitude of its work is such as entitle it to recognition and its work and insignia to protection by Federal incorporation." The rest of the House and the Senate concurred, unanimously passing the BSA's federal charter that session. For many Americans and communities, Scouts ably performing emergency service and daily Good Turns demonstrated the value of the BSA's modern civic training and the readiness of its boy members for future political leadership positions.[20]

Good Scouts Are Neither Pro- nor Antimilitary

Military preparedness and being a soldier in wartime, given its longstanding linkage in Western societies to political leadership, offered a potential disruption to the BSA's modern civic teachings. American Scout administrators' solutions to the preparedness debate, particularly concerning the appropriateness of military training for adolescent boys, emphasized that "Peace Scouting" and nonmilitary civic service was more essential to modern men's citizenship than was martial training or physical aggression. The original British Boy Scout uniform and program, created by General Baden-Powell to better prepare boys to defend the British Empire, had come heavily laden with military imagery and teaching methods. In response to both the declining American enthusiasm for overseas territorial expansion and criticisms from labor and women's groups about the militaristic tone of Scouting, BSA administrators tacked away from military drill and dummy rifles in the early 1910s and adopted a stance of being patriotic but neither pro- nor antimilitary. This shift defused the concerns of most critics of the BSA and also helped distinguish the organization's plan to prepare boys for constructive public service and participatory daily citizenship from the narrow military focus of some rival American Scout organizations. While the occasional Scoutmaster used military drill, relatively few BSA troops emphasized drill, and national administrators discouraged it. Discussions about militarism in the BSA centered on four key areas: uniforms, drill, rifles, and what services Boy Scouts should perform during World War I.

BSA national leaders' policies and statements on these issues differed noticeably from those made by Scout organizations in most Western or colonized countries in the 1910s. Many historians have argued that the early British, Canadian, and Australian Boy Scout programs consistently emphasized militarism, drill with rifles, soldier imagery, defending the empire, and protecting the homeland against invasion by foreign powers. These historians have typically argued that emphasis on traditional class hierarchy and elite leadership, strict obedience, and social control of both boy members and the lower classes accompanied these martial values, and that such beliefs paralleled mainstream British and European culture and politics in this era. Such works have also highlighted the predominance of military men among early British Empire Scoutmasters and national council members as well as the outspoken, ongoing criticisms by labor unions and socialists about British Scouting's overtly military teachings. A few historians, however, have countered that Baden-Powell and British Scouting placed more emphasis on character development and civilian duties to the nation during the 1910s, foregrounding Baden-Powell's insistence on broader character education and not allowing Scouting to be subsumed under the military's leadership during World War I. Several historians have also noted that British Scouting, and Scouting in the world as a whole, became more internationalist and peace oriented in the 1920s. These historians have cited Baden-Powell's de-emphasis on martial imperialism as well as the growth of international Scout associations, international exchanges, and World Scout Jamborees as evidence of this shift.[21]

What is clear from these historians' debates and evidence sources about foreign Scouting is that overall, the BSA began and remained noticeably and intentionally less militaristic than mainstream Scouting in the British Empire, Europe, and most other studied areas, such as South

America and Palestine. The BSA also emerged as a moderate on military issues relative to rival American Scout organizations. Few military men were on the National Council or its Executive Board. The lack of military training and martial emphasis in the evolved BSA also prompted several military men, such as Adjutant General William Verbeck and Colonel Peter Bomus, to quit their positions as BSA National Scout Commissioners. As historian David Macleod pointed out, BSA leaders toned down soldiering and martial rhetoric partly because many of the key American troop-sponsoring institutions—such as churches and schools— were nonmilitary in the early 1910s. Before the United States' entry into the Great War, most BSA national and local leaders tried to steer the organization toward the majority American preference for isolationism and away from universal military preparation (especially for the young teens who dominated the organization's membership). The outbreak of the Great War challenged the BSA's neutral stance on military preparedness. Scout organizations in other countries armed boy members to guard bridges and coastlines, but BSA national leaders held fast.[22]

Faced with the heritage of militarism in British Scouting and its uniform on the one hand, and criticisms against militarism on the other hand, BSA administrators quickly staked out a successful position of being a daily-life civic leadership training program that was neither pro- nor antimilitary. The BSA's first handbook emphasized Baden-Powell's recent defense of Scouting against militarist charges: "There is no military meaning attached to the name scouting. Peace scouting comprises the attributes of colonial frontiersmen in the way of resourcefulness and self-reliance and the many other qualities which make them men among men. There is no intention of making the lads into soldiers or of teaching them bloodthirstiness." However, the 1910 BSA handbook stated that patriotic citizens must do their share of defending the homeland against aggression in order to maintain their safety and freedom. James West reached out in 1911 to the New York Peace Society and its president— steel magnate Andrew Carnegie—to try to get the organization's endorsement of Scouting, but the BSA rejected the society's suggestion to change the Scout fleur-de-lis to something pacifist, like an olive branch and a compass. West also encouraged Stanford University president David Starr Jordan, a leading figure in the American peace movement, to join the BSA National Council in 1911 and become a BSA Vice President in 1913. The 1919 Boy Scout handbook stated that Scouting trained boys in character and personal efficiency so that they can be prepared to fulfill peacetime citizen obligations, but that some of these activities "are included in the ordinary preparation for responsibilities of the life of the soldier," making the Scouts "as strong a factor as any other one agency which the country now has for preparedness." The handbook claimed that the Boy Scout uniform, patrol and troop units, and special drills were not primarily intended for military purposes but rather to teach boys uniformity, harmony, and rhythm of spirit. BSA national leaders downplayed outright military drill and discouraged the use of rifles or even dummy guns in Scout training. Instead, the BSA encouraged the use of civilian drills in First Aid, signaling, camp making, and other Scout skills to replace military drill while still teaching members the group discipline and efficiency modern men needed. Minneapolis Scout leaders even adopted a policy that only physical fitness directors were allowed to lead Scouts in drill after local units were criticized for marching in a 1911 Memorial Day parade. National BSA administrators successfully requested that the U.S. Congress pass a bill in 1916 prohibiting every organization other than the Boy Scouts from wearing uniforms like the Army or Navy, but emphasized that the uniform helped the Scouts learn broad character and civic values while encouraging brotherhood among members.[23]

The uniforms of Boy and Girl Scouts and Guides across the world simultaneously served as a potential unifying force and point of conflict among members, an area of contestation between its members and the broader public, a form of individual expression for the wearer, and a powerful vehicle for pursuing minority rights and status. National leaders of Scout and Guide organizations in many countries often stated that having a common uniform built ties of brother/sisterhood among members and loyalty to the organization and the country. Since the uniform also gave the wearer public authority and recognition, Scout and Guide administrators in various nations debated and disagreed for years and even decades over whether or not different racial and religious minority groups could become formal members and wear the full, official uniforms. The Scout uniform in British Africa was key to British colonial officials' efforts to teach Africans loyalty to and pride in the British Empire, as well as to African Scouts' (and imposters') labors to use their visible Scout membership in combination with the Fourth Law that a Scout was a brother to every other Scout to assert Africans' rights and pursue individual opportunities within the colonies' system of racial segregation and subordination. Not only did boys and men in Scout uniforms experience better treatment from British officials and other white residents in Africa, but African community members often ceded them more status and respect because they assumed the African Boy Scouts were part of the British military. The American Girl Scouts' replacement of Girl Guide blue bloomers and sateen ties with a Boy Scout–like khaki uniform in 1913 empowered girl members to seek larger social and political roles, but garnered criticisms from some BSA administrators and the broader public. Some early British Scout and Guide members viewed their uniforms (which they often had to work to purchase themselves) as an expression of personal pride and age hierarchy, and a site of cultural negotiation with parents and their local community. Members could distinguish themselves by earning rank and merit badges and purchasing additional uniform accessories. Some working-class British Scout members, however, had to defy verbal ridicule and physical abuse from community members who believed Scouting was anti-labor and pro-militarist.[24]

In the BSA, uniform debates emerged over criticisms of teaching boys aggressive militarism, whether to allow racial minorities to wear the uniform, and proposals to adopt a cheaper uniform or do away with it altogether. Early BSA local councils could and sometimes did deny minority groups permission to wear the official uniform—especially African Americans in the southeastern United States. Some Local Councils did not allow African American troops to wear the uniform until they had proven themselves reliable and respectable members from the perspective of white locals, while other councils completely denied them uniform access through the 1930s. BSA national and local officials periodically debated whether to adopt a cheaper uniform or even do away with the uniform to make membership more accessible to working-class and destitute youth—a problem on which other countries' Scout and Guide officials also remarked. It was a large, up-front, and reoccurring expense as a child grew (in addition to the annual membership fees and any weekly troop membership fees or activity expenses imposed). Some working-class boys viewed the Scout uniform as feminine and childish. The BSA might have attracted more working-class boys and parents by simplifying or doing away with the uniform, but such a move would have undercut the program's distinctive prestige and thereby decreased middle- and upper-class boys' interest in Scouting. Most BSA national and local leaders quickly stifled the occasional plea to eliminate the uniform or simplify it to just a cheap badge by insisting on its unique ability to ease class and ethnic tensions and build esprit de corps among members. A 1911 article in *World's Work* magazine, for example, reported, "There is comradeship and fraternity in a uniform, but the uniform of the boy scouts is by no means essential to membership. It has its advantages: it is picturesque and distinctive, as well as serviceable. It tends to develop a democratic feeling. It checks snobbishness and helps the boy to feel the force of the scout law that, 'a scout is a friend and a brother to every other scout.' Social distinctions are not permitted in scouting, and a common uniform does much toward obliterating them." Despite initially claiming that the uniform was not required, the author suggested that every member needed to buy a uniform in order to develop the Scout brotherhood in which class differences could be overcome. A poor boy who joined the BSA but could not afford to buy the uniform therefore risked being called undemocratic and un-American for calling attention to class disparities in his troop or council. Unlike the broad range of clothing and hat qualities and prices for British Scout and Guide uniforms—the choice of which also highlighted a member's economic class—BSA administrators maintained a single, relatively pricey uniform and hat type in the face of suggestions that a cheaper uniform would be as serviceable and that many working-class and destitute boys could not easily afford the traditional uniform. Beyond insisting that all boys pay for their own uniforms, national leaders allowed local officials to make their own decisions about requiring uniforms—but most Local Councils kept with the standard uniform requirement. The BSA did not lower uniform prices until well into the Great Depression.[25]

While Scout officials in other countries increased military drill of troops and enlisted them directly in armed defense during World War I, most BSA officials preferred that American Scouts contribute to the war effort in civilian ways that demonstrated their versatile political leadership skills. Drawing on the daily Good Turn and the annual Scout service days initiated in the early 1910s, BSA national and local leaders partnered with federal government officials to roll out a broad range of civilian service drives for Scouts to support the nation's war effort and to develop useful modern skills, such as efficient organization, data collection, persuasion, salesmanship, and scientific management. As a BSA news bulletin titled "Washington Believes in the Scouts" explained, no Washington, D.C., government officials needed to be told what the BSA was, since they already knew and had seen the Boy Scouts doing their many war service campaigns: "These busy, burdened men didn't talk of the Scouts as men talk of the high school football team, but more as they talk of the Chamber of Commerce and the Board of Trade. To them a troop of Scouts is not a bunch of youngsters doing spectacular stunts, but a civic organization, a permanent and necessary part of the machinery of Government." Liberty Bond and War Savings Stamp sales campaigns provided the BSA's most public and successful civilian war drives. The partnership between the federal government and the BSA produced staggering results: Boy Scouts sold 4,650,000 subscriptions for Liberty Bonds and War Savings Stamps totaling $407 million (around $5 billion in 2015 terms). One report found that the national sales average was about $900 per Scout—in excess of $10,000 *per boy member* in 2015 terms. In response to President Wilson's request that Boy Scouts be dispatch bearers to aid the federal Committee on Public Information (CPI), boy members delivered more than 300 million pieces of government literature. Many Scout troops answered Acting Secretary of War Benedict Crowell's request to collect fruit pits and nutshells to make gas masks. Scouts joined other civic organizations in collecting old tires and rubber scrap to fuel the war effort. Scouts located 20 million feet of standing black walnut lumber for propellers and gun stocks. Scouts also planted twelve thousand Liberty Gardens in 1918 alone, and helped Herbert Hoover and the U.S. Food Administration conserve food consumption in American homes. In recognition of the many services Scouts provided to the nation during the war, President Wilson designated a special anniversary week in early February to be national Boy Scout Week—a tradition that continues to this day.[26]

President Wilson's and Theodore Roosevelt's cooperation with BSA national leaders and men's service organizations on a nationwide campaign to recruit those men ineligible for military service and those returning from military service to become Scoutmasters composed one of the most dramatic linkages between World War I public service and the BSA's vision of modern citizenship. In a 1918 letter to BSA President Colin Livingstone, reproduced and distributed nationally, President Wilson urged the public to support the BSA with money or as volunteers to help replace those Scoutmasters who had left for military service, since Scouts' service would help win the war. Letters from the secretary of the treasury, the secretary of agriculture, and General Pershing reinforcing the vital importance of Scout training accompanied Wilson's letter. Moreover, an essay from Theodore Roosevelt insisted that all men who could not be soldiers should volunteer to be Scoutmasters to fulfill their patriotic duty to the country and to replace those who have been "going to fight for American manhood and civilization on the other side of the water." He argued that those men who would not join the military nor volunteer to be Scoutmasters were not entitled to the privileges of American citizenship or voting. After the war, the BSA partnered with the federal government to recruit returning soldiers to continue serving the nation through becoming Scoutmasters. In exchange, the assistant secretary of war, Colonel Arthur Woods, teamed up with the BSA's James West on a national campaign to get Scouts to enroll employers in an agreement to take back returning soldiers who had quit their jobs to serve in World War I.[27]

While some explicitly military American groups and youth organizations fell out of fashion after 1919, the BSA—having supported the war through civilian service drives and maintaining its patriotic but neither pro- nor antimilitary stance—continued to prosper as mainstream political sentiment shifted toward peaceful global trade and mediated diplomacy. BSA literature, public statements, and training sessions placed somewhat more emphasis in the late 1920s on promoting international peace and arbitration instead of war—paralleling international policies such as the Kellogg-Briand Pact as well as efforts by foreign Scout leaders such as Robert Baden-Powell. The 1928 Boy Scout handbook's "Citizenship" chapter characterized war as wasteful and stated that nations should hold conferences and have differences mediated instead of going to war. The 1929 Scoutmaster's handbook shortened the section on drill but maintained the suggestion to use it to develop troop discipline and morale—as long as it did not supersede other, more vital Scout programs. Throughout its first two decades, BSA programming and ideology remained focused on teaching boy members broader skills for modern civic leadership and the privileges it would convey.[28]

The Privileges of Playing for "Uncle Sam's Team"

In a discussion at the first National Training School for BSA Executives in 1925, the staff leader explained that officially registering to be a member of the organization was essential, especially for the boy, because he then "has a card showing he is a member of Uncle Sam's team, because the President of the United States signs it, and says so." Furthermore, the many kinds of civic services and Good Turns for which federal and local officials depended on uniformed Scouts, during times of both peace and war, gave boy members a quasi-official status as government representatives. This ongoing and pervasive arrangement allowed BSA administrators to argue not only that communities should give resources to prioritize Scout training but also that America's future leading citizens deserved special political benefits. What, then, were the privileges of leading citizenship that Scout training offered to its boy members? An active Boy Scout could expect to be a priority for local and national public recognition and funding support; serve as an honor guard for a wide array of public events; meet government officials, such as the local mayor and even the U.S. president; be a municipal leader for a day; apprentice for government staff positions; and access a spectrum of government land and equipment. BSA officials' equation of service leadership with political privileges paralleled their linkage of learning modern manhood with future control over material resources and higher-echelon jobs in the corporate-industrial economy.[29]

U.S. presidents and many other government leaders regularly accorded Boy Scouts special recognition and benefits. In addition to President Wilson calling out Scouts as servants of the nation on key tasks during the Great War, other presidents provided public relations and status boons when delivering lengthy speeches at BSA events, such as President Coolidge's 1926 speech and Herbert Hoover's 1929 speech for National Council gatherings. The individual Boy Scout felt he enjoyed a special, meaningful relationship with these presidents, who served in turn as honorary Presidents of the BSA. As hundreds of pairs of letters and telegrams between Scout troops and the American presidents and their ensuing meetings in the 1910s and 1920s demonstrated, being a Scout literally gained boys admission to the White House to meet the president of the United States. Figure 3.2 captures just a small sliver of the thirty-five hundred Scouts occupying the White House lawn for a picture and conversation with President Calvin Coolidge in 1926. Pictures of each president in the 1910s and 1920s visiting with troop-sized groups at the White House, public parades, and summer camps abound. These visits could be particularly motivated, such as when a troop of mounted Boy Scouts from Custer, South Dakota, visited President Coolidge at his summer home on the Fourth of July in 1927 to give him a horse with a special saddle, Navajo blanket, bridle and spurs, boots, red shirt, and purple bandanna for his birthday. The grateful president took the horse for a ten-mile ride the next day. The public relations support that President Herbert Hoover extended to the BSA in national speeches and in greet-

Figure 3.2 President Coolidge's boys at home on the White House lawn. *Coolidge with Boy Scouts* (1926). (Courtesy of Library of Congress Prints and Photographs Division)

ing troops visiting the White House fit this general pattern, but he was more cognizant of the importance of girls' civic training due to the active leadership of his wife, Lou Henry Hoover, as President of the Girl Scouts. Cross-branch and local political recognition and benefits filtered down from the ongoing presidential relationship with the Boy Scouts. For example, Vice President Charles Dawes (who won a Nobel Prize for authoring a plan to resolve World War I's German reparations conflict) helped form a new troop in Evanston, Illinois, and was elected honorary President of the Local Council in 1927. Inspired by an Eagle Scout who became a senate page because of his reputation in Scouting, U.S. senators from both parties and a senate chaplain organized a troop of Boy Scouts in 1929 that met weekly in the basement of the Capitol.[30]

The U.S. Congress unanimously granting the BSA a huge prize with the second-ever federal charter in May 1916 helped facilitate material support and recognition for Scouting from both local and national government officials. As the 1929 Scoutmaster's handbook exclaimed, "Departments of the local, state and national governments, nationwide organizations and various institutions are ready and willing to give the Scoutmaster valuable aid for the asking." The author suggested that local

Scout leaders should feel free to request support from fire departments, Boards of Health, schoolteachers, playgrounds, athletic fields, museums, American Legion armories, government conservation agencies, and the Red Cross. Based on the charter, federal and local government agencies could and did donate significant amounts of land, camping equipment, training, and transportation privileges to Scout troops and councils across the country. The U.S. Army provided new tents, cots, blankets, and other camping equipment to outfit the entire BSA delegation to the 1929 World Scout Jamboree in England, which drew comments from foreign Scouts that perhaps the BSA should have just sent a regular U.S. Army unit to the event instead. The U.S. Navy provided over five hundred sailing charters for every port in the country to the BSA's Sea Scout branch for older boys. The surgeon general of the War Department offered Boy Scout units low-cost First Aid kits for camping and hiking. These are just a few of the many examples of government aid to Scouting in the 1910s and 1920s that illustrated the organization's semi-public status.[31]

Building on the precedent of federal government sponsorship of Scouting, local and state political officeholders developed even more intimate and frequent partnerships with the organization. BSA leaders quickly realized the public relations value of having the active support of the town mayor or state governor for Scouting. In return, backing Scouting demonstrated politicians' proactive concern about the community and its youth to their constituents as well as new potential voters. Local officeholders often visited Boy Scout camps for public reviews and awards events. Mayors and governors regularly hosted public rank and badge ceremonies for Scout troops and councils, at which many became official honorary Boy Scouts. Over thirty state governors received their honorary Tenderfoot badges in 1922 Scout ceremonies at their respective state capitol buildings during Boy Scout Anniversary Week, first declared by President Wilson. A 1923 *Scouting* article and photograph showed the entire Arizona legislature joining the governor in taking the Scout Oath and ascribing to the Scout Law in a large ceremony at the state capitol building, "publicly announcing that they, too, '*Agree that Boy Scout leaders are producing for the Nation its greatest need—men of character trained for citizenship.*'" Even as they wrangled over every bill and political method, politicians across the spectrum could agree on the importance of Scouting's practical citizenship and modern manhood in the 1910s and 1920s.[32]

Governors throughout the country published glowing statements of support for the BSA's character and civic training, particularly the Scout Laws and civic service work. By the organization's fifth year, its annual report presented lists of state governors of different political parties recommending Scouting. In 1915, New York governor Charles Whitman predicted, "You Scouts are to be the men of the coming generation, who will be called on to take our place in public life, and I feel sure that your watchword, 'Be prepared,' will help you in fitting yourselves for the life work which you will take up when your time to serve arrives." Wyoming governor John Kendrick elaborated on this connection between Scout manhood and leading citizenship: the Boy Scout Law "is a creed which embraces the outlines of all good and true things, not only in boy life, but in that of adults. The boy who adopts it as his motto and lives up to it cannot help but prove a valuable citizen in the years to come. It is the sort of man he will be caused to become, who will prove the mainstay and backbone of the citizenship of the future." West Virginia governor Henry Hatfield insisted that Scouting made the best men as well as a more noble and efficient future for the nation: "Out of boys who are learning to be trustworthy, loyal, helpful, friendly, courteous, kind, obedient, cheerful, thrifty, brave, clean and reverent, are made the best and noblest men and citizens. That is the kind of training which fits boys for lives of efficiency, helpfulness and happiness in this world of ours. It develops the kind of men we need, both in public and in private life. It makes for national efficiency. It is a conscious social effort toward the development of a higher type of humanity." The increase of national Scout service drives during World War I prompted even more notes of support from state governors in 1918. Ohio governor James Cox, who would later run for the American presidency, may have summed up the governors' sentiments most succinctly: "In our state notable service has been rendered by the Boy Scouts of America. In a sentence it can be truthfully stated that no one organization has rendered more evident help to every worthy cause."[33]

As the 1926 article in *American City* magazine titled "Boy Scouts as City Fathers" highlighted, an expanding number of Boy Scouts in cities across the nation became honorary mayors and councilmen, establishing mutual recognition between government officeholders and the Boy Scouts, presumed to be America's future leaders. President Harding sent a telegram explaining his appreciation to Chicago government officials for handing over city government posts to Boy Scouts for the day: "I want to express my personal hope for your success, because I believe this is one of the effective ways of doing most useful work for the generation that very shortly will be in command of our nation's destinies." The Pennsylvania cities of Lancaster, Oil City, Franklin, McKeesport, and Chester turned over their mayor jobs and municipal administrations to local Scouts elected by fellow Scouts one day in 1923. The Scout mayors held sessions at city council chambers and performed such duties as planning traffic and safety at local schools, asking the chief of police to investigate anti-cigarette law enforcement, preparing a bill for a $1.5 million street widening project, and proposing that city officials be required to take the Scout Oath in connection with their municipal oath of office. Some councils, such as the Yakni Scout Council in northeast Mississippi, held formal Scout elections with campaign speeches and voting, often enlisting men's business and service clubs, such as Rotary, to help facilitate the elections and temporary government takeovers. Philadelphia; New York City; Atlanta; Helena, Montana; and El Paso, Texas, were among the many cities across the country that granted Scouts this recognition of their fitness to lead the government, a tradition that continued for decades in many councils.[34]

"The Great Gate of Service": Scout and Scoutmaster Reflections on BSA Civic Teachings

Surveys of thousands of boy and adult members, local council histories, and individual memoirs suggest that a significant number of regular Scouts, Scoutmasters, and other supporters highly valued and absorbed the modern civic teachings that BSA administrators and publications emphasized. Many saw citizenship training as the primary goal of Scouting and the program's most important contribution to society. Responses to a 1928 survey of 697 Scoutmasters from across the country (a mix of those characterized as exemplary and average by their Executives) laid out some of the main currents of troop leaders' and boys' perspectives on BSA civic training. "Citizenship training" constituted the most common troop-leader answer to an open-ended question about the main objective of Scout training and troop activities, written in by 18.6 percent of respondents. Even this statistic underplayed the importance Scout leaders placed on citizenship training, since related but separately tallied answers also scored high in the survey results, such as "leadership development" (the third most common response at 8.5 percent), "the Scout Oath and Law" (the fifth most common response at 6.3 percent), and "love for God and country" (the sixth most common response at 4.1 percent). Other surveys and reflections of Scouts and their adult supporters reinforced the responding Scoutmasters' insistence that training in active but nonpartisan citizenship and corresponding opportunities for service leadership, Good Turns to the community, and adult-like adventure formed a vital and effective aspect of early Boy Scouting.[35]

The 1976 memoirs of William Harrison Fetridge, a prominent businessman and civic activist, demonstrated that he was among those many boy members in the 1910s and 1920s who embraced the early BSA's vision of active, practical citizenship and fulfilled those ideals as adults. The citation accompanying the honorary degree of laws bestowed on him in 1954 by Central Michigan University (an award his connection with fellow Scout activist and CMU president Dr. Charles Anspach helped earn) emphasized that the university's trustees and professors deemed him a "good citizen." Fetridge, however, felt that "perhaps a better phrase would have been 'active citizen' for certainly during most of my life I have been active in many causes, probably too many." In a 1965 speech he gave to help start the annual United Fund social work fund-raising drive in Williamsport, Pennsylvania, he insisted that Scout volunteer leaders, YMCA workers, Red Cross drivers, political party precinct workers, and other regular folks consistently involved in community affairs were ideal active citizens. In words that closely paralleled the participating citizenship teachings of the BSA organization of which he had been such an avid and dedicated member as both a boy and an adult, Fetridge explained, "In effect, he is the citizen who realizes he is not doing his share merely by obeying the laws and doing his daily work. Instead, he does these things and, more, he makes a conscious effort to help others, to help his community, to support his country. He is not a citizen drone; he is a citizen worker." Such civic ideals probably infused the fifteen or twenty Scouting speeches he delivered each year at national and international conventions and local meetings across the country. He served for years as the chairman of Scouting's Midwest Region Seven, on the National Executive Board, as BSA Vice President, and as founder of the Boy Scout National Museum.[36]

In his 1958 memoir, reflecting on over three decades of work as an adult Scout volunteer, August Kietzman emphasized how an individual could be faithful to Scouting's principle of engaged but nonpartisan citizenship while being dedicated to a particular political party. In response to a common question in Scouting circles as to whether an adult Scouter should be involved in politics, Kietzman affirmed that adult Scouters had a special duty to be active in supporting a political party and its candidates, since that was the way American democracy worked best: "You have heard it said that a man performs his whole duty when he goes to the poll and votes. . . . But he who does only that does not measure up entirely to the ideal of our Constitution. . . . The man who carried his rifle forward during the war was not undutiful. But the one who, in addition, inspired and helped others to do their utmost did his full duty." Along with reaffirming the early BSA standard that voting and even serving in the military did not constitute a man's full civic obligation, Kietzman argued that it was essential for adult Scouters to be regularly involved in a party of his choice and, even better, run for political office because "the Adult Scouter who reaches a position of influence in a political organization will, to [the] extent of his influence, be able to line up that part in support of the principles laid down in the Boy Scout Oath and Law and the Constitution of the Boy Scouts of America. I go further. I maintain that it is only through those of our number who secure large political influence that we can ever hope for an American government equal to the aims of our Scout movement." It is striking how Kietzman held up the Boy Scout Oath, Law, and Constitution as a model that the United States government and its officials would have to work hard and stay diligent to match. However, he stressed that it was essential that the name of any specific political party, candidate, or platform should never be mentioned at a Scout meeting or event, since "the Scout movement is irrevocably non-partisan." He concluded, "America will always need her wisest, most powerful and most public-spirited sons for leadership. Where shall she find her truest guides if not in the rank and file of the Boy Scouts of America and their leaders."[37]

Surveys of boy members done in the 1920s and Boy Scouts' later memoirs highlighted that service leadership was not just a standard for the adult stage of their lives; belonging to the BSA organization gave youth adult-like status and leadership authority in their communities. To many boys, being initiated into Scouting conveyed the personal force of becoming a respected, essential young adult citizen of the United States. In the 1928 BSA survey of over two thousand boy members from across the country, a fifteen-year-old Second Class Scout declared, "I believe my entrance into Scouting was as I now realized one of the greatest events in my life. I never knew how much I was ignorant of till I joined Scouting. I have gained knowledge in every way and all this has helped to make me a better citizen. This, after all, is the final object of Scouting." A fifteen-year-old First Class Scout stated, "When I first started the Scouts I was determined to do a Good Turn daily and take an active part in all Scout activities and have tried to do so ever since." Another fifteen-year-old First Class member explained that becoming a Scout granted a boy public status and authority in both peer and adult eyes; Investiture "makes you proud to be a Scout and have authority." In his memoir of fifty-two years of Scouting experiences, J. Hurley Hagood recalled that a new Scout Executive appointed in 1928 to the Tom Sawyer Area Council in Hannibal, Missouri, often sent Hagood and another veteran Boy Scout as official delegates to help stir up interest in new units and to solidify fledgling troops that were having difficulties. Hagood and his young friend "helped organize new Troops, train new leaders, and were active in all Scout activities in Hannibal. If a Troop lost its leader, or was having difficulty in handling troop programs, we would be sent out to get the Troop meetings functioning properly. This status of being accepted as an equal by adult leaders was very gratifying. I enjoyed it." In a survey of 288 teachers, principals, and professors by a BSA National Commission in 1928, respondents emphasized that the organization benefited the development and practice of new educational theories by providing boys with civic leadership training through practical Scouting experiences and increasing student participation in school government associations.[38]

Early Boy Scout and adult Scouter surveys and memoirs both emphasized that the primary path for a young member to earn civic leadership status required fulfilling the Scout duty to do a daily Good Turn as well as engaging in organized community service projects. In the 1928 BSA survey of over two thousand boy members, respondents ranked the daily Good Turn and community service as the third most important of twelve program elements for building Scout character, but cited it first in the number of practical experiences they encountered in which a Scout Law or Oath was directly involved. The surveyed Scouts reported that they fulfilled the Scout Oath and Laws (particularly the trustworthy and helpful Laws) in these Good Turns and community service events at a ratio five times greater than they broke the Scout Oath and Laws. Several Scouts noted that at first they did Good Turns to show off or because they were supposed to, but later it developed into a regular habit of helping others that they enjoyed. Scouts remarked that the Good Turn enabled them to be contributing members to the broader community—participating citizens. A thirteen-year-old new Tenderfoot already noticed, "It gives me a feeling of wanting to help a lost child, the underfellow, or the weakling. It gives me a new importance, that of being of use to others." A fourteen-year-old First Class Scout remarked, "It taught me how to do Good Turns without making a big fuss over it, and taught me how to be a good citizen." Surveyed boy members frequently remarked that reminding themselves of the Scout's duty to do a Good Turn prompted them to choose to help others in need rather than be selfish and pursue their own enjoyment or interests. A thirteen-year-old Tenderfoot explained how his new loyalty to Scouting and its civic values overrode other group loyalties, such as to his baseball team: "One hot day when I came home from school my dad asked me a favor which would take a half hour; our team had an important ball game that day and I was to play. I refused to do it, and I went into my room to put on my baseball clothes. The first thing I noticed was my Scout uniform on the chair. I went out and ran the errand." Some surveyed Scouts noted how the daily obligation to do a Good Turn was difficult to meet and could be counterproductive if not met regularly, while other Scouts recalled doing individual Good Turns and troop community service frequently. J. Hurley Hagood's memoir of Scouting as a boy in Hannibal, Missouri, in the late 1920s explained, "We practiced the Boy Scout slogan, 'Do at least one Good Turn Daily.' Sometimes this required a bit of imagination, and it is possible that my interpretation of a Good Turn was a bit questionable at times. But gradually, I did get the right idea of the Good Turn as being an unrewarded helpful act. Our Troop was frequently called upon to help in civic activities, thus giving its members opportunities for being of service to the community. These Troop good turns were important community activities, and gave Scouts a sense of importance." Paul Painter, a Texas Eagle Scout in the second half of the 1920s, explained in an interview decades later that his troop "was always doing civic projects. Doing other projects always brought out a majority of the Scouts in uniform." He believed this led "a lot of former Scouts in adulthood to be more involved in the civic and charity affairs of their community."[39]

Reflections by and surveys of local council Scout Executives and Scoutmasters suggest that civilian service leadership made a better organizing focus than did teaching boys militarism. Charles L. Weaver, who served as the Scout Council Executive of Richmond, Virginia, from 1915 until his death in 1938, stressed the centrality of service to Scouting in his 1917 annual report to the council (written after America's entry into World War I): "I like to think of Scouting as a great gate of Service, held in place by Good Turn hinges firmly riveted against a solid post, 'the Scout Oath,' with long, sharp and penetrating staples, 'the twelve Scout laws'—a wonderful gate is service . . . swinging back and forth as it often opens allowing the individual Scout to pass through on the road to his 'daily Good Deed.' Sometimes it swings far back, until the old 'Good Turn' hinges fairly creak, to permit hundreds of Scouts to jam through bent on their mission of service [in large-scale community engagement activities]. In this little figure I have reported to you what to me is scouting . . . because all else in Scouting is second to, and trivial beside 'The Good Turn.'" Leaders of the Middle Tennessee Scout Council recalled in their local history that deflecting charges of militarism was a concern for area Scouters in the 1910s: "The first uniformed scouts on the streets of Nashville were sometimes ridiculed as 'baby soldiers.' Scoutmaster Fitzgerald of Troop 3 explained: 'One dear old lady who wore a deaconess cap gave me a high moral lecture on the wickedness of training such beautiful children to be cannon fodder in the next war.'" Nashville Scout leaders, with support from the BSA national office, worked hard to defuse such concerns by stressing the broader character development and service leadership goals of the organization. After a decline in Scout membership and enthusiasm during America's participation in World War I, Nashville Scouting rebounded in the early 1920s with heavy sponsorship and promotional support from the Rotary Club under the banner of service leadership rather than militarism.[40]

The majority of the one thousand Scoutmasters from around the country surveyed in 1928 by a BSA National Commission agreed that military experience was not a primary motivation for them being troop leaders. Even though 33.3 percent of respondents noted having had some military experience (likely during World War I), only 1.3 percent of the Scoutmasters reported that their time in the military was their key motivation. Much more common motivations listed included general interest in boy development, duty to others, and previous experience as Boy Scouts themselves. The same survey reported that 34.1 percent of the Scoutmasters had been Scouts as boys, 22.9 percent of which had earned the highest rank of Eagle Scout. Eighty percent of the total number of Scouts-turned-Scoutmasters had held troop offices as boys.[41]

Paralleling the statements made in early BSA teachings and publications, Boy Scouts fondly recalled the unique opportunities and material benefits that being a member and adhering to its civic code garnered. In an interview with a reporter years later concerning his Scouting experiences as a northern Mississippi youth in the late 1920s, Dr. W. A. Spearman highlighted that his troop was allowed to meet in the local courthouse and frequently went on adventure trips. In 1927, the troop and other local Scouts traveled to Biloxi to escort Confederate and Union veterans in their joint reunion. As a Scout, Spearman was able to take and pass his Red Cross swim instructor test a year early and hold his own Red Cross swimming camps to earn money. In 1930, he saved thirty dollars to participate in the third annual Eagle Flight trip of 2,473 miles to Washington, D.C., and used passes obtained by Congressman Rankin to tour such sights as the Smithsonian, Lincoln Memorial, Washington Monument, and Naval Academy. Mississippi senator Pat Harrison personally showed the visiting Scouts around the Capitol, but according to Spearman, "When the president [Herbert Hoover] came down on the back lawn [of the White House] and shook hands with us, and posed with us for the picture, that was the highlight." Being a boy member and doing Good Turns could also benefit Scouts in monetary ways. A new Dallas Scout explained in a 1929 survey response that the respect adults in the community accorded Scouts, particularly for their Good Turns, and the superior job opportunities available to Scouts over non-Scouts encouraged him to join the organization: "I noticed that the boys in my neighborhood who were scouts had many good times together, of their desire to do 'good turns,' to help someone some way, and that they tried to live up to scouting standards. I noticed that these boys conducted themselves more mannerly than the boys who were not scouts. And I saw that grown people had respect for Scouts. . . . It was easier for these boys to get jobs than for other boys, because people believed them to be the best. For these reasons I was attracted to scouting."[42]

As both Boy Scout and adult Scouter memoirs noted, the annual ritual of Boy Scouts around the country being elected to take over municipal governments and their functions for a day constituted one of the most direct and lasting linkages between Scout citizenship ideals and future political leadership. In a 1983 history of the Middle Tennessee Council of the BSA, author Wilbur Creighton Jr. recalled the personal impact of becoming the first Boy Scout to serve as Tennessee governor for the day in 1924: "[I] took the job seriously, acting upon a petition for parole during [my] hour in the governor's chair, and the event left an enduring impression upon [me]." Creighton stated that he and other

Scouts who served in government positions for a day in the 1920s often issued proclamations about local issues of special concern to area youth. Eagle Scout Beverly Briley served as Tennessee boy governor in 1927, and later became a Davidson County judge and the first mayor of the Metropolitan Nashville government. Briley, also a veteran Scoutmaster, was fond of explaining that he began planning the metropolitan government system for Nashville while working at Scout camp. In his 1952 memoirs, Scoutmaster and District Scout Chairman Willard Adams of Rigby, Idaho, highlighted the intricacy and importance of Boy Scouts operating the local government for a day: "The first time the Scouts of this area were privileged to take over the city government was on May 25, 1929. . . . An election was conducted with printed ballots, furnished by *The Rigby Star*. Much excitement was manifested in the election," in which young Scouts were chosen to take over the positions of mayor, town clerk, town treasurer, town councilmen, chief of police, city attorney, fire chief, and health officer. The thirteen elected Scouts made sixty-eight arrests for traffic and parking violations, proposed a new city sewer system and health improvement program, and did a fire inspection of the town's business district. Adams concluded, "The city officials were well pleased and asked the Scouts to take it for a week next year." To Adams, managing the town government was a culminating feature of local Scouts' broader civic service program, which included such efforts as helping area farmers thin their beet crops, cleaning up cemeteries, saving lives, and meeting with visiting dignitaries, such as President Harding.[43]

Reflecting on his long stint leading a wayward Illinois group of Scouts into becoming an exemplary unit designated as a National Council Laboratory Troop, August Kietzman's memoir captures the high stakes that many early BSA supporters believed Scouting's civic vision of active, nonpartisan service leadership held. He argued that the very future of the country and its well-being depended on developing in boys upstanding character and unselfish civic virtues: "They must possess those qualities contained within the theme of Scouting. They must be 'physically strong, mentally awake and morally straight.' Then, indeed, and then only, in our national defenses shall we 'Be Prepared.'" He insisted that it was of paramount importance to train all developing boys in Scouting, since the government policies set today would have to be carried out by them: "Even if you make leagues and treaties, he will have to manage them. He is going to sit at your desk in the Senate, and occupy your place on the Supreme Bench. He will assume control of your cities, states, and nation. . . . We have been forty-eight years in Scouting in the United States, and we have turned out millions of young men who have been subject to the training of Scouting. We have made of them, better citizens than they otherwise could have been or might have been." Kietzman stressed that the Scout program and its daily Good Turn taught boys essential civic lessons such as responsibility, accountability, cheerful work, patriotism, leadership, and service—"the supreme commitment of life."[44]

THE RITUALS OF GOVERNORS becoming honorary Scouts and Boy Scouts shaking hands with the president and becoming mayors for a day sanctified the recognition from government officials across the political spectrum that the BSA was a key training ground for leading men and citizens. Scouting helped promulgate a modern vision of practical, engaged citizenship that emphasized leading by serving. Individual Good Turns and council and national service drives upheld Boy Scouts as exemplars of organized efficiency and scientific expertise. Being nonpartisan and neither pro- nor antimilitary while contributing to the war effort, patriotic festivals, and voter turnout helped Boy Scouts withstand political shifts and appear above the divisive fray of narrow partisan or military organizations. Scout civic training and activities offered a prized supplement to the school curriculum, family, and church after the early twentieth century's removal of youth from most of the political and public realm. The third pillar of Scout training—a structured, scientific engagement with the outdoors and natural resources—provided a key space and metaphor for developing Boy Scouts into these leading citizens and men of modern character.

4

Nature, Conservation, and Modern Manhood

The 1917 *Boys' Life* sketch by staff artist Frank Rigney in Figure 4.1, re-produced widely in BSA publications and local pageantry, perhaps best illustrates the multiple audiences to whom the organization appealed as well as the emphasis on modern rather than primitive values in Scouting's nature ideology and practices. In the lower left-hand corner, a "gang" of adolescent boys has been left unsupervised to gamble and smoke on the city streets. The relaxed boys do not seem to mind this arrangement, but many parents, educators, and urban reformers in this era would have remarked that such boys had no discipline, positive character influences, or good career prospects. Child development theorists and male educators worried that "feminized" clergy, admonishing mothers, and female schoolteachers and their textbook platitudes might be incapable of stemming the pernicious influences of the era's tide of independent youth and urban mass culture. Such adults often preferred that adolescent boys learn character and civic values and skills like those listed along the lower right to upper left diagonal axis of the sketch, which comprise the Scout Oath, Laws, and tests for rank advancement. Drawn by Scouting's outdoor life and strong men's leadership, the boys willingly choose to leave their corrupting street life behind to climb the ladder of the Scout Oath and learn the twelve Laws' character values as well as the foundational civic duties to country, God, self, and others. Scout campers in the inset at the top right practice modern skills, such as order, time discipline, personal hygiene, efficiency, group cooperation, balanced fitness, and serving others. The stair steps labeled with the sequential Scout rank tests and merit badges in the top left quadrant of the sketch illustrate that the end goal of the BSA's outdoor programming was not savage virility or Romantic contemplation of a scenic waterfall but to become honorable citizens and reintegrate into modern society. The sketch prompted ongoing progress and advancement through individual effort by asking boys, Are you climbing? However, the question, Are you helping others up? encouraged the peer loyalty and teamwork good Scouts developed, which were conducive to America's interdependent cities and corporate-bureaucratic workforce. The sketch highlights that while outdoorsmanship

Figure 4.1 A synopsis of Scouting. Frank Rigney, "Every Step Means Progress," *Boys' Life*, February 1917, 29. (Courtesy of Boy Scouts of America National Scouting Museum Archival Collection)

was a key appeal to boys who joined the organization, learning to adapt successfully to a changing society and government constituted the ultimate purpose of Scouting.[1]

The fact that early BSA publications and leaders talked frequently about the outdoors while only one of the twelve Boy Scout Laws dealt directly with it suggests that the organization taught boys modern manhood and civic leadership through—but not for—nature. As with its intertwined gender ideology, the mature BSA's environmental teachings contrasted significantly with those of the Woodcraft Indians and the Sons of Daniel Boone. Five of Seton's ten Woodcraft Indian Laws emphasized camping or nature, while nearly all of the eight elements of the Sons of Daniel Boone pledge focused explicitly on them, including, "I will give all creatures a fair show for life, liberty, and the pursuit of happiness," killing game only within the conservation laws and that could be rightfully used; not cutting live trees for campfires; preserving the forests, since they are the retreat of many beasts and birds; not setting forest fires; being careful with firearms around people and animals; and abiding by the game laws (again!). Of the twelve American Boy Scout laws, only the Sixth Law (inherited from the British program) on being kind to animals mentioned nature values—and even it was carefully hedged by most early BSA leaders, who preferred that boys learn natural resource conservation's firm scientific and monetary judgment instead of sentimental, indiscriminate attitudes toward all animals, regardless of their value to humans.[2]

British and Canadian Boy Scouts and Girl Guides, Jewish Boy Scouts in Palestine, and American Girl Scouts placed more emphasis on notions of the imperial frontier and the heroic pioneer settler than did most BSA national leaders and their primary teaching methods and publications in the 1910s and 1920s. One historian argued that the frontier myth and the martial pioneer-soldier best explained the appeal of early Boy Scouting in the British Empire because it responded to popular beliefs, such as the virility crisis, fear of German invasion, Social Darwinism, and seeing nature as the solution to many urban social ills. Early American Girl Scouting balanced scientific inquiry, nostalgic pioneering paired with an idealized local indigenous folklore, and a sentimental friendship with nature. While BSA publications and local officials occasionally employed a pioneering motif or theatrics from frontier lore specialists like National Scout Commissioner Dan Beard, the organization more often stressed scientific approaches to nature and conservation of natural resources—practices that many BSA leaders (including Dan Beard) directly contrasted against wasteful, excessive, and selfish pioneering practices. A modern and efficient nature mind-set became increasingly dominant in American Scouting between 1915 and 1930.[3]

As Figure 4.1's sketch suggests, the ways in which early officials taught the BSA's rank and merit badge tests and rhetorically framed their larger purposes helped bridge any potential gap between the boys' outdoor fun and the modern Scout character laws and civic virtues that garnered adult approval. Practicing for and passing these rank and badge tests was the key feature of most Scout troop meetings and hiking and camping sessions across the country in the 1910s and 1920s. According to the 1929 Scoutmaster's handbook, eighteen of the twenty-six tests for Tenderfoot, Second Class, and First Class Scout ranks as well as the majority of required Scout merit badges for Life, Star, and Eagle Scout ranks were best taught and demonstrated outdoors. Even if the lessons were taught indoors at school or church troop meeting rooms, BSA literature and spokespersons emphasized that the rank and merit badges tested outdoor skills needed to hike and camp productively, while enabling boys to develop the character and civic attributes outlined in the Scout Laws and Oath.[4]

As the BSA matured and grew more influential over the course of the 1910s and 1920s, its leaders honed four key nature activities to attract boy members and teach them Scouting's modern character and practical citizenship: Nature Study, hiking, camping, and conservation of natural resources. Scouting discouraged boys from "feminine," Romantic sentimentalization of nature and from "unproductive" primitivism. Scouts instead practiced scientific categorization, observation, and data collection through Nature Study. Approved forms of "hiking with a purpose" encouraged Scouts to make productive use of their leisure time by learning quantitative assessment and mapping, time discipline, and even appreciation for industrial production. The "Pine Tree Patrol" method, perhaps the pinnacle of early Scout outdoorsmanship, divided camping into Taylorist, specialized work roles to develop boys' hierarchical loyalty and efficient teamwork on standardized tasks under the disciplined eye of the stopwatch. Conserving natural resources taught Scouts expert management, monetary evaluation of nature, and service to the nation. Scouting appealed to boy members by offering the opportunity to experience the outdoor life and learn men's skills and values—a far cry from the increasingly isolated and feminized realms of the school and privatized home. From the perspectives of administrators, adult supporters, and many boy members, Scout nature programming provided boys an intense and effective preparation for modern living that replaced the nineteenth century's job apprenticeship and engagement with the public realm, which compulsory schooling and child labor laws were undercutting.

Nature Study: Scouts "Must Not Be Satisfied with the Mystery and Romance of It All"

BSA administrators argued that Nature Study taught Scouts to scientifically master and engineer nature for humans' material benefit instead of befriending nature or spiritually contemplating its great mystery. Nineteenth-century Romantics and transcendentalists such as Henry Thoreau and John Muir had insisted that appreciating nature's beauty and mystery led each individual to spiritual and creative growth, and that nature's deepest secrets were and should remain unknowable. The first handbook for American Scoutmasters, published in 1912, promised that new boy members would be instinctively interested in their first outdoor troop meeting because they "are yearning to know their world. To unlock the mysteries of nature and to know their relationship to them." The author, though, echoed the era's leading theorists of adolescence by cutting short any suggestion that a Scout's purpose for contemplating nature's mysteries should be creativity or spirituality: "They must learn to recognize the forces and the laws of operation which underlie the manifestations of nature. Their wonder and interest must not be satisfied with the mystery and romance of it all but their ability to use and master these forces must be impressed upon them. This mastery will give knowledge and power for later life-work." A 1920 *Scouting* article by a Connecticut troop leader applied William James's theory of the moral equivalents of war to encourage Boy Scouts to develop men's work skills by engaging in "the struggle with nature. To coal and iron mines, to freight trains, to fishing fleets in December. To road-building and stoke holes and to the frames of sky-scrapers would our gilded youth be drafted to get the childishness knocked out of them and to come back to society with healthier sympathies and soberer ideas." President Calvin Coolidge echoed this sentiment in a 1926 speech for the BSA National Council meeting at which he argued that the struggle against the forces of nature that Scouting helped provide was essential to the physical and mental growth of the modern race, and especially its youth.[5]

BSA publications claimed that Scout Nature Study activities served a threefold purpose: increasing scientific knowledge of nature, helping identify valuable natural resources for the common good, and—most importantly—teaching capable boys the masculine values and skills needed to lead a modern society and its expert-managed government. For example, a 1919 *American Review of Reviews* article about a troop sponsored by the American Museum of Natural History stated that Nature Study helped improve Scouts' observation, deduction, patience, accuracy, and precision. One First Class rank advancement test required fully classifying and explaining the material uses of a set of plants and animals. Scouts could then continue with Nature Study in merit badges like mining, fishing, zoology, rocks and minerals, astronomy, beekeeping, botany, forestry, insect life, stalking, and taxidermy. In a 1926 *Scouting* article on Nature Study emphasizing "The Economics of It," the author instructed Boy Scouts to carefully distinguish between useful plants and animals, destructive pests, and those "which are merely ornamental or quite useless. . . . In fact, it is *all-important* that scouts obtain *practical* information through Nature Study. . . . One of the best services scouting can render the country is to greatly increase the number of boys who know the differences between harmful and harmless insects, birds and other forms of small life of the fields and woods, and also know how to help in the perpetual campaign to exterminate destructive pests of all kinds." From the perspective of many early BSA leaders, studying nature too intimately or loving it sentimentally risked clouding a boy's ability to discriminate among valuable, destructive, and useless beings. American Girl Scouts' Nature Study practices, on the other hand, blended scientific categorization with friendly, personal intimacy with the animals and the rest of the outdoors.[6]

BSA officials especially encouraged tree and bird study because of the observable ways humans benefited from them as well as the lessons on scientific classification they offered members. As a 1925 *Weekly News Bulletin* declared, "America's trees and birds are the special wards of scoutdom. Yearly an increasing number of trees are being planted and tended by troops everywhere; and each Spring witnesses 'a building boom in birdtown.'" Large handbook sections on tree identification and various activity suggestions emphasized the human uses of different tree species—and prioritized appreciating and conserving those that were more valuable. According to a 1919 *Scouting* article promoting the new BSA ornithology merit badge pamphlet, bird study was an important Scout activity, since it helped boys evolve from a childish approach to nature as simply a "huge playground" to a man's scientific study of nature and protection of materially valuable species. The author argued that bird study had the greatest chance of converting boys from wildlife killers to wildlife protectors because birds were readily available, easily identifiable, beautiful, and economically useful to man. In another *Scouting* article that year, George Gladden differentiated scientists focused on orderly classification of birds from sentimental "Nature Faker" writers who invested birds with humanlike characteristics that they did not possess. Gladden referred to anthropomorphizing animals as a passing madness, similar to a parlor lecture or dog show. Whereas sentimental bird lovers never truly came to know nature or understand its real value, Gladden encouraged Boy Scouts to follow the example of scientific bird observers such as naturalist John Burroughs (who wrote articles for a regular *Boys' Life* column). As Figure 4.2 from that year's BSA Annual Report to Congress suggested, observing birds in the wild also allowed boys to engage in the increasingly popular Scout "specimen hunts" and create scientific collections for display in troop meeting rooms, council offices, and public buildings and fairs.[7]

Analyzing patterns in the four major editions of the American Boy Scout handbook in the 1910s and 1920s highlights the growth of material, scientific, and expert management motivations for doing Nature Study at the expense of moral and Romantic concerns. Romantics insisted that sublime landscapes and nature's mysterious essence offered universal moral lessons and spiritual truths to the individual seeker who was at one with his or her surroundings. Seton's original 1910 Boy Scout handbook, for example, contained a large section on studying star constellations to convey moral tales of Native Americans and classical Western societies. However, the 1911 Boy Scout handbook quickly replaced most of Seton's moralistic, Native American lore–based nature philosophy with a segmented series of Nature Study topics written by a committee of expert authors—including government biologists, zoologists, and conservationists—who stressed humans' scientific and material uses of various plant and animal types. For example, the new section on reptiles explained which species were hunted to make purses, luggage, and delicacies. The U.S. Bureau of Entomology emphasized the production of silk cloth in its new handbook essay on insects and butterflies. The U.S.

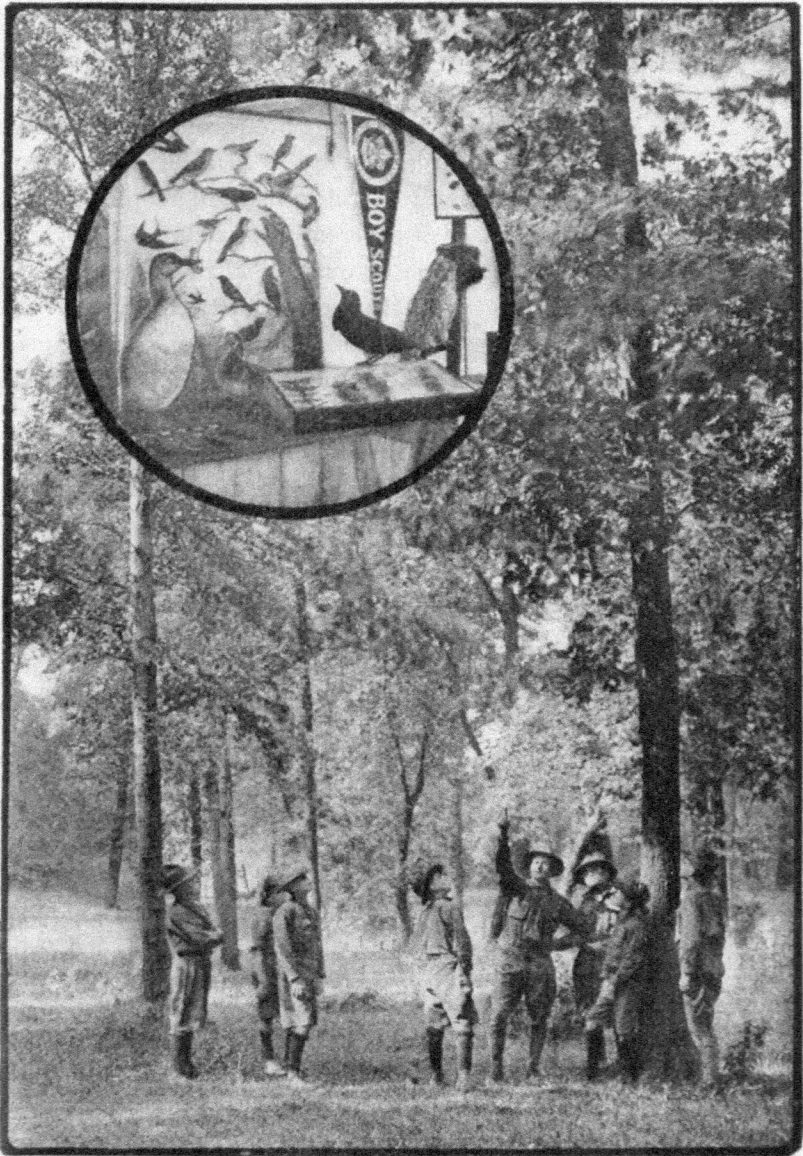

Studying nature at first hand to afterward construct and preserve educational exhibits

Figure 4.2 A bird in the display is worth two in the trees. "Studying Nature at First Hand," 1919 BSA Annual Report to Congress, 95. (Courtesy of Boy Scouts of America National Scouting Museum Archival Collection)

Fisheries Deputy Commissioner's section highlighted food and game fish, while the U.S. Bureau of Plant Industry pointed out the species best for timber, juice, gum, and resin production. The third major edition, in use from 1914 to 1927, completed the expulsion of Seton from the BSA's Nature Study program. The fourth edition of the handbook in 1928 reserved special praise for those birds that ate noxious insects, weed seed, and small rodents, and that helped maintain the "fine balance of Nature without which human life might become very difficult, if not impossible . . . a vast and aggressive army that is constantly fighting in the interests of our farmers and fruit-growers." The hard-science-based Nature Study chapter grew to a larger portion of the BSA handbook's pages with each new version.[8]

Nature Study taught Scouts a modern, scientific way to view and engage with not only the environment but also human society. In a 1927 *Scouting* article titled "Good and Bad Citizens in Nature," author C. A. Edson argued that Nature Study's lessons that evaluated the worth of specific animals and plants should be applied to judging and managing different groups of humans. Edson suggested that hiking Scouts divide into two groups: one looking for good "nature citizens" and one looking for bad nature citizens. "Good" nature citizens provided some use to humans, such as lumber, nuts, fruit, and the snakes that ate crop-destroying rats. "Bad" nature citizens—such as ivy, tree moths, tent caterpillars, rats, and mosquitoes—damaged valuable trees, invaded human dwellings, and infected people with diseases. The article encouraged Scoutmasters to talk with their boys about how utility to humans should be used to classify each nature citizen as good or bad, and how to apply that same standard to evaluating the character and civic worthiness of good and bad people. Edson also suggested that the Scoutmaster discuss with his troop how bad people and nature citizens could be improved, and what role Boy Scouts could learn to play in those processes.[9]

Hiking the Scout Trail to Manhood and Citizenship

The 1925 "Boy Scout Trail to Citizenship" sketch in Figure 4.3, one of the most enduring images for early leaders and members, conveyed the centrality of structured hiking activities for teaching Scouts modern manhood and participating citizenship. The artist, like many other BSA officials, depicted Scouting's overall program as a regulated hiking trail through the otherwise bewildering woods of adolescence. In this image,

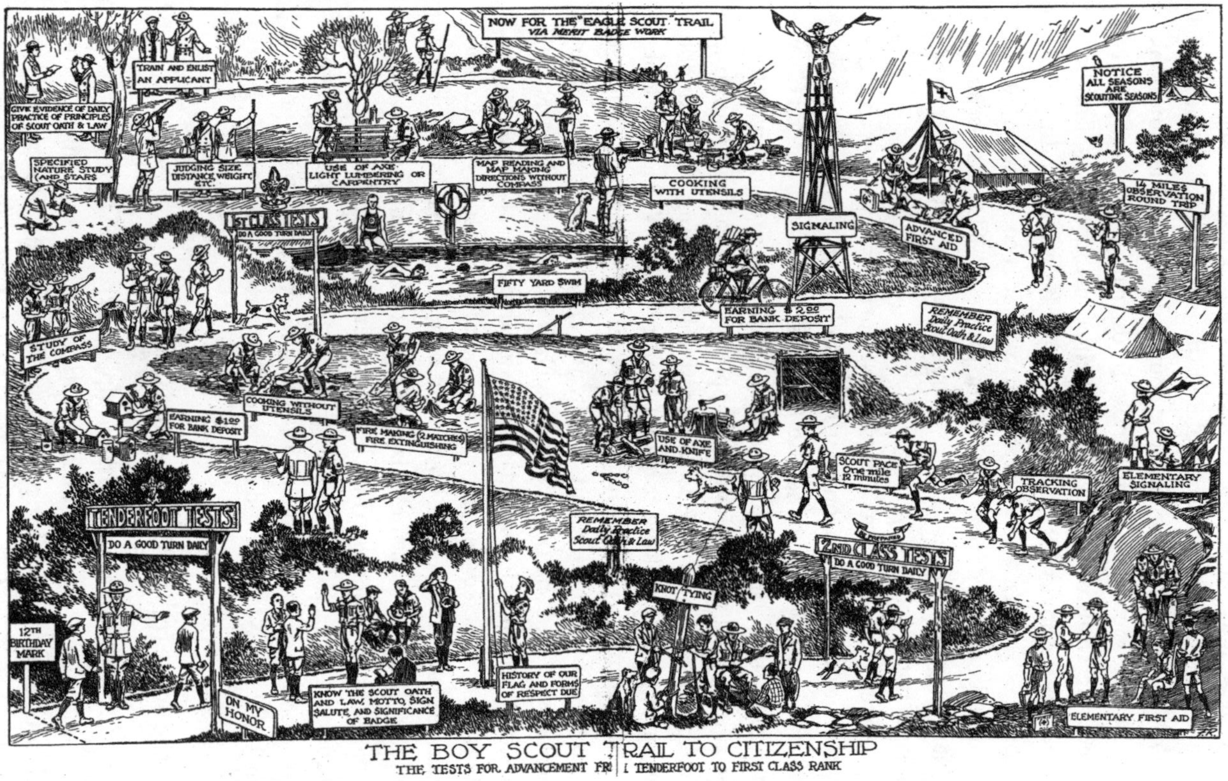

Figure 4.3 Scouting's trail of advancement tests. Frank Rigney, "The Boy Scout Trail to Citizenship," *Scouting*, November 1925, 25. (Courtesy of Boy Scouts of America National Scouting Museum Archival Collection)

a boy in street clothes enters on his twelfth birthday, ushered in by an upright, uniformed Scoutmaster. Guided by the Scoutmaster and older peers at regular stations along the woodsy path, the new member hikes through the Scout rank test lessons as he advances from Tenderfoot to First Class Scout. BSA administrators successfully encouraged local leaders to teach boys these skills outdoors on hiking trips, so the metaphor was both symbolic and reflective of actual practices. Many of these required rank lessons employed a scientific or mathematical approach to nature, such as compass orienteering, the fourteen-mile "observation hike," map reading, judging size and distance, and Nature Study. First Aid prepared the troop to be self-reliant while hiking and to serve the community by saving the lives of others. Some reprinted and reimagined versions of this vignette highlighted that the end of Scouting's adolescent trail leads back to the city and its skyscrapers. The hiking trail to citizenship metaphor proved to be popular with local officials and troops; many used similar sketches and even live reenactments of this scene to promote Scouting and to enlist public and government support.[10]

Hiking in and of itself did not guarantee that Scouts would learn proper character and civic lessons; BSA leaders constantly warned that there were both useful and ineffective kinds of hiking. American Scout publications insisted that strolling aimlessly through the woods or just arriving at a scenic destination would not turn a boy into a good man but would encourage idleness and frivolity. A trained Scout would have recognized that the boy in Figure 4.4 from a 1922 issue of *Boys' Life* violates nearly every Scout Law and modern virtue taught by the program. Although this boy is traversing across a field on a beautiful day unaided by car or horse, his carefree attitude and lack of constructive character goals means that he is not *actually* hiking in Boy Scout eyes. Instead, the poor African American country boy is tramping or hoboing. By constantly borrowing things such as the hoe and not returning them, the tramp fails to be trustworthy, friendly, or courteous. He violates the Law on obedience, since not promptly returning borrowed items was considered stealing. The tramp appears to be a victim of his own selfish, shortsighted urges rather than someone who uses self-control to be helpful or loyal to others, his superiors, and the nation. He appears cheerful, but it is a cheerfulness that stems from ignorant laziness and taking advantage of people rather than from a good Scout's conscientious focus on working hard and making other people happy. In the accompanying poem, the boy casually recommends always trying

"Try yo' bes' ter borrer it,
Frum som' un e'se, Ah s'pose;
An' jus'
keep up
'at borrerin',

Figure 4.4 The carefree tramp. "Try yo' bes' ter borrer it,"
Boys' Life, August 1922, 16. (Courtesy of Boy Scouts of
America National Scouting Museum Archival Collection)

to borrow things from someone else (instead of being thrifty and paying
his own way). He displays no courage, since he is not standing up for what
is right, and appears incapable of even knowing what is right or wrong.
This barefoot African American tramp cannot be reverent or clean in
mind or body since he has shunt off moral decency and self-respect.
The sketch and poem imply that such a boy would never be a proper
Scout hiker, upstanding man, or future civic leader.[11]

The 1929 Scoutmaster's handbook, as had previous manuals, instructed troop leaders that constructive hiking was essential for developing modern manhood: "The Scoutmaster who does not have his troop
make as many 'hikes' as possible is, to that degree, not a real Scoutmaster.... The purpose of the 'hike' is of course to make the Scout self-
reliant, observant, and efficient in the open, and by the close contact with
other boys, to rub off his rough edges." What, then, made for a constructive Scout hike? Tellingly, a good Scout hike did not require walking at
all. The handbook explained, "The week-end outings of troops—although
often involving little or no actual walking—are commonly called 'hikes'"
because of the lure of the outdoors, even if most of the troop's time was
spent in a sedentary fashion practicing woodcraft or campcraft skills and
passing rank tests. The handbook's suggestion for a good fourteen-hour
Scout hike included only two thirty-minute walking periods. The author told Scoutmasters to use the other thirteen hours at stations along

the way giving instructions on rank and merit badge tests, Scout games, signaling, pioneering, and campfire ceremonies—thus bringing the "Scout Trail to Citizenship" sketch to life. Part of this emphasis on short hikes stemmed from the BSA's belief in a modest, conserved boyhood rather than the strenuous physicality and virility that extreme hiking entailed: "The Scoutmaster should not strain the body nor the interest of the younger boy by a long hike." However, it was still essential that "a Scout 'hike' is distinguished from a picnic by the fact that mother does not put up a lunch. A Scout must be able to take care of himself. . . . On every hike each Scout should cook his own meals." Excluding women took precedence in early BSA hiking over whether or not the boys actually walked.[12]

At a Scouting conference hosted by Columbia University in 1917, New Jersey Scout Commissioner Joseph Carstang insisted that the most important consideration in planning a hike was to know precisely what you were going to do on the hike and to fill it with constructive Scout activities and lessons: "So many hikes are taken for the mere purpose of hiking, but [Boy Scouts] should have some object in view in starting off on a hike." The boys should "know they are headed for some definite place, and when they get there they are going to do such and such a thing. And then if that is accomplished the boys will know the hike has been a success." BSA national leaders and teaching publications recommended that Scoutmasters choose a specific type of hike that met a clear Scout character building or civic training goal. The desired Scout character value also dictated the location, pace, and tone of a proper hike. For example, the 1929 *Handbook for Patrol Leaders* advised choosing the hike location based specifically on the type of terrain and distance most appropriate for practicing the designated Scout skill, such as wooded country for tracking exercises or open spaces for semaphore signaling.[13]

In addition to designing a hike of core Scout activities, such as the daily Good Turn or Nature Study, common types of "worthwhile" hikes in the early BSA included the Scout's Pace hike, the mapping and orientation hike, and the industrial hike. These hikes taught skills and values boy members needed to develop into future work and civic leadership for a modernizing society: efficiency, endurance, standardization, quantification, and appreciation of modern industry and cities. Scout council histories, local newspaper and national magazine accounts, troop charter renewal applications, and leader training conference discussion sessions suggest that most American Scouts in the 1910s and 1920s participated in these specific hiking types with particular character and civic goals rather than in unstructured hikes or Romantic strolls through the woods.

The widespread popularity of Scout's Pace—a hiking drill alternating fifty walking steps with fifty jogging steps—reflected early BSA leaders' emphasis on boys learning time efficiency, self-discipline, and consistent work on assigned tasks. Scout's Pace aligned more closely with the goals and methods of Henry Ford's mass-production moving assembly line and Frederick Taylor's standards of scientific management than with spiritual, aesthetic hiking purposes. Scoutmasters often had troops hike using Scout's Pace in order to cover one mile in precisely twelve minutes, no more and no less. BSA teaching publications instructed Scoutmasters and Patrol Leaders to hold a stopwatch and keep a strict time account of how long each boy traversed one measured mile. Some patrols or troops competed against each other in achieving the perfect twelve-minute mile hike in unison—regardless of weather or terrain. Since Scout's Pace hiking was a required test for rank advancement, every successful American Scout did this type of hiking in the 1910s and 1920s. Intentionally, Scout's Pace was neither too physically strenuous nor a leisurely stroll conducive to contemplating the infinite, God-in-nature, or sublime landscape views.[14]

Frequent map making and compass orienteering hikes taught Scouts quantitative analysis and a visual and physical mastery of nature and its useful resources. Boys learned to calculate distances and follow directions while orienteering by compass. Scoutmasters often had boys make maps of terrains they had hiked, including the precise locations of transportation barriers and aids as well as natural resources. The 1914 Scoutmaster's handbook instructed troop leaders to have their boys make a map of the country covered on a recent hike, showing the route taken, landmarks, streams, tree groves, and so on. This activity emphasized observation, teamwork, and recall skills. Some Scouts also practiced orienteering on urban terrains where they lived, since the skill and associated values were more important than nature itself.[15]

Embracing the 1928 Boy Scout handbook's declaration that "hikes need not be to the woods," BSA officials successfully encouraged and led what they termed "industrial hikes" and "city hikes," which explicitly connected Scout hiking to appreciating corporate industries, mass production, and natural resource development. Industrial hikes culminated in visits to modern sites, such as mass transportation hubs, river dams that produced electric power, and oil well drills. BSA leaders also offered city hikes as a method of teaching essential Scout skills and values to urban boys with limited access to the outdoors. A 1917 *Scouting* article suggested that urban Scouts could get a good dose of nature by visiting factories to see natural resources being manufactured into goods. The BSA's Director of Volunteer Training explained at a troop leaders' training course, "The city Scoutmaster dealing with 'steam heated' Scouts will find adventure for his boys in patrol hikes to industries, museums, historical points and overnight hikes to the week-end Council Camp." Rather than aesthetic wandering, Scout hiking was more akin to a sequential journey, advancing through the masculine skills and values associated with BSA rank and merit badge proficiency tests. The ability to hike within the adult-led troop to achieve constructive character and civic building goals distinguished a good Scout from the carefree masses. A successful Scout hiker learned and demonstrated essential modern values like time efficiency, self-discipline, and quantitative analysis.[16]

Camping Gives Functioning Citizenship, Which in Large Cities Is Difficult to Comprehend

Early BSA leaders prized camping because it could provide the extended time, regulated space, structured schedule, and select company needed to best teach the hierarchical group loyalty and participating citizenship that America's urban-industrial society and modern democracy required. Officials often stressed that the Scoutmaster who failed to take his troop outdoors was in danger of stunting proper boy character and civic development. The 1929 Scoutmaster's handbook explained, " 'Parlor Scouting' is not real Scouting. The boy who cannot take care of himself in the open, who has not had the practical training and the experience in self-reliance which hikes give, is not a real Scout. . . . Scoutcraft can be taught indoors but most of it can be practiced only in the open. It has been said that, a week in camp brings more Scouting to a boy than a year of indoor meetings. . . . It is the imperative duty of every Scoutmaster to give his troop as much outdoor work as possible." However, good Scout camping did not foster extreme survival skills or individualism. Like a casual, purposeless stroll through the woods, BSA sources suggested that primitive camping and eking out a bare survival was for hobos and tramps. Instead, members learned as a group to efficiently make themselves comfortable using available resources while practicing core Scout character and civic skills. The handbook explained that the true objectives of Scout camping included discipline, troop loyalty, advancement, preparation for saving lives, and balanced physical development through group calisthenics and swimming. According to the author, camp taught both self-reliance and interdependence with the troop. Proper Scout camping also developed leadership skills and provided opportunities for public service to nearby communities. While not all Boy Scouts could attend camp regularly, many did. One hundred and sixty thousand Boy Scouts—45 percent of members—camped at least one week in 1920, and Local Councils continued to build and acquire additional camps to accommodate more members. Moreover, each boy member going camping was not actually essential, since he would be learning the modern masculine skills and values associated with Scout camping during the year-round weekly meetings and other troop activities.[17]

As BSA National Camping Director L. L. McDonald explained in his "Camping in America" speech at the first BSA Executives National Training School in 1925, camping offered a key opportunity for Scouts to develop practical citizenship for an urbanizing democracy: "Camping develops a sense of citizenship; a realization of functioning citizenship, which in the large city is difficult for the mind of youth to comprehend." He explained that the camp community, during the time the boy attends, is civilization, is America. A boy's participating membership in the camp community helped him practice citizenship, since any single boy's failure was felt by all, and he was thus more inspired to do his duty among a group of his own fellows. Early Scout camps isolated boy members from females and the increasingly diverse populations of America's growing cities, which distinguished camp training from other Scout citizenship lessons, such as the daily Good Turn and community and national service, which engaged the broader public. However, both forms of Scout citizenship training reinforced the notion that the nation's political decision makers were and should be males. McDonald warned that an unstructured outdoor environment could just as easily give refuge to the criminal to become the worst type of man, so Scout Executives must direct camps aggressively with a purpose, the right place, the right motive, and the "kind of activities which develop resourcefulness and self-control." He concluded, "It is self-control we want to teach, if we are going to make real patriots, real citizens of Boy Scouts in camp." The transcript recorded the audience's enthusiastic shouts of approval for McDonald's vision of a proper Scout camp.[18]

American Scout supporters often argued that the properly run camp was an ideal place to teach boys modern patriotism. Instead of dry school lectures, Scout camping with its natural landscapes and flag ceremonies would enable boys to actively love their country: "No finer setting can be found for a flag recognition ceremony than in the out-of-doors. Some picturesque spot may be dedicated in a particular way and used for no other purpose. Many of the great crisis periods in our national life are connected with the patriotic work of the old scouts, pioneers, plainsmen, explorers. They lend a unique atmosphere to the flag exercise and are capable of unusual ceremonial remembrance." Photographs and sketches of Scout camps in the 1910s and 1920s often highlighted the central flagpole grounds with orderly tents arranged around it. However, just learning to revere the American flag at camp did not make a Scout a complete citizen. BSA administrators insisted that camping's group loyalty, advancement by merit, and hierarchical obedience represented other essential traits for modern democratic leadership.[19]

BSA camping directors frequently pointed out that the most important part of a proper Scout camp was not scenic vistas or fresh air but a structured schedule of troop activities and progress in rank and badge work. Scouting's camping routines and its advancement scheme paralleled broader accreditation and professionalization trends in early twentieth-century American work and government. Like leaders at other types of American and British summer camps in the 1910s and 1920s, BSA camp directors and staff packed the Scout schedule with character and civic training exercises to make an intensified version of the regular troop meetings that were held throughout the rest of the year. The typical Scout camp schedule included at least two hours of formal rank and merit badge test preparation and completion. Specialists visited camps to help boys refine particular required skills. General preparation for other rank and merit badge tests consumed most of the rest of the Scout camp day, although some local leaders employed Indian or pioneer lore in campfire ceremonies and other evening activities. According to Local Councils and the BSA's national annual reports, one could quantitatively assess whether or not a Scout camp session was good by how many rank and merit badge tests were passed by the boys. BSA administrators insisted that hosting friendly efficiency contests between patrols at camp was the best way to spur advancement and group camaraderie. Published American Scout literature and statistics from annual troop reports revealed that local camp leaders made frequent use of the suggested patrol and troop efficiency contests on Scout skills. Some boys passed more skill exams at camp than in all the troop meetings during the rest of the year.[20]

Scout camping's length, isolation, and need for order and safety helped instill the virtue of peer group loyalty paired with willing obedience to the Scoutmaster's authority. As the Cave Scout column explained in a 1916 *Boys' Life* article, the most important rule for a successful camp was to "'Follow Orders.' Camps where everybody does just as he pleases are no good at all." Although the author noted that he liked to see a camp where boys were given some share in making up the program and were told in advance why different things were done, he concluded, "But scouts should understand that at times it is necessary for the officers to give orders without taking time to explain them. A good scout always jumps right in and follows orders first and asks his questions afterwards. He takes it for granted that his officers know what they are doing and that the orders they give are for the best interests of the whole camp." A Scout Executive from the Louisville Council stated in his speech on "Educational Aspects of the Camping Program" at the 1926 BSA Executives National Training Conference that camping helped promote civic responsibility, since participating in making and enforcing camp rules would inspire a Scout to respect city and national laws afterward. Solo or extreme survival camping failed to teach group loyalty or hierarchical obedience, so it was less valued by most early BSA officials.[21]

James "Kimo" Wilder's Pine Tree Patrol camping method diagrammed in Figure 4.5 represented the zenith of the group efficiency contests, hierarchical loyalty, and Scouting's modern engagement with nature. The sketch and accompanying explanations in his popular pamphlet distributed by the BSA national office suggested that the best way to interpret this style of camping is in light of the contemporary Taylorization of industrial work practices. Frederick Taylor perfected a system of work management that subdivided production into small roles that unskilled laborers could be quickly trained to perform. Taylor employed the stopwatch and slow-motion photography in his intensive studies of workers' body mechanics and the layout and equipment of various job sites in order to design the most efficient production methods. Taylorism helped make goods cheaper and quicker, but it did so at the expense of the work satisfaction and ability of the individual employee to understand and carry out the entire production process. Wilder's Pine Tree Patrol pamphlet provided numerous drills with exact diagrams to teach differentiated tasks to eight boys in a Patrol to achieve the greatest group and time efficiency in setting up and striking down a complete Scout Patrol camping layout. The script even specified the precise number and

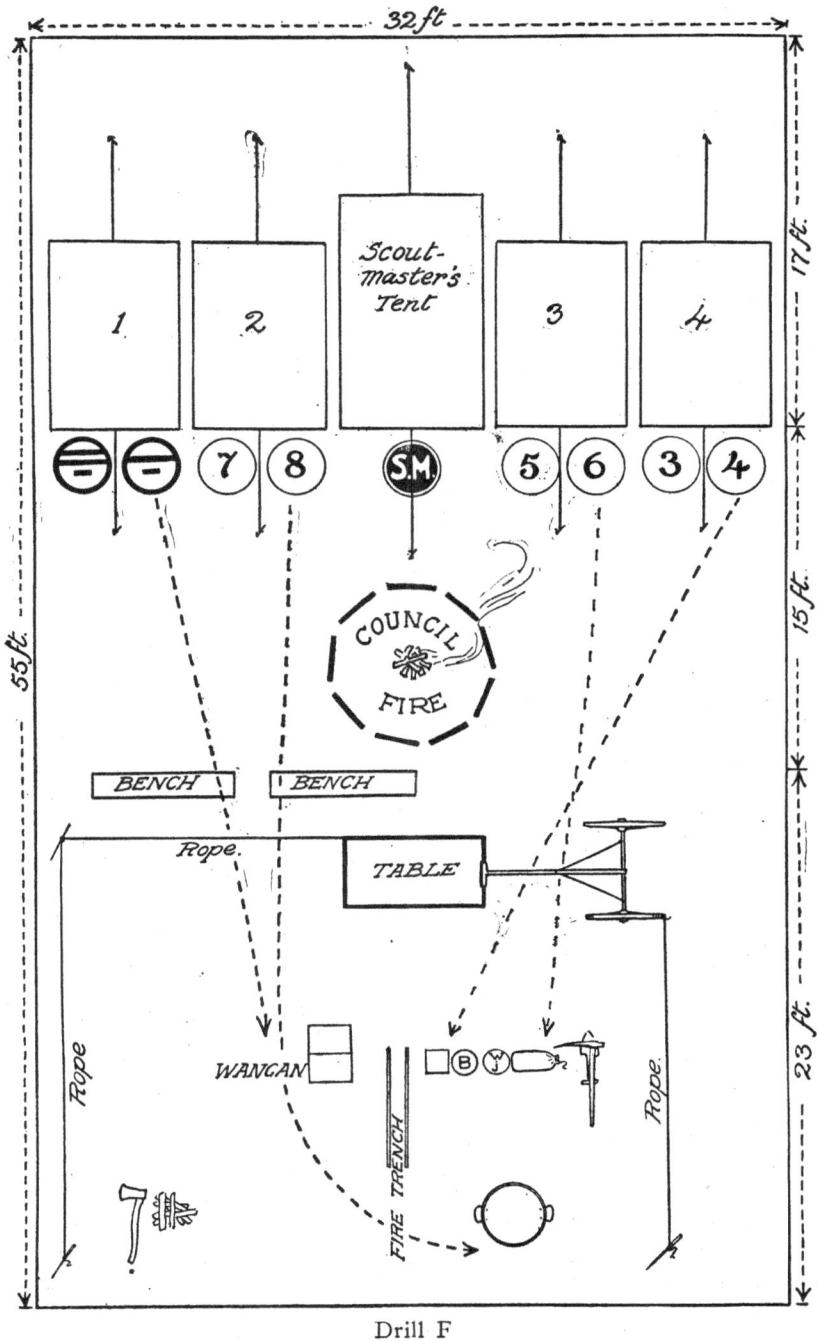

Drill F

Figure 4.5 Diagramming a successful camping trip. James Wilder, "Drill F," *Pine Tree Patrol* (pamphlet) (1918): 45. (Courtesy of Boy Scouts of America National Scouting Museum Archival Collection)

direction of paces each Scout was allowed to take in this choreographed dance of modernity. Wilder emphasized that Pine Tree camping was one of the best ways to teach boys precision, efficiency, effort-saving actions, thoroughness, and "individual and co-operative obedience, the foundation of Good Scouting." He stressed that "the standing and efficiency of the Troop should be [the Scoutmaster's] greatest pleasure in life and he should watch it with jealous care. He 'fires' the hopeless slacker, remembering that Scouting is not a reformatory institution." The managing Scoutmaster delegated authority through his Pine Tree Patrol Leader, "his foreman." In scenes that would have impressed Frederick Taylor as well as Henry Ford's Model T factory engineers, Boy Scout troops across the country practiced and competed on the Pine Tree Patrol camping method. Encouraged by the National Camping Department, many Local Councils held troop competitions on who could perform the process fastest and most precisely—with the award often being permission to go to the regional encampment or the World Scout Jamboree. At the first World Scout Jamboree in England in 1920, the Miami Council, which then held the world record, had the honor of showcasing America's ultimate camping method to the tens of thousands of Scout representatives and visitors from across the globe. Sponsored by the local Rotary Club, the Miami Council shipped its own trek cart to England so it could tirelessly demonstrate Wilder's method. Its best Patrol could set up a complete campsite (including tents for eight boys, cooking equipment, a campfire, and even a sanitary disposal trench) in perfect order in just four minutes, ten seconds. The BSA National Camping Department made extending the Pine Tree Patrol method to every Local Council a departmental objective in 1927. Proper Scout camping thus taught efficiency, self-discipline, cleanliness, well-rounded bodily development, and rank advancement through group cooperation. Moreover, good troop camping trained boys in the patriotism, hierarchical loyalty, and participating citizenship needed to lead America's expert-managed system of government.[22]

Conserving Natural Resources: "A Scout Is Kind, He Is Kind but Firm"

Early BSA officials encouraged members to conserve natural resources because it helped accomplish three intertwined goals that hiking, camping, and Nature Study by themselves could not fully achieve: showcasing to the broader public the scientific analysis and quantitative efficiency skills Boy Scouts developed, serving the nation to bolster the argument that Scouts were tomorrow's leading citizens, and reinforcing the racial and gender hierarchy embedded in the BSA's vision of modern manhood. As Americans recognized the limits to the nation's resources and set aside more public lands and water supplies by the turn of the twentieth century, the ability to expertly manage scarce resources became a key marker of leadership. Conserving natural resources taught boy members expert regulation, scientific knowledge, data collection, and careful implementation—skills that aided their success in modern management and professional jobs as well as bureaucratic forms of government. BSA officials shifted the emphasis in the original British Sixth Law to be kind to all animals toward scientifically discriminating between productive species that good Scouts protected and destructive species that good Scouts destroyed. Starting in the early 1910s, a growing number of Boy Scouts across the country partnered with state and national conservation experts to manage the country's forests and wildlife. Conservation's firm judgment distinguished Scouts from females, whom some American Scout leaders stereotyped as being too sentimental and selfish toward nature to manage it properly. Early BSA officials suggested that African Americans and Native Americans, like young children, were too savage and self-absorbed to be capable of deliberate resource conservation. Some Scout conservation sources also implied that working-class European immigrants lacked the intelligence and foresight needed to protect the nation's resources, but that they might develop such skills through joining Scouting. BSA officials claimed that capable boys who honed the ability to scientifically conserve the nation's natural resources deserved to control them as tomorrow's future leaders.

BSA officials suggested that women were too self-involved and sentimental to conserve natural resources, while Boy Scouting helped members develop the firm reason and scientific judgment needed to distinguish between useful and destructive species. In Baden-Powell's original 1908 British handbook, the Sixth Scout Law instructed, "A SCOUT IS A FRIEND TO ANIMALS. He should save them as far as possible from pain, and should not kill any animal unnecessarily, even if it is only a fly—for it is one of God's creatures." This explanation offered an expansive view of wildlife protection reinforced by the notion that nature was God's special preserve and that even the fly was connected to the divine. Many BSA leaders, however, feared that being kind to all animals and insects was a feminine liability and a threat to the productivity standard set by scientific natural resource management. In 1913, the BSA National Council unanimously resolved that troops cooperate with public authorities "in the conservation of those forms of plant and animal life which are useful, and the prevention and destruction of those animals and pests, such as flies, mosquitoes, rats and so forth, that are harmful." National Scout Commissioner Dan Beard best articulated the relationship between firm manhood and conservation contained in the Americanized Sixth Law: "A Scout is kind, but that does not mean that he will not kill [creatures that] are enemies to the plants." He argued in 1917 that being kind to harmful animals and insects was "slushy sentimentalism, which is neither the pure water of truth and kindness nor the hard cold ice of decision. A Scout is kind, he is kind but firm."[23]

BSA leaders equated being kind to "dumb," "weak," and female animals while being firm against noxious pests with chivalry, linking animal conservation with Boy Scouts' provision of service to "helpless" women, the "deserving" poor, and invalids. Arthur Astor Carey argued that a key part of a medieval knight's chivalric duty was "to bring order out of confusion,—to kill the wild beasts that interfered with flocks and herds and made farming difficult." He compared the extermination of savage predators to a knight's duty to overpower the highwaymen and robbers who made traveling unsafe for women and children: "It goes without saying that dangerous or noxious animals should be killed. . . . By killing them we are really protecting far more life, and life of a higher order, than we destroy. The motive of the killing is really constructive or upbuilding." Carey differentiated conscientious pest extermination from a young boy killing harmless squirrels or songbirds, a primitive instinct that a mature Scout sublimated. Being firm with pests paralleled the National Park and Forest Services' widening predator extermination campaigns in this era, although the BSA placed particular stress on pest extermination's capacity to build boys' firm character and civic leadership. National Park and Forest Service staffers eliminated predators in these reserved lands to protect and increase plant and animal species deemed to be of more material or aesthetic value to humans, but only gradually realized (through the groundbreaking work of Aldo Leopold) that their targeted kills resulted in dangerous overpopulation of the favored species, which could not be maintained without artificial feeding and further ecological imbalances.[24]

The BSA's emphasis on bird protection demonstrated how conserving natural resources could also help reinforce a masculine hierarchy of race and class groups. In their support for the Migratory Bird Act and bird sanctuaries, Boy Scouts and their leaders prioritized elite sport hunting, bird-watching, and farming over market and subsistence hunting. A 1913 *Boys' Life* article urged Scouts to get their fathers to write congressmen in support of the McLean Bill for federal protection of migratory birds. The author criticized how, despite robins' service to humans in eating hordes of crop-damaging insects, "we are right now, this very month, allowing the negroes and the poor whites of seven Southern states to slaughter the robins for the pot." The BSA's advocacy of bird conservation extended far beyond the successful McLean Bill. Scout troops policed and even created their own bird sanctuaries, reporting violations of game laws to authorities. National Scout Commissioner Dan Beard lamented in 1916 that native birds had been pushed to extinction because "our dear mammas, our lovely sisters and our darling sweethearts and wives wanted the beautifully upholstered skins of these poor birds as ornaments for their hats." He contrasted women's superficial fashion urges with Boy Scouts' wise protection of endangered native birds, but in doing so he ignored middle-class and elite women's demonstration of self-control and conservation during a successful boycott of the millinery trade from the 1890s to the 1910s.[25]

BSA sources occasionally criticized working-class European immigrant boys for being too selfish and shortsighted to protect valuable resources like birds, but also left open the possibility that they could learn through Scouting to live up to conservation's standard of sustained development and responsibility to the nation and future generations. Early Scout plays and stories employed the working-class immigrant street tough as a stock character. The tough exhibited aggressive virility, like a pioneer, but his impoverished background hinted at delinquent tendencies arising from an ingrained lack of self-control. A 1929 play written by a boy member for the *Scout Executive* centered on a conversation between an Eagle Scout—the BSA's highest boy rank—and a tough with a heavy accent, poor grammar, and "several front teeth missing." The tough reported that he spent his free time "smokin' cigarettes, ridin' box cars and shootin' birds. Shot a robin and a canary this morning." He asked the Eagle Scout how many birds he had to shoot in order to earn the Marksmanship merit badge on his uniform. The Scout retorted that the badge judged accuracy and consistency in shooting inanimate targets, since "one of the first things a Scout pledges is not to kill harmless creatures for the mere pleasure of killing." The play hinted that the tough's savage treatment of innocent birds revealed further character shortcomings. His inquiry about other merit badges gave the Eagle Scout a chance to lecture him on safety, nutrition, hygiene, and school study habits. However, the fact that the tough expressed interest in Scout advancement and that the Eagle Scout began to teach him proper masculine and environmental values demonstrated that outdoor Scout training might be able to redeem the tough.[26]

BSA literature suggested that white men's advanced character and commitment to civic responsibilities enabled them to protect the nation's valued natural resources better than could "primitive" nonwhites. U.S. Forest Service dendrologist George Sudworth, for example, contrasted white western ranchers' intentional burning of public forests to create grazing land against Native American hunters' practice of burning forests to scare out wild game in the revised 1914 Boy Scout handbook. He stated that both groups were equally to blame for selfishly killing millions of trees. Ranchers, however, were also guilty of what might be deemed environmental treason to the white race: "Wanton destruction of this sort is excusable in the case of Indians, because they were uncivilized and thought only of their own immediate needs. But in the case of white people such useless waste of what, in most cases, did not belong to them, is criminal-uncivilized." In this handbook's new section on "Conservation of Wild Life and Forests," prominent conservationist and author William T. Hornaday cast civilization as nature's main enemy but maintained that deliberate conservation was exclusively a white man's trait: "The natural tendency of civilization is to destroy the products and the choicest handiwork of nature. Civilized man exterminates whole species of wild birds, beasts, and fishes as no savages have dreamed of doing." Hornaday, who also served as the director of the world-leading Bronx Zoo, singled out reckless game hunters and people who started forest fires as the primary culprits in civilization's "Army of Destruction." While the passage hinted that primitive nonwhites might serve as a model for a broader and more inclusive Scout environmental and social philosophy, he posited the intentional conservation of remaining wild life and forests as a "white man's burden" that Boy Scouts "should manfully take up."[27]

World War I greatly expanded the political significance of and opportunities for Scouts' natural resource conservation work. Boy Scouts cooperated with government officials and other civic organizations on a wide range of resource conservation drives to support the war effort. In addition to helping enlist mothers for Herbert Hoover's food conservation drives, Scouts collected scrap rubber, newspapers, and metal; stockpiled peach pits and nutshells for soldiers' gas masks; and grew castor beans in waste places to make airplane motor oil. The black walnut tree census and soldier memorials, however, provided Scout conservation work with its most powerful political symbolism. Boy Scouts across the country helped locate stands of black walnut trees for the military to use in manufacturing gunstocks and airplane propellers. During and after the war, the Scouts planted black walnut trees to replenish supplies for future military production and to cooperate with such groups as the American Legion to memorialize dead soldiers and the Scouts' own war conservation efforts. Pennsylvania forester Robert S. Conklin referred to this process as planting "living memorials" to the fallen men. The Scouts also cooperated with the American Tree Association to send seeds to reforest battlefields where the American army had fought in France. British Boy Scouts similarly memorialized soldiers through tree planting and other public commemorations after the war.[28]

In addition to the Scout service drives to support America's World War I effort, local and national government officials' frequent requests throughout the 1910s and 1920s for the BSA's aid on a wide range of natural resource protection and pest extermination projects reinforced the likelihood that Boy Scouts would become the country's future political leaders. Government officials throughout the nation gave BSA troops special privileges—in the form of equipment, instruction, and transportation—in exchange for their help with conservation work. They often allowed Boy Scouts to use the public lands they helped conserve to hike and build campsites. The BSA appointed Gifford Pinchot, former head of the U.S. Forest Service and America's leading advocate of natural resource conservation, as the organization's Chief Scout Forester. Pinchot started a troop in his hometown and, as governor of Pennsylvania, helped designate over thirty thousand Boy Scout Forest Guides by 1925. The federal government granted members semiofficial status, such as the 1915 National Forest Aide badge for Boy Scouts who rendered at least ten days service during the fire season. The BSA worked fervently during these two decades to hold up its end of the bargain with the government. Scouts across the country engaged in campaigns to eliminate pests, including mosquitoes, tent caterpillars, and flies. They fought actual forest fires and served as park police—guarding prized tree groves and enforcing game conservation laws. Scouts helped protect valued wildlife by erecting grain feeding stations for deer, stocking trout and other fish, surveying wildlife populations, serving as junior wildlife game rangers at state parks, and building countless birdhouses. BSA troops conducted frequent tree censuses and did scientific identification and labeling of plant species in public lands and parks. Scouts helped with government fire-prevention campaigns and distributed forestry literature. By 1930, Boy Scouts were planting more than 1 million trees annually in cooperation with state and federal officials. Conservation activities acted as both community service projects and career apprenticeships for the many participating Scouts.[29]

Reflecting their use of conservation to reinforce a masculine hierarchy of character and citizenship, BSA leaders suggested that the benefits of the country's natural resources should flow primarily to those best able and trained to manage their development. Gifford Pinchot argued that every person had a duty to conserve resources to benefit the most people for the longest time, whereas some BSA sources depicted conservation as a privilege of leading citizens. In the cover sketch of the 1920 *Conservation* merit badge pamphlet, for example, the cornucopia gourd swallowing up natural resources and the coin wealth they represented hinted that Boy Scouts should practice conservation in part to enrich themselves. As the embodiment of America's future, Boy Scouts deserved to control the country's resources. Indeed, BSA leaders often argued that America's boyhood was the nation's most valuable resource, and thus the country should privilege boys' development through Scouting and in reserved natural areas.[30]

"Time Will Never Erase the Impressions of Those Occasions"

Published memoirs and surveyed boy members and adult supporters confirmed that Scouting's scientific Nature Study, efficient natural resource conservation, character-building hikes, and total immersion in the Scout camp community formed key appeals and developmental benefits for boys and men in a modernizing society. At the 1922 BSA Executives National Training Conference, the "Report of Commission on Turnover" noted a study by a Toledo, Ohio, Council that asked schoolboys who quit Scouting to comment on the program. Sixty-six percent stated that their favorite part of Scouting was the outdoor life, hiking, and camping. Twenty-five percent of those who quit the program did so because they had hoped for even more outdoor emphasis. In a survey of one hundred Scoutmasters from thirty-eight states in 1929, Charles T. Johnson found that Scoutmasters believed the outdoor part of the program to be what appealed most to boys. Fifty percent of the Scoutmasters ranked it as the boys' primary motivation to Scout, while the next most prevalent category merited only 6 percent of the votes. One hundred fifty-two out of 159 parents of San Francisco Boy Scouts responding to a 1924 survey replied that Scouting had stimulated their sons' interest in the outdoor life, with some parents noting specific activities commonly found in BSA publications, such as bird study, botany, hiking, and camping. A significant majority of those parents (120 out of 159) reported that hikes and overnight camping were beneficial to boys. Many noted that outdoor activities improved their sons' physical health and strength. The main two points made by those surveyed parents who expressed concerns were that good adult supervision was necessary for effective outdoor Scouting, and that hikes should not be too long or arduous for adolescent boys. In contrast to some Scout leaders in other countries, BSA national officials and teaching publications mirrored the parents' concerns by constantly stressing the need for trained adult supervision and modest, constructive hiking and camping activities.[31]

Other surveys of Scoutmasters, boys, and non-BSA community leaders done in this era reported what might appear on the surface to be a disjuncture when they found that love of nature was not a primary goal or outcome of the Scout program. Of 1,609 religious, professional, business, and educational leaders from twenty-eight cities surveyed in 1928 on the key effects of Scout training, only 105 listed "love of nature" as a trait that Scouting helped develop. The survey's questions and most of the respondents' answers instead emphasized character values from the twelve Scout Laws, such as trustworthiness, bravery, loyalty, obedience, courtesy, and helpfulness. In a survey that year of 697 Scoutmasters from across the country, only 3.5 percent answered that love of nature was the main objective of Scouting. That answer was ninth on the list of primary objectives reported, following such choices as citizenship training, leadership development, the Scout Oath and Law, love of God and country, and vocational guidance. Only 4.5 percent of those surveyed Scoutmasters listed "love of nature" as their own primary motivation for being troop leaders. Interest in boys, duty to others, and being asked by other BSA or institutional leaders to serve Scouting motivated more of the surveyed Scoutmasters. Boy members' survey responses and memoirs that emphasized the modern character and civic values Scout outdoor programming taught suggest, though, that the question was simply worded wrong.[32]

Memoirs of early Boy Scouts and Scoutmasters, for example, remarked on both the immediate joys and long-term career training offered by Scouting's scientific Nature Study. Eagle Scout Hohn Mehlhop reported that Nature Study was a favored activity and unique opportunity at his council camp near Roswell, New Mexico, in the late 1920s. He noted the large number of bird species, the more than two dozen species of trees, and the seventy-plus kinds of wildflowers that camping Scouts found and classified. Some campers frequently woke at five o'clock in the morning to study birds when they were active and could best be seen and heard. Mehlhop stated that he and other campers also observed and classified animal, tree, and flower species during other activities, such as hiking and horseback riding, and discussed unusual sightings at evening campfires. He and fellow Scouts hoped to erect a separate camp nature building and museum to house permanent species collections they had made. A bird specialist from Lubbock, Texas, even came out to the camp for several days to help identify and discuss new birds and reptiles. Many other early Scout council camps had Nature Study projects, special staff, and species museums like those Mehlhop described. Scoutmasters such as veteran Illinois troop leader August Kietzman recalled that Scout nature merit badges and intense study of these subjects at camp helped many of his boys identify a productive career path, "*Vacations* and *vocations* have more to do with each other than may appear. Holidays in camp may be the deciding time for the Scout as to what he would like to be when he grows up." Kietzman stated that Scouts enjoyed studying ornithology, botany, forestry, and surveying.[33]

Local council histories and Scoutmaster memoirs recalled similar practical uses and future benefits of Scouting's natural resource conservation training. Kietzman discussed the results of his Gilman, Illinois, Scout troop studying forestry and fire prevention at their 1926 encampment. The owner of the private forest in which the boys camped, who was impressed by their study of fire prevention and building of firefighting equipment, enjoyed visiting the troop to learn more about Scouting. When the troop was packing up to leave, a rapidly growing fire broke out in a nearby forest. Boy members quickly jumped in to adeptly control and put out the fire, saving the surrounding forest. Several years later, the appreciative owner provided 120 acres of that forest to the council for building a camp to train Scouts in camping skills, Nature Study, and conservation.[34]

Scout-style hiking drew consistent praise from adult staffers and surveyed boy members for its ability to reinforce modern educational theory and build good character. The author of the BSA National Commission's Character Values in Scouting study, which surveyed over two thousand boys in 1928, linked Scout hiking to key educational reform sentiments of the era, such as experiential education, active learning, and engaging with nature and real-life situations. The author stated that the troop hike "represents the pilgrimage in quest of adventure. It takes the Troop out of the artificial into the natural. It enables the scout to depart from the theory into practice." According to the Commission, troop and patrol hikes offered unique opportunities to learn constructive use of time to hone character, practice leadership, and develop respect for property owners' rights. The surveyed boys' answers for how Scout hiking helped build character mirrored explanations from BSA teaching publications, leader training sessions, and surveyed parents. A fifteen-year-old Star Scout reported, "An interesting hike accomplishes more than two meetings. Tests can be passed, knowledge of country gained and boys like better to do something outside than to listen to talks." A sixteen-year-old First Class member was one of many surveyed boys who emphasized Scout hiking's ability to develop self-reliance within the company of peers: it "teaches confidence in my ability to take care of myself, fellowship, to do my part and avoid mistakes made by others." Hikes seemed particularly effective at reinforcing boys' interdependence: "They make you know that the other fellows depend upon you for something and you depend upon them for something else." A sixteen-year-old Second Class Scout, however, placed more emphasis on hiking's ability to sort members into a hierarchy of character: "Here's where we learn to study character. By these hikes one soon finds out who are the real Scouts and who are slackers." The line between living up to Scouting's and the Scoutmaster's expectations and not sometimes caused rifts between hiking boys and close friends: "I went on a Buddy hike once and thought I was with an excellent Scout, a Scout who would not stoop to lower himself. After the second day of our hike, my Buddy becoming tired flagged a ride home [hitchhiked]. I walked, although I was smaller and less strong than he. Our Scoutmaster had told us not to flag as it was a test of endurance. The deed was never reported, but a warm friendship was broken off suddenly." In this account,

Nature, Conservation, and Modern Manhood   149

the hiking boy made the hard choice to end a friendship because he placed more value on his Scout Oath and living up to the Scoutmaster's expectations. Overcoming adversity and building endurance through the long hike also allowed this particular boy to overcome his small and weak stature and best a larger, stronger boy. Stick-to-itiveness trumped brawn in the Scout world.[35]

Early Scoutmaster memoirs frequently highlighted hikes and the ensuing troop encampments as the apex of Scouting for boy development, group camaraderie, and the troop leader's enjoyment. The typical American Scoutmaster memoir—especially in the 1910s, before larger-scale and more developed Scout council camping became common—reads like an adventure story. Veteran Scoutmaster Stuart Walsh recalled in his memoir *Thirteen Years of Scout Adventure*, "The officers of the 23rd [Chicago] troop believed that hikes were the most vital of scout experiences, and that with plenty of hikes included in the program the troop's spirit, technique, and traditions would grow and flourish. . . . Here tenderfeet got their first introductions to outdoor scouting; here merit badge aspirants struggled with lean-tos, camp kitchens, bridges and derricks; here inter-patrol cooking contests and flag-raiding games were staged; here all sorts of outdoor sports adapted from the scout Handbook were tried out. . . . Those evenings in the woods, and those nights under the stars with timid tenderfeet, how thrilling they still seem in recollection, even since the experiencing of much larger adventures. . . . Time will never erase the impressions of those occasions."[36]

Many of the two thousand boys surveyed by the 1928 Commission on Character Values in Scouting praised camp sessions as a total immersion in Scout ways and prime opportunities for developing a work ethic and good character. The increasing number of American town boys who attended school and did not have a job seemed to need Scout camping in locales removed from urban settings to learn the importance of and practice a strong work ethic. The opportunity and requirement to do physical work cheerfully in order to make a needed contribution to the camp community stood out in many boys' responses: Troop Camping "in my mind does the most to bring out the true Scouting qualities. A boy must show the right spirit, be willing to work, be willing to help others, and do this cheerfully. It is here that the Scout Oath and Law are best lived up to." As a fourteen-year-old Eagle Scout noted, camp's isolated setting also allowed boys to develop their broader character attributes with fewer modern distractions, "because up here at camp there are not as many temptations as in the city and this gives a boy a chance to live a square and clean life while in Camp." Several Scouts remarked on the ability of the council camp to foster comradeship, hierarchical loyalty, and leadership by modeling instead of imposing harsh discipline: "I picked this one first because of the good fellowship in an organized camp. It tends to make a boy follow the good example of the better trained and more experienced fellows." A twelve-year-old Second Class Scout explained, "We learn respect to elders, pass tests and respond for work as well as play. We are kept so we have no chance to do wrong and corporal punishment is not needed here."[37]

Discussions of camping in early Boy Scout memoirs often paralleled other goals stressed in BSA literature and training: rank and badge progress, internalizing the Scout Oath and Laws, and associating with boys and men of good character. Al Herbert, in an interview done approximately seven decades after his Scout tenure for a history of the local Harrisburg Scout Council, stated that late 1920s Scout camping for him and fellow Pennsylvania boy members was designed primarily to advance them through the Scout ranks "as quickly as they could learn. To get all the merit badges they could." He recalled that the council camp and its leaders placed particular focus on the Camping, Swimming, and Life Saving merit badges, which were otherwise hard to earn. He estimated that 90 percent of the boys at the local Hidden Valley Scout Camp learned to swim there, because it was only one of two places in Harrisburg to swim—and many community social activities at the time were conducted on the Susquehanna River, such as ethnic food festivals, boat races, and water stunts. In an interview years later as an adult, Gifford Walcutt (a Boy Scout camper in New Jersey from 1913 to 1916) emphasized the influence of good troop leaders as role models in his memories of Scout camping experiences. Walcutt remarked, "The boys were devoted to [Scoutmaster Frank Gray]. It is wonderful to recall the influence he had over them. . . . Mr. Gray had an uncanny way of sizing up the Scouts and making every Scout toe the mark by subtle disciplinary measures. . . . He never used violent language, slang or cursed. The impression he left was that we were associated with a real gentleman. He seemed to have a great store of learning. I was deeply impressed with that."[38]

These memoirs of early Boy Scouts and Scoutmasters help explain the seeming mismatch between surveyed troop leaders and adults stating that the outdoors was a key appeal to boys but that the program did not teach them a love of nature. The key to understanding this issue may lie in the surveys' incorrect or misleading phrasing of that particular nature question. As this chapter has argued, the majority of early BSA national leaders and teaching publications emphasized using the outdoors to teach boys modern character and participating citizenship values rather than to love nature. Community leaders and Scoutmasters were thus correct in saying that love of nature was not a primary goal or outcome of early Scouting. If the surveys had instead used the phrase "using the outdoors to help teach modern character and citizenship," then many more troop leaders and community leaders would have chosen it. As the memoirs and interviews demonstrate, camping and hiking was not a separate activity to trick boys into stomaching character lessons but a primary and highly effective method for teaching American Scouting's modern character and practical citizenship to developing boys and their adult leaders.

BSA OFFICIALS USED Nature Study, hiking, camping, and conservation activities not only to teach boy members modern masculine and civic skills but also to distinguish between the relative capacities of various gender, racial, and class groups. American Scout sources claimed that women were too sentimental and selfish to engage nature constructively or conserve its valued resources. BSA officials suggested that Native Americans and tradition-minded working-class immigrants were too aggressive and destructive to manage nature properly, while depicted African Americans seemed fit only for manual labor in the outdoors. The organization attracted broad government and popular support by promising to train select boys in modern manhood and leading citizenship while safeguarding the nation's natural spaces and raw materials. In return, the organization promised Scouts future control over the nation's landscapes and resources. BSA officials stated that Nature Study's and conservation's assessment of the relative values of productive, harmless, and noxious species could also be applied to understanding the capacities and worth of different human groups. The second half of this book expands on this concept by tracing BSA officials' debates on whether and how to include working-class European immigrants, rural farm boys, and African Americans in Scouting's outdoor-based training in modern manhood and leading citizenship.

Part II **Reconfiguring Social Hierarchies through Scouting**

5

Mainstreaming White Immigrants and the Industrial Working Class in the BSA

Lyman Beecher Stowe, a prominent minister in the Social Gospel movement, trumpeted the BSA's inclusive promise in 1911: "Rich boys, poor boys; boys African American, white and yellow; Protestant boys and Roman Catholic boys and Hebrew boys; nice boys and bad boys; boys born in this 'Land of the free, and home of the brave,' and boys born in other and quite different lands. In fact, any and every old kind of a boy may join, if he can pass the test and will take the oath." BSA national leaders echoed Stowe's democratic sentiment and claimed that the program was open to all boys, regardless of race, class, or creed. The organization drew widespread praise and government support for its plan to ease the growing tensions in America's urbanizing, industrializing society by promulgating a universal model of modern manhood and participating citizenship. Outside of those with severe mental or physical handicaps, the basic requirements indeed barred no boys over the minimum age of twelve. Although nonwhite boys and men encountered resistance from some early local Scout officials, the BSA's membership outreach efforts and public statements suggest that dominant American manhood was opening to non-Protestant, southern and eastern European immigrant, and other working-class males by the early 1910s. The ability and willingness to adapt to America's modern values and skills began to replace older notions of permanent racial differences—at least among light-skinned groups—as key determinants of masculine status.[1]

Some early twentieth-century white Anglo-Saxon Protestant leaders worried that the southern and eastern European working-class groups that increasingly permeated the nation's urban centers resisted integrating into modern American life, but many reformers and educators believed that immigrants' sons were more willing and able to join the white male mainstream. While public school advocates hoped to Americanize the growing tides of new urban immigrants, some critics doubted the ability of the female-dominated public schools to teach immigrant boys participating citizenship and men's skills for a modernizing society—especially when some immigrant parents kept their children in private Catholic, Jewish, or foreign language schools to help teach them cultural heritage and loyalty. Moreover, as Julia Grant's recent study on *The Boy Problem* noted, some working-class immigrant boys resisted compulsory education through truancy and defying teachers. In the eyes of some middle-class and elite white Protestants, new immigrant and working-class boys' homes and tenement "enclaves" inhibited their development and made them more prone to juvenile delinquency.[2]

Prominent juvenile court judges and settlement house leaders, however, claimed that Boy Scouting's powerful lessons in character development and active citizenship could prevent or even cure juvenile delinquency and cultural defiance, particularly among European immigrant and working-class boys. Denver judge Benjamin Barr Lindsey—father of the American juvenile court system and a friend of such prominent reformers as Theodore Roosevelt, G. Stanley Hall, and Lincoln Steffens—served as a key early advocate of Scouting. He argued in 1914 that juvenile courts were only capable of handling delinquency cases after it was too late, whereas the BSA was "our greatest hope, the greatest single activity in this country promising a solution, not only of the boy problem, but the girl problem, for the best protector of girls is the youth who lives up to the laws and ideals of the Boy Scouts." Lindsey suggested that Scouting could prevent juvenile delinquency by redirecting boys' innate energies and gang instincts from harmful associations and aimless activities to building good character and serving the broader community. He predicted that if enough people supported the BSA's efforts, the juvenile court system would disappear altogether. Reformer Jane Addams, the head of America's leading immigrant settlement house in Chicago, wrote to Judge Lindsey that since Scouting did not allow guns and focused on outdoor skills and trade instruction, it gave working boys the "pleasure and also the training which comes from military drill, without any touch of the military spirit." She stated that the Hull House's Scout troop was particularly useful in maintaining the interest of the "rough sort of boy." A host of other juvenile court judges, educators, and sociologists echoed these sentiments. A few argued that Scouting might even reform boys who had already become delinquents.[3]

From 1908 to 1930, Boy and Girl Scout and Guide organizations in other countries adopted a variety of policies on ethnic and religious minority and working-class group membership, including attempts to actively integrate and assimilate minorities, segregated troops and camps, separate but federated organizations, or exclusion of minorities and non-recognition of their Scout and Guide associations or units. Several historians have argued that white superiority was central to the ideology and methods of Scouting and Guiding in the British Empire. For example, white South African Boy Scout and Girl Guide officials tried but failed to garner interest from white Dutch Afrikaners in a broadened white Scouting program, while resisting mergers or even formal affiliation with growing local nonwhite Scout and Guide associations until 1936. British Boy Scouting and Girl Guiding, influenced by Baden-Powell's emphasis on good deeds and morality over specific religious principles, tended to be more flexible on religious denomination, yet their memberships did not significantly diversify until the 1920s. More intense church practitioners in many other countries expressed concern over the relative laxity on religious requirements in the British Scout and Guide model. The uniform, Oath and Laws, and church services at camps and training sessions became hot-button religious issues on the international Scouting stage. Two primary response patterns emerged: separate Guiding/Scouting sections or associations for different religious groups in countries like Sweden and France, or a single mixed association with flexible rules and accommodation for different denominational leadership and practices in areas such as the United States.[4]

Relative to Scout and Guide organizations of other Western or colonized countries that historians have studied, the early BSA (as well as the American Girl Scouts) adopted one of the more inclusive and tolerant sets of minority policies and practices in terms of both religious denominations and lighter-skinned working-class and immigrant groups. BSA leaders made significant gestures to welcome working-class laborers, Catholic and Jewish immigrants, and Polish nationalists into dominant manhood and citizenship starting in the early 1910s—years before the 1924 Immigration Restriction quota law curtailed the flow of such immigrants, or the peak of African Americans' movement from the rural South to the urban-industrial North and Midwest made the "negro problem" a more pressing national concern. By allowing such groups flexibility prior to World War I in terms of religious teachings, running their own exclusive Scout troops, and even the language of Scout instruction, BSA national administrators helped attract labor union leaders, Jewish and Catholic clergy, and European immigrant groups to Scout training. European immigrant churches, schools, businesses, and community organizations sponsored BSA troops that allowed boys to simultaneously demonstrate their American patriotism, learn mainstream and modern masculine values, and reinforce their parents' religious practices and cultural traditions. Inclusion in Scouting helped accelerate the shifting focus of light-skinned new immigrants' status from permanent, physical "racial" differences in character and civic capacity to voluntary, permeable ethnic differences in religion, social custom, and language. World War I eroded a bit of the latitude BSA leaders had initially granted European immigrants on matters of dual patriotism and language of instruction, but administrators continued to assert light-skinned immigrants' right to full participation in Scouting and its many privileges. The war seemed to increase the importance of European immigrant boys belonging to the organization, albeit with some occasional concerns about the loyalty of German American Scoutmasters. However, even after two special 1922 BSA Commissions on the Underprivileged Boy and Scouting in Industry revealed obstacles to Scout participation faced by immigrant and poor boys, such as high costs and the fixed troop schedule requirement, national leaders discouraged making wholesale changes in program activities and membership policies to accommodate specific groups. To do so might have shown favoritism and set them up as a distinct and thus antidemocratic class in Scouting and society. BSA administrators insisted that conceding individualism and embracing Scout lessons in modern interdependence was the price of earning mainstream manhood and civic status for working-class and European immigrant males of different faiths.[5]

The Trade Movement and the BSA Are "Heartily in Accord," 1910–1913

Prominent middle-class and working-class American men came to articulate an overlap via Scouting on masculine and civic values suited to a corporate-industrial economy and modern democracy: balancing self-reliance with social cooperation, individual honor with loyalty to the greater good, and a strong work ethic with smoothing out labor tensions and political strife. Responding to British and American unions' criticisms that early Scouting was antilabor and promoted violence, BSA administrators worked for and achieved a common ground by 1913 on Scouting's modest, full-orbed manhood with labor union leaders and even some Socialists by adopting a neutral stance on capital-labor conflicts and offering white working-class and immigrant males a path to mainstream civic leadership and dominant men's status. BSA officials systematically eliminated offensive remarks about the working classes from their teaching literature and public announcements to placate labor critics and to substantiate the organization's classless rhetoric of democratic manhood. Working-class and European immigrant groups appreciated American Scout leaders' statements that rich boys' tendencies to be selfish, snobbish, and dependent on servants meant they also needed Scout training and could benefit from intermixing with more self-reliant working-class boys. The BSA's welcoming gestures toward working-class and European immigrant boys contrasted with the emphasis on elite boys' leadership and the derision of working-class boys' character in early British Boy Scout publications. BSA national administrators' efforts to alleviate labor leaders' concerns and American Scouting's universal promise to teach modern manhood and leading citizenship attracted wide union support and encouraged a number of working-class and European immigrant boys and men to join.[6]

British and American labor union and Socialist leaders initially criticized Scouting for teaching boys slavish militarism, uncritical obedience to employers, and hatred of the working class. The American Federation of Labor (AFL) and other unions argued that Scout training undercut a boy's developing self-control and independent political judgment. By October 1911, at least thirteen labor unions in Massachusetts, Pennsylvania, New Jersey, Illinois, Indiana, Michigan, Wisconsin, Missouri, and Colorado had gone on record opposing Scouting because of its presumed martial tone and antiunion bias. The United Mine Workers of America even issued a ban in 1912 refusing union membership to anyone connected with either the National Civic Federation or the Boy Scouts, suggesting that the unions saw the BSA as a junior military arm of employers. On the surface, this was not an unreasonable conclusion, since so many leading businessmen and financiers contributed money and public relations support to the early BSA and served on national and local Scout councils.[7]

Labor and Socialist leaders' complaints that some early Scouting groups in the United States taught boys to be militaristic and violent appeared to have merit. Some military men served as Scoutmasters (partly because of their training in outdoor living). The Boy Scout uniform looked suspiciously like the one worn by the American National Guard, which had been used for decades to repress strikers. In the early 1910s, newspapers occasionally carried tragic accounts of Boy Scouts shooting other boys. A December 1910 article in the *Chicago Daily Tribune* reported a fatal clash between two rival factions of Scouts in Covington, Kentucky. In 1912, a twelve-year-old Bronx Scout carrying a loaded rifle from a drill session came upon three other boys. He ordered them to throw up their hands; one of the boys dared him to shoot. The Scout shot and killed a nine-year-old. The Scout later defended himself by saying that the victim had been throwing stones. These armed Scouts likely belonged to one of the more militaristic competing Boy Scout organizations, like Hearst's American Boy Scouts, but the mass media's failure to distinguish between the programs contributed to working-class suspicions of all Scouting as a training ground for soldiers that might later be pitted against unions and strikers.[8]

Labor and Socialist critics of the program also expressed dismay about the harsh characterization of working-class and unemployed men in Baden-Powell's first British Scout handbook (published in 1908 and used by many troops in the United States prior to the triumph of the second, "Americanized" BSA edition of 1911). Baden-Powell declared that men's poverty was the result of bad character and habits—notably drinking, smoking, and wasting of valuable time. The British Scout Laws overtly emphasized loyalty and obedience to employers. Baden-Powell referred to striking workers as wasters and bad citizens who did not deserve to be saluted; he insisted that joining labor unions and striking was not a manly way of improving one's lot in life. He instructed better-off boys to be charitable to the worthy poor, but not to the 99 percent of street beggars who were frauds. Baden-Powell held up bees as the model civic community, since they obeyed their queen and killed off their worthless unemployed. Labor and Socialist leaders resented Baden-Powell's instruction that each boy should know and keep his place by being a "brick" in the wall of the nation and the British Empire. In the fledgling BSA's rushed attempt to meet the demands of American boys and youth organizers for teaching literature and programming ideas, officials replicated some of Baden-Powell's diatribe against working-class men in their cobbled-together 1910 manual (which spliced the original British Boy Scout handbook with Seton's Woodcraft Indians manual).[9]

However, in addition to the resulting complaints from American labor union leaders, highlighting fixed class divisions did not sit well with many middle- and upper-class white Protestant American men's rhetoric of unlimited opportunity and their hope for a democratic, mobile society distinct from Europe's tradition of fixed hereditary classes. Two men suggested at the first annual meeting of the BSA National Council in 1911 that American boys could best be taught democracy by learning Baden-Powell's vision of proper class hierarchy, but they were outvoted. National leaders instead chose to eliminate Baden-Powell's overt references to class hierarchy from BSA literature, and to carefully guard against harsh criticisms of the working class in future publications and statements. Administrators corresponded and met with the AFL's influential leader, Samuel Gompers, and the BSA soon adopted a policy of not favoring either side during labor strikes. Many BSA officials argued that "peace Scouting" activities, such as pioneer craft and training in First Aid and Life Saving, distinguished the BSA from militaristic groups like the American Boy Scouts, which emphasized rifles and martial drilling. Seton's criticism of the effects of militarism and overly specialized industrial jobs as well as his promise that Scouting's outdoorsmanship and woodcraft could serve as a release for strained laborers also appealed to some union members. Adopting less militaristic activities and less antagonistic rhetoric and actions toward the working class set the BSA apart from the British Boy Scouts, who continued to regularly drill and shoot rifles while also directly engaging in strike breaking through the 1920s.[10]

BSA supporters' statements that wealthy boys' tendencies toward snobbery, selfishness, and having everything done for them by servants left them needing Scout training reassured working-class and European immigrant groups. American Scout leaders hoped to ease the country's growing class tensions by teaching poor and rich boys cooperation and service to the greater good, a key component of which was learning to avoid dwelling on economic inequality or partisan differences. BSA writers and speakers insisted that class conflict and political strife resulted not from material differences but from individuals' unwarranted belief in or undue emphasis on social distinction. A 1910 article in *Outing* magazine claimed that denying social distinctions was the Scout's mark of true chivalry: "Above all he must never be a snob, and snobbishness in the scout's eyes is two-edged. It may be despising the rich as well as the poor. In short, social distinctions are to be obliterated." At the first annual meeting of the BSA National Council in 1911, a representative of the Big Brother organization that served urban working-class boys argued that Scouting not only provided poor boys with opportunities for wholesome play and companionship with men of good character but also benefited the rich boy by having him "mix in with some of the rougher diamonds . . . to have some of his more objectionable characteristics, such as selfishness, polished off." BSA literature frequently characterized rich boys as suffering from being "overprivileged." Their dependence on house servants feminized and infantilized them, thus interfering with their learning of manly self-reliance, efficiency, independent judgment, and service to others. Given the BSA's initial reliance on financial support and leadership from the elite, such statements held special meaning for the laboring classes.[11]

Early BSA officials' efforts to stake out a universal vision of modern manhood and cooperative citizenship drew solidarity from most labor and even Socialist critics. James West's explanations of how the BSA was distinct from Hearst's American Boy Scouts organization and had recently altered the Boy Scout Laws to remove antilabor sentiments, "which did not conform with American conditions," along with meetings with local BSA officials, helped persuade the Central Trades and Labor Union of St. Louis to rescind its union band boycott of the 1911 parade for President Taft's visit and to instead endorse cooperation with Boy Scout marchers for the event. In 1912, the AFL made a study of the BSA and interviewed its national leaders. The investigators concluded that some of the confusion indeed resulted from the existence of the militaristic American Boy Scouts organization. They expressed approval of the BSA's expunging of Baden-Powell's offensive remarks about working-class men from the Scout Laws and its de-emphasis of martial training and drill. The AFL voted at its 1912 annual meeting in Rochester to retract its denouncement of the BSA. AFL leaders promised to promote the organization while helping it guard against militarism. The AFL's softening stance toward the BSA paralleled its philosophy of "business unionism," in which leaders increasingly cooperated with businessmen and their government allies to gain wage increases and other tangible benefits for workers while downplaying political conflict and violence between capital and labor. Despite greater differences, the Socialist Party also withdrew its protest of the BSA in 1913 due to the overlap between the two organizations on such masculine ideals as outdoorsmanship and cooperative loyalty. In a 1915 letter to a fellow Socialist, Eugene Debs confessed to liking Scouting's "teaching of manliness, its attention to bodily health and vigor, its stimulating out-doors program and its inculcation of principles of mutual kindness and mutual help among its members." BSA editors' reprinting of Debs's letter in the 1922 Executives' handbook helped solidify this cross-class cooperation on Scouting's balanced manhood and modern work ethic.[12]

"A Catholic Has Equal Rights": Integrating European Immigrant Boys, 1912–1915

In addition to actively recruiting working-class union support, the BSA was working by 1912 to expand the boundaries of dominant white manhood and participating citizenship to also include southern and eastern European immigrant Catholics, Jews, and Polish nationalists who embraced Scouting's ideals. Some new white immigrants initially hesitated to join the organization because they feared it was a militaristic white Anglo-Saxon Protestant conversion factory. BSA administrators encouraged Local Councils to accept light-skinned immigrants and other white "outsiders," regardless of religious denomination, as equal members and to give them some leeway to practice their traditional cultures and faiths. Between 1912 and 1914, administrators granted Catholic, Jewish, Polish, and Mormon organizations' requests to run exclusive BSA troops with their own appointed leaders, practice their religions at Scout camps, and have representation on local and national Scout councils. BSA administrators justified such concessions in the early 1910s as being nonpartisan and allowing institutional sponsors democratic self-determination in troop matters. White immigrant Scouting in the early 1910s thus offered a more lenient and tolerant form of "soft Americanization" than that of the public schools and the growing number of supervised urban playgrounds. A decade before the culmination of African Americans' Great Migration and the 1924 Immigration Restriction quota law, the BSA facilitated European immigrants' transition to an enlarged white manhood if they adopted Scouting's modern American character and civic values.

Active cooperation with leaders of major religious denominations and the pairing of local troop autonomy with full integration in the national Scouting body marked the early BSA as distinctly more welcoming of boys of different faiths than Scouting in some countries. It was not uncommon in other nations for each of the major religions to form its own separate Scout organization, but BSA national leaders worked hard and effectively to include boys and churches of varied faiths. In James West's introductory statement to *Scouting and the Jewish Boy*, published in 1928 by the BSA and its national Jewish Committee on Scouting, he stressed that the provision of the Twelfth Scout Law on being reverent—that Scouts should "respect the convictions of others in matters of custom and religion"—had made a large contribution to the Scout movement and "furnishes a platform upon which all of us may unite in working for the development of the future citizenship of our country." West argued that Scouting "has been developed on such broad lines as to impress all classes and creeds and at the same time allow the greatest possible independence to individual organizations, officers and boys. The fact that there are now three Committees on Scouting, representing Catholic, Protestant and Jewish bodies, each extending to increasing numbers, indicated the willingness of the Boy Scouts of America to cooperate with all religious bodies."[13]

Key leaders of American Catholic churches had initially expressed concern in the early 1910s that the BSA would teach their boys martial values and try to turn them into Protestants. In 1912, the *Holy Name Journal* of New York suggested the formation of a separate "Holy Name Scouts" organization to ensure that Catholic boys lived up to their religious responsibilities without falling prey to the influence of Protestantism or atheism. At the very least, Catholic leaders wanted the power to appoint their own Scoutmasters and exclude boys who were not members of their parishes.[14]

The predominantly white Protestant BSA national leadership made significant membership and council leadership concessions to win over Catholic immigrants and incorporate them on egalitarian terms. James West denied the charge that Catholics were barred from BSA membership or leadership in 1912: "In fact, we will not recognize a Scout council unless the Catholics are proportionately represented on the Council. . . . A Catholic has equal rights and is just as eligible to an office as a Protestant, and has never been and never will be discriminated against in any way." The BSA national office stated that Local Councils should have Catholic representation on their boards and should admit Catholic boys as equals. BSA administrators appointed Victor Ridder as National Commissioner for Scout Work in the Catholic Churches in 1913 and created the Catholic Bureau in 1914. BSA officials also agreed to the demand of Catholic troop sponsors that they be allowed to exclude boys who did not belong to their parishes. Local Councils facilitated Catholic Mass services at their camps. Given that many American Catholics were immigrants from southern and eastern Europe or Mexico, the gradual growth of Catholic troops set in motion by BSA national leaders' concessions from 1912 to 1914 reflected a modest increase in the number of light-skinned European immigrants in the BSA.[15]

Building on the special policies being created for Catholics, Mormon leaders pursued mainstream American masculine and civic status by adopting Boy Scouting as the religion's official youth program. The BSA's modest manhood and emphasis on civic and spiritual duty fit neatly with Mormon teachings. Support for Scouting allowed Mormons to demonstrate their good character and patriotism in an era when some Protestants still considered them to be outside the mainstream. The Mormon's Young Men's Mutual Improvement Association (YMMIA) initially maintained a separate Scouting organization under its direct jurisdiction from 1911 to 1913, using the BSA handbook and similar methods, and holding Scout meetings before or after its regular YMMIA sessions. By January 1913, YMMIA Scouts boasted fifteen hundred troops and twenty thousand boy members. However, in response to increasing questions from within its organization about why they should not merge with the BSA and some Mormon boys' decision to join both Scout organizations, the YMMIA began negotiations with the BSA. The merger agreement confirmed Mormon leaders' ability to exclude non-Mormons and the joint appointment of the YMMIA's Dr. John Taylor to oversee all Mormon Scout troops—eventually throughout the United States, Canada, and Mexico. According to a recent published history of Mormon Scouting, "Within a few years Scouting was woven into Church curriculum and culture." Mormons soon recruited a higher percentage of their boys for Scouting than any other church denomination, and Utah Scout Councils came to enlist a greater portion of the state's boys than any other state. Being a Mormon boy became synonymous with being a Boy Scout, to the point that today it is one of the largest single blocks among BSA troop sponsors.[16]

In contrast to some white Anglo-Saxon Protestant groups that excluded, ridiculed, or assaulted Jewish Americans in the early 1910s, BSA national administrators welcomed them into the fold as members and leaders. Many immigrant and native-born American Jews came to embrace Boy Scouting and other types of youth summer camp programs in the 1910s. Mortimer Schiff (the Jewish president of Sears, Roebuck and Company and an important early BSA donor) served actively as one of the organization's Vice Presidents from 1910 to 1931. The BSA even appointed him President of the organization in 1931, but he died a few months later. Three other Jewish men sat on the BSA National Council by February 1911. The BSA appointed Jewish businessman Sigmund Eisner to make the official BSA uniform and other Scout items. While some Orthodox leaders established separate Jewish BSA troops, many reform Jewish leaders hoped Scouting in religiously integrated community troops would directly mainstream and Americanize Jewish boys. With support from the BSA national office, some Local Council camps facilitated the creation of kosher mess halls and offered Jewish religious services, helping Jewish Americans balance religious and cultural traditions with learning mainstream manhood and citizenship. The Young Men's Hebrew Association formed a Scouting Committee in 1915, which helped increase the number of distinctly Jewish troops. Only forty BSA troops of the 7,375 U.S. total that year were sponsored directly by Jewish synagogues, but the percentage increased noticeably afterward.[17]

In 1914, BSA national leaders employed both more elaborate concessions and legal tactics in their attempt to take over the independent Polish Scouts of America (PSA), a branch of the Polish National Alliance (PNA). The PNA, a men's fraternal organization with approximately 100,000 members, advocated Polish national independence and maintaining Polish culture and language in America. The PSA modeled itself after the Harcerstwo Scouting organization in Poland. James West argued in 1914 that the PSA should merge into the BSA because it had infringed on Scout copyright by publishing three of its own pamphlets. The BSA offered the PSA two spots on the National Council and one Special Field Scout Commissioner if they would agree to adopt the full program and transfer its nine thousand existing members to BSA rolls. BSA national leaders also conceded that its American Scout handbook could be translated into Polish, and that Scout instruction at troop meetings could be done in Polish. The merger, however, failed when BSA officials refused PNA leaders' new demand for an independent branch with a separate badge and rules. The PNA insisted that it needed to maintain a distinct branch due to the trouble its people encountered both in America and abroad, but officially approving a separate division might have encouraged more minority groups to form separate branches and undercut the BSA's claim to offer the universal character and civic training program for all American boys. Instead, BSA administrators happily granted a request to train men belonging to a related fraternal organization, the Polish Falcons Alliance of America, to lead regular BSA troops. The Falcons, formed by PNA members and once linked to that organization, combined physical education and drill with instilling Polish language and

cultural pride into its young men. BSA national leaders sent a field officer who, aided by a translator, guided a two-month-long Scoutmaster
training course in the summer of 1914 for fifty-eight Falcons. The PNA
showed its approval of this arrangement by providing facilities for the
Polish Falcons' Scoutmaster training at its new Alliance College in Pennsylvania.[18]

BSA national leaders' agreement with the Polish Falcons helped solidify three important procedures for including light-skinned immigrants
in Scout training in modern manhood and participating citizenship. First,
the national office demanded that all troop-based Scouting groups be
under its direct jurisdiction; thus, it refused requests for independent
branches. Second, national leaders stipulated that Local Councils appoint
Catholic, Jewish, and Mormon leaders and accept their troop applications. Finally, early BSA administrators worried about finding men from
minority groups whom they deemed worthy of leading troops, so they
focused on selecting and training white immigrant Scoutmasters instead
of on actively recruiting as many white immigrant boys as possible. Many
Catholic, Jewish, Polish, and Mormon leaders seemed content with
these stipulations in exchange for representation on Scout councils and
permission to run exclusive BSA troops in which they could control
the appointment of Scoutmasters, religious content, and language of
instruction. Gaining access to Scouting's masculine and civic status and
privileges without having to give up their denominational or cultural traditions represented a significant step toward white immigrants' incorporation into the American mainstream.[19]

Scouting's "Great Melting Pot of Boyhood," 1915–1921

BSA administrators grew more anxious about encouraging single-minded
American patriotism among its members during World War I but also
more confident that Scout training could meld the working class and
various light-skinned immigrants into a unified American manhood
and civic leadership. As National Scout Commissioner Dan Beard informed boy members in 1919, it was their duty to learn more about America so that they could inform people of foreign birth about its meaning:
"This is the melting pot of the world, all races come here, but when
they come they must leave their race behind, they must come here to
join us, to be one of us." The organization's Americanization rhetoric,
which peaked alongside broader society's "100% Americanism" movement

Reprinted from "Chicago News"

Figure 5.1 Uncle Sam's solution to Gilded Age corruption and immigrant loyalty. "A Little Comfort for the Old Man," 1915 BSA Annual Report to Congress, 113. (Courtesy of Boy Scouts of America National Scouting Museum Archival Collection)

between 1915 and 1921, revealed BSA leaders' concern as well as hope about new white immigrant males' work ethic and patriotism. While World War I increased Anglo-American suspicions of German immigrants, BSA officials continued to actively embrace immigrant boys and allow exclusively Catholic, Jewish, and nation-of-origin troops. BSA supporters argued that Scout troops served as a key civilian Americanizing force akin to a military regiment, and that immigrant Scouts would spread these lessons at home to their families. Administrators also confirmed their cooperation with labor union and Catholic leaders on nonpartisan citizenship and the overriding duty of all American males to support the war effort.[20]

The sketch in Figure 5.1 from the *Chicago News*, reprinted in the 1915 BSA Annual Report, juxtaposes the Boy Scout's patriotism and kind service against the false patriotism and selfishness of those immigrants who chose to be disloyal to America. Uncle Sam's worries about "hyphen stuff" and "foreign spies in U.S." refers to native-born white fears that immigrants might be more loyal to their mother countries than to the

United States. The sketch associates disloyal immigrant men's character with political corruption and the late 1800s patronage system in the forms of graft and pork. Instead of being patriotic, the hyphenated Americans remain either apathetic or selfish in their partisan greed. Uncle Sam gazes in a fatherly manner at a young Boy Scout while holding a list of his virtues. Since Uncle Sam's "worry index" focuses on correctable behaviors rather than innate character deficiencies such as stupidity, laziness, or natural criminality, he smiles in recognition that Scouting could teach immigrants the loyalty, chivalry, courage, and kindness needed to make them patriotic Americans.[21]

In a 1917 screenplay that was turned into a popular movie, James Wilder (the white Hawaiian artist who created the Pine Tree Patrol system of camping and later revamped the BSA's Sea Scout program for older teenagers) suggested that working-class, European immigrant boys' courage and group loyalty—*if redirected* via the Scout troop's training in modern manhood and civic responsibility—could be redeeming qualities. After his thieving father is accidentally killed during a robbery, Pug (the leader of a gang of working-class toughs) is "filled with promptings of the old tribal code that demands revenge for injury done to any member of the family no matter how despicable the member may be" and attacks the policeman who killed his father. The scenario hinted at the unbridled violence and excessive partisanship associated with European immigrants and machine politics in the minds of some white Anglo-Saxon Protestants at the time. The policeman lectures Pug that right is more important than brute strength and that his father was appropriately penalized for breaking the law: "The state killed him—not I!" Pug later gets involved in a robbery to keep a younger gang member out of trouble and ends up badly cut. The policeman tracks Pug to his lair and demands that his gang reveal his whereabouts. They refuse: "We've took a swear, an' we stick! You can kill me before I'll tell!" The policeman thinks for a moment and then replies, "I guess you're right, boys! If you swear anything, sticktoit [*sic*]!" A local Scoutmaster arrives with his trained, prepared troop to help the injured Pug. The Scoutmaster and the policeman agree that the street gang is worthy of becoming a Boy Scout troop because they have shown courage and group loyalty: "Well, that's half the battle!" The policeman, upon learning that the Scoutmaster is also the busy president of the Metropolitan Trust Company, decides that he can also find time to be a Scoutmaster. It seems fitting for the troop of working-class toughs to be led by the Irish policeman, representing the Americanized immigrant who shows his loyalty to the United States by helping maintain law and order. The un-Americanized gang of immigrant toughs had positive but misplaced virtues, which an apprenticeship in modern manhood under a worthy Scoutmaster could channel into improved character and contributing citizenship.[22]

BSA national leaders worked diligently during the Great War to maintain the good relationship they had established earlier in the decade with labor union officials; both parties agreed that cooperative patriotism and war production should be the immediate priorities of all American men. BSA administrators actively reassured labor leaders of their good intentions. In a 1916 national press release, James West reminded workers that the BSA had quickly made every change labor leaders suggested in its 1911 Americanization of the Scout Oath and Laws. West persuaded the President of the Boston Boy Scout council to retract his statement that the BSA should work to counter labor's aggressiveness after the war. After a thorough examination of the matter and several meetings with local BSA officials in 1916, a special investigating committee appointed by the Massachusetts branch of the AFL and the Central Labor Union announced their endorsement: "The Committee is finally convinced that the Boy Scouts of America do not sanction attacks upon the Trade Movement, but are heartily in accord with it. We find that the leaders of the Boy Scout Movement in this vicinity are men of sterling character and have the welfare of the boys' future at heart; they have invited representatives of the Trade Union movement to take an active part in helping them to make better men and citizens of the boys." The investigating committee expressed particular satisfaction with a BSA national office statement sent to labor union leaders that Scouting was "entirely non-class, non-military, non-sectarian and non-partisan." A June 1919 *Scouting* article reiterated the BSA policy forbidding members from helping either side of labor strikes. Such gestures even softened the militant United Mine Workers of America. The union removed its ban on members' sons belonging to the BSA, stating that the Scouts contributed to the country's essential war needs.[23]

Cooperation between BSA officials and key Catholic leaders also expanded during the war era. In 1917, the National Catholic War Council helped increase the number of Catholic Scout troops as part of the American bishops' patriotic drive to support the war effort. The troop drive offered proof that immigrant Catholics would be loyal to the United States. Even the pope added his blessing in 1919 for Scouting in "distinctly Catholic troops." Notre Dame University began offering a Scout-masters' training course in 1920. The Knights of Columbus—the Catholic men's fraternal organization—adopted Scouting as the association's official youth program. The cooperative efforts of BSA and Catholic leaders during World War I helped cement Scouting as an appropriate character, civic, and religious training experience for European immigrant and other American Catholics.[24]

BSA national leaders claimed that Scouting could help win the war and the subsequent peace by blending the variety of white immigrant strains into a unified and modern American manhood. BSA Executive Board member Theodore Roosevelt Jr. (the son of the former U.S. president) argued in an early 1919 speech at the National Council's annual meeting that Scout troops and camping would have a democratizing and Americanizing effect on immigrants, similar to that of World War I army regiments: "All those men considered themselves Americans and nothing else. They would not have tolerated a question of any allegiance to any so-termed 'old country.' . . . It got him right out of the frame of mind that he belonged to any particular strata. It de-internationalized him, but—it nationalized him." *Scouting* magazine defined "Americanization" that year as an emphasis on thrift, patriotic but safe celebrations, use of the English language, cooperation through the troop and patrol spirit, and maintenance of American standards of nutrition and child care. The author added that Americanization efforts should resist antagonistic propaganda, eliminate causes of immigrants' misunderstanding, and work to reduce cultural prejudice and the segregation of immigrant communities.[25]

The 1920 BSA Annual Report to Congress concluded that white immigrant boys who participated in Scouting's "great melting pot of boyhood" helped sow the seeds of sympathy and loyalty for America among their parents and bring "scout lessons of cleanliness, health, safety and happiness into practical application in their own homes." A key example of this was the 1921 national service drive in which Boy Scouts helped the federal commissioner of naturalization in the Department of Labor distribute pamphlets to forty-five thousand immigrants in 338 communities. The publications encouraged adults to attend English language and citizenship classes and apply for naturalization. BSA administrators also succeeded in encouraging many local units to perform the "melting pot" skit as a public fund-raiser. In the most popular version, boys of various European nationalities (or native-born white American boys dressed as immigrant minorities) entered into a cauldron of Americanism or a

Scout camping tent and emerged as neatly uniformed Scouts. At least for light-skinned immigrants, participation in Scouting's character and civic training provided a means by which they could voluntarily shed their ancestral race and become a part of America's dominant white manhood.[26]

Debating Policies for the "Underprivileged" and "White Nationalities," 1922–1929

The September 1922 second National Training Conference for Local Council Executives witnessed a peak in BSA administrators' awareness of the life obstacles that America's modernizing society created for immigrant, industrial working-class, and other underprivileged boys. While confirming some existing policies that constricted fuller participation by such groups, their statements also marked the maturation of administrators' belief that European immigrant, non–white Anglo-Saxon Protestant, and working-class boys were capable of developing mainstream masculine character and civic traits in Scouting without special treatment. Encouraged in part by a resolution the National Council had forwarded to its Executive Board in March—that reaching immigrant boys should be emphasized in Scout literature and that instructions should be provided to local officials on how to do so—two special BSA commissions announced the findings of their studies at the conference. Based on input from the leaders of the Boys Club Federation and the Big Brother Movement (two organizations that targeted urban working-class and immigrant youth), the Commission on the Underprivileged Boy reported to attendees that the Scouting program was not well adapted to the varied needs of underprivileged boys. The commission argued that "inherited mental slackness," physical defect, "inherited vicious qualities," racial prejudice, foreign-born parentage, or having to work to bolster the family's income all hindered a boy's life opportunities. However, the commission's report presented a narrower list of key problems in reaching underprivileged boys with Scouting: the "old military bugaboo" (the assumption that some working-class immigrant parents and labor union leaders still worried that Scouting promoted militarism), finding willing adults in these underprivileged districts to lead troops, the boys' long working hours, and the high cost of Scout fees and equipment. This second list belied the difficulties posed by racism and physical or mental disability. Moreover, the chairman claimed that one major type of handicap was "the boy that is restrained from full privilege by a class consciousness of being a poor boy," and that the uniform cost and the troop fee problems were "largely a state of mind," since many boys who claimed that they could not pay for them spent the same amount of money every week attending movies. The commission concluded, "We find no apparent reason so far as the Scout program is concerned, for recognizing the underprivileged boy as a type or class to whom any special appeal should be made to enter the ranks of Scouting." The commission instructed Executives to avoid special treatment of underprivileged boys. The audience of white local Scout Council Executives reinforced the commission's arguments and policy advice. The first respondent earnestly declared, "I seriously object to the use of the term underprivileged boy as it relates to the Boy Scout Movement. We are teaching democracy. . . . I don't believe the Boy Scout Movement should set up any class of distinction. We can run the clubs in [the working-class immigrant] East Side just as well as on [the elite] Fifth Avenue, if we provide leadership. I don't like this term." Arguments like this one carried the day, as they had since the organization's second year, 1911. Although the statement underplayed the life obstacles faced by underprivileged boys, it did confirm that BSA leaders wanted to and did run troops of working-class and European immigrants on equal standing with middle- and upper-class white Anglo-Saxon Protestant troops.[27]

The chairman of the 1922 conference's Commission on Scouting in Industry argued that rich boys were equally disadvantaged as working-class boys: "We disagree on what is the underprivileged boy. Some of us believe that the boy with an automobile is far more under-privileged than the boy in industry." Only a few local BSA officials bothered to respond to the commission's survey about their councils' efforts to recruit working-class boys in industry, suggesting either that most Executives did not want to respond to a questionnaire about special treatment of certain local groups or that they had no such recruitment programs to report. The commission instructed local Executives to not allow a company's welfare worker to serve as a Scoutmaster for boy employees or let business owners pay for the expenses of company troops, since that would accustom working-class boys to wait for free handouts: "You absolutely are not going to make Scouts that way." The fact that some major corporations, such as Western Union, had been running successful Scout troops on this basis for several years made this warning particularly striking. The commission's leaders wanted to put a stop to this type of outreach, since paying for boys to Scout and adjusting the program to better fit the schedule and budget of factory boys would set them up as a special class of Scouts and thus be un-American—exacerbating rather than resolving class and political conflict.[28]

Despite awareness that such costs as that of the regulation uniform might be limiting participation of some poor and immigrant boys, BSA officials demonstrated their faith that Scouting could meld together different light-skinned groups by increasing rules on wearing the official version over the course of the 1920s. A Los Angeles council Executive complained that troops wearing incomplete or mismatched uniforms contributed to misbehavior and negative publicity. In a 1923 bulletin to local officials, James West agreed that the standard uniform should be better enforced. Later that year, West instructed boys to borrow money if they had to in order to acquire a proper uniform: "If necessary incur an honorable debt to somebody for the price, and then keep everlastingly at it until you pay up." This would demonstrate the boy's thrifty consumer habits as well as his stick-to-itiveness and trustworthiness. A 1927 study suggested that a lower-priced, medium-quality uniform and shoes would suit Scouts' needs, discourage boys from buying low-quality knock-offs, and allow more poor boys to join—but the BSA did not lower uniform prices until well into the Great Depression.[29]

Most BSA national and local leaders continued to actively defend the right of Catholic, Jewish, Polish, and other light-skinned immigrants to be a part of regular Scout training through the 1920s. As the report on the proceedings of the 1922 Executives National Training Conference declared, "On the Boy Scout platform we can erect a great non-sectarian Cathedral of Humanity. . . . Scouting provides a platform for bringing people of all faiths together without giving up one bit of their faith or convictions." BSA administrators did not advocate restrictions on European immigration, and they clearly distanced themselves from the revived Ku Klux Klan's (KKK) virulent nativism. KKK members sent a letter to the 1924 BSA Executives National Training Conference threatening to pull their children out of Scouting if the organization continued to accept Jewish, Catholic, and African American boys. James West wrote to a prominent Scout supporter that, despite the fact that both organizations emphasized 100 percent Americanism, the BSA wanted no affiliation with the KKK because the Twelfth Scout Law on religious tolerance "so definitely covers the principle involved that there can be no question where the Boy Scouts of America stands." Some local urban

"Cosmopolitan" Boy Scout Troops

Many nationalities are represented in this unique unit. Top row, left to right, Bertram Ruffino, patrol leader; Edwin Zecher, troop scribe; William Giambastiano, patrol leader. Bottom row, left to right, Roque Belaunde, senior patrol leader; Washington J. Bray, scout master, and Benjamin Baderacco, assistant scout master.

Figure 5.2 The diversity of immigrants in Scout troop leadership.
"'Cosmopolitan' Boy Scout Troops," *San Francisco Chronicle*, January 29, 1922, 7.

councils touted highly diverse international or "cosmopolitan troops" that mixed different European immigrant nationalities with white Anglo-Saxon Protestant boys, as the 1922 photograph from the *San Francisco Chronicle* in Figure 5.2 demonstrates. The accompanying article, "Scout Troop Boasts Many Nationalities," explained that the active troop of twenty-two boys contained nearly that many nationalities, including boys from Ireland, Italy, Portugal, Slovenia, Serbia, Germany, and the Philippines, all of whom had either full- or part-time jobs. The author praised this troop of Scouts, which was formed in 1915 by a Catholic

White Immigrants and the Industrial Working Class   175

church and whose Scoutmastership was successfully taken over by an insurance broker.[30]

The 1926 formation of the national Jewish Committee on Scouting represented a culmination of earlier efforts at welcoming Jewish and other non–white Anglo-Saxon Protestant light-skinned boys and institutions into the organization. Twenty rabbis and laymen met with BSA officials that year and voted to establish the new committee to produce special literature for Scouting with Jewish boys and to encourage more Jewish institutions to form troops. The committee soon published the key booklet, *Scouting and the Jewish Boy*, which provided statements of support for the movement's religious diversity and inclusiveness from the BSA's Jewish Vice President Mortimer Schiff, prominent Jewish rabbis, BSA Chief Scout Executive James West, Dean James Russell of Columbia University's Teachers College, and U.S. president and honorary BSA President Calvin Coolidge. The booklet offered several pages of comparisons between the Scout Laws and Jewish traditions to help persuade parents and institutional leaders, highlighting the overlap on such staple values as trustworthiness, dutifulness, obedience to parents and those in authority, friendliness, helping those in need, being kind to animals, serving others without pay, and learning a trade through merit badge work. The booklet recommended that in the formation of new troops, "something may be gained in personal dignity and racial loyalty by incorporating with the Troop number the name of some outstanding Jewish personality, ideal or historical place." The author recommended that boys be taught the meaning or importance of that person or ideal for which the troop was named. An excerpted letter from Rabbi Julian Morgenstern, who served as president of Hebrew Union College in Cincinnati, summarized the spirit of enthusiastic cooperation between the BSA national office and Jewish leaders, which the booklet and new committee embodied: "I feel [Scouting] to be one of the supreme movements making for the development of a right boyhood and a healthy manhood and citizenship in America. Its religious work I find to be broad, constructive and truly spiritual and absolutely free from all denominational partisanship. I believe that all the churches of America ought to give loyal and eager support to this movement; particularly to the Jews of America and to our Jewish congregations I commend the movement most heartily and unqualifiedly. I would like to see at least one Scout Troop organized in every synagogue in the land. I find the movement to be in complete sympathy with the aims of Judaism in

America, and feel convinced that the presence of a Scout Troop in a synagogue can make only for the deepening and intensification of the spirit of loyalty and positive Jewish observance of all its members." Jewish leaders promoted Scouting so well that between exclusive troops and boys in "mixed" community troops, they became overrepresented in the BSA relative to their portion of the U.S. population.[31]

BSA ADMINISTRATORS' GROWING USE of the term "white nationality groups" and their decision to not treat European immigrants as a group in need of intensive outreach effort or policy exceptions exemplified their belief that light-skinned immigrants could be incorporated into dominant white manhood and full American citizenship. In contrast to the term "white races," which implied permanent biological difference and inferiority, the term "nationality groups" emphasized country of origin and suggested that these boys were capable of advanced character and civic development through Scouting. In 1927, the BSA national office stated its intention to expand outreach to white nationalities. However, two years passed before even two information pamphlets on Scouting were translated into Spanish, Lithuanian, and Polish. Officials placed more emphasis on mixing "foreign-born boys" with native-born white boys where possible, to "bring them more quickly into full American citizenship with respect for our laws and institutions and a desire to upbuild the community." A 1929 survey found that Local Councils across the country were open to white nationality boys and tallied one hundred Spanish troops; one hundred Polish troops; and a "large number" of Lithuanian, Italian, and other white immigrant troops. An even greater number of European immigrants probably belonged to the cosmopolitan troops. BSA leaders soon seemed to lose interest in the idea of special recruitment of white nationality groups—perhaps a casualty of the dislocations and budget cuts caused by the Depression as well as the success of New Deal programs in helping "whiten" and Americanize these groups of European immigrants. For those working-class and European immigrant boys who joined, Scouting offered a broadly respected and accessible path by which to become leading white American men. Traditional rural farm boys (many of whom were Anglo-American or older immigrants from Scandinavia and Germany) proved to be a more difficult match with the BSA's modern manhood and teaching methods.[32]

6

Rural Manhood and Lone Scouting
on the Margins of a Modernizing Society

The Norman Rockwell sketches in Figure 6.1 and the play they accompanied in a 1915 issue of *Boys' Life* exemplified not only the faith BSA administrators had in Scouting's ability to bring urban working-class "new immigrants" into modern white manhood but also the difficulty they had incorporating traditional rural manhood and farm boys—regardless of their race. The sketches and play positioned the modest, efficient Boy Scout camp orderly as the facilitator between the shortsighted, pleasure-seeking working-class immigrant tough from the city and his uncle, a backward and nearly feminine rural farmer. The play, *A Strenuous Afternoon: A Short Scout Play That Any Troop Can Enact*, opens on a Scout camp scene with a raised American flag. The Scoutmaster explains to an Assistant Scoutmaster of another troop that his strenuous afternoon will be filled with writing a full report of his Scouts' rank and merit badge test progress and other successes from this camp session to submit to the Executive at the Local Council office (an obligation that highlights BSA camping's increasing bureaucratization and hierarchical chain of command). The Assistant Scoutmaster asks the Scoutmaster if his troop wants to play flag raiding, but the Scoutmaster replies that they had better not, since his boys prefer to finish their merit badge work. He summons his troop with a whistle to find out the Patrols' plans for their remaining time. As the efficient manager and delegator of his troop workforce, the Scoutmaster approves the three Patrol Leaders' requests to lead their units on sketching camp maps, semaphore signaling, practicing First Aid, and bridge building. A tough from the city who has been hanging around the camp for several days shuffles across the stage and asks, "How much does it cost tuh jine de scouts? . . . I likes de look o' de uniform." The Scoutmaster explains the costs, annual registration process, and rank and badge tests: "Why, you have to learn a few things and do a little work." The tough responds, "Eh? D'yuh say work? I t'ought it wuz all play. Gee, if it's work, not fer mine! I gets 'nuff work in de city. I'm out here [in the woods] fer fun." The Scoutmaster explains

Figure 6.1 Balancing the city tough and the rural farmer. Norman Rockwell, "The Tough, the Orderly, the Farmer," *Boys' Life*, October 1915, 20. (Courtesy of Boy Scouts of America National Scouting Museum Archival Collection)

that the program's outdoor skill tests are fun, and has the Scout orderly who was assisting him show the tough around camp to see the Patrols in action. A farmer (who turns out to be the tough's uncle) enters, gruffly pulling two Scouts by the ear, and demands that the Scoutmaster explain why they were making a path through his oat field and damaging his crop. One Scout picks up the farmer's dropped handkerchief, while another returns his dropped purse with the money intact without accepting a tip, and both boys apologize for possibly spoiling his oat field while they were studying the nest of a bird (probably for a scientific Nature Study merit badge). The surprised farmer says he has never seen such polite and respectful boys in his life, and that they have not done any permanent damage. When the impressed farmer asks if his tough nephew could join the Scout troop, the Scoutmaster readily agrees. The tough gleefully returns from his camp tour, praising the Scouts' outdoor merit badge work. When the tough spits on the ground, the orderly explains, "We don't do that in this camp. It isn't healthy." The ashamed tough states that he wants to join the troop. The Scoutmaster instructs the orderly to start teaching him the initial Scout tests and asks the tough if he wants to stay for supper. The tough (who catches and stops himself from spitting a second time) has already begun the process of correcting his primitive ways just by being around boys and men of good character in the structured Scout camp environment. "Yuh betcher—I mean, t'anks, mister." The tough quickly learns the Scout Oath and Tenderfoot skills, and is allowed to join the Troop before the curtain drops. This parable illuminates several key aspects of early Scout teachings, perhaps the most striking of which was that the farmer, with his traditional agricultural work and rural lifeways, was no longer able to bring his nephew up into respectable American manhood.[1]

The tough and the Boy Scout troop clearly rejected traditional rural boyhood. The tough, uninterested in his uncle's farm work and the traditional masculine values it conveyed, had come to the rural area "to play." However, upon being educated about the more constructive but "fun" outdoor tasks that Scout campers engaged in, he jumped at the chance to join. The troop (whom the reader assumes were urban or town white Anglo-Saxon Protestants due to their lack of an accent in the script) quickly embraced the working-class city boy and began to fold him into the mainstream. The Scoutmaster, operating a camp apparently just a few feet away from a working farm, did not bother to encourage the Scouts or the man's nephew to learn any masculine values or work skills from the farmer or his way of life. The farm itself was out of the mainstream, irrelevant to a rapidly changing society. By contrast, the Boy Scout camp offered modern, exciting, and worthwhile opportunities to the city tough and the troop. While the new Lone Scouts of America and other organizations such as the 4-H Club successfully attracted large rural boy memberships by reinforcing the farm occupation and individual self-reliance, this play juxtaposed Scouting's outdoor activities and masculine teachings *against* those of the traditional farmer.

From colonial New England through the late 1800s, the self-made yeoman farmer, making an independent living for his family out of sheer determination and personal thrift, had represented an ideal: the respected American man and citizen. According to such authorities as Thomas Jefferson and Abraham Lincoln, his ability to provide for the household from his own land and by his own hands without being beholden to any employer or landlord gave the yeoman farmer the independent political judgment essential for contributing to America's democratic government. However, the frontier of unsettled territory began to disappear, and corporations and mechanization began to take over farmland and food production by the 1890s. These trends pushed many rural dwellers to give up family farming and move to the growing cities in search of corporate-industrial jobs and exciting social and leisure outlets. Historians of the idea of American success have argued that the yeoman farmer's social authority and place in the pantheon of heroes for American manhood was seriously challenged by the turn of the twentieth century. The play and sketch suggested that the Boy Scout's modern relationship with nature and interactions with his troop might fill this void and save country boys, but analyzing the early BSA administrators' rural boy debates and policies reveals otherwise.[2]

The BSA's ineffective early outreach efforts to mold rural boys with standard Scouting and, especially, their failed takeover of the Lone Scouts organization highlighted the extreme disjuncture between modern, dominant manhood and the yeoman farmer's traditional values. Early BSA administrators and publications discussed farmer manhood infrequently, and when they did, their critiques sometimes suggested that farmers' isolated rural environment made them inefficient and ignorant of the ways of modern men. This incongruity also marked the era's shift toward child labor restrictions and lengthened compulsory schooling. New labor restriction laws exempted children's farm work, and rural districts were slow to enforce required schooling for boys. Scout officials stated that rural farm boys were resourceful and self-reliant, but too individualistic and set in the old ways. Boy Scout supporters argued that it was difficult to teach modern society's group hierarchy, public service, and scientific efficiency to rural boys—especially when their parents objected to key Scout methods, like the troop and its adult leadership requirement. Therefore, until 1923, most BSA officials did little to effectively recruit rural boys—despite the fact that many rural boys were either white Anglo-Saxon Protestants or from older immigrant areas, like Germany and Scandinavia. A Pioneer branch for rural Boy Scouts and the rural-based Area Councils had attracted few boys from the open country, so in 1924 BSA administrators pushed through the absorption of the competing Lone Scouts organization, which had more effectively recruited country boys. Despite internal and external experts' advice that Lone Scouting's primitive, individualistic manhood and programming better met the needs of rural boys, BSA administrators quickly squandered the old Lone Scout members' allegiance by trying to bring Lone Scout masculine and environmental teachings in line with regular Boy Scout values. The BSA's greater willingness to accommodate working-class and European immigrant boys suggests that modernization redrew the bounds of dominant manhood to include light-skinned immigrant groups who lived in industrial towns and cities to the exclusion of traditional farmers of all ethnicities.[3]

Scouting for the Country Boy, 1910–1923

The tensions surrounding the early BSA's persistent failures to effectively recruit rural boys and BSA founder William D. Boyce having to start a separate Lone Scout organization to better meet the needs and interests of country boys help demarcate the emerging parameters of modern manhood. The few BSA national publications that addressed rural manhood between 1911 and 1924 tended to depict the small independent farmer as ignorant, inefficient, and unscientific—the opposite of Scout manhood. Because the BSA failed to attract or even consistently take rural boys into account, Boyce felt compelled to start an independent Lone Scouts of America organization (LSA) for them in 1915, with a primitive Indian focus and no adult leader or troop membership requirements. The LSA quickly recruited a large following; it appealed to many more rural farm boys than did troop-based Boy Scouting, with its emphasis on scientific efficiency and hierarchical loyalty. The BSA soon countered by creating a new Pioneer Scout branch and later Area Councils for rural boys, but they failed to garner much interest because they stuck to standard Boy Scout programming as well as troop membership and schedule requirements. Even after nearly a decade of rural programming, a 1925 survey estimated that the BSA recruited only one out of every fifty-seven available rural boys. The national average was then close to one Scout for every eight available boys, so BSA rural recruitment was dismal compared to town and urban rates. BSA administrative debates and policy decisions prior to 1924 suggested that the key obstacle to engaging country boys was that the isolated rural environment and traditional family farm produced boys unfit for an increasingly urban, industrial, and interdependent society.[4]

The conflict between rural boys' needs and the BSA's vision of modern manhood created distinct problems for an organization whose leaders claimed to provide a universal character and civic training program useful for and welcoming to all American boys. In the early 1910s, a few national administrators tried to excuse poor rural recruitment rates with the argument that country boys had less need for Scout character training because they were busy doing heavy farm work under their fathers' tutelage. Farm boys being too spread out to form a full troop or partake of its modern lessons in cooperative team building and hierarchical leadership, though, formed a more important practical concern for BSA administrators. In a 1916 *Scouting* article, two New York State Scoutmasters bluntly explained that the lack of competent merit badge examiners, willing troop leaders, effective methods to deliver instruction, and Good Turn opportunities further hindered rural recruitment. The shortage of competent examiners and willing Scoutmasters suggested that the BSA's program did not match up well with farm men's skills and interests. The two Scoutmasters noted that troop hiking and camping did not appeal to rural boys who were already able to do that on their own. The relatively high cost of Scout uniforms and equipment also discouraged some rural boys from joining, as it did working-class and nonwhite boys.[5]

Boyce had consistently argued that the BSA needed to significantly modify its methods and teaching emphases to attract and benefit rural boys. James West and the Executive Board disagreed, insisting that the troop experience was essential to Scouting and that the BSA's farm merit badges and the federal 4-H Club youth program met the needs of country boys. Boyce, frustrated by their disdain for rural boys and by the BSA's growing bureaucracy, modeled the independent Lone Scouts of

America organization in January 1915 on the British Lone Scout program, created by maverick Scout leader John Hargrave in 1913. Hargrave had borrowed heavily from the primitive masculine teachings, critical-thinking emphasis, and moralistic nature ideology of Ernest Thompson Seton's Woodcraft Indians (which BSA national administrators had almost finished expunging from its official recommended program). Boyce hired Frank Allan Morgan, the popular Scoutmaster of Chicago's largest BSA troop, to develop the LSA's seven progressive degree booklets and to edit a new *Lone Scout* magazine. Morgan stated that a focus on primitive Indian lore and boy self-government was more appropriate for and appealing to country boys than was regular Scouting. Rural boys across the United States quickly gravitated to Lone Scouting. The LSA registered 30,000 in its first few months and 133,000 in its first year.[6]

Lone Scouting—which emphasized Indian lore to teach rural and other marginalized boys individualistic, primitive manhood—stood in stark opposition to American Boy Scouting and its modern, dominant manhood. Unlike regular American Scouts, Lone Scouts served as masters of their own apprenticeships in good character and civic development while providing most of their own content and programming ideas through the national *Lone Scout* magazine and numerous local newsletters. Lone Scouts, who joined as individuals, enjoyed much more autonomy and flexibility than did the troop-based Boy Scouts, who were directed firmly by Scoutmasters through a standardized program. The LSA had no immediate adult supervisors or intermediary local offices, whereas the BSA continued to expand its bureaucracy, paperwork requirements, and local and regional offices led by trained professionals. Lone Scouts did most of their work individually using Boyce and Morgan's degree pamphlets and magazine, while the BSA added increasing layers of adult supervision and testing through the Scoutmaster, Troop Committeemen, and merit badge experts. LSA boys paid a one-time fee of five cents (or sold a small number of Boyce's newspapers), worked the program at their own pace and schedule, supervised their own examinations, and asked the LSA national office for the appropriate badge insignia when they passed. Most BSA Scoutmasters managed the whole troop's activities and tests directly; before the late 1920s, some BSA national officials discouraged boys from even leading a Patrol on a short outing. The BSA offered polished publications created by paid professionals and expert committees, but LSA boy members sent in so many letters and articles that were published in the *Lone Scout* magazine that the post office had to establish a separate branch for its editors. With Boyce's encouragement, the boys also set up over two thousand independent, amateur Lone Scout newsletters, ranging from one handwritten page to fifty typed pages.[7]

The creation of the LSA apparently motivated the BSA to start its own rural branch, but BSA administrators had serious misgivings about rural boys' fitness for training in modern manhood and leading citizenship. BSA officials originally called the proposed program Lone Scouts—perhaps an effort to persuade Boyce to give up his separate organization. BSA leaders settled on the name Pioneer Scouts by August 1916. Any individual boy could join Boyce's LSA, but the BSA's Pioneers accepted only those who could demonstrate that it was impossible for them to join a regular Scout troop. In seeming ignorance of the needs of rural boys and the significant obstacles to their participation in regular Boy Scout troops, a 1916 *Scouting* article explained that the BSA did not want a boy who "didn't get along with the fellows . . . doesn't like the scoutmaster," or was just too lazy to hike a few miles to go to troop meetings. Even after they were admitted, Pioneers had to make every effort to join an existing troop or to start a new one. BSA administrators heavily curtailed Native American imagery in the Pioneer Scouts, just as they had done with regular Boy Scouting. Pioneers studied the regular Boy Scout advancement tests and had to find a teacher, a pastor, or an employer to judge them on their competency.[8]

In short, Pioneering eliminated the very things that made Boyce's Lone Scouting distinct and appealing to rural and other marginalized boys, because BSA administrators believed it was inappropriate to teach members individualism, self-government, and primitivism in a modernizing nation. They may have also feared that having too many farm boys in the organization would skew the development or discourage the participation of regular town or city boys. Even with the World War I boom in the BSA's overall membership total, the number of Pioneers barely topped one thousand in 1918. BSA administrators created an official Pioneer Division headed by Armstrong Perry in 1919, new Area Councils with Regional Deputies in 1923, and Railroad Scout Executives, but refused to loosen requirements or invest enough money or time into developing a more appropriate program for rural boys. These changes represented a slight improvement over the original Pioneer program in bringing Scouting to country boys; however, the BSA's high costs, fixed schedule, and continued emphasis on modern masculine skills and troop hierarchy over self-reliance and Indian primitivism resulted in only small gains in the organization's rural recruitment rates. For the BSA's first fourteen years, most of its national leaders had great difficulty attracting country boys and seemingly little interest in rural manhood.[9]

The BSA's Failed Modernization of Lone Scouting for Rural and Other Marginalized Boys

The BSA's unsuccessful absorption of William D. Boyce's independent Lone Scouts organization and its many rural members best illuminates the mismatch between dominant, modern manhood on the one hand, and the traditional masculine virtues of the self-reliant yeoman farmer and the primitive Indian hero on the other. The 1924 takeover stemmed partly from BSA administrators' desire to monopolize American Scouting and expand its membership, but the masculine values and teaching methods that administrators employed when attempting to merge Lone Scouts into the parent organization revealed a lack of awareness of rural life and a stubborn desire to radically transform and modernize the character of country boys. Despite being informed by several of their own officials as well as outside experts about why Lone Scouting succeeded where Boy Scouting's Pioneer Branch had failed in recruiting such boys, BSA administrators insisted on converting Lone Scouting into regular troop Boy Scouting, with its focus on modern manhood, and, as a result, promptly lost most of Boyce's membership by the late 1920s.

Before the merger, Lone Scouting's emphasis on individualism, initiative, self-government, and primitive Indian lore made the program far more attractive to rural boys than was the BSA's Pioneers. The BSA Pioneers peaked at 1,224 boys, whereas Boyce's Chicago office staff boasted that they had served a total of 523,470 LSA members at the time of the merger with the BSA (although this figure may have included every boy who ever subscribed to *Lone Scout* magazine or paid the small, one-time membership fee). Since a Lone Scout did not register annually and had no adult troop leaders, it was difficult to define and pinpoint active membership. Perhaps 150,000 Lone Scouts considered themselves engaged members at the time of the merger, although some BSA officials had lower estimates by their standard of active membership.[10]

Since the key September 1910 Waldorf Astoria banquet honoring Baden-Powell, BSA administrators had worked to absorb other Scout organizations in order to have a monopoly on American Scout programming and to prevent competing interpretations of dominant manhood and citizenship. A recent biography of Boyce argued that his 1915 creation of the LSA prompted BSA administrators to resume their efforts to get a federal charter, which was achieved in June 1916. The BSA particularly benefited from the federal charter's granting of a legal monopoly to the organization on the use of the word "Scout" and its derivatives in the United States. This helped BSA administrators absorb some independent Scout organizations and discourage new Scout associations from forming. However, trying to eliminate the LSA proved to be trickier. The BSA's own corporate founder had started the LSA before the granting of the BSA's federal charter, so he had some "vested right" to its distinct name and unique program. Moreover, the LSA did not directly compete with the BSA for membership, since the LSA was designed primarily to serve a rural clientele, whom most BSA national administrators had shown relatively little interest in recruiting. Predictably, BSA officials' early efforts to persuade Boyce to merge the LSA into the BSA made little headway.[11]

Rather than being motivated solely by the needs of rural boys, one growing impetus for absorbing the LSA appeared to be that its existence came to threaten an essential source of income for the BSA national office: product royalties for use of the word "Scout." From 1916 to 1924, BSA administrators had used the monopoly on the word "Scout" provided by the organization's federal charter to persuade over four hundred companies to stop producing items carrying the name Scout or to pay the BSA a royalty for doing so. In 1924, the BSA national office drew almost $64,000 (approximately 18 percent of its income for the year) from royalty fees on these Scout items. The BSA drew another $65,000 from Scout supplies and publications that it sold directly. In other words, over a third of the BSA national office's income hinged on its monopoly of the word "Scout" in manufactured items and publications. Owning the word was easily worth over $1.5 million annually to the national office in 2015 equivalencies.[12]

This practice, however, ran aground in 1923 when the Winchester Arms Company refused to pay the BSA a royalty for producing its Winchester Scout rifle. Winchester defense lawyers argued that the BSA, by knowingly permitting the Lone Scouts and the American Girl Scouts organizations to exist and produce their own Scout literature and materials, had forfeited its monopoly on the word "Scout." Furthermore, the Girl Scouts had made arrangements with several companies to produce knives, axes, and other items with Scout names. If Winchester lawyers could convince a judge that the BSA had indeed forfeited its legal monopoly on the word, then other groups would be free to form new Scout organizations, and other companies could produce Scout items without paying the BSA a royalty. To undercut Winchester lawyers' claims, BSA national leaders followed their own lawyers' advice and quickly ramped up their efforts to take over the LSA and to put the Girl Scouts out of business (the latter of which was never achieved).[13]

Boyce agreed to the merger, and at first it seemed from statements made by experts on rural manhood that the BSA might retain Lone Scouting's successful country boy character training methods. Armstrong Perry, the veteran Scoutmaster and former secretary of the Brooklyn YMCA, who had headed the BSA's small Pioneer Division since 1919, delivered the first prominent speech on Lone Scouting by a BSA official at the 1924 National Training Conference for Local Council Executives. He stated that Boyce's old program had allowed boys to be "self-governing" and "not dominated by adults." Perry noted that though they were "crude and boyish," the LSA publications and rallies represented the boys' own work, were paid for out of their own pockets, and showed initiative. Boy leadership also reduced office overhead and the need for large membership fees. In an unsubtle jab at the heavy emphasis on adult leadership in regular American Boy Scouting, Perry argued that the polished, adult-led BSA rallies and publications contradicted the methods by which many of America's great historical leaders had learned to do things for themselves. He voiced the concerns of many existing Lone Scouts with the BSA merger: "All of a sudden, without a moment's warning, you hear that your organization has been turned over to another, in which the governing principle is not self-government but adult leadership." Perry read an excerpt from a letter written by a North Carolina Lone Scout who demanded to know on whose authority the merger was enacted, since the LSA was "advertised as an organization of, for and by boys." Building on the Lone Scout writer's use of American men's traditional individualism to critique the BSA's takeover, Perry concluded that the BSA had "no right to assume that the merger has passed over to us, as so many chattels, 50,000 boys or more to do with as we please." He urged other BSA leaders to be democratic and take the opinions of existing Lone Scouts into account.[14]

Earlier at the conference, rural boys' work expert Dr. Charles J. Galpin had suggested to the hundreds of BSA Local Council Executives and national office staff in attendance that they cooperate with and learn from existing farm boys' organizations instead of trying to promote troop-based Boy Scout character training in rural areas. He reported that he had written agricultural college leaders to ask if regular Boy Scouting could be "powerfully injected" into rural boys. They all replied, "No!" They explained that the farm boy did not need Boy Scouting, could not afford it, and was already being better served by such organizations as the Lone Scouts and the 4-H Club. Dr. Galpin pointed out that existing rural youth organizations had broad popular and governmental support and totaled between three and four hundred thousand members. Farm parents appreciated the low cost of these programs, their emphasis on farming methods, and the fact that they kept boys under parents' super-vision instead of turning them over to "strangers." Galpin concluded that any effort to challenge rural organizations with traditional Boy Scout-ing would end in certain failure.[15]

In 1926, the BSA national office hired O. H. Benson, the influential rural educator and father of the 4-H movement, to direct a new Depart-ment of Rural Scouting. Benson sought additional input from the U.S. Department of Agriculture, farm journals, the Grange, rural schools, the 4-H Club, and other agencies in his efforts to bring Boy Scouting to rural boys. Benson interviewed over four hundred boys on why they had chosen to be Lone Scouts instead of regular Boy Scouts. Some rural boys, as expected, stated that there were not enough other boys around to make a regular Boy Scout troop. Benson's farmhouse-to-farmhouse survey along a typical Iowa road also found that some boys "had tried to join scout troops but had given up the idea because of parental objections, transportation reasons during the winter, and work and chores during the summer [Boy Scout camping] months." Furthermore, Benson's sur-vey revealed that many urban working-class, handicapped, and younger boys had joined Lone Scouting because they felt ostracized by the BSA's adult-led troops for adolescents. He reported that urban working-class boys who labored all day "have found it impossible to belong to scout troops and have therefore accepted lone scouting as their opportunity to become scouts." Physically handicapped Lone Scouts told Benson that they "can not without embarrassment undertake the work of a vigorous troop program and therefore naturally welcomed the lone scout method." Given strict BSA test requirements such as swimming and hiking profi-ciency, many physically handicapped Scouts could not earn First Class Boy Scout rank or pursue merit badges for which only advanced Scouts were eligible. A large number of eager boys under twelve also became

Lone Scouts, but some of these might have joined the BSA if they had been allowed. Unlike Scout officials in Great Britain and other countries, BSA national leaders refused for over a decade to start a Cub Scout program because they did not want to have to include women leaders and believed that preadolescents were the evolutionary equivalent of primitive Indians and therefore incapable of learning regular Scouting's modern manhood and participating citizenship.[16]

These men and other consultants concluded that Boyce and Morgan's individualistic, primitive, Indian-lore-based character ideals and training methods effectively reached rural and other marginalized boys whom modern troop Boy Scouting had failed to recruit in large numbers. They argued that officials had a duty to study Boyce's methods and create alternative policies to help these groups find a home in the BSA. Despite these glaring reports, BSA national leaders claimed in a 1927 issue of the *Scout Executive* that they had discovered that rural boys did not need a different type of program like Boyce's old Lone Scouting but rather regular BSA troop Scouting on a smaller scale. The author argued that the BSA had met the LSA halfway by adding twelve more farm merit badges that year. The BSA had offered farm merit badges since 1911 with little success, so administrators probably knew that creating more of them without changing the basic Scout requirements, troop format, and modern character and civic emphases would not attract many rural boys. The farm merit badges remained relatively unpopular.[17]

BSA national administrators worked diligently in the late 1920s to force Lone Scouting into the Boy Scout mold by increasing adult supervision, de-emphasizing individualism and Indian lore, and encouraging Lone Scouts to form troops and participate in BSA Local Council activities. BSA leaders eliminated the distinctive Lone Scout Indian-lore degree programs and tacked their names onto regular Boy Scout rank tests. They made Lone Scouts adopt the BSA Oath and Laws and its more expensive handbook. The BSA raised Lone Scout membership fees from a small one-time outlay to fifty cents annually. The LSA had allowed males of all ages to be regular members and had quite a few active men in their twenties and thirties when the BSA took over. BSA administrators suggested that older Lone Scouts become Tribe Chiefs or Guides. The BSA removed boys under twelve, who had constituted almost a third of Lone Scouting's membership. By 1929, the BSA national Constitution had been amended to prevent giving an official charter to a small rural Farm or Home Patrol. Although it allowed such Patrols of two to eight boys to form, headquarters required them to have an adult Scoutmaster and to agree to merge with other Patrols to form a proper troop as soon as it was possible.[18]

The change that most upset veteran Lone Scouts, however, was the diminution of authority and independence granted to regular members. BSA Chief Scout Executive James West correctly identified that the major problem with the merger was that the Lone Scout boys were used to "self-government": the "essence of the Lone Scout plan is the boy absolutely on his own resources—'of boys, for boys and by boys.' The essence of the Boy Scouts of America plan is in the provision and requirement of responsible *adult male leadership*." National policy bulletins distributed to BSA Local Council Executives acknowledged that many Lone Scout journalists and boy leaders resisted the merger because they feared that their voice in running the organization would be taken away, especially with the discontinuance of member-led rallies and the *Lone Scout* magazine and local newsletters that depended heavily on readers' contributions. BSA national administrators insisted that Local Council Executives move to take full control of Lone Scouts and rural Scouting as soon as was practical. The BSA's sympathetic Lone Scout Chief Totem Armstrong Perry resigned in January 1926, insisting that Lone Scout members should "kick" if they felt they were being treated unjustly in the takeover by BSA leaders, "who are not quite ready to let you go ahead unsupervised as you did before the merger."[19]

Despite these private acknowledgments to Local Council Executives, BSA sources claimed to members that Lone Scouting still operated through "self-government" after the takeover. A Grand Council, featuring elected representatives from different geographical regions of the country, had guided Boyce's Lone Scout organization. After the merger, the BSA national office moved all Lone Scouts into Region Thirteen, which consisted of boy members in America's territories and in foreign countries. Thus, the BSA reinforced the idea that rural manhood was outside the American norm, literally placing Lone Scouts beyond the bounds of the nation with noncitizens and citizens abroad. BSA national administrators appointed their own adult representative for this "region," claiming that it was too far for any actual members of these groups to communicate with or travel to. The national office's Region Thirteen representative also served as the new Chairman of the Lone Scout Grand Council. All Lone Scout business and official actions had to be originated by him, whereas in Boyce's program the Lone Scouts whom members elected to the Grand Council had the power to originate motions. Elected Lone Scout boy officers could make suggestions for consideration under the BSA, but it was up to the Chairman whether or not to place a suggestion on the agenda for discussion. In other words, the Lone Scouts' Grand Council went from being run by democratically elected boys and young men to being controlled by an adult appointed by the BSA national office. Administrators also tried to commandeer local Lone Scout publications by deciding which ones to officially endorse.

The BSA was not nearly as successful as Boyce and Morgan had been at recruiting or retaining rural and other boys marginalized by modernization. After transferring some boys to troops and eliminating men, boys under twelve, and the "deadwood" who no longer appeared active, the BSA's Department of Rural Scouting tallied 68,756 Lone Scouts at the end of 1927. Despite expanding their efforts to engage rural boys, the BSA reported that only 14,361 registered Lone Scouts remained in 1928. Many Lone Scouts resented the program changes enough to quit. Significantly, many former LSA members continued their advancement programs and communication with one another outside the purview of the BSA. The Elbeetian Legion and the Lone Indian Fellowship formed to maintain traditional Lone Scouting masculine virtues, bonds, and publications. By 1930, there may have been more active rogue Lone Scouts than official BSA Lone Scouts. Some Lone Scouts have maintained their relationships and connection to the LSA for over eighty years; veteran members set up a museum dedicated to Lone Scout activities, newspapers, and memorabilia in North Carolina, while some still write letters and hold reunions to this day.[20]

THE BSA'S FAILED ATTEMPT to transform the Lone Scouts suggests that extreme self-reliance and Indian primitivism appealed to boys on the margins of American society but was increasingly at odds with modern, dominant manhood. It is difficult to understand how BSA national leaders could have assumed that these changes would increase rural membership, since the BSA Pioneers—a program that was very similar to what Lone Scouting became under the BSA—had barely topped one thousand members during its decade of existence. In spite of BSA administrators' claims to be working to expand rural recruitment, the changes they made to Lone Scouting in the late 1920s suggested that some officials continued to hold a deprecatory view of rural manhood and paid little real attention to rural boys' character needs. Early BSA national leaders seemed to pigeonhole farm boys into a domestic role—similar to that which they envisioned for girls and, by 1930, for preadolescent Cub Scouts. The BSA's version of Lone Scouting emphasized rural boys' home duties and orientation: "The Lone Scout Program is a very distinct family circle program of Scouting. . . . Lone Scouting is a distinct 'Back-to-the-home' movement, where boys who become Scouts are from the beginning encouraged in every way to 'hike back home' with Scouting and all of its benefits and through the home to build a better and finer Scout community." BSA national leaders prodded town and urban adolescent boys to leave the feminized, sentimental home behind to better learn advanced character for urban-industrial careers and modern civic engagement, but they argued that Lone Scouts, Cub Scouts, and girls (whom they hoped would join the domestic-oriented Camp Fire Girls rather than the feminist Girl Scouts) should stay in or return to the home. Such statements may have been an effort to alleviate rural parents' expressed concern that Boy Scout troops would undercut parental authority, although it was painfully at odds with most BSA pronouncements about home life. Encouraging rural Scouts to stay on the family farm recalled the country-life movement championed by Liberty Hyde Bailey, which romanticized farm life to bolster rural populations, but this left rural boys out of step with both a modernizing society and regular Boy Scout training in full-orbed manhood and leading citizenship. While the "backward" influence of rural living also entered BSA administrators' discussions about the role of African Americans in Scouting, white officials' concerns about deficiencies in African American males' character and civic capacities also came to the fore.[21]

7

The Right Sort of Colored Boy and Man

African American Scouting

Among the groups of males that helped BSA national leaders formulate and enact their vision of modern manhood in the 1910s and early 1920s, the stereotyped African American boy encapsulated a negative mirror image of the proper character and work ethic of the Boy Scout. American Scout literature depicted leading white boys distancing themselves from the home to learn men's work skills and serve the broader community, but the lazy African American boy in the 1921 *Boys' Life* sketch in Figure 7.1 still required his mother's prodding to work. The mother criticizes Robertson Crusoe Jones for not showing initiative or a sense of obligation to do consistent work. Instead, the oversleeping boy appears content to put off his responsibilities and let others do the work while he just eats, plays, and sleeps. It went without saying that such a boy would be incapable of responsible voting or political office holding if he did not change his ways when he grew up. The characterization of African American boys in this sketch typified a range of other early BSA images, blackface performances, and jokes—and was also linked to Local Councils' exclusion of most African Americans boys from Scouting in the 1910s and their subsequent placement in segregated troops with restricted privileges in the late 1920s.[1]

Despite some disparaging BSA stereotypes and the slow establishment of African Americans troops, some members of this population grasped the opportunity to Scout because it offered more hope for status than did many other available avenues in a modernizing society. By the late 1800s, white Southerners had instituted an effective new method of racial repression based on African American disfranchisement, antimiscegenation laws, segregated schools and neighborhoods, extralegal lynching, and forced labor though vagrancy laws. Many African American men did not have access to the advanced schooling, voting rights, and modern scientific or management jobs needed to acquire mainstream masculine status and privileges. Instead, many southern African American males faced a lifetime of poverty through cotton sharecropping or poorly paid manual-labor jobs. The nation's increas-

"LIS'N' Robertson Crusoe
Jones—
Ah's sumpin ter aks
yo' 'bout—
When yo' goner shake yose'f,
An' clean 'at hen-house out?
Does yo' fink all
yo' has ter do
Is eat, an' sleep,
an' play?
Well, Ah'll havter
get er doc-
tor,
Ef yo' 'magin's
that-a-way.
Kase mah min'
tells me,
Missis Jones,
'At li'l boy ob
your'n,
Is got er lot ob
fings ter do,
Jus' es sho's
yo' born.
He! Wha's 'at
you's mum-
lin'?
'At hen-house slipped yo' min',
But yer reckon, long's it mus' be did,
Termorrer's plenty time!

Figure 7.1 A wake-up call from mother. "Robertson Crusoe Jones," *Boys' Life*, August 1921, 7. (Courtesy of Boy Scouts of America National Scouting Museum Archival Collection)

ingly segregated cities did create a small window for African American men to move into professions like church leadership, medicine, and law, or even run their own small businesses, such as grocery stores and barber shops—though their clientele consisted primarily of poor African Americans. Some African Americans invested hope in working to gain respect through white-led institutions like the military and the Boy Scouts of America, which at least offered the potential that all American males could partake in the same ideal of manhood and civic leadership.

Recent histories of early Boy Scouting and Girl Guiding in Africa, India, and Syria suggest that African Americans who became official BSA members or formed independent Scout troops may have seen it as a vital path to asserting minority rights and pursuing opportunities in America's system of racial hierarchy. Early white British Scout officials hoped that the program would mitigate some of the detribalizing and individualizing effects of the colonial education and industrial system while teaching African Scouts to become efficient and loyal functionaries of the empire. However, African Scouts, independent troops, and individual Scout impostors seized upon the status membership granted and the Fourth Law's statement that a Scout is a brother to every other Scout to assert their rights and challenge the legitimacy of European colonization. White South African Scout and Guide officials initially refused requests for membership from nonwhite Africans, Indian settlers, and "Cape Coloureds," but fear of their autonomy and the growing Scout and Guide rhetoric of peaceful internationalism in the 1920s gradually pushed white officials to federate these groups as unequal partners in 1936. African Scouts and Guides associated themselves with modern progress and Western education to meet their own needs and to take advantage of opportunities for status and material privileges within the growing apartheid system. Even segregated and subordinated Scouting and Guiding offered racial minorities hope and a gradual path toward political and cultural status in the early 1900s.[2]

While skin color formed an important male membership and character divide in the early BSA, its leaders gradually moved toward more inclusive policies for and optimistic characterizations of African American males by the late 1920s. From 1910 to 1924, white BSA officials and boy members deployed backward, lazy, carefree, and untrustworthy African American stereotypes in jokes, published sketches, songs, leader training sessions, and theatrical performances that highlighted character flaws that good Scouts scrupulously avoided if they wanted to succeed in a modernizing society. The visibility of such BSA stereotypes in the available historical record declined but did not completely disappear in the late 1920s. Two stages of BSA national policies concerning African American members paralleled the racial hierarchy embedded in Scout foil imagery and the organization's vision of modern manhood. From 1910 to 1924, BSA administrators quietly allowed each of the several hundred Local Councils the democratic right of "self-determination" to decide whether and how to include African American boys. While few Local Councils in the rural

South allowed African Americans to join the organization, Local Councils in other regions enrolled almost five thousand African American Scouts by 1925. A few controversial white southern BSA officials helped initiate the second major African American Scouting phase that year when they applied for a grant from a Rockefeller family foundation. The resulting creation of the BSA's Inter-Racial Service marked a significant shift in recruitment methods, but some of the policies it advised for African American Scouts still hinted that they might possess suspect character and civic capacity. The Inter-Racial Service actively encouraged local southern councils to experiment with segregated African American troops, which emphasized a narrower set of masculine skills than did regular Scouting and whose access to key Scout privileges—such as uniforms, camps, rank and badge advancement, and public service leadership—could be withheld. This BSA method was more inclusive of people of African descent than was British-led Scouting in areas like South Africa, but it fell short of the more active welcome the BSA extended to light-skinned European immigrants and those of different religious faiths in the 1910s. Many African Americans still worked to overcome obstacles to Scouting because they associated it—even in segregated troops without full privileges—with men's equality and independence. Restrictions placed on their advancement and privileges placed them in Second Class Scout membership and manhood, but the increasing number of African American Boy Scouts and Scoutmasters in the late 1920s represented a modest improvement in their public stature.[3]

Scout Foils, 1910–1924

Early white BSA staff and members at various levels of the organization invoked common cultural stereotypes to suggest that African American boys possessed inferior masculine character and to warn members against behaviors that were anathema to Scouting's modern manhood. Boy Scouts' and national and local officials' deployment of these figures (who, along with the backward farmer, the hobo, and the working-class-immigrant tough, might be referred to as "Scout foils") cast African American males as unfit for leadership and power in a modern economic and political system. Early BSA publications and national leaders offered no positive, identifiable images, such as African American intellectual leaders, civil rights activists, or the brave Zulu scout warrior in Baden-Powell's original British Scout manual. Despite the era's massive migration of African Americans to northeastern and midwestern cities for factory jobs and military service, BSA sources usually characterized African American males as backward rural dwellers who had heavy southern accents. Boy and adult members across the country parodied African American manhood in jokes, sketches, poems, fiction, songs, and minstrel shows. The use of African American blackface characters in skits and songs at Boy Scout camps and meetings did not reveal a yearning for a carefree, preindustrial past. Instead, blackface performance and other stereotyped literary and verbal forms enabled BSA leaders to caution boy members about the pitfalls of not developing the values and skills essential for success in America's corporate-industrial, urban mainstream.[4]

The deployment of African American foils in jokes could be found anywhere from the organization's highest echelon of administrative training conferences to some local troops' camp sessions and weekly meetings. Some Scout leaders and supporters began speeches with jokes about stereotyped African American men who were stupid or cowardly. At the first BSA National Training Conference for Local Council Executives in 1920, guest speaker Dr. Herman H. Horne (a prominent author and New York University professor of philosophy and education) told a joke about a fight between an African American boy and a white boy. The white boy won both the physical contest and the exchange of verbal insults. Unable to keep up with the big names the white boy called him, the African American boy exclaimed, "O! dem der t'ings you call me you is 'em." The large white audience laughed, as they did at an earlier speaker's joke: when a judge instructed an African American defendant that he had sixty minutes to get out of town, the African American man replied, "Judge, I hand you back fifty nine." While the BSA's modern manhood and civic ideals valued efficiency and obedience to authority, the defendant's response instead hinted at his poor character.[5]

The few prominent images of black boys (besides "savage" Africans in safari tales) that could be found by this researcher in BSA national publications from 1910 to the mid-1920s informed readers that being industrious and thrifty would be rewarded, while suggesting that African Americans were too lazy and lacking in self-reliance and thrift to become good Scouts, good workers, or good men. The "Pickaninny" sketch and accompanying caption in the 1919 BSA Annual Report to Congress, for example, explained that this African American boy was unprepared for a good career opportunity and would fall into any job he was offered. The barefoot Pickaninny, wearing ragged clothes and swinging from a tree, seems not to have evolved very far from his "monkey ancestors." BSA publications frequently depicted white Scouts learning the organization's key motto to "Be Prepared" while scientifically conserving natural resources and camping and hiking efficiently, but the rural Pickaninny ironically seemed lost outdoors. His lack of self-control and forethought might later leave him unemployed and dependent on charity, swallowed up by the depicted river alligator representing modern work and life's struggle for the survival of the fittest. The sketch's caption warned that Scouts had to make a conscious choice to either select and pursue a good career, or be like the Pickaninny and fall into a dead-end job if they failed to plan ahead, set goals, and acquire the necessary training for better positions. This image ignored African American males' lack of access to quality schooling and better jobs and unions, which most white Scouts could take for granted.[6]

The rare African American character in published BSA fiction, such as the 1917 *Boys' Life* story of "Smokey the nigger," buttressed the notion that African American males were natural servants or lackeys to white males. BSA fiction frequently cast white boys as heroic Scouts, but primarily depicted black males in safari fiction as savage Africans or guides for white explorers. Smokey the African American newspaper boy shared a big-city tenement dwelling with a white orphan newspaper boy named Jimmy, a drunken janitor, an Italian organ-grinder, and a monkey. Their urban basement abode seemed to exacerbate the faulty work ethic and poor substitute parenting skills of the organ-grinder and the drunken janitor, so Smokey and Jimmy fled to the fresh air and health of the Adirondack Mountains to recover from a city-borne illness. A local Scout troop included Jimmy as a full member but made Smokey the troop mascot. This linked African American boys to the animal totems or boys under twelve who served as real Scout troop mascots in this era. Smokey, who appreciated simply being part of the white troop, seemed blissfully unaware of his inferior status: "I'se just a li'l nigger, sir, but de all's a moughty good bunch and de don't mek no difference 'cause I ain't white." Smokey's inclusion in a subordinated fashion in which he did not have access to Scouting's prized uniform, rank and merit badge advancement, and prestige foreshadowed the restricted ways in which African American boys in the South would be admitted to the BSA in the late 1920s.[7]

White Boy Scouts asserted their own superior status and recruited members and funding support by parodying African American males

during minstrel shows and the singing of black spirituals. Such performances, which were common white American forms of popular entertainment in this era, helped distance Boy Scouting's use of the outdoors
to develop modern work and character values from the lazy and carefree rural lifestyle of African American characters. Boy Scout minstrel
shows consisted of skits that sometimes stereotyped African American
males as ignorant, superstitious, and lacking a productive work ethic.
Guided by advice from BSA national magazine articles with titles such
as "African American Faces Make Green Backs," a number of councils
and troops used minstrel shows as public fund-raisers and recruitment
events. Some Boy Scouts and their leaders also sang African American
spirituals and work songs. The lyrics of the particular songs white Scouts
chose tended to reinforce the belief that African Americans were primarily fit for manual farm labor and were happy with their subordinate
position in society. Published BSA song books categorized "Negro songs"
like "Massa's in the Cold, Cold, Ground" and the docile and humble "Old
Black Joe" as "Old Quiet Songs" that were best used when "the Fire Burns
Low." Another favorite declared, "Carry me back to Old Virginny. . . .
There's where I labored so long for old master, Day after day in that
field of yellow corn; No place on earth do I love more sincerely." The
days of yearning for the preindustrial life, though, had passed; being
undisciplined and carefree—like the African Americans depicted in BSA
skits, sketches, and jokes—was no longer a positive or even an ambivalent
character or work attribute for modern American men. The stereotyped
rural African American male thus served as a cautionary tale for good
Scouts from 1910 to at least the mid-1920s. These negative BSA images
of African Americans, though, became less harsh and more difficult to
locate in the historical record of the late 1920s. Not coincidentally, this
era witnessed a significant shift in African American Scout membership
policies and recruitment efforts.[8]

"Fundamental Virtues" for African American Scout Troops, 1925–1929

In spite of BSA national leaders' public claims to be open to all boys, early
administrators initially maintained restrictive membership policies that
reflected the Scout foil imagery and its presumption that African
American males possessed inferior character. In one of its earliest major
decisions on race and membership in 1910, the BSA Executive Board

determined—but did not broadly publicize—that Local Councils could decide whether or how to admit African American boys and Scoutmasters, and that the national office would not charter African American troops in areas not governed by a Local Council. The national office justified the exclusion of African American males with the democratic principle of Local Council self-government, or "self-determination" on "local matters." While local autonomy on race policies represented a better possibility than in many white institutions in this era, relatively few local Scout councils in the 1910s and early 1920s encouraged African American boys to join. The Executive Board resolution's second clause may have had an even greater effect in the 1910s, when many areas (especially in the rural South) were not yet under local Scout council jurisdiction. Very few African American troops existed in the southeastern United States, where the majority of African Americans still lived in 1920. Northern and midwestern Scout councils allowed some scattered African American troops, but they generally segregated them from white Scouts. Councils that admitted African American boys sometimes denied them full membership, such as not allowing them to wear the official uniform. Neither the participation of African American soldiers in the Great War for democracy nor the early stage of the Great Migration of African Americans from the rural South to northern and midwestern cities for industrial jobs had significant effects; BSA administrators refused to make any substantial changes to policies or recruitment methods for African Americans through 1924. In the second half of the 1920s, however, a few exceptional white southern Scout officials would draw BSA national leaders into a cautious plan to recruit southern African American boys for a simplified and segregated version of Scouting, which would train them to be dutiful laborers and loyal to the nation rather than economic and political leaders like regular Scouts.[9]

In his January 1925 letter requesting funding for this vision from the Laura Spelman Rockefeller Memorial (LSRM), a white investment banker and founder of the local Memphis BSA council named Bolton Smith argued that the strictly segregated Scouting plan being used by the Louisville, Kentucky, council since 1916 "is a good illustration of what can be done" in "helping to develop the right sort of colored boy and man." His proposal emphasized white concerns, like public safety, social order, and racial purity. Smith claimed that letting African American boys join Scouting in segregated units, if it could be done gradually and voluntarily by local white southern officials, was the best way to improve the tense relations between the races in American society. He stated that the differences between African Americans and whites were so great that there would be little intermarriage or "mingling of blood" for generations. Smith argued that while he eventually hoped for "at least potential equality and definite sympathy and kindliness of attitude," considerable segregation was advisable under present conditions. He speculated that other southern councils might be persuaded to copy the Louisville model if the right white man gently persuaded local leaders to quietly start one or two African American troops. Smith recommended Stanley Harris, the white BSA Assistant National Field Director for Southeastern Region Five since 1917, who (alone) had argued at the first National Training Conference for Scout Executives in 1920 that all African American boys had a *right* to Scout. Smith suggested that having African American boys in Scout uniforms would prompt white Southerners to give them a modicum of respect and be kinder to them, just as African American soldiers' uniforms had done in World War I. Furthermore, he stated that African American Scouting "will perhaps keep a larger number of negroes in the south. Besides, the negro Scout will rarely, if ever, be guilty of any of those acts which bring about racial conflict." Smith concluded, "The Boy Scout movement seems to me to be the most effective method by which contact between the negro and white ideals of civilized conduct can be established."[10]

LSRM representatives questioned BSA officials on how—and even if—African American boys should be included in the organization. Leonard Outhwaite asked Stanley Harris in February 1925 whether it would be better to have an independent Scout-like organization for African American boys, with a different name, uniform, and program. Harris replied that BSA national leaders had considered that idea but felt that it was inadvisable, since some African American leaders would criticize it as racial discrimination. Harris added that there were already thousands of African American Scouts (outside the South) and that the BSA had worked hard in the past to eliminate independent Scout organizations so that it could control the quality of American Scout programming. LSRM official Beardsley Ruml pressed Bolton Smith on how African American intellectual leaders might respond to segregated BSA troops, and whether they should be consulted. Smith replied in March that African American leaders' criticisms might be avoided if the recruitment plan was superficially extended to include other regions of the country and other minority groups: "It seems to me we had better call the proposed service one to be rendered to 'under privileged boys.' In my region there are the Arcadian or French families . . . which require special effort to become interested in Scouting for their boys . . . though the underprivileged boys we have in mind are the negro boys above all as presenting a more serious problem than any other boys." Smith's idea blurred the line between two distinct recruitment issues: those socioeconomic groups, such as the rural French Arcadians, who were underrepresented in the BSA because they were not interested in joining, and those groups, such as African Americans, who were clamoring to be admitted but were often being excluded. Outhwaite solicited the opinions of several leading race and education experts before finally approving funding. The LSRM awarded the BSA a $40,000 grant (approximately $500,000 in 2015 terms) to use between 1926 and 1928 to start an Inter-Racial Service (IRS) that would encourage Local Councils to recruit African American boys into segregated BSA troops.[11]

Smith, Harris, and the generous Rockefeller grant offer convinced the rest of the BSA Executive Board to start the IRS, but the plan was less far-fetched in 1926 than it had been in the 1910s, when such ideas had first been quietly discussed. Harris, who would become the first director of the IRS, pointed out to Outhwaite that the time was ripe for expanding African American Scout recruitment because of the good feelings after the resolution of the Great War and the waning of the second Ku Klux Klan. By 1925, postwar race and labor tensions had eased some. New immigration restriction laws slowed the flow of immigrants from Asia and southern and eastern Europe. The immediate shock of the Great Migration of African Americans to midwestern and northern cities had passed. The social scientific theory championed by anthropologist Franz Boas and sociologist Robert Park—that character and behavior were influenced by environment and culture rather than just innate racial biology—had gained ground. The economy was thriving, and Republicans dominated the White House with pro-business agendas. International and domestic peace and prosperity had become the order of the day.[12]

Stanley Harris based the IRS's resulting "Louisville Plan" on the lessons he drew from his March 1925 study of the Louisville Scout Council's methods. He concluded that African American Scouting should be started voluntarily, slowly, and with no publicity. Interested councils should begin with only one or two African American troops to demonstrate that they could be successful before trying to expand. African

American boys should be in segregated troops with African American leaders. They should have completely separate meetings, Courts of Honor, camps, and training sessions: "The activities of the colored department parallel those of the white but are kept distinctly separate ... to avoid any possible clash between white and colored scouts." In addition, a separate African American Scout headquarters should be established in the African American area of town, since they might be "reluctant" to visit the white council office. IRS staff told Local Council leaders that it was essential to enlist good institutional sponsors, usually African American churches. A white or an African American man could be the immediate supervisor of African American Scouting, serving as a special assistant to the white Local Council Executive. White council leaders should select cooperative African American men for an advisory council, but final authority on African American Scouting would rest with the white Executive and the white Local Council.[13]

Despite BSA administrators' reports that African American Scouts in Louisville excelled in recruitment rates, advancement, community support, Good Turns, patriotism, and reducing Scoutmaster turnover, IRS staffers emphasized that African American boys should Scout in order to train them to be loyal and efficient laborers, reduce juvenile delinquency, and curtail southern sanitation and disease problems. White IRS men suggested that African American boys' training should particularly stress the Scout Laws on being trustworthy, loyal, courteous, obedient, cheerful, and clean. White national Scout leaders rarely spoke of African American boys developing bravery, reverence, self-reliance, or leadership. Harris happily reported to the Inter-Racial Committee in 1927 that the African American boy who Scouted was very much improved "as a laborer. He is more industrious, more courteous, and generally more efficient." He added that teaching African American Scouts cleanliness and sanitation would help solve southern disease problems. The 1927 BSA Annual Report to Congress contained an IRS statement titled "Compelling Reasons for Pushing Forward," which emphasized Scouting's ability to transform African American boys from state liabilities to labor assets: "To be the most useful to his community, each individual must be taught the dignity of labor, the importance of industry and the obligation to do well each task he undertakes. [Scouting] seems ideal as an agent to supplement the school in giving the Negro youth these fundamental virtues." This plan paralleled the emphasis in many African American schools and colleges on preparing students for basic industrial and farm labor rather than advanced professions, business ownership, or political leadership. The 1928 Inter-Racial Service report explained that crime cost the nation $10 billion annually and that 85 percent of it was done by African Americans and immigrant Americans. Intriguingly, the author argued, "Students agree that these people are no more criminal in nature and intent than native-born whites and that the large amount of crime among them is due to environment and lack of moral training. Scouting does reduce crime and would undoubtedly improve the boy's surroundings." By suggesting that bad environment and parenting rather than biological inferiority caused delinquency, this statement represented a modest change from those made by BSA leaders in the 1910s. This recognized the possibility that African American boys' character could be improved through a structured development program led by trained Scout men in the outdoors.[14]

BSA national leaders strongly encouraged councils starting an African American troop to require their African American leader to undergo intensive training before granting him a Scoutmaster commission and troop charter, whereas administrators had never required white Scoutmasters to undergo formal training. BSA national leaders stated that it was difficult to find African American men with worthy character and a strong work ethic, so they had to be trained by white men before being ready to run a Scout troop. Bolton Smith argued in a 1928 letter to LSRM officials that the insufficient support and leadership provided by institutional sponsors for African American troops also made extensive training and ongoing supervision of African American Scoutmasters necessary: "Therefore, we must not only instruct these Scoutmasters but we must keep track of their work and patch it up where it fails." African American institutions such as churches and colleges had already demonstrated their eager and active support for Scout troops, so it remained unclear whether Smith doubted African American Scoutmasters' and institutional sponsors' ability to guide Scouting, or whether he exaggerated the situation to ensure approval for IRS efforts and the LSRM's continued financial support for promoting African American troops.[15]

The IRS began running segregated training schools for African American Scoutmasters in 1926 to meet the "deficit" in African American character and sponsorship, as well as to deflect white criticisms of the outreach program. As Figure 7.2 highlights, the Hampton Institute in Virginia and the Tuskegee Institute in Alabama hosted early African American Scoutmaster training sessions; other southern African American

Figure 7.2 African American Scoutmaster training course. *Scout Executive*, September 1927, 6. (Courtesy of Boy Scouts of America National Scouting Museum Archival Collection)

colleges soon followed suit. Since many attendees at these early training sessions were studying to be schoolteachers, educated, lower-middle-class African American men often led the early African American BSA troops. Some Local Councils ran their own African American Scoutmaster training sessions. The General Education Board—a philanthropy led by John D. Rockefeller Jr. that focused on improving schools and farming methods in the rural South—also actively supported African American Scoutmaster training and the expansion of African American troops. The General Education Board offered thirty-five Local Councils $500 each to help pay the salary of an administrator for new African American troops. Thirty-three of the councils eventually accepted. The General Education Board paid the expenses of African American teachers to attend Scoutmaster training if they had been nominated by officials at the state level. The policy of requiring African American Scoutmasters to undergo extensive training held at least through 1936.[16]

Finally, white IRS leaders suggested that a man needed less character to direct a Local Council's African American division than it took to direct white Scouting and the overall council. IRS Director Stanley Harris described R. M. Wheat, the white Louisville administrator in charge of African American Scouting, as "limited enough in ability to make his success in work with white boys very questionable, yet strong enough to be of undoubted service [in heading the African American Scout branch]. He is much too much a super-Scoutmaster to be a large executive under any conditions." Harris suggested that Wheat made a good leader for African American Scouting because he was a charismatic "boys' man," implying that Wheat was not enough of a "men's man" to be an effective Executive in charge of the overall council and white Scout men and boys. Harris, however, may have just been trying to preempt the potential criticism that having a good white man like Wheat direct the African American division came at the expense of white Louisville Scouts, who would not be able to benefit from Wheat's leadership. Harris added that African American Scouting in other councils could be directed by a trained African American man who possessed unusually high executive ability *for his race*. It went without saying that most white officials at the time deemed it inappropriate for African American men to direct white Scouting or the overall council.[17]

The creation of the IRS and its successful efforts to encourage southern councils to admit African Americans marked a significant step in national leaders' efforts to diversify the organization and a departure from the long-standing policy of passively allowing Local Councils to exclude African Americans from BSA membership. However, it differed from BSA national leaders' concessions to recruit more white southern and eastern European immigrants and working-class boys in the 1910s. The BSA allowed Catholic, orthodox Jewish, and Polish leaders to run exclusive troops, because some new white immigrants preferred to teach their sons Scouting's modern character and civic values while maintaining their traditional religious and cultural heritage. By joining such a troop or by being a member of one of the mixed-nationality troops, southern and eastern European immigrants moved toward inclusion in the American mainstream and dominant white manhood. African American leaders, on the other hand, were forced to undergo Scoutmaster training in order to run involuntarily segregated troops—often with restrictions on uniforms, camping, and other privileges. The higher echelons of Scout manhood and civic leadership remained closed to them in the 1920s. Although the IRS helped increase African American membership, its segregation plan shuffled African American boys into an inferior branch in which Scouting was a different experience than it was for most native-born white or light-skinned immigrant members. Given these limitations, one might wonder why African Americans persisted in joining the organization.

The Value of Second Class Scouting for African Americans

The fact that African American leaders named their Scout troops and divisions after heroes like Frederick Douglass and Crispus Attucks suggests that their work to overcome obstacles to Scouting should be viewed as an important part of African American males' long labors to achieve full manhood and citizenship rights. Since being a Boy Scout carried significant status in the eyes of the American public, government officials, and employers, even Scouting with restrictions represented a halfway step to demonstrating modern manhood and civic leadership that many African American boys and men eagerly grasped. The opportunity to sponsor approved Scout troops rallied key African American institutions, including churches, schools, and men's fraternities. For the most part, African Americans were able to control what was taught in their troops while also competing (at least in theory) on the same universal standards for rank and badge advancement as white Scouts did. African American Scouting in segregated troops appeared to be both gradual enough to suit cautious reformers and solid preparation for W. E. B. DuBois's "talented tenth" to lead the African American community. Those African Americans who achieved Scout membership encountered a surprising array of white responses as well as continued obstacles in the forms of public harassment; violent threats; high costs; and discrimination in pool, camp, uniform, and rank and merit badge advancement access. Despite its limitations, African American Scouting grew gradually in the South and around the country, becoming a source of masculine and civic pride for its members and sponsors.[18]

Three decades before the major push for racially integrating schools and public accommodations, African American Scouting served as a battleground for civil rights and equal access issues that not only pitted white and African American males against each other but also divided some white men from each other and from white boys. White Boy Scouts' responses at the local level to the growing number of African American Scouts around the country ranged from outright resistance to courageous support. There appeared to be some truth to the frequent claim made by southern Scout leaders that some white boys refused to admit African American boys. Other white boys, even in the South, facilitated African American inclusion by giving them uniforms or teaching them Scout skills. Some white Boy Scouts acted bravely to include new African American members, even stepping across racial segregation lines drawn by local adults. When the first group of African American Louisville Scouts earned the organization's highest boy rank of Eagle Scout in 1925, eleven local white Eagle Scouts came of their own accord to the African American Court of Honor ceremony to congratulate them and wish them well. In Mississippi, African American and white adults agreed that new African American Scouts should not be allowed to purchase or wear uniforms, but some local white Boy Scouts defied this decision by buying uniforms for them. Five white Miami Boy Scouts challenged their Local Council Executive in 1928 on why there were no African American troops, while white Atlanta Scouts offered to help organize African American troops.[19]

A well-trained African American Boy Scout wearing his uniform publicly and giving service to the community seemed threatening to some white males because he demonstrated his capacity for advanced character, thus undermining justifications for America's racialized hierarchy of manhood and citizenship. IRS Director Stanley Harris informed LSRM officials in 1927 that white adults with whom he had spoken who opposed

African American Scouting "admit they would like to keep the Negro down where they can control him and scout training and organization are detrimental to their keeping him down in the sense they want to treat him, as a brute." Local Ku Klux Klan chapters occasionally intervened against African American Scouting, particularly troop camping sessions. A Pennsylvania Klan group, for example, burned a cross and fired shots to break up an encampment of African American Scouts. The fact that African Americans persisted under the real threat of violent reprisal reveals how crucial they saw Boy Scouting for their status as modern men and full citizens.[20]

Even if a council admitted them, African American Boy Scouts still faced significant obstacles to advancing through the program and fully employing its privileges. The costs of Scouting and racial discrimination in access to swimming pools, camps, and Scout uniforms blocked many African Americans from opportunities for advancement, leadership, and adventure made available to most white members. Some local southern councils subsidized registration fees for African American troops, but this only reinforced the assumption that African American boys could not be self-reliant or thrifty. Few African Americans in the South had ready access to public or BSA swimming or camping facilities, making it difficult for them to participate fully in Scouting or pass rank and badge tests. The swimming test—for which the national office allowed no exemptions despite some local officials' requests—barred some African American Scouts from First Class and advanced ranks. IRS officials recognized this problem but did not suggest any exemptions or replacement tests to fix it. As late as the 1950s, discrimination surrounding swimming pool use prevented African American Scouts in areas such as Richmond, Virginia, from advancing. Segregated Scout camping or the outright exclusion of African American members from camps served as an additional barrier to their progress. Camp constituted the year's most intensive period of instruction for passing Scout tests and badges. Attendees had access to special instructors, often for the only time that year. Moreover, the entire Scout program was geared toward the summer camp apex. Not being allowed to camp or swim probably discouraged some African American boys from advancing or even wanting to join, although they rarely fared better at non-BSA white summer camps in this era.[21]

Some white males, especially in the South, resented African Americans attempting to wear the Scout uniform because of its strong association with leading citizenship and intimate brotherhood with other members. BSA teaching publications and training consistently instructed Scouts to recognize and salute any fellow Scout in uniform, so if and when African American boys and men could wear the uniform formed a pivotal concern. The IRS told Local Councils starting African American troops to withhold uniforms until local white residents approved. IRS Director Stanley Harris suggested in 1925 that Local Councils even delay the granting of African American troop charters until they were fully accepted by the white public. He explained that African American troops must understand that there would be no mixing of races and that they should not expect recognition from white Scouts. Local Council uniform policy varied, but most southern councils restricted African American members' access to uniforms in the 1920s and beyond. These conditions required many African American Scouts to submit to the stigma of inferiority carried by troop segregation and the lack of official charters and uniforms. The 1928 IRS annual report argued that withholding the uniform ensured the safety of African American boys, who would bear the brunt of any white opposition to their presence in Scouting. The report added that not allowing uniforms might encourage more African American boys to join, since most would be too poor to buy them if they were required. Administrators had made similar rhetorical claims about attracting working-class and European immigrant boys by not requiring them to have uniforms, but the flood of BSA publications and speeches on the centrality of the uniform to building manhood and troop camaraderie made it obvious that those lacking uniforms were inferior members or perhaps not real members at all.[22]

Pool, camp, and uniform discrimination thus hampered African American boys' progress to First Class and advanced ranks and their many privileges, literally marking them as Second Class Scouts. Since merit badges were typically reserved for First Class Scouts, if a boy did not have access to a swimming area then he could never advance beyond Second Class Rank to start on merit badges. Merit badges offered boys the chance to explore new areas of interest and develop special job skills and employment contacts and references. Advancement by merit and effort formed the crux and goal of Scouting, so boys who could not advance in rank or gain merit badges for their uniforms looked less capable of good character and leading citizenship. The ties among local and national elites, government agencies, and the BSA created many unique leadership opportunities for select Scouts, such as serving as the honor guard for the town mayor in a parade or even meeting the president of the United

States. Boy Scouts also competed in the 1920s for prestigious awards, scholarships at Ivy League and other colleges, and grand adventures, such as African safaris and Arctic expeditions. However, BSA leaders always gave these honors to highly decorated and uniformed Scouts. African American boys barred by pool and camp discrimination from advancing in Scout rank could rarely compete for such elite merit awards.

The combination of IRS staff efforts, cooperation by some white local officials and boys, and African Americans' determination to participate in the organization gradually expanded this version of Scouting for African Americans. Troops met particular resistance in the areas where the percentage of African American residents in the total population was greatest: Mississippi, South Carolina, and Georgia. Southern Illinois and Indiana, where the second Ku Klux Klan flourished in the 1920s, also opposed African American Scouting. By 1930, though, every southern state had at least one African American troop. If they had not already developed segregated Scouting, most Local Councils eventually fell in step with the Louisville Plan. While some northern and western African American boys joined integrated troops, local racial prejudice and the institutional sponsor requirement combined to segregate the majority of African American Scouts.[23]

IRS recruitment of southern African American Scouts constituted a brave and forward-looking effort in an era of rampant racial discrimination, but the ways in which African Americans were incorporated into the organization tended to reinforce their second-class status instead of directly challenging the BSA's racial hierarchy of manhood. Although the Depression facilitated somewhat greater awareness of the economic obstacles that African American boys faced, it created little change in BSA policies. In 1931, Chief Scout Executive James West upheld white Local Council leaders' right to exclude or segregate African American boys, claiming that it was impossible to do otherwise. Some local officials continued to restrict African American members' access to uniforms and camping. Some councils, even outside the South, racially segregated troops until the 1960s. Despite these obstacles, the number of African American members in the BSA increased to 100,000 by 1944. African American boys remained underrepresented in Scouting relative to their portion of the population, but the 1944 figure marked a major improvement. However, closing some African American schools after the Supreme

Court's 1954 *Brown v. Board of Education* decision undercut African American Scouting, since many of these schools had sponsored troops.[24]

THE STORY OF AFRICAN AMERICAN Scouting demonstrated that the BSA was much more than a leisure organization to occupy children in their free time; it is more apt to describe early Scouting as a new means of allocating power and privilege between and among generations and socioeconomic groups of males in an era in which most children were being removed from the realms of political engagement and production work. Scouting offered its full members real status, authority, and material benefits—both as teenagers and in their adult lives. White American and African American males actively pursued Scouting's many privileges: camps, pools, uniforms, new knowledge, adult-like training, and opportunities for job advancement and civic leadership status. The lack of access to some of these incentives may have slowed the growth of African American Scouting as effectively as did white resistance.

Epilogue

Scout Manhood and Citizenship in the Great Depression

One might expect the Great Depression to have derailed the BSA, but the organization managed to adapt and increase its membership while continuing to provide boys and men with a viable standard of masculine values and behavior for daily living. Financial shortfalls prompted cuts in staff pay, council expenses, and even uniform prices. Camping and Good Turns took on even greater significance during this period of economic deprivation. The Depression raised BSA officials' awareness that larger structural factors might be the cause of some boys' and men's poverty rather than a lack of innate character capacity. The Inter-Racial Service expanded its scope to partner with the federal government to bring Scout troops to Native American boarding schools in the early Depression. BSA leaders debated ideas for new outreach efforts to "White Nationality" groups, but they ultimately decided not to deviate from the standard program and policies for light-skinned urban immigrant groups, whom they already considered sufficiently within the American mainstream. Scouting's modern character and participating civic leadership norms persisted and were held in high esteem by many members and supporters. Moreover, the continued tight affinity between government officials and Scouting during the Depression may help illuminate some of the controversies that have surrounded the BSA in recent decades.

Given the organization's reliance on voluntary contributions from donors and discretionary spending of members and parents, the precipitous decline of national wages and investment values during the Great Depression created difficulties for BSA funding and staffing. Council budgets dwindled as Community Chest drives and other donations decreased. The national office's staff had to be reduced, and remaining personnel took pay cuts in 1932. BSA regional and local offices adopted similar cutbacks in staff and expenditures, especially since many Local Councils had engaged in deficit spending in the second half of the 1920s. An average of two councils disbanded in each state, with some regions losing nearly half their councils. Stronger councils, however, tried to pick up the abandoned areas. Some troops lost their meeting place as schools and community centers closed or limited their hours. A number of Scoutmasters lost their jobs and moved in search of work, leaving some troops leaderless. On the bright side, some college students and fathers who were out of work had more time to volunteer for Scouting. Troop leadership helped uphold these men's masculine identity and civic status during the economic chaos of the 1930s. Shortages of male Scoutmasters in the Depression also helped ease women's entry into BSA leadership via the new Cub program for boys under the age of twelve. Den Mothers could officially register in 1936, and headquarters published a handbook for them in 1937. Some councils set up leader training sessions, which Scout husbands and Cub wives attended together. Even with reduced budgets and staff, the number of total BSA members increased from 834,000 in 1929 to over 1,000,000 in 1935 and 1,358,000 in 1939 (though 200,000 of the latter figure were Cubs).[1]

Economic turmoil helped highlight two key components of the BSA's traditional character and civic training: Good Turns and camping. In response to President Franklin D. Roosevelt's special radio address urging Boy Scouts to help in the national emergency, BSA members across the country provided a wide range of Good Turn services that garnered momentum and support for the organization. One of these services involved acting as messengers and gathering data for social workers and relief agencies. San Diego Scouts, for example, distributed thirty thousand forms in 1931 to prospective employers who might have odd jobs available. Boy Scouts around the country collected nearly two million clothing, food, and household items. Such community services reinforced the belief that Boy Scouts were the leaders of the future. The Depression also provided a boost to Scout camping. Camps sometimes offered better and cheaper food and shelter than did the outside world, so many parents were glad to send their sons. Over twenty-seven thousand Scouts from around the country attended the first National Scout Jamboree in 1937, camping for ten days in the shadow of the Washington Monument in the nation's capital. The quadrennial encampment would become a highlight of many members' Scouting careers. In 1938, oil tycoon Waite Phillips donated thirty-five thousand acres in New Mexico, which was eventually developed into Philmont Scout Ranch, the BSA's first national high adventure camp. Today, it serves as the apex of Scout camping and outdoor lore.[2]

Building on the policies and momentum of encouraging local southern councils to allow African American troops, the BSA's Inter-Racial Service partnered with the federal government's Indian Bureau beginning in 1929 to establish Scout troops at Native American boarding schools. The BSA national office and the federal Indian Bureau believed Native American boys had a natural affinity toward Scouting and its outdoor program, but ultimately hoped that the program would mainstream and modernize Native American boys in line with the boarding schools' curriculum and goals. The initiative achieved rapid growth in the number of Native American Boy Scout troops, rising from about five to forty in the first year of concentrated effort, along with another four hundred or so Native American boys in "mixed" race troops. The number of Native American reservation troops climbed to 150 by 1932, which very possibly could have made Native American boys overrepresented in Boy Scout membership relative to their portion of America's population. New Indian Bureau head John Collier's efforts to shift Native American children to mixed-race public schools and engage more with white communities beginning in 1933, however, decreased the number of Native American boarding schools and therefore their Scout troops.[3]

BSA officials continued to debate the respective influence of biological inheritance and cultural environment on boy character development in the 1930s. A special BSA Commission on Inter-Racial Activities' report to Local Council Executives at their 1936 National Training Conference demonstrated that the Depression had made the organization's leaders more aware of the obstacles to Scout participation faced by nonwhites, immigrants, and poor boys—but few changes in national standards or membership policies resulted. This commission's division into three subcommittees revealed BSA administrators' masculine worldview: White Nationality Groups; Indians, Mexicans, Japanese, and Chinese; and Negro Work. Weaver Marr, the Atlanta council Executive who chaired the subsection on Negro Work, argued that while Scouting had a special responsibility in times of economic depression to help African American boys who faced prejudice and real restrictions in life opportunities, "local conditions and attitudes continue to be the determining factors in the method of promoting the Scout Program. Local custom shall determine the extent to which activities shall be [racially] separate." The subcommittee also recommended adhering to the requirement that African American Scoutmasters undergo extensive training before receiving their troop commissions.[4]

In the 1936 conference's discussion sessions, however, some Local Council leaders disagreed with these policy recommendations. Linn C. Drake of Washington, D.C., argued against Local Council autonomy on race issues, since "it certainly is not their province to refuse to recognize that there is a problem." In the large city councils' discussion session, Mr. Green stated that he would only vote for requiring African American Scoutmasters to take training courses if the resolution was changed to include men of all races. The Executives in the discussion session for councils that had both rural and urban boy membership voted to reject requiring only African American Scoutmasters to undergo formal training, but the existing national race policies were upheld.[5]

Harry K. Eby, the Chicago council Assistant Executive who chaired the commission's subcommittee on White Nationality Groups, stressed in his report at the 1936 Executives' conference that although the United States had been built on immigration and different cultural groups merged into American society, Scouting was still not readily available to new white immigrants. He stated that most of the new white immigrant Scouts belonged to "mixed" community or Rotary-sponsored charity troops, but he suggested that each white nationality group be encouraged to run more of its own troops. This subcommittee recommended that work with white immigrants should proceed similarly to rural boy outreach efforts but be distinctly separate from Inter-Racial work, since "they are not distinct races. They are people of the white race, whose ancestry is traceable to other nations." This statement demonstrated that the BSA's twenty-five years of efforts to bring southern and eastern European immigrants into the white mainstream had made tangible gains. In their discussion sections, though, local Executives expressed continued division on such issues as whether or not to translate informational pamphlets on Scouting into foreign languages to ease the fears of immigrant parents. Some leaders' desire to downplay social divisions and encourage the use of the English language prevented adoption of Eby's special outreach suggestions.[6]

The Depression prompted a few minor adjustments in the BSA's class-based policies, but continued belief in the importance of self-reliance, thrift, and voluntary service for training boy members in modern manhood and practical citizenship limited the changes most officials were willing to make. The national office finally reduced the price of the uniform to ease costs for members. Some troops eliminated the uniform requirement and weekly dues. Scattered evidence suggests that financial shortfalls in the Depression may have prompted a few Local Councils to racially integrate Scout camps or administration to save money. Local Scout leaders and institutional officials gradually increased the number of troops in reform schools, handicapped institutions, and working-class Boys' Clubs. BSA leaders attempted to start more troops in destitute areas, but sociological studies found that the majority of Scouts still came from better-off socioeconomic groups. Some local leaders suggested that the Second Class rank requirement to deposit a dollar in a bank account be waived for poor Scouts, but James West refused and insisted that Troop Committeemen should instead create jobs so that boys could earn the money. At the 1939 BSA Executives National Training Conference, West strongly reiterated that donated money should not be used to pay registration fees or uniform costs for "less chance boys." Attendees had difficulty even pinpointing a definition of the less chance boy and what methods might be used to approach him. Some stated that the less chance boy was characterized by his family's and community's levels of income, while others suggested including all white immigrants and nonwhites in the category of less chance boys. Attendees also debated whether companies or labor unions could effectively sponsor Scout troops, and whether a labor representative should be put on each Local Council.[7]

Despite—or perhaps because of—the difficulties the Great Depression imposed on Boy Scouting, the organization's public stature, advancement program, and opportunities for leadership and character development continued to hold great appeal for many members. Ralph Casperson's life memoir, *A Northern Boyhood*, emphasized how he learned the rewards of advancement and leadership as a Northern Minnesota Boy Scout in the 1930s. Scouting offered a boy unique opportunities for both peer and community status: "Until I joined the Scout movement I had never received any public recognition. . . . To be noticed by a whole circle of my peers or the general public began in the Boy Scouts." Casperson insisted that Scouting as a boy provided the foundation for his worldview and future adult life: "My ego gauge rested on zero for thirteen years until I learned the Scout Oath. A number of times during the next four years the gauge went off the chart. The Boy Scout movement provided the spark that energized my life and was the nutrient that stimulated my growth. From a seedling in a planting where all looked alike, scouting allowed me to develop into a full-sized plant, to stand out in the row." He particularly cited the rank and merit badge advancement scheme as a key stimulant to his and his troopmates' striving for achievement and public stature in life. For Casperson, Scouting's badges and honors offered tangible rewards, which each boy could pursue according to his own initiative: "The movement fit me like an old shoe. I discovered my competitive spirit in the scout troop and scouting provided an environment in which I could compete to my heart's content. Also, advancement through the classes was not hampered by artificial structures. The only barrier to advancement was the individual scout's lack of ability or initiative." According to Casperson, Scouting taught many values and skills that he and the other boys used later in life, including learning to influence others through serving as a Patrol Leader and Assistant Scoutmaster: "This knowledge was beneficial to me in the army and in corporate life after the war." He noted, though, that his leadership ability was sometimes counterproductive in that he did not work well in a group unless he led it. Raising funds to attend Scout camp provided him business and sales knowledge. Finally, Scouting brought Casperson (who was of Norwegian descent) into close contact with boys and men of different ethnicities. He reported on the local Scout Executive of the Gitchee Gumee Council in 1936: "A slim Adonis with jet black hair and dark complexion, obviously of Italian descent, Anton was revered by all of his Scouts and emulated by some—a real role model." He contrasted his experiences in Scouting against the Order of DeMolay fraternity he later joined in high school: "I enjoyed the fellowship but didn't have the opportunities for self-expression there that I had in the Scouts. For me, the possibility of developing leadership skills was not as great in DeMolay as in Troop 32. In the Scouts we had to memorize the Scout Oath and the twelve Scout Laws. I can still, over fifty years later, recite them, but of the reams of words I memorized in DeMolay, I remember nothing today.... The Scout program allowed a free-play of imagination and personal initiative, and was made to order for me.... In the Boy Scouts I did it all and have been rewarded with the benefits for a lifetime."[8]

A FINAL DEPRESSION-ERA STORY about the establishment of a permanent Philadelphia Boy Scout Local Council office and recent complications surrounding the enduring government-BSA partnership established in the 1910s may shed new light on the controversies surrounding the organization today. The narrative begins in 1910, the BSA's first year, when Mayor Reyburn of Philadelphia hosted a meeting to organize what would become one of the larger and more vocal local Boy Scout councils. He helped attract twenty-five prominent men in the city to support Scouting financially and serve on its Local Council board. For the years 1911 to 1917, the mayor gave two rooms in Independence Hall, which had been used by the nation's first Supreme Court "in the shadow of the Liberty Bell," for the local BSA council to use as a headquarters and supply office. The city's decision to restore the historic building to its original state meant that the local Scout council would have to move, yet a satisfactory permanent office location eluded the council for over a decade. As early as 1920, the council had hoped to establish a new, single-purpose building: "It should be of dignified architecture and good material and would, for all time, make Scouting permanent in the eyes of the public and go far to make it permanent in their hearts as well. With such a headquarters our very own, all of us would have a perpetual inspiration to carry on to the greatest heights the vast opportunities for good as yet scarcely begun." It took nine years to gather the funds from over three hundred subscribers and final authorization from the municipal Fairmount Park Commission to erect the building (which would become city government property), the ground for which was broken in 1930.[9]

The seventy-year anniversary history book of the council proudly described the impressive two-story Italian Renaissance style building and its inclusion of ample offices, a library, a boardroom, file space, a trading post, and display vaults. More impressively, the builders covered the outside and interior of the building with numerous Scout symbols and carvings to signify the public stature and dignity of the BSA. The front of the building carried inscriptions reading: "YOUTH SAFEGUARDS THE NATION. This House, Dedicated to the Training of Boys for Useful Citizenship, was Built by the Boy Scouts and their Friends." Images and inscriptions of the Scout Oath; the twelve points of the Scout Law; the Silver Buffalo Award for lifetime service to Scouting; the badges for Life, Star, and Eagle ranks; a local Service Medal; and the National Life Saving Award also adorned the front of the office building. Stone carvings of the lower Scout rank badges as well as key merit badges—such as First Aid, Personal Health, Camping, Physical Development, and Civics— covered the sides. The Golden Book of Scout Heroes, with its parchment pages and Moroccan leather, into which the names and stories of local Scouts who earned medals for saving the lives of others were inscribed, rested on a special mantle in the grand lobby. The interior also included "an exquisite carving of the coat of arms of the United States, which we proudly have the right to use, as being chartered by the Government of the United States." The interior's coat of arms of both the Commonwealth of Pennsylvania and the City of Philadelphia reinforced Scouting's ties to local and state government agencies and officials. A prominent replica of the famous bronze statue *The Boy Scout*, done by Local Council member Robert McKenzie in 1915, was erected in front of the building in 1937. The 1980 Local Council history claimed, "The Scout Headquarters building provides a sense of council unity, and demonstrates to the public that Scouting is a permanent program. Being a thing of beauty, the building makes a lasting impression upon all who have visited it during the past half century . . . a home around which will center all Scout life and knit the bonds of Scout comradeship even closer."

However, this government-BSA cooperation and the impressive Philadelphia office came under public scrutiny in 2003 when Scouters Greg Lattera and R. Duane Perry led an effort to challenge the national organization's exclusion of openly gay members and the Local Council office's occupation and use of city-owned land. At one point America's third largest Scout council tried to adopt a local policy of not discriminating in terms of sexual or religious preference (partly in response to the withdrawal of funding from the United Way), but the city government indicated that the organization's policies violated the city's 1982 Fair Practices law and asked the council to vacate its historic office, pay market rent, or accept homosexual members. However, the fact that the city of Philadelphia let religious groups use city land, combined with the federal 2002 Boy Scouts of America Equal Access Act and the 2005 Support Our Scouts Act, which required government officials and government-funded schools to continue to support the organization in ways they traditionally had, complicated the situation. Several years of political and legal wrangling ensued. The BSA pursued legal recourse against the city and claimed its civil rights were being violated by the eviction request, and in 2010 a federal jury sided with Philadelphia's Cradle of Liberty Council and ordered the city to stop its eviction efforts and pay the BSA's sizable legal fees for the case. After several counteroffers, the city agreed to pay the local Scout council $825,000 for improvements it had made to the building over the past eighty years in exchange for the council vacating the office.[10]

The early history of the BSA suggests, though, that the organization has often evolved and adapted to include diverse peoples. While BSA publications and available sources from the 1910s and 1920s did not prominently feature discussions of homosexuality or atheism, the organization and its administrators did actively design policies to accommodate and welcome groups then on the margins of society, beginning with southern and eastern European immigrants, non-Protestants, Mormons, and working-class labor union families. The BSA national office and several white southern Scout leaders helped lead a groundbreaking and successful movement to form more African American troops. The national office then cooperated with the federal government to expand outreach efforts to Native American boys at isolated boarding schools. In an era in which nativism against non-Protestant immigrants and extreme racial segregation and violence permeated American society and politics, many early BSA officials came to embrace a very progressive and inclusive vision that all boys and men could and should learn the same standard of modern manhood and participating citizenship. Early American Boy Scouting developed into a powerful force, bringing together men and boys of different ethnic, religious, and class groups for a common project of character and civic development. Although national Boy Scout membership declined in the 1970s, its national office and Local Councils embarked on vigorous outreach campaigns to recruit more ethnic minority boys and even opened its older youth division to girl members. Moreover, the BSA has recently changed its policies to allow gay boys to join—and at the time of this writing, the Philadelphia Scout council's website affirms its nondiscriminatory policies—so the organization's latest cycle of adaptation and membership diversification appears to be under way. Its evolution and continued social relevance for turning adolescent boys into men of good character and involved citizens would fit rather than depart from its long, storied history.

Notes

Introduction

1. Figure I.1 in J. P. Freeman, "Typewriter vs. Ax," *Scout Executive*, February 1926, 15.

2. On Carey's petition and Seton's criticisms, see Macleod, *Building Character*, 156; and Rowan, *To Do My Best*, 58–67, 91. BSA founder William D. Boyce and Lee Hanmer also left the organization about this time for related reasons. Dean, "Scouting in America," 59.

3. For statistics on annual and cumulative BSA membership, see 1930 BSA Annual Report, 211–13. (What is labeled in this book as the 1930 Annual Report covered reports and statistics from the completed 1930 year and was published early the following year, 1931.) James Galt-Brown estimated that 358,000,000 boys had been members of a Scout organization by 2002; this figure was based on an extrapolation of Nagy's 1977 estimate of 250,000,000 Scouts to date. Galt-Brown, "Baden-Powell," 292; and Nagy, *250 Million Scouts*, 177. For current Boy Scout statistics, refer to the World Organization of the Scout Movement's official website, http://www.scout.org, and "Fact Sheet: Scouting Around the World," http://www.scouting.org/FILESTORE/pdf/02-505.pdf. On sales of the BSA handbook, see the *Scout Executive*, March 1928, 1. Ray O. Wyland reported that when the BSA placed an order for a million copies of the new 1927 Boy Scout handbook, the printers were so surprised that they researched and concluded that it was the largest single order of a book ever given to any publisher. The previous handbook editions went through thirty-seven editions in seventeen years, with 3,100,000 copies through 1926, placing it, according to Wyland and the publishers, second only to the Christian Bible in the history of American printing to date. Wyland, "The Knighthood of Youth," 857. Gary Ink, librarian for *Publisher's Weekly*, reported that the Boy Scout handbook still ranked fourth in all-time American book sales in 1999—behind the Bible, *The Guinness Book of World Records*, and *Dr. Spock's Baby and Child Care*. Robert Peterson, "The Perfect Book for a Desert Island," *Scouting*, September 1999. Chapters 1, 3, and 6 discuss the BSA's federal charter and Scout term monopoly further. To standardize the usage of Scout names and terms and to highlight their importance, the national office instructed publishers and local administrators to consistently capitalize all terms and titles related to Scouting, such as "Scoutmaster," "Local Council Executive," "Twelfth Law," and "Good Turn." Headquarters issued an editors' guidebook in the 1920s that asked rhetorically that since titles like "Congressman" and "Reverend" were capitalized, why should BSA positions and titles not be capitalized as well? In this book, I have tried to be consistent with the early BSA's typical usage

concerning particular Scouting terms and their capitalization. BSA, *Standard Capitalization and Terminology*, 3–9.

4. For changes in middle-class and elite children's duties, see Macleod, *Age of the Child*; and Zelizer, *Pricing the Priceless Child*. On the history of American fatherhood, refer to Griswold, *Fatherhood in America*; and Mintz and Kellogg, *Domestic Revolutions*.

5. Juvenile courts eliminated youth offenders' right to a lawyer or jury trial and broadened the scope of offenses to include minor ones, like incorrigible stubbornness. Nasaw, *Children of the City*; Kett, *Rites of Passage*, 254–64; and Mintz, *Huck's Raft*, 172–78.

6. Robert Grinder offered a succinct synthesis of Hall's theory of adolescence in "The Concept of Adolescence." See also Demos and Demos, "Adolescence in Historical Perspective"; Stocking, "Lamarckianism in American Social Science: 1890–1915"; Ross, *G. Stanley Hall*; and Green, "Savage Childhood." For the early BSA's synthesis of recapitulation theories, see Boy Scouts of America, *Handbook for Scout Masters* (1914), 97–102; and Macleod, *Building Character*, 5–26, 97–103, 112–13.

7. Hantover, "Sex Role," 14–53; and Hall, *100 Years and Millions of Boys*.

8. On Progressive Era education and critiques, see Mintz, *Huck's Raft*, 174–75; Kett, *Rites of Passage*, 234–44; Spring, *American School*, 169–218; Schlossman, "G. Stanley Hall"; and Cavallo, *Muscles and Morals*. Educators surveyed in Kimball, "Dividends of Scouting," 1928 biennial national Executives Conference Report (hereafter referred to as ECR), 604. Most of the other fourteen did not answer that particular question. Only 0.3 percent answered that Scouting had no effect on education theory and practice.

9. For historiographical reviews arguing that the typical characterization of American masculinity as a performance in crisis has underplayed native-born white men's stable power over others, see Banner, Review; Traister, "Academic Viagra," 284–99; and Ditz, "The New Men's History," 2–19. For studies of American masculinities history emphasizing the crisis theory, consult Filene, *Him/Her/Self*; Dubbert, *A Man's Place*, 2–11, 111–13; McGovern, "David Graham Phillips," 334–55; and Kimmel, *Manhood in America*. Gail Bederman argued that masculinity was not in crisis in fin de siècle American society, but she still described the period as one of "unusual obsession" with masculine identity. Bederman, *Manliness and Civilization*.

10. BSA leaders used the term "character" interchangeably with "manliness" and "manhood." 1920 ECR, 152–62. On the rise and decline of the Victorian self-made man and yeoman farmer models of American success in the 1800s, refer to Wyllie, *Self-Made Man*, 21–61, 86–87, 96, 133–82; Cawelti, *Apostles of the Self-Made Man*, 47–63, 101–23, 201–48; Burns, *Success in America*; and Hilkey, *Character Is Capital*, 50, 71, 78–82, 136–51. For examples of masculinity works citing Boy Scouting as evidence of the virile, primitive, strenuous masculinity model, see Kasson, *Houdini, Tarzan, and the Perfect Man*, especially 191; Roberts, "The Strenuous Life," 111–14; Filene, *Him/Her/Self*, 241; Pleck and Pleck, *The American Man*, 25–26; Stearns, *Be a Man*, 19, 22, 68; Dubbert, *A Man's Place*, 148–53, 191–92;

Rotundo, *American Manhood*, 227–32, 258; Kimmel, *Manhood in America*, 168–70; Rodgers, *The Work Ethic*, 143–47; Martin Summers, *Manliness and Its Discontents*, 126–27; and Watts, *Rough Rider in the White House*, 27–30. For other works stressing the shift from Victorian self-control to virile, aggressive masculinity in fin de siècle American society, consult Bederman, *Manliness and Civilization*, 173–83; Putney, *Muscular Christianity*; Mangan and Walvin, *Manliness and Morality*, 1–3; Testi, "Theodore Roosevelt," 1, 509–33; Higham, "The Reorientation of American Culture," 73–102; Nash, "American Cult of the Primitive," 517–37; and Syrett, *The Company He Keeps*, 1–11, 121–228. A number of books have been written about the history of the BSA but surprisingly few of an academic nature and none by a gender historian. This book also disputes the characterization of Boy Scouting as individualistic, antimodern, and nostalgic for rural living and primitivism presented by the two main academic works that address early BSA gender dynamics. Macleod, *Building Character*, xiii–xvi, 30–34, 51–55, 108, 144, 206–11, 265–66, 283–90. Hantover, "Sex Role," 3–13, 54–75, 118–24, 210–57. See also Gilbert, "Controlling Boys," 529–32; Macleod, "Act Your Age," 10–14; and Hantover, "The Boy Scouts," 184–95. For other useful histories of the BSA's development, see Peterson, *The Boy Scouts*; Murray, *History of the Boy Scouts*; Dean, "Scouting in America"; Wagner, "The Boy Scouts"; Wills, *Boy Scouts*; Scott and Murphy, *The Scouting Party*; and Bolland, "Magazine Coverage of the Boy Scouts," 24–34.

11. Parsons, *Race, Resistance and the Boy Scout Movement*; Bragg, "The Boy Scout Movement in Canada," 60–66, 106, 125; Proctor, *On My Honour*, 16–19, 107–8; Proctor, *Scouting for Girls*, 32–45; and Miller, *Growing Girls*. On Baden-Powell's critique of the BSA's bureaucratization, see Pote, *Fifty Years of Scouting*, 15–16. For other key works on Scouting in Great Britain and its empire, refer to Rosenthal, *The Character Factory*; MacDonald, *Sons of the Empire*; Jeal, *Baden-Powell*; Crotty, *Making the Australian Male*; and Crotty, "Scouts Down Under." Bragg and Crotty argued that Canadian and Australian Scouting emphasized virile, aggressive masculinity.

Chapter One

1. For varied descriptions of the attendees, banquet, and other early key BSA organizational developments and events, see Oursler, *The Boy Scout Story*, 34–36; Macleod, *Building Character*, 146; James E. West, "Historical Statement concerning the Early Days of the Boy Scouts of America," for BSA National Training School (Sept. 24, 1934), folder of same name, Boy Scouts of America National Archive (hereafter referred to as BSANA); Edgar M. Robinson letter to Herschleb (Aug. 24, 1942), folder "First Troops," BSANA; William D. Boyce, "Memorandum concerning How Scouting Came to America as Told by W. D. Boyce," folder "History of the B.S. of A.," BSANA; and Scott and Murphy, *The Scouting Party*, 4, 101–17.

2. "Boy Scout Leaders Dine Baden-Powell," *New York Times*, September 24, 1910, 8; "To Dine Baden-Powell: Boy Scouts of America to Honor the Head of Their English Cousins," *New York Times*, September 23, 1910, 8.

3. Beard overtook Seton as the BSA's charismatic outdoorsman and public figurehead, but he never possessed the authority West had. Beard became the only remaining National Scout Commissioner after the involvement of two military officials, Bomus and Verbeck, declined. For central office moves, including the 1928 relocation to a much larger space in the new No. 2 Park Avenue Building, see "Boy Scouts of America Move National Office in New York," *Weekly News Bulletin of Boy Scout Activities*, December 10, 1927. On West's background, see Rowan, *To Do My Best*; Oursler, *The Boy Scout Story*, 47–52; and *Boys' Life*, June 1926, 46. Seton's disaffection (or ouster) from the BSA took several years, but significant tensions were present by the September 1910 BSA trial camp at Silver Bay and October's Waldorf-Astoria banquet. For accounts of Seton, his Indian hero, and their ouster, refer to Wagner, "The Boy Scouts," 142–52; Macleod, *Building Character*, 130–56, 180–81, 239; Scott and Murphy, *The Scouting Party*, 16–19, 36, 103–25, 141–55, 208–10; Deloria, "Playing Indian," 261–81, 298–301; Wadland, "Ernest Thompson Seton"; Huhndorf, *Going Native*, 11, 72–77; Anderson, *Ernest Thompson Seton*; and Braude, "Making Men," 123–24.

4. Most gender historians have emphasized Scout quotations about manhood and antimodernity made by Beard, Seton, Alexander, and Baden-Powell between 1903 and 1910, before the major changes in BSA gender ideology and teaching methods. Some early BSA leaders occasionally encouraged boys to play pioneer or Indian in order to learn a dose of self-reliance and outdoorsmanship, but most officials hesitated to use either figure as a complete model of manhood, since neither self-reliance nor outdoor survival was the organization's ultimate goal. As Macleod argued, "Beard's berserker spirit . . . though attuned to American dreams of individualistic frontier manhood, was too anarchic and willful for an age groping towards social control." Macleod, *Building Character*, 145. On Beard's life, the Sons of Daniel Boone, and their relationship to early Scouting, consult Beard, *The Boy Pioneers*; Beard, *Hardly a Man Is Now Alive*, 352–57; Whitmore, "Beard, Boys and Buckskins"; and Kahler, "An Historical Analysis."

5. For BSA histories stressing the importance of its bureaucracy, see Wigginton, "The Boy Scouts"; Dean, "Scouting in America"; and Rowan, *To Do My Best*.

6. Baden-Powell, *Aids to Scouting for N.-C.O.s.* On Baden-Powell's role as a Boys' Brigade inspector and the influence of that organization and militarism on Boy Scouting, refer to Oursler, *The Boy Scout Story*, 27–28; Blassingame, *Story of the Boy Scouts*, 31–32; Macleod, *Building Character*, 89–93; and Galt-Brown, "Baden-Powell," 20–22, 84–136, 233–35, 295.

7. For details on Baden-Powell's career, the Mafeking siege, and the growth of Boy Scouting in England, see Jeal, *Baden-Powell*; Dan Lipton, "Where Scouting Began," *Scouting*, May–June 1983, 16, 38–39, 43; Galt-Brown, "Baden-Powell," 231–44; and Oursler, *The Boy Scout Story*, 30–33. In 1909, the British Boys' Brigade had perhaps sixty thousand members, the Sons of Daniel Boone had twenty thousand, and the Woodcraft Indians had less than twenty thousand. For membership statistics on these and other boys' organizations of this era, see Rosenthal, *The Character Factory*, 230–52; Jeal, *Baden-Powell*, 351–67; and Macleod, *Building Character*, 83–93, 189–90. Scouting also spread quickly to Germany, Spain, Sweden,

Norway, Denmark, Austria, Hungary, Chile, Canada, Australia, Belgium, Brazil, Greece, India, Italy, the Netherlands, New Zealand, the Philippines, and Sweden. Arthurs, "Boy Scouts Building for Manhood," 281; and Boy Scouts International Bureau, *Facts on World Scouting*. By 1929, Scouting spanned at least fifty-seven nations, which together accounted for 90 percent of the world's population. The number of active Boy Scouts in the world reached 2 million by the end of 1930. Hurt, *Handbook for Scoutmasters*, 2. The United States and Great Britain formed Scouting's early strongholds and global leaders. The United States accounted for 850,000 members, the British Empire 650,000, and Japan nearly 50,000. "World Boy Scout Membership Now Nearly at 2,000,000 Mark," *Weekly News Bulletin of Boy Scout Activities*, September 20, 1930.

8. It remains difficult to calculate the exact number and location of early, independent Boy Scout troops in the United States. Peterson, *The Boy Scouts*, 29–30; "Baden-Powell's Boy Scout Plan Invades America," *New York Times*, April 24, 1910, SM11.

9. Boyce, a Chicago publisher who had made a fortune producing weekly newspapers such as the *Saturday Blade* and the *Chicago Ledger* for a rural clientele, established the Boy Scouts of America in February 1910. For details of the BSA's founding, see Oursler, *The Boy Scout Story*, 36–43; Petterchak, *Lone Scout*, 63–64, 72–75; and Boyce, "Memorandum concerning How Scouting Came to America." On Boyce's failed early BSA efforts, see also Robert Peterson, "The Man Who Got Lost in the Fog," *Scouting*, October 2001. For the influence of Hearst's organization, consult Macleod, *Building Character*, 146–59. For the pre-BSA YMCA Scout troops, see Robert Peterson, "The BSA's 'Forgotten' Founding Father," *Scouting*, October 1998. YMCA local branches hosted many of the first BSA recruitment stations. Even as late as 1918, five out of six district Scout heads and over one-fourth of Local Council Executives were former YMCA employees. On YMCA-BSA relations, see also Murray, *History of the Boy Scouts*, 15–32; and Hurt, *Community Boy Leadership*, 378–79.

10. A temporary governing board, led by Seton, was appointed until the National Council's Executive Board plan was put into place. Oursler, *The Boy Scout Story*, 55. On the early BSA office's disarray, see Macleod, *Building Character*, 146–59; and Wills, *Boy Scouts of America*, 38–40. For Robinson's role in bringing in the Woodcraft Indians and Sons of Daniel Boone, see Petterchak, *Lone Scout*, 68; and Robinson letter to Herschleb (Aug. 24, 1942).

11. On the elite's funding of the BSA, see Petterchak, *Lone Scout*, 70–71; and Macleod, *Building Character*, 147–48.

12. Keith Monroe, "Ernest Thompson Seton: Scouting's First Spellbinder," *Scouting*, October 1977, 28, 70; Murray, *History of the Boy Scouts*, 27–28, 140; "American Boy Scouts," *Washington Post*, May 22, 1910, E4; "To Teach Yegg Signs: Peace Aids, Not Military," *Washington Post*, March 26, 1911, 81; and Narragansett Council BSA, *25 Years of Scouting in Rhode Island*. Chapter 3 of this book explores the Scout militarism issue. Hearst apparently distanced himself some from the American Boy Scouts organization after accusations of false representation and fund-raisers being given 40 percent commissions for their ABS solicitations

surfaced. Scott and Murphy, *The Scouting Party*, 135. For the key June 1910 reorganization meeting, see Oursler, *The Boy Scout Story*, 34–36; Macleod, *Building Character*, 146; and West, "Historical Statement concerning the Early Days of the Boy Scouts of America."

13. On the Boy Scout–Girl Scout controversy, see Rothschild, "To Scout or To Guide?"; Groth, "Scouts' Own," 17, 44, 65–66, 82, 98–121; Biegert, "Woman Scout," 187–94, 225–27, 280–85; Miller, "Trademark: Scout"; and Rowan, *To Do My Best*, 68–71, 105–6. On the development of the Girl Guides and Girl Scouts, their growth during World War I, as well as Boy and Girl Scout and Guide organizations working together in other areas, see Choate and Ferris, *Juliette Low*; Proctor, *Scouting for Girls*, chaps. 1–2, 52–55; Proctor, *On My Honour*, 107–30; Miller, *Growing Girls*, 13–47; Wade, *The World Chief Guide*, 63–68, 90–99; and Kerr, *The Story of the Girl Guides*, 46–48.

14. On the growing emphasis on bureaucratic forms, processes, and committees in the BSA championed by West (and his lawyer-like tendencies in making policies and statements), see Macleod, "Original Intent." The professionalization and volunteerism issue also surfaced in Girl Scouting and Guiding in this era. Proctor, *Scouting for Girls*, 39–40.

15. Using 1925 as an example, the BSA tapped 163,760 adult volunteers and fewer than 1,000 paid staff. Around 99 percent of adult Scouters from 1910 to 1930 volunteered their services. 1925 BSA Annual Report, 143; and Hurt, *Handbook for Scoutmasters*, 534. Peterson tabulated just 4,000 professional Scouters among 1,130,000 adult Scouters (0.35 percent) in the BSA in 1984. Peterson, *The Boy Scouts*, 214. For Wilson's January 14, 1918, letter to BSA President Livingstone, see the two-sided poster titled "295,262 Boys Through Scouting Help Uncle Sam Win the War: Training for Citizenship through Service," folder of same name, BSANA. Pamphlet, "Scout Leaders Reserve Corps Boy Scouts of America Wanted 100,000 Men for Leaders of Uncle Sam's Boys," folder of same name, BSANA. Clergy formed the largest initial group of volunteer Scoutmasters, though their portion of applicants declined over time. The percentage of clergy Scoutmasters dropped from 29 in 1912 to under 8 by 1931; YMCA men dropped from 5.7 percent of Scoutmasters in 1912 to less than 1 percent just four years later. The percentage of national Scoutmaster applicants claiming "Mercantile" occupations jumped from 19 to 48 between 1912 and 1931. Part of this may have resulted from the recategorization of "miscellaneous" occupations, which dropped from 21 percent of Scoutmasters nationally in 1911 to less than 1 percent in 1931, but the trend also paralleled the growth in sponsorship of Scout troops by businessmen's service organizations, such as the Rotary Club. Educators accounted for a relatively consistent 12 percent of Scoutmasters nationally, while college students hovered around 3 to 5 percent of applicants except during World War I, when many served in the military. Skilled "mechanical" workers increased from 7 percent nationally in 1911 to over 13 percent in 1925. A significant number of farmers as well as upper-middle-class professionals such as engineers, lawyers, and doctors also served as Scoutmasters across the United States in the 1910s and 1920s. For leaders' occupational statistics, see Macleod, *Building Character*, 150–60, 201–7; Dean, "Scouting in America,"

106–9; 1911 BSA Annual Report, 10; 1912 BSA Annual Report, 19; 1916 BSA Annual Report, 34; 1925 BSA Annual Report, 143; and 1931 BSA Annual Report, 221.

16. On the Bureau of Municipal Research's analysis, see Macleod, *Building Character*, 155–56. On the bureau's mind-set, see Haber, *Efficiency and Uplift*, 110–14. The Bureau of Municipal Research's 1914 report, however, criticized the disorganization and inefficiency of the local New York City Boy Scout councils. Quotation in *Report on the Boy Scouts of America* (New York: Bureau of Municipal Research, 1914), 14. For the BSA's early and continued dependence on paid staffers, which contrasted with Scout organizations in many countries, refer to Davis, *Men of Schiff*, 3–5, 14–15, 21–27, 37–39, 85–162. For British Boy Scouting's professionalization conflicting with its attempts to help members escape from modern work, see Proctor, *On My Honour*, 112–13.

17. Macleod, *Building Character*, 159–62, 201–7; and Dean, "Scouting in America," 106–9. Ex-Scoutmasters still made up a majority of the Executives in 1922, but the tide was turning in favor of businessmen with no youth-work experience. 1922 ECR, 78. On the Executive reporting to the Commissioner, see BSA, *Handbook for Scout Masters* (1914), 14–15. Murray, *History of the Boy Scouts*, 259. During the 1930s, First Class Councils began to consolidate, while the number of Second Class Councils and Scouts not under council remained quite low. On the qualifications of the ideal Scout council Executive, see Hurt, *Community Boy Leadership*, 21–43, 102–6, 195; and "Qualifications of the Scout Executive," *Scout Executive*, March 1920, 1.

18. For examples of hedging the Scoutmaster's autonomy with the Local Councils and their paid Executives, see 1926 ECR, 187–90; and Macleod, *Building Character*, 161–63.

19. For characterizing the BSA's administrative structure and particularly its National Council as democratic, consult Hurt, *Community Boy Leadership*, 1. Mark M. Jones, "Report on a Survey," 96–97, 105–7, 116–19. With the exception of the Finance and National Court of Honor committees, the Executive Board appeared to control most of the National Council's somewhat limited functions. The "Constitution of the Boy Scouts of America" explained the makeup and powers of the National Council and its Executive Board. This chapter uses the version of the Constitution and By-Laws reported in BSA, *Handbook for Scout Masters* (1919), 356–404. For BSA leaders' occupational statistics, see Macleod, *Building Character*, 150–60, 201–7; Dean, "Scouting in America," 106–9; 1911 BSA Annual Report, 10; 1917 BSA Annual Report, 70; and 1931 BSA Annual Report, 221.

20. Although the BSA occasionally modified its structure, its basic operations remained consistent. See "A Glimpse of National Headquarters," *Scouting*, May 15, 1913, 3; and Hurt, *Handbook for Scoutmasters*, 505–19, 551–56. On the heavy influence of West and the Executive Board subcommittee as well as the organization of national Scout departments and their problems, refer to Macleod, *Building Character*, 150–63; Jones, "Report on a Survey," especially 96–99, 122–25, 273–75; Wigginton, "The Boy Scouts," 72; Rowan, *To Do My Best*, 14–17, 96–97, 117–97, 209; and Macleod, "Original Intent," 13–27. On the development of the organization's prolific range of publications and media relations, see Murray, *History of*

the Boy Scouts, 392–417; John T. Dizer, "The Birth and Boyhood of *Boys' Life*," *Scouting*, November–December 1994; Levy, *Building a Popular Movement*, 117; and "Educational Publicity Number," *Scout Executive*, April 1927, 1–3.

21. The BSA national office cut expenditures temporarily in the early 1920s until the quota system gelled. The 1929 expenditure figures used here represent adjustments to include the total funds spent by the Supply, Magazines, Publications, and Field Departments. Annual reports in this period switched to reporting spending by these departments in terms of profits and losses instead of how much total money each took in or spent. To track national office income sources and expenditures, see 1912 BSA Annual Report, 46; 1915 BSA Annual Report, 98; 1920 BSA Annual Report, 52–56; 1926 BSA Annual Report, 35; 1929 BSA Annual Report, 64–70; Jones, "Report on a Survey," iv–v, 262; Murray, *History of the Boy Scouts*, 67–75; Oursler, *The Boy Scout Story*, 77–78; and Shaver, *Notes from a Pioneer's Journal*, 174–77. The Local Councils paid their operating expenses and quota pledges through a combination of boy and troop dues, private donations, admission fees at Scouting exhibitions, and contributions from local Community Chests (the forerunner of today's United Way). BSA headquarters established an Education Department in 1916 to produce training literature and to direct the increasing number of national and local training conferences for Scoutmasters and Local Council administrators.

22. West estimated in February 1911 that there were two hundred informal local Scout committees across the United States. Oursler, *The Boy Scout Story*, 44. Pote argued that the Executive Board chartered Local Councils after mounting difficulty keeping up with requests for help from individual Scoutmasters. Pote, *Fifty Years of Scouting*, 7–8.

23. On West's limitation of councils to one municipality each and the Executive Board working to maintain authority over the Local Councils, see Macleod, *Building Character*, 121, 150–52; and Wigginton, "The Boy Scouts," 64–65. For the 1913 changes, see also Boy Scouts of America, "Fact Sheet: Historical Highlights," 2001, 1. For the functions of a typical BSA Local Council, refer to the El Paso example in the *Scout Executive*, February 1922, 2; the Cedar Rapids Area Council's annual calendar in the *Scout Executive*, May 1930, 7; and the organizational chart in Hurt, *Handbook for Scoutmasters*, 501. For suggestions on the formation of a proper Local Council's membership, see Hurt, *Handbook for Scoutmasters*, 580–81; and Boy Scouts of America, *First National Training School*, 590–601, 620–25.

24. Figure 1.1, "Local Council Forms," *Scout Executive*, November 1920, 8.

25. Mortimer Schiff provided matching funds to help the national Field Department set up the twelve regional offices with paid Executives. For duties and development of the Regional Councils, see Hurt, *Community Boy Leadership*, 189–93; 1918 BSA Annual Report, 75; and Murray, *History of the Boy Scouts*, 276–79. Physician Dr. George J. Fisher, president of the New York City Kiwanis Club in the late 1920s, served as head of the expanding Field Department and Deputy Chief Executive to James West from 1919 to 1936. Dean, "Scouting in America," 72–73; and Pote, *Fifty Years of Scouting*, 11. Unfortunately, the regional offices this

researcher contacted for information kept very few older records. At the time, the BSA had a schedule instructing that the offices throw out most types of documents after a period of seven years to conserve space.

26. On the formation of new Local Councils, see Mark Jones, "Report on a Survey," 129–31. On council statistics and foci, see Murray, *History of the Boy Scouts*, 259; Boy Scouts of America, *Handbook for Scout Masters* (1914), 13; and Boy Scouts of America, "Fact Sheet: Historical Highlights."

27. For the troop-sponsoring institution's responsibilities, refer to Boy Scouts of America, *Handbook for Scout Masters* (1914), 197–200.

28. The churches' portion dropped from a peak of 68 percent of total troops in 1915 to 47 percent in 1930, in part reflecting the broadening of Scouting's appeal to other institutions. For the comparative troop-sponsorship statistics, see 1930 BSA Annual Report, 232–35. The change in percentage of total troops sponsored by churches from 1915 to 1925 is reported in 1925 BSA Annual Report, 443. For service club troop sponsorship, see Dean, "Scouting in America," 74. Macleod notes that 17 percent of Scout troops in 1921 met in schools, while only 7 percent of troops were actually sponsored by schools. Macleod, *Building Character*, 199–200.

29. Macleod, *Building Character*, 153; Boy Scouts of America, *Handbook for Scout Masters* (1914), 17–18; Boy Scouts of America, *The Troop Committee*, 6–8; and "The Duties of a Troop Committee," *Scouting*, April 1927, 12.

30. The exact number of Scouts is difficult to ascertain before the registration system was installed in 1913. Peterson, *The Boy Scouts*, 55–56. The number of boy members dropped slightly to 896,484 for 1930. The inclusion from 1925 to July 1927 of an inflated rural membership figure of boys absorbed from the independent Lone Scouts of America organization, and its subsequent correction, helps account for the 1925 jump and the apparent decrease in total membership after mid-1927. For statistics on annual and cumulative BSA membership and ratios of Scouts to available boys, see 1930 BSA Annual Report, 211–13. For the number of adult volunteer Scoutmasters per year through 1926, see Hurt, *Handbook for Boys*, 590–96.

31. For a discussion of the gender, race, and environmental dynamics in the development of Sea Scouting and Cub Scouting in the 1910s and 1920s, see Jordan, "Savages and the 'SHE PERIOD.'" Boy Scout headquarters offered the Sea Scout program for boys over the age of fifteen, but relatively few joined. Sea Scouting denied the autonomy and dating that many teenagers sought, because administrators felt that these were pernicious influences on the development of older boys. Administrators reluctantly developed a separate Cub branch with an Indian motif in 1930. Cubbing for seven- to eleven-year-old boys overtook the number of traditional Boy Scouts in the 1950s—a dominance it has maintained to this day. For age statistics, see Macleod, *Building Character*, 280–96. For Cub growth, see Peterson, *The Boy Scouts*, 104–8, 135, 163. For Sea Scouting, consult Macleod, *Building Character*, 296–97; Peterson, *The Boy Scouts*, 100–105; and Hurt, *Community Boy Leadership*, 475–86.

32. For a visual sketch of the geographical spread of Scout troops by 1928, see Hurt, *Handbook for Boys*, 15. For growth areas and troop density over time, see

1911 BSA Annual Report, 6; 1913 BSA Annual Report, 12; 1915 BSA Annual Report, 40; 1921 BSA Annual Report, 110–37; 1925 BSA Annual Report, 169–70; and 1930 BSA Annual Report, 215–18.

33. Town-based Local Councils also maintained a higher ratio of adult supervisors and spent more money per boy member than did big city councils. Hurt, *Community Boy Leadership*, 306. Macleod, *Building Character*, 224–29. See also 1921 BSA Annual Report, 8–9; and 1930 BSA Annual Report, 276–79.

34. Mark Jones, "Report on a Survey," 43–47. For information on the class makeup of BSA boy members and Scoutmasters, consult Hantover, "Sex Role," 168–223; Macleod, *Building Character*, 206–22, 302–303; 1912 BSA Annual Report, 20, 50–53; 1; 1917 BSA Annual Report, 70; 1921 BSA Annual Report, 142; "Institutions with Which Troops Are Connected," *Scouting*, July 1925, 5; 1925 BSA Annual Report, 160–61; Gorman, "A Comparative Study"; Fairchild, *Conduct Habits of Boy Scouts*, 35–43; Wyland, *Scouting in the Schools*, 106–25; and 1936 ECR, 741–43. On British efforts with the working class, see Proctor, "(Uni)Forming Youth," 103–34.

Chapter Two

1. The BSA has retained the twelve Laws, Oath, and Motto as adopted in May 1911 to the present day, although some explanations of their meanings have been modified. For the revised BSA version of the Laws and Oath, see Murray, Pratt, and Jameson, *Official Handbook for Boys*, 15–16. For comparison against the original British Boy Scout Laws, see Baden-Powell, *Scouting for Boys*, 1:49–51. On Americanizing the Scout Oath and Laws, see Murray, *History of the Boy Scouts*, 49–64; and Hurt, *Handbook for Scoutmasters*, 482–86. For early BSA Law consistency, see Hurt, *Handbook for Boys*, 34–37. For a recent explanation of the meanings of the BSA Laws, refer to Boy Scouts of America, *The Boy Scout Handbook*, 47–54. The British Boy Scouts added the BSA's new Law on being clean to its own program in 1912. Most BSA leaders described this new constellation of modern values as developing a well-rounded "happy medium," a "modest manliness," and a "full-orbed manhood." On "full-orbed manhood," see *Scout Executive*, April 1922, 1. On "happy medium," see Ripley, *Games for Boys*. These phrases and the term "modest manliness" were repeated in various forms throughout BSA literature and programming activities of the 1910s and 1920s.

2. For the British interpretation, see Rosenthal, *The Character Factory*.

3. BSA standard explanation in Murray, Pratt, and Jameson, *Official Handbook for Boys*, 15. Carey's popular book explaining the Scout Laws to boy readers was quite helpful in formulating this chapter. Carey, *Scout Law in Practice*, 67–69. Baden-Powell, *Scouting for Boys*, quotation on 1:49.

4. Emphasis in original. Baden-Powell, *Scouting for Boys*, first quotation on 1:50. Murray, Pratt, and Jameson, *Official Handbook for Boys*, second quotation on 15. "Loyalty," *Boys' Life*, July 1930, 24. For Scoutmaster's discipline instructions, see Boy Scouts of America, *Programs for Scout Masters*, 5. For other forms of Scout drilling, consult *Boys' Life*, September 1913, 34; *Boys' Life*, October 1913, 18; Hurt,

Handbook for Scoutmasters, 138, 354–58; and Wyland, *Principles of Scoutmastership*, 101–2. For examples of large Scout drills and skills public rallies, see *Scouting*, April 1922, 8; Boy Scouts of America, *Handbook for Scoutmasters*, 237; San Francisco Area Council BSA, *Twenty Years of Progress*, unpaged entries for 1923, 1924, 1931; and Narragansett Council BSA, *Scout Trail*, 23–24, 59.

5. Chapter 5 will further explore the relationship between the BSA and labor leaders. Baden-Powell, *Scouting for Boys*, first quotation on 1:49. "Suggestions by Joseph Lee," "Standardization Scout Oath and Law" volume, second quotation on 88, BSANA. Murray, Pratt, and Jameson, *Official Handbook for Boys*, third quotation on 15. Figure 2.1 sketch in Hurt, *Community Boy Leadership*, 352. For an excellent discussion of Ford Motor Company factory workers' fraternal loyalty management method, see Lewchuk, "Men and Monotony."

6. Hurt, *Handbook for Scoutmasters*, 175–77; Hurt, *Handbook for Boys*, 387–89; and Hurt, *Community Boy Leadership*, 502.

7. Murray, Pratt, and Jameson, *Official Handbook for Boys*, first quotation on 15. The Cave Scout, In the Scout Cave, *Boys' Life*, August 1920, 41. Colin Livingstone, "The Uniform of the Smile," in Hurt, *Handbook for Boys*, quotations on 80–81.

8. Richardson and Loomis, *The Boy Scout Movement*, first quotation on 353. See also the Cave Scout, "The Scout Who Will Stick," In the Scout Cave, *Boys' Life*, February 1915, 13; and the Cave Scout, In the Scout Cave, *Boys' Life*, May 1922, 38. Boy Scouts of America, *Programs for Scout Masters*, second quotation on 201. On hobos' failed work ethic, see John Rolfe, "Prize Essay," *Weekly News Bulletin of Boy Scout Activities*, May 29, 1925. On strikers' character, refer to "Lawlessness and the Training of the Young: Apropos of the 'Boy Scouts of America,'" *Century* 81, no. 3 (January 1911): 472–73.

9. Murray, Pratt, and Jameson, *Official Handbook for Boys*, first quotation on 15–16. Eliot, *The Training of Boy Scouts*, second quotation on 7. The BSANA's copy of Eliot's pamphlet was attached to a board with the typewritten note. See also *Paradise of the Pacific*, November 1919, 26. John D. Rockefeller Jr., "Scout Ideals," *Boys' Life*, July 1921, third quotation on 5.

10. A Buffalo Scout leader suggested a new clause for the Scout Oath in 1918: "On my honor I will be efficient in everything I do." Although the BSA's national Badges and Awards Committee rejected this formal change, efficiency pervaded most aspects of the program. Minutes of "Badges and Awards Committee, July 30, 1912–Nov. 13, 1928" (Nov. 26, 1918), 92. Macleod argued that Boy Scouting "matched the turn from moralism towards efficiency which observers have noted in Progressive Era ideology around 1910 to 1912. But it did not bring full-blown technocracy." Macleod, *Building Character*, 144, quotation on 165. For sample troop meetings, see the following issues of *Scouting*: October 3, 1918, 6; April 1922, 2; and December 1924, 15. See also Hurt, *Handbook for Scoutmasters*, 68–69; and Charles T. Johnson, "Study of the Boy Scout Organization," 132–38, 212–18.

11. Figure 2.2 in Boy Scouts of America, *Handbook for Boys*, 475. Second advertisement in Boy Scouts of America, *Handbook for Boys*, May 1927, quotations on 495. See also William D. Murray, "Why a Boy Is Like a Watch," *Boys' Life*, March 1921, 1;

and E. P. Beebe's speech for the Convention of Efficiency Society, "Scouting and Raw Material," *Scouting*, January 1, 1916, 15.

12. "—And Spending," *Boys' Life*, April 1929, quotation on 24. On spending thriftily, see Dan Beard, "A Scout Is Thrifty," *Boys' Life*, September 1917, 22; Boy Scouts of America, *Handbook for Scout Masters* (1914), 85; and Carey, *The Scout Law*, 135. On beggars, refer to "The Question of 'Begging' by Scouts," *Scouting*, February 1, 1917, 7; Dan Beard, "Some Straight Talk for Scouts," *Boys' Life*, May 1913, 32; and sketch in *Boys' Life*, February 1925, 14.

13. On British Scout and Guide modernity, see Proctor, *On My Honour*, 2–3, 107–8, 122.

14. *Tenderfoot Helps* (New York: BSA Service Library, 1930), quotation on 21.

15. *Physical Development* (New York: BSA, 1929), 23–24, quotations on 24. Carey Watt argued that early British and colonial Indian Scouting emphasized a supple and useful body for the emerging citizen over the showy muscles of extreme body-builders. Watt, "'No Showy Muscles.'"

16. Baden-Powell, *Scouting for Boys* 6:338; Seton and Baden-Powell, *A Handbook of Woodcraft*, xi–xii; Hurt, *Handbook for Scoutmasters*, 309–10; and Carey, *The Scout Law*, 44–46. Jacob Riis, "The Boy Scouts," *Outlook*, October 24, 1913; reprinted in *Improvement Era* 17, no. 9 (July 1914): 872. For one of the rare examples of Boy Scout sport leagues, see *Boys' Life*, December 1912, 36. On the continued BSA national leaders' rejection of sport competitions, see "Speech of James West before Joint Sessions of Department of Physical Education and Department of School Patrons" (Jul. 7, 1916), folder C-39-01, BSANA; and Dr. F. W. Johnson speech, "Educational Objectives," in Wyland, *Principles of Scoutmastership*, 43.

17. Carey, *The Scout Law*, 44–46. Fisher, "Health and Endurance." Despite discouragement from the national office, a few early local Scout leaders continued to run track meets and sport leagues. For a photograph of setting-up drill at camp, see Bowers, *"On My Honor,"* 37.

18. Italics in original. Seton and Baden-Powell, *A Handbook of Woodcraft*, xii, first quotation on 3. Boy Scouts of America, *Handbook for Boys*, second quotation on 11. Hurt, *Handbook for Boys*, third quotation on 11.

19. Fisher, "Health and Endurance," quotations on 232–33. Barker-Benfield, "The Spermatic Economy," 45–74. Macleod noted BSA leaders' confusion between semen and testosterone and their lack of frank discussion on sexuality and masturbation, despite being concerned about such matters. Macleod, *Building Character*, 49, 260–61; Macleod, "Act Your Age," 7; and Hantover, "Sex Role," 141–43. For an early decision to remove discussion of continence and purity from the Scout Laws so that boys would not be led to even think of such things, see minutes of BSA National Council (Feb. 14–15, 1911), 92–93. See also Hurt, *Handbook for Scoutmasters*, 34, 313; and Carey, *The Scout Law*, 47–59.

20. Fisher, "Health and Endurance," quotations on 223–27. This essay was repeated verbatim in the following two major handbook editions: Boy Scouts of America, *Handbook for Boys*, 305–19; and Hurt, *Handbook for Boys*, 495–512.

21. Baden-Powell, *Scouting for Boys*, 1:20. Murray, Pratt, and Jameson, *Official Handbook for Boys*, first quotation on 14. On the revision of the Oath and its mean-

ing for boys' lives, see 1922 ECR, 29; Hurt, *Handbook for Scoutmasters*, 33–34; and Carey, *The Scout Law*, 47–59. Previous historical accounts of the BSA have credited YMCA leaders or James West for the American addition to the Boy Scout Oath. Macleod, *Building Character*, 29, 149; and Rowan, *To Do My Best*, 38. Despite the presence of YMCA International Boys' Work director Edgar Robinson on the revision committee, the original version of the Scout Oath the committee sent out to leading educators, clergymen, and businessmen for suggestions did not contain the additional clause. In the collection of letters sent to the BSA revision committee, Hall's wording best approximated the revised Oath. For the BSA committee's original draft of the Scout "Vow," see "Standardization Scout Oath and Law" volume, hand-numbered page 90, BSANA. G. Stanley Hall letter to BSA national office (February 10, 1911), second quotation on hand-numbered pages 47–48, and G. Stanley Hall letter to James West (April 21, 1911), third quotation on hand-numbered page 164, both in "Standardization Scout Oath and Law" volume, BSANA.

22. For merit badge development and woodcraft and campcraft activities, see Murray, Pratt, and Jameson, *Official Handbook for Boys*, xiii–xiv, 16–18; Boy Scouts of America, *Handbook for Boys*, xiii–xiv; Hurt, *Handbook for Scoutmasters*, 176–77; Curtis, "The Boy Scouts," 495–97; Peterson, "Evolution of the Eagle Scout Award"; and Macleod, *Building Character*, 251–59, 376, 537.

23. Baden-Powell, *Sea Scouting*, first quotation on 7. On Scouts earning their own money, see Dillon Wallace session on "Troop Administration," transcript of Scoutmasters' training conference, Columbia University, February 2, 1917, hand-numbered page 187, BSANA; and "Bureau to Help Boy Scouts Get Occasional Jobs," *Los Angeles Times*, March 29, 1925, 18. Dan Beard essay draft, "Boy Pioneers Expect to Earn Their Own Living," 5–7, second quotation on 5, folder 9, "Boy Scouts of America (origins)," Box 209, Daniel Carter Beard Papers (hereafter referred to as DCBP). Emphasis in original.

24. Thornton W. Burgess, "Making Men of Them," reprinted from *Good Housekeeping* by the BSA, July 1914, first quotation on 10. The BSA reproduced this article as a pamphlet for distribution. See also Boy Scouts of America, *Handbook for Boys*, 16. "What's a Boy Scout?" *Boys' Life*, December 1915, second quotation on 26. Emphasis in original. See also Dr. H. H. Horne speech, "Methods of Education," in Wyland, *Principles of Scoutmastership*, 70.

25. "Honesty," *Boys' Life*, October 1930, first and second quotations on 24. John D. Rockefeller Jr., "Character and Business," *Boys' Life*, July 1928, third and fourth quotations on 39. On courtesy, see Hurt, *Handbook for Boys*, 24, 184–85. See also Macleod, *Building Character*, 201–3; and Wigginton, "The Boy Scouts," 59–69.

26. On boys' judging themselves, see Hurt, *Handbook for Boys*, 181, 382, 391. See also Cheley, *Practice of the Oath and Law*, 6; Hillcourt, *Handbook for Patrol Leaders*, 157; and "Loyalty," *Boys' Life*, July 1930, 24. On safaris, expeditions, and Lindbergh, see *Weekly News Bulletin of Boy Scout Activities*, May 25, 1929; "Scout Explorers," *Weekly News Bulletin of Boy Scout Activities*, September 6, 1930; Hurt, *Handbook for Boys*, cover sketch; and West, *Lone Scout of the Sky*. For the handicraft revival in Scouting, see George W. Goodard Jr., "Craftsmanship: What Part

Does Handicraft Take in Your Troop?" *Boys Life*, December 1930, 319. See also 1917 Scoutmasters' training conference, Columbia University, February 2, 1917, hand-numbered pages 178–79.

27. Figure 2.3, Frank Rigney cover sketch, *Business* (merit badge pamphlet) (New York: BSA, 1928): cover. The Square Deal recalled Theodore Roosevelt's successful 1904 presidential campaign slogan, part of which meant that the federal government would deal with everyone fairly and equally.

28. President Coolidge speech in Hurt, *Handbook for Scoutmasters*, 644–45. See also Hurt, *Community Boy Leadership*, 17, 161–63, 233. Charles Eliot's 1913 speech provided one of many examples of BSA supporters' belief that cooperation promoted work efficiency. Charles Eliot, "President-Emeritus of Harvard Speaks in Praise of Scout Work," *Scouting*, December 15, 1913, 3. On the balance between the individual and cooperation in the BSA, see Macleod, "Act Your Age," 8–9; Macleod, *Building Character*, 105; and Wigginton, "The Boy Scouts," 1–24. On the 1920s youth subculture's balancing of cooperation and competition, see Fass, *Damned and the Beautiful*, chap. 5.

29. For several of many statements claiming that Scouting was noncompetitive, see Hantover, "Sex Role," 131–38; Seton and Baden-Powell, *A Handbook of Woodcraft*, 13; and Oursler, *The Boy Scout Story*, 40–41. James Wilder, "Report of Commission on Sea Scouting," 1922 ECR, first quotation on 129. See also 1920 BSA Annual Report, 67; Wyland, *Principles of Scoutmastership*, 32; and Hurt, *Handbook for Scoutmasters*, 240–41, 319–34, 672–75. For the practice council design discussion, see Boy Scouts of America, *First National Training School*, 634.

30. Italics in original. Hurt, *Handbook for Scoutmasters*, quotation on 672.

31. First quotation and progress grid sketch in Scoutmaster M. M. Babcock, "Good Troop Records Make for Progress," *Scouting*, October 1928, 7. For information on the credit system, refer to Hurt, *Handbook for Scoutmasters*, 195. Boy Scouts of America, *Handbook for Scout Masters* (1914), 129–36, 239–45, 293, last quotation on 253.

32. Wyland, *Principles of Scoutmastership*, 56, 227–34, quotation on 228. For other warnings against badge grabbers, see Stuart P. Walsh, "A Scout's Advancement" speech, 1926 ECR, 105; and *Troop Spirit* (New York: BSA, 1930), 3, 6–7. On competing without developing a haughty or defeatist attitude, see Hillcourt, *Handbook for Patrol Leaders*, 52–53. On the importance of individual ambition, willpower, and aggressiveness for self-made manhood and success in the 1800s, consult Wyllie, *The Self-Made Man*, 34–41; Cawelti, *Apostles of the Self-Made Man*, 47–52, 101–23; and Hilkey, *Character Is Capital*, 78–82, 142–51.

33. Emphasis in original. Boy Scouts of America, *Programs for Scout Masters*, 79–80, 89–90.

34. Emphasis in original. Ibid., 7, 47–52, 201, quotations on 185. See also Boy Scouts of America, *Handbook for Scout Masters* (1914), 33, 62; and 1926 ECR, 105.

35. Emphasis in original. Murray, Pratt, and Jameson, *Official Handbook for Boys*, first quotation on 15. Ashley Piper, "A New Moral Force," *Outlook*, February 12, 1919, second quotation on 265. See also "Boy Scouts and Service," *Chicago Daily Tribune*, July 6, 1911, 8. Many BSA and mass media sources discussed the impor-

tance of the Scout's Good Turn, such as *Chicago Daily Tribune*, December 18, 1913, 1; Boy Scouts of America, *Handbook for Scout Masters* (1914), 21–22, 89, 156, 312; "Old Lady Adopted," *New York Times*, March 2, 1924, X12; and Ray Sisley, "A Thanksgiving Day 'Good Turn,'" *Chicago Daily Tribune*, November 21, 1925, B13.

36. For one of many iterations of the masculine values learned through Life Saving, see Hurt, *Handbook for Scoutmasters*, 144. "Boy Scout Dives into Bay and Saves Woman While Men Stand Helplessly on the Sea Wall," *New York Times*, June 10, 1928, first quotation on 1. "Scouts Find Three Lost Men," *Boys' Life*, January 1914, second quotation on 19. See also "Week's Best Good Turn," *Los Angeles Times*, October 28, 1923, X2; and "Scout Rescue Unit Formed," *New York Times*, February 10, 1929, 142.

37. "A Scout Is Courteous," *Boys' Life*, April 1926, initial quotations on 22. See also Murray, Pratt, and Jameson, *Official Handbook for Boys*, 15; and Hurt, *Handbook for Boys*, 35. "Race Chivalry," *Boys' Life*, June 1927, middle quotation on 24. "Help Aged Negro," *New York Times*, April 11, 1926, X22. 1924 BSA Annual Report, last quotations on 26–27.

38. Baden-Powell, *Scouting for Boys*, first quotation on 1:49–50. BSA version in Murray, Pratt, and Jameson, *Official Handbook for Boys*, 15. "Scout Law. III: General Differences Noted," Standardization Scout Oath and Law volume, second quotation on hand-numbered page 247, BSANA.

39. Carey, *The Scout Law*, 96–103, quotations on 96, 98.

40. Murray, Pratt, and Jameson, *Official Handbook for Boys*, first quotation on 16. By contrast, see Beard's Sons of Daniel Boone Top Notch award for bravery explanation in "Mark Twain Top Notch," Folder 3, Box 209, DCBP. Recent BSA handbooks have specified that defending the rights of others demonstrates bravery and that one should befriend those of other races. Boy Scouts of America, *The Boy Scout Handbook*, 49, 53. For examples of knight, Pilgrim, and pioneer bravery against savage men, see Andy Janson sketches in Hurt, *Handbook for Boys*, 20–23; and "Our Inheritance of Courage and The Tenth Scout Law," *Boys' Life*, March 1926, 24.

41. For a sketch of a Scout standing up to working-class toughs to protect an innocent boy, see S. H. Wainwright painting, *Boys' Life*, April 1922, 2. For real incidents of Boy Scouts standing up against street toughs, see "Show Courage," *Boys' Life*, October 1912, 28; and *Boys' Life*, January 1914, 18.

42. Murray, Pratt, and Jameson, *Official Handbook for Boys*, first quotation on 16. Of the three new American Scout Laws, Baden-Powell only adopted the Law on being clean to the British Boy Scout program. *Paradise of the Pacific*, November 1919, second quotation on 26. *Tenderfoot Helps* (New York: BSA Service Library, 1930), third quotation on 23–24.

43. Wyland, *Principles of Scoutmastership*, 240–41, quotation on 140. See also Carey, *The Scout Law*; and 1922 ECR, 30, 238–39. For the patriotic and reverent pioneer, see Sidney Risenberg sketch, *Boys' Life*, November 1926, 16. On Baden-Powell and British Boy Scouting placing more emphasis on general morality and good deeds rather than religion, while the BSA stressed religious reverence and duty more explicitly, see Proctor, *Scouting for Girls*, 17; Macleod, "Original Intent," 19–25; and Mechling, "God and 'Whatever' in the Boy Scouts of America."

44. Murray, Pratt, and Jameson, *Official Handbook for Boys*, quotation on 16. For West's role in creating the Law on reverence, see 1922 ECR, 29–30. On troop sponsorship, consult Macleod, *Building Character*, 23, 43–44, 93. Early BSA sources reveal little domestic dissent on the reverence policy, although the Law stirred some debate at the international level, since Scout organizations in some countries followed Baden-Powell in downplaying focus on religion, while others copied the BSA's new reverence Law. However, once Catholic, Jewish, and Mormon leaders were convinced to support Scouting, few Americans appeared to raise serious religious complaints on a public level toward the BSA in the 1910s and 1920s.

45. Von Allman, "A Study of the San Francisco District Council," 78–81. "Dividends of Scouting," 1928 ECR, 603–5. See also Dr. Lindley Kimball, "Character Values of Scouting: Part II," in Wyland, *Principles of Scoutmastership*, 182–87.

46. 1928 ECR, 569–71.

47. In a separate Table D of the boys' 1928 survey, respondents reported the most difficulty complying with the Scout Laws on being friendly at troop and patrol meetings, council camps, and Scout games, and being obedient at troop meetings and council camp. 1928 ECR, 565–72.

48. 1928 ECR, 602–9.

49. Kelly interview in Yater, *A History of Troop 1 (201)*, 116–18. Utter interview in Price, *Thirty Years of Scout Camping*, 26.

50. Geiss, *Youth—the Hope of the World*, 6–15, 20–26, first quotation on 22. Shaver, *Notes from a Pioneer's Journal*, second quotation on 37.

51. 1928 ECR, 596–98.

52. Ibid., 587–91. See also Johnson, "A Study of the Boy Scout Organization," 201.

53. Emphasis in original. Geiss, *Reminiscences of a Berks County Rural Boy*, 1–5, 55–74, 63–64, quotation on 55–57. Geiss, *Youth—the Hope of the World*, 46–69. Edwards, "The Hatching of an Eagle," in *Slices from My Life*, stories 49, 65. Henderson, *A Thousand Campfires*, 22. Longtime Scoutmaster August Kietzman stated that it was better for Scouts to learn cooperation, since competition was destructive and anti-Christian. Kietzman, *Why I Became a Scoutmaster*, 29–31.

54. Lamb, *My Scout and Other Poems*, 83–84. 1928 ECR, 573–75.

55. Fetridge, *With Warm Regards*, 117, 170, 173–74, 241–46.

Chapter Three

1. Baden-Powell, *Scouting for Boys* 1:9–12, 6:335–36. Woodcraft Indians vowed obedience only to their own elected council's decisions, not to all authorities. Seton, *Birch-Bark Roll of the Woodcraft Indians*, 2–13. Seton, *Birch Bark Roll of the Outdoor Life*, 6–13. Seton and Baden-Powell, *Handbook of Woodcraft*, 8–10, 47. Wadland's fine examination of Seton summarized the program's civic thrust succinctly: "The Woodcraft Indians were supposed to become a body of critical youth, challenging accepted values and suggesting constructive alternatives." Wadland, "Ernest Thompson Seton," 459. On Seton, Beard, and Robinson's recruitment of Roosevelt to the early BSA, see Robert Peterson, "The BSA's

'Forgotten' Founding Father," *Scouting*, October 1998; and Beard, *Hardly a Man*, 355–59. Roosevelt's citizenship essay reproduced in Murray, Pratt, and Jameson, *Official Handbook for Boys*, 353–56. For West's requests to Roosevelt to edit the new draft of the Boy Scout Laws and handbook chapter on citizenship and to write an introductory note for the handbook, see James West letters to Theodore Roosevelt (Feb. 23, 1911; July 14, 1911; July 15, 1911; July 22, 1911; Aug. 4, 1911; Aug. 24, 1911), and Roosevelt reply to West (July 20, 1911), Theodore Roosevelt Papers, Reels 100, 109–10, 368. Roosevelt letter to West (Feb. 10, 1911), Roosevelt Papers, Reel 364. For letters West forwarded to contribute ideas for Roosevelt's handbook essay, see O. W. Price letter to West (May 23, 1911), Judge Ben B. Lindsey letter to West (June 19, 1911), and J. Horace McFarland letter to West (June 23, 1911), Roosevelt Papers, Reels 107–9.

2. The American middle class had been gradually removing their children from paid work since at least the mid-1800s, but the expansion of age-segregated children's spaces and socialization programs by the early twentieth century completed the separation of children (including the working classes to a significant degree) from many aspects of adults' productive work and political engagement. Zelizer, *Pricing the Priceless Child*.

3. On broad political changes of the late 1800s and early 1900s, see Schudson, *The Good Citizen*, 146–217; and Cawelti, *Apostles of the Self-Made Man*, 54–55, 168–69.

4. Murray, Pratt, and Jameson, *Official Handbook for Boys*, 323–56; Boy Scouts of America, *Handbook for Boys*, 11–12; and H. W. Hurt, "Citizencraft," in Hurt, *Handbook for Boys*, 524–32. Social geographer Sarah Mills argued that Baden-Powell and other early British Boy Scout officials envisioned youth members as both future citizens-in-training and community members with a distinct, active civic role to play during their youth, such as performing the Scout's daily Good Turn and voluntary character development through the Scout rank and badge process. Mills, "'An Instruction in Good Citizenship,'" 120–34.

5. First quotations in Hurt, *Handbook for Scoutmasters*, 9, 498, 521; see also 540, 642. For nonpartisan resolution, see *Scouting*, August 1, 1916, 6. See also Boy Scouts of America, *Handbook for Scout Masters* (1914), 6. Macleod argued that the BSA's nonpartisanship resembled the conservative end of Progressivism. Most national Executive Board members were Republicans, outside of a few southern Democrats. Macleod, *Building Character*, 185.

6. Nicholl, *The Golden Wheel*, 222–25. Proceedings of the Ninth Annual Convention of the International Association of Rotary Clubs (Chicago: International Association of Rotary Clubs, 1918), 486–501, quotations on 489, 497. On the range and motivations of businessmen's clubs that supported Scout troops, see "Business Men and Boy Scouts," *Los Angeles Times*, August 5, 1923, IX3; "Kiwanis Club as Civic and National Force," *Los Angeles Times*, March 22, 1918, III3; and "News of the Men's Clubs," *Chicago Daily Tribune*, December 4, 1921, G11.

7. Boy Scouts of America, *First National Training School*, 168–69, 263–77. For Boy Scouts helping lead and guide parades, see Kansas City Area Council BSA, *Trail to Eagle*, 12, 13, 14; and San Francisco Area Council BSA, *Twenty Years of*

Progress, 3. For an example of voter registration drives, see West, *Bulletin to All Scout Officials*, August 20, 1924, 3.

8. *Civics* merit badge pamphlet (New York: BSA, 1930), 2–16, 43–47, 53–58, 62–65.

9. "Scouting Program Helps Develop Civic Responsibilities," *Scouting*, February 20, 1919, 2. 1922 ECR, 322–27. For a leading sociologist's analysis of Scouting's modern civic training, see Dr. Edward A. Ross speech, "How to Teach Participating Citizenship," 1926 ECR, 42–44, 248–54. House of Representatives report of bill 755, 1917 BSA Annual Report, 144; and "Scouting," *Friend*, September 1916, 209–11.

10. George J. Fisher, "Boyhood and Citizenship Training," *Scout Executive*, February 1923, 7. For a BSA critique of the lack of practical civic training in schools, see James West, "Training Young America for Citizenship," *Playground*, April 1923, 18–20. Hurt, *Handbook for Boys*, 392. Murray, Pratt, and Jameson, *Official Handbook for Boys*, 349–53. For a broad sampling of the many local and national lists of the kinds of services and projects Boy Scouts completed, see Hurt, *Handbook for Scoutmasters*, 219–33. For other historical interpretations of the BSA's civic service activities, see Macleod, *Building Character*, 173–75, 253–55; and Hantover, "Sex Role," 135–37.

11. Boy Scouts of America, *Programs for Scout Masters*, first quotation on 10. Boy Scouts of America, *Handbook for Scout Masters* (1914), second quotation on 44; see also 73, 89. Hurt, *Handbook for Scoutmasters*, third quotation on 436.

12. William B. Ashley, "The Local Council Civic Service Committee," *Scout Executive*, June 1930, quotation on 6–7; "One Good Turns Deserved Another," *Scouting*, March 1927, 13–14; and Boy Scouts of America, *The Good Turn Test* pamphlet. For one of the most extensive reports on Boy Scout Good Turns, see "Report of the Chief Scout Executive for 1927" to the BSA National Council, 12–33, folder "Boy Scouts of America—Boy's Life 1927–1928," SIII-4 B-12, Laura Spelman Rockefeller Memorial Collection (hereafter referred to as LSRMC).

13. Stuart Walsh, "Vitalizing the Good Turn," *Scouting*, December 1927, 5. For equating Good Turns with Scout manhood and citizenship training in BSA and popular media sources, see "Scouting and Citizenship," 1926 ECR, 275–81; Moffat, "Volunteer Citizens," 317–19; "What Boy Scouts Are Good For," *Literary Digest*, February 17, 1923, 41–44; Gladden, "Some Practical Aspects of Scouting," 573–75; and Helen Jones, "The Boy Scouts of America," 562–63. On public event and parade Scout service, see 1913 BSA Annual Report, 28; and "Service at Fairs and Conventions," 1922 BSA Annual Report, 24–25.

14. James West, "Trained for Citizenship: The Boy Scout," *American Review of Reviews*, December 1916, 643–48; Figure 3.1 on 645. L. F. Kimball, "Plan of Cooperation with the Police Department as Worked Out by the Brooklyn Council," *Scout Executive*, April 1925, 3. For other apprentice patrols and troops, see 1926 BSA Annual Report, 24–25; "Scouts as Aids to Firemen and Policemen," 1922 BSA Annual Report, 30; and E. S. Martin, "Educating the Public in Safety," *American City*, February 1927, 180.

15. "Headquarters Correspondence on Questions of Policy," *Scouting*, June 15, 1916, 6; "And as Special Police Aides," *Scouting*, June 1921, 4–5; "Scout Traffic

Police for Greater Safety at Schools: Courts Uphold," *Weekly News Bulletin of Boy Scout Activities*, November 20, 1926; and "They Shall Not Pass," *Scout Executive*, August 1922, 1–2.

16. "Scouts Take an Active Part in 'Safe and Sane' Celebrations," *Scouting*, August 1, 1914, 3; "Let Your Scouts Be the Leaders in Sane Celebrations this 'Fourth,'" *Scouting*, June 1, 1914, 1–2; and Lee Hanmer, "Scouting for a Sane Fourth," *Scouting*, June 1, 1913, 3.

17. *Scouting*, August 1924, 1–3, 6; "Scouting's Greatest National Good Turn," *Scouting*, September 1924, 1–3, 5; West, "Citizenship Training," *Bulletin for All Scout Officials*, September 24, 1924; "Scouts Help Raise Voting Average," *Scouting*, November 1924, quotation on 2; and "Boy Scouts after Vote Slackers," *Literary Digest*, September 20, 1924, 57–58.

18. On San Francisco Scouts helping as nurses and messengers during the influenza epidemic of 1918, see San Francisco Area Council BSA, *Twenty Years of Progress*, 1918 entry. See also Shaver, *Notes from a Pioneer's Journal*, 66–67.

19. "The Florida Hurricane," 1926 BSA Annual Report, 15–16. "The Mississippi Flood," *Boys' Life*, July 1927, 25. See also "Boy Scouts Work Effectively in Mississippi Flood Disaster," *Weekly News Bulletin of Boy Scout Activities*, July 9, 1927; and "Report of the Chief Scout Executive for 1927" to the BSA National Council, 31–33. For examples of cooperation between the Red Cross and the BSA, see Wilbert Longfellow, "The Red Cross and the Boy Scout Movement," *Scout Executive*, March 1928, 5.

20. House of Representatives report of bill 755, 1917 BSA Annual Report, 144. On the BSA's efforts to achieve the federal charter and some of its ambiguities, see Macleod, "Original Intent," 17–19.

21. For some of the many works arguing that British, Canadian, and Australian Scouting in the 1910s was highly militaristic, see Wilkinson, "English Youth Movements"; Morris, "Ernest Thompson Seton"; Springhall, "The Boy Scouts, Class and Militarism"; Rosenthal, "Knights and Retainers"; Springhall, "Baden-Powell and the Scout Movement"; Anne Summers, "Scouts, Guides and VADs"; MacDonald, "Reproducing the Middle-Class Boy"; and Hill, "Building a Nation of Nation-Builders." For opposing arguments that British Boy Scouting emphasized broad character training more than it did militarism, see Warren, "Sir Robert Baden-Powell"; Warren, "Baden-Powell"; Jeal, *Baden-Powell*, 409–11, 510–17; and Galt-Brown, "Baden-Powell and His Boy Scouts." For additional works arguing that British Boy Scouting and Girl Guiding shifted some from military defense preparation toward service and internationalism after World War I, see Proctor, "Gender, Generation, and the Politics of Guiding and Scouting in Interwar Britain"; Proctor, *On My Honour*, 85–102; and Bragg, "The Boy Scout Movement in Canada," 88, 114–19, 127. Crotty argued that militarism remained a much more vital aspect of and problem for Australian Boy Scouting than it was in mainland British Scouting after World War I. Crotty, "Scouts Down Under," 74–88.

22. On the BSA's statement that it was neither pro- nor antimilitary, see Peterson, *The Boy Scouts*, 57–59. For a stronger BSA national statement that it was

nonmilitary in 1914, see BSA Executive Board meeting minutes (Mar. 20, 1914), 3. On the militarism debate and the low numbers of military men in BSA leadership, see Wills, *Boy Scouts of America*, 49–57; Hantover, "Sex Role," 251–52; and Macleod, "Original Intent," 16–17. On the unfulfilled desire of Bomus and Verbeck for the BSA to take a stronger stance in favor of militarism and martial training, see "American Boy Scouts," *Washington Post*, May 22, 1910, E4; and "To Teach Yegg Signs: Peace Aids, Not Military," *Washington Post*, March 26, 1911, 81.

23. While the majority of Baden-Powell's serialized 1908 handbook emphasized military training and imagery, his sixth volume hedged this tone slightly. Baden-Powell, *Scouting for Boys*, 1:9, 37, 52–57; 3:182; 5:321–28; 6:340–42. The first 1912 proof edition of the American Scoutmaster's handbook contained a section on using military drill with Scout troops, reprinted from a British Boy Scout drill book written by Baden-Powell. However, subsequent editions of the American Scoutmaster's handbook downplayed it. Seton and Baden-Powell, *A Handbook of Woodcraft*, 50–51. Boy Scouts of America, *Programs for Scout Masters*, 22–37. The 1914 Scoutmaster's handbook rewrote this section but still discussed drilling. Boy Scouts of America, *Handbook for Scout Masters* (1914), 276–93. On the BSA reaching out to peace organizations and Jordan, see Scott and Murphy, *The Scouting Party*, 173–82. Boy Scouts of America, *Handbook for Boys*, 12–13, 439. On civilian Scout drilling, consult Hantover, "Sex Role," 251–53; and Arthurs, "Boy Scouts Building for Manhood," 276–77. On physical fitness directors leading Scout drills, see Kenney, *Honor Bright*, 9–10. The BSA maintained a Marksmanship merit badge but discouraged the use of guns in drilling. The 1929 Scoutmaster's handbook even suggested that guns not be allowed at camp at all, since they would make it difficult to ensure the boys' safety. Hurt, *Handbook for Scoutmasters*, 388. On congressional bills allowing only the BSA to wear military-like uniforms, see Army Reorganization Law, Section 125, in Boy Scouts of America, *Handbook for Boys* (1919), 31; Hurt, *Handbook for Scoutmasters*, 364; and Dean, "Scouting in America," 48.

24. Parsons, *Race, Resistance, and the Boy Scout Movement*, especially 23–25, 69–71, 87–88; Miller, *Growing Girls*, 31–43; and Proctor, "(Uni)Forming Youth," 103–34.

25. Sherman, "The Boy Scouts 300,000 Strong," quotation on 1487o. For one of several statements on not needing a uniform, see Murray, Pratt, and Jameson, *Official Handbook for Boys*, 46. The Boy Scout handbook in use from 1914 to 1927 was more typical of BSA literature in arguing that "the scout uniform should be an outward expression of the scout's inward feeling of friendliness to every other scout, no matter to what class in society the other scout belongs. It represents the spirit of true democracy." Boy Scouts of America, *Handbook for Boys* (1919), 77. See also Kenneth A. Wells, "The Scout Uniform," *Scouting*, October 1927, 2. On BSA uniform debates and policies, see Boy Scouts of America, "Minutes of the Annual Meetings: February 14–15, 1911 to May 28–29, 1925" volume (1911): 68, BSANA; Boy Scouts of America, *Handbook for Scout Masters* (1914), 126. On British uniform prices and class distinctions, see Proctor, "(Uni)Forming Youth"; and Proctor, *Scouting for Girls*, 15–16.

26. For a good overview of statistics and documents related to the many Scout civilian service drives during World War I and Wilson's Boy Scout Week declaration, see pamphlet, "Service Record in the First World War," BSA, 1941, box "BSA World War One: Liberty Bond & War Savings Stamp Materials," BSANA. For second quotation, see news bulletin, "Washington Believes in the Scouts" in same archival box. On Scout war bond sales, see Dean, "Scouting in America," 60; and "Boy Scouts after Vote Slackers," *Literary Digest*, September 20, 1924, 57–58. For Wilson's letter on the Scout bond drive, see folder "665 2nd Liberty Loan Application" (Sept. 20, 1917), BSANA. On government dispatch bearing and peach pit, nutshell, and black walnut service drives, see Cronin, "Ninety-Two Years of Service," 24–31; and Brittain, *The Spirit of Scouting '76*, 16. For Scout gardens, see "'A Scout Is Hungry': But He Need Not Be," *Boys' Life*, April 1917, 34; and R. N. Berry, "Scout Garden Leadership," *Scouting*, June 1, 1918, 6–7. On the home-front food conservation Scout campaign and last quotation, see folder "293,000 Boys Aid the Nation by Hermann Hagedorn," box "BSA World War One: Liberty Bond & War Savings Stamp Materials," BSANA.

27. On the Scoutmaster recruitment campaign during World War I, see folders 295 and 262 documents: "Boys Through Scouting Help Uncle Sam Win the War," "Every Scout to Save a Soldier—Emergency Circular #7," "Scout Leaders Reserve Corps Boy Scouts of America 'Wanted 100,000 Men for Leaders of Uncle Sam's Boys,'" and "Roosevelt Appeals for Scoutmasters—News Release" (Sept. 11, 1917), box "BSA World War One: Liberty Bond & War Savings Stamp Materials," BSANA. On the Scout campaign to get veterans' jobs back, see "Emergency Circular No. 66 to Scoutmasters Helping Soldiers Get Their Old Jobs Back," BSA National Council, New York City, letter from James West to Scoutmasters (Aug. 20, 1919), folder KAU 19/2 Haw, C, General Correspondence—1919–1920, in Hawaii Sugar Plantations Association papers, Honolulu.

28. On the peace Scouting emphasis in the BSA, see also Arthurs, "Boy Scouts Building for Manhood," 277. Hurt, *Handbook for Boys*, 536–37. Hurt, *Handbook for Scoutmasters*, 69, 74, 138, 218–19, 354–57, 543. On Baden-Powell's shift toward peaceful internationalism in the 1920s, see Vallory, "Status Quo Keeper or Social Change Promoter."

29. Quotation in Boy Scouts of America, *First National Training School*, 230.

30. Hurt, *Handbook for Scoutmasters*, 436. "Coolidge Praises Boy Scout Ideals," *New York Times*, May 2, 1926, 18. 1930 BSA Annual Report, 56. 1929 BSA Annual Report, 344–45. Figure 3.2 photo at Library of Congress Prints and Photographs Division. For the South Dakota Boy Scouts' horse gift, refer to *Weekly News Bulletin of Boy Scout Activities*, July 16, 1927, and August 29, 1927. See also "Visit to the White House," *Boys' Life*, June 1926, 26. For Taft with New Haven, Connecticut, Scouts, see Bogan, "No Larger Fields," 66. For Harding at inauguration as BSA honorary President with other Scouts and officials, see *Scouting*, March 1921, 8; and Boy Scout Fact Sheet, "The Presidents of the United States and the Boy Scouts of America," 2001. For Lou Henry Hoover's leadership of the Girl Scouts of the United States, consult Miller, *Growing Girls*, 49–56; and Proctor, *Scouting for Girls*, 40. For Dawes's troop sponsorship, see *Weekly News Bulletin of Boy Scout Activities*,

November 12, 1927. For the Senate troop, see "United States Senate Pages Organize Own Boy Scout Troop," *Weekly News Bulletin of Boy Scout Activities*, December 21, 1929; and "A Troop of Senate Pages," *Boys' Life*, March 1930, 25.

31. Hurt, *Handbook for Scoutmasters*, 230–33. For state and national forest Scout camps, see 1925 BSA Annual Report, 25. On Navy charts gift, refer to *Weekly News Bulletin of Boy Scout Activities*, June 15, 1929. For First Aid packets, see *Scout Executive*, December 15, 1922, 7. On surplus military camping equipment, see "Army Supplies for Scout Use," *Scout Executive*, June 1922, 3. For the 1929 Jamboree army equipment, consult folder "1929—Jamboree Diary by E. L. Vickery (Original at Museum)" transcript, 10–11, BSANA.

32. For lists of state governors supporting the BSA, see 1913 and 1914 BSA Annual Reports. For state governor Scouts, see "The Wrong Governor," *Boys' Life*, June 1922, 54; and "Governors Who Are Now Scouts," *Boys' Life*, April 1922, 28. For Arizona legislature joining Scouts, see "Patriotism the Keynote of the Coming 14th Anniversary Week Celebration," *Scouting*, December 1923, 1 (italics in original). See also *Scouting*, February 15, 1918, 7, 13.

33. "Governors Send Messages to Scouts," *Boys' Life*, November 1915, 9–13; and 1918 BSA Annual Report, 58–60. See also "Governors of Many States Send Greetings to the National Council," *Scouting*, February 15, 1914, 5.

34. "Boy Scouts as City Fathers," *American City*, February 1926, 184–86. "President Harding an Active Exponent of Scouting," *Scouting*, June 1921, 3. For Pennsylvania Scout Mayors for a Day, see "National Council News," *Boys' Life*, June 1923, 34. On Yakni Council Scout elections, see Watkins, *Yakni*, 15. Wesleyan University, Temple University, and the University of Pennsylvania were among the colleges awarding special scholarships to accomplished Scouts by the mid-1920s. Philadelphia Council BSA, *Seventy Years of Scouting*, 29; and Narragansett Council BSA, *Scout Trail*, 62.

35. The other two frequent responses included "building character," with 13.4 percent of Scoutmasters' responses, and "developing self-reliance," with 7.2 percent of responses. "Scoutmaster and His Job," Commission report appendix, 1928 ECR, 55–56. Johnson's 1929 survey of one hundred leading Scoutmasters from thirty-eight states reported fairly similar findings about what troop leaders identified as the strongest part of the Scout program. Johnson, "A Study of the Boy Scout Organization," 61–63.

36. Fetridge, *With Warm Regards*, 237–41, 251–62.

37. Kietzman, *Why I Became a Scoutmaster*, 152–57.

38. 1928 ECR, 569–71, 604. Hagood, *52 Years of Adventure*, 43. See also Charles T. Johnson, "A Study of the Boy Scout Organization," 25.

39. 1928 ECR, 565–68, 591–94. Hagood, *52 Years of Adventure*, 25–27. Yater, *A History of Troop 1 (201)*, final quotations on 118.

40. Dillon, *On My Honor*, 27–31. Creighton and Johnson, *Boys Will Be Men*, 26–30, 37–53, quotation on 28.

41. 1928 ECR, 54–56, 70–72.

42. Watkins, *Yakni*, 19–22. Charles T. Johnson, "A Study of the Boy Scout Organization," 210.

43. Creighton and Johnson, *Boys Will Be Men*, 55–56. Adams, *My Thirty Years in Scouting*, 4, 7, 13, quotation on 45.

44. Kietzman, *Why I Became a Scoutmaster*, foreword, 7–11, 47–48, 107.

Chapter Four

1. Figure 4.1, Frank Rigney sketch, *Boys' Life*, February 1917, 29.

2. Seton, *The Birch-Bark Roll of the Woodcraft Indians*, 12–13; 2–3, 47–66; Seton, "Laws of the Seton Indians," in Chesley, *Social Activities*, 263; and Beard, *The Boy Pioneers*, 112–14. BSA leaders and publications most often explained being kind to animals in terms of domesticated animals like dogs and horses rather than wild animals. Murray, Pratt, and Jameson, *Official Handbook for Boys*, 15–16; and Baden-Powell, *Scouting for Boys*, 6:343, 351.

3. On the strong influence of frontier imagery in Boy Scouting in other countries and Girl Guiding/Scouting, see Proctor, *Scouting for Girls*; Miller, *Growing Girls*, 52–56, 122–57; Bragg, "Boy Scout Movement in Canada"; Pryke, "Popularity of Nationalism," 309–23; Rosenthal, *Character Factory*, chap. 2; MacDonald, *Sons of the Empire*; and Bar-Yosef, "Fighting Pioneer Youth." The growing emphasis on science and efficiency in BSA nature ideology at the expense of pioneering imagery is analyzed in Jordan, " 'Conservation of Boyhood.' "

4. Hurt, *Handbook for Scoutmasters*, 372. The two best recent works on the history of summer camping argued that early twentieth-century camps were primarily antimodern or distanced children from adult production work and public life. Van Slyck, *A Manufactured Wilderness*, xx–xxvi, 7–8, 158, 176–77; and Paris, *Children's Nature*, 4, 8–46, 103, 122, 165–88, 240–42, 276. For other discussions of Scout nature philosophy, see Sterne, "Formation of the Scouting Movement," 228–31; and Wagner, "The Boy Scouts of America," 217–22, 240.

5. Boy Scouts of America, *Programs for Scout Masters*, 4–6, 16–18, 61, quotations on 19. Richard Braunstein, "From a Scoutmaster's Duffle Bag," *Scouting*, February 12, 1920, 11. President Coolidge's speech in Hurt, *Handbook for Scoutmasters*, 638–39. Amy Green argued that male advocates of adolescent theory believed boys evolved to domination of nature while girls reached a plateau at the primitive stage of nature intimacy. Green, "Savage Childhood," 113.

6. Armitage argued that early twentieth-century Nature Study blended scientific modernity with a Romantic, spiritual critique of the narrow, instrumental view of society embedded in corporate industrialization, but few BSA sources conveyed a sentimental or Romantic tone or motivation for Nature Study activities. Armitage, *The Nature Study Movement*. For the American Museum of Natural History Troop, see "Boy Scouts as Naturalists," *American Review of Reviews*, June 1919, 627–29. For examples of Scout Nature Study activities and purposes, consult Murray, Pratt, and Jameson, *Official Handbook for Boys*, 85–142; Hillcourt, *Handbook for Patrol Leaders*, 321–26; Boy Scouts of America, *Handbook for Scout Masters* (1914), 59–60; and Boy Scouts of America, *Programs for Scout Masters*, 44–45, 82–83. "Nature Study: A Year-Round Troop Project," *Scouting*, April 1926, quotation on 2. On early Girl Scout Nature Study emphases, see Miller, *Growing Girls*, 125–34.

7. First quotation in "Trees and Birds, Scouts' Wards," *Weekly News Bulletin of Boy Scout Activities*, April 23, 1925. "The Bird Study Booklet," *Scouting*, June 26, 1919, second quotation on 6. *Bird Study* merit badge pamphlet (New York: BSA, 1919). George Gladden, "John Burroughs," *Scouting*, July 3, 1919, 10–11. Figure 4.2 in 1919 BSA Annual Report, 95. See also Murray, Pratt, and Jameson, *Official Handbook for Boys*, 85–94. For two of the many publications advocating specimen hunts, consult "What to Do with Your Nature Study Collections," *Boys' Life*, October 1921, 23; and Denslow, *Making Nature Collections*.

8. Seton's key Nature Study sections in Seton and Baden-Powell, *Handbook of Woodcraft*, 99–114, 127–42. Murray, Pratt, and Jameson, *Official Handbook for Boys*, 85–142. Boy Scouts of America, *Handbook for Boys*, 164–231. The fourth Scout handbook's tree identification section opened with an ill-fitting sketch and poem by Joyce Kilmer, alluding to a Mother Earth breastfeeding female trees that wore robins' nests in their hair. An expanded plant section explained that it was important because plants are the food makers and make human life possible. Hurt, *Handbook for Boys*, 456, 283, quotation on 334.

9. C. A. Edson, "Good and Bad Citizens in Nature," *Scouting*, February 1927, 12.

10. Figure 4.3, Frank Rigney sketch, "The Boy Scout Trail to Citizenship," *Scouting*, November 1925, 25. For an example of Local Councils reenacting this "Trail to Citizenship," see the Little Rock plan for a public demonstration at the Arkansas State Fair in "Scout Trail to Citizenship," *Boys' Life*, October 1930, 44.

11. Figure 4.4 in *Boys' Life*, August 1922, 16.

12. Hurt, *Handbook for Scoutmasters*, 127, 51, 64, 105, see also 59–63, 103–5. The handbook did explain, though, that longer trips of ten miles or more were adventurous hikes.

13. "Hiking and Trekking" discussion group transcript, Scoutmasters Conference, Columbia University Teachers College, New York City, 10:30 A.M. session, February 3, 1917, quotations on hand-numbered 273–75 in conference report volume, BSANA. Hillcourt, *Handbook for Patrol Leaders*, 166, 189–90. For two of the many other sources instructing leaders to have a specific character or skill goal in mind for each hike, see Joseph Ames, "The Manhood of To-morrow," *Saint Nicholas*, February 1923, 348–51; and "Scouting for Historic Secrets," *Boys' Life*, December 1925, 30.

14. Hurt, *Handbook for Scoutmasters*, 95–96.

15. Boy Scouts of America, *Handbook for Scout Masters* (1914), 248; and *New York Times*, August 12, 1923, X6. One required First Class test involved hiking fourteen miles and mapping the territory traversed.

16. Hurt, *Handbook for Boys*, quotations on 101. For examples and instructions for factory, dam, and oil field hikes, see "On the Hike," *Scouting*, May 1, 1917, 1; Many Eventful Scout Hikes, *Boys' Life*, November 1913, 23; *Boys' Life*, December 1914, 18; and "Know-Your-City Hikes," *New York Times*, April 29, 1923, X13. BSA Director of Camping L. L. McDonald explained at a troop leaders' training course that city boys could benefit from hiking to the fish market, printing establishments, commercial warehouses, and industrial plants. Berg speech, "A Scout Pro-

gram Which Meets the Boy's Needs," and McDonald speech, "Adequate Yearly Outdoor Program of a Scout Troop," in Wyland, *Principles of Scoutmastership*, latter quotation on 30, 114.

17. Hurt, *Handbook for Scoutmasters*, 374, 667, quotation on 51. On Scout camping's ability to build good character, a strong work ethic, and cooperative loyalty, see Murray, *History of the Boy Scouts*, 420; and Charles B. Horton, BSA Director of Training Schools and Camps, "What the Old Scout Said," *Boys' Life*, July 1912, 7–10. For the 1920 BSA camping statistic, refer to Paris, *Children's Nature*, 45. Miller's examination of early girls' organizations and summer camping argued that most leaders saw girls' camps as a balance between extreme wilderness survival and overcivilization. Miller, *Growing Girls*.

18. L. L. McDonald speech, "Camping in America," in Boy Scouts of America, *First National Training School*, 413–17.

19. Hurt, *Handbook for Scoutmasters*, 37–40, 73, quotation on 40. Hillcourt, *Handbook for Patrol Leaders*, 289–90. 1925 BSA Annual Report, 25.

20. On other American summer camps' busy activity schedules by the 1910s and 1920s, see Paris, *Children's Nature*, 12, 113–22, 230–33; and Van Slyck, *A Manufactured Wilderness*, 41–63. For a Local Council judging the success of its camping sessions by rank advancement progress, see Kansas City Area Council BSA, *Trail to Eagle*, 18. See also L. L. McDonald, "Me for the Country This Year!" *Scouting*, March 27, 1919, 25. On British Boy Scout and Girl Guide camps' balance of structured efficiency and primitivism, see Alexander, "Similarity and Difference at Girl Guide Camps."

21. The Cave Scout (F.J.P.), "With the Cave Scout in Camp," In the Scout Cave, *Boys' Life*, June 1916, 7. Thorton Wilcox, "Educational Aspects of the Camping Program" speech, 1926 ECR, 157–58.

22. Figure 4.5 in James Wilder, *Pine Tree Patrol* (New York City: BSA, 1918), 2–3, 6, 9, 45. James E. West, "The Miami Pine Tree Patrol," *Boys' Life*, November 1920, 28. 1926 BSA Annual Report, 116. 1927 BSA Annual Report, 136, 142.

23. Emphasis in original. Baden-Powell, *Scouting for Boys*, 1:50. Minutes of BSA National Council Annual Meeting (Feb. 11, 1913), quotation on 117. For wording of BSA Sixth Law, see Murray, Pratt, and Jameson, *Official Handbook for Boys*, 15. Dan Beard, "From Dan Beard's Duffel Bag," *Boys' Life*, June 1917. See also Beard letter to James West (Jan. 11, 1912), folder 6, "correspondence West 1912 Jan.–Mar.," Box 128, DCBP.

24. On showing chivalry by caring for dumb, weak, and female animals, see "Gift to Boy Scouts," *Los Angeles Times*, April 17, 1917, II5; and Boy Scouts of America, *Handbook for Boys*, 222. Carey, *The Scout Law*, 3, 111. On the National Park and Forest Services' predator campaigns, see Dunlap, *Saving America's Wildlife*.

25. "A Double-Barreled Announcement," *Boys' Life*, January 1913, first quotation on 1. On the McLean Bill, see "Federal Protection at Last," *Boys' Life*, April 1913, 20. On BSA bird sanctuary efforts, see 1922 BSA Annual Report, 20, 74; 1925 BSA Annual Report, 115; "Posted Game Preserve," *Weekly News Bulletin of Boy Scout Activities*, January 13, 1926; and 1930 BSA Annual Report, 159. Dan Beard, "American Birds First—the First Conservationist," *Boys' Life*, March 1916, second

quotation on 20. On the convergence of diverse groups on protecting birds, see Mighetto, *Wild Animals*; Doughty, *Feather Fashions*; Price, *Flight Maps*, 57–109; and Armitage, "Bird Day for Kids," 528–51.

26. Forrest Bennett, "A Sketch on Scouting," *Scout Executive*, May 1929, 9–10.

27. Boy Scouts of America, *Handbook for Boys*, quotations on 165, 170–71, 227–28 (the 1919 printing's wording on these topics had been used since the last major revision in 1914).

28. On the BSA's World War I conservation drives, see Murray, *History of the Boy Scouts*, 101–36; Boy Scouts Enter Castor Bean Drive," *Los Angeles Times*, March 26, 1918, I5; and Oursler, *The Boy Scout Story*, 59. On planting soldier tree memorials and the French project, consult Boy Scouts of America Publicity Department, "Weekly Pictorial Poster: October 1922 to October 1923," 31–34, Oct. 1922 to Oct. 1923 (New York: BSA); Robert S. Conklin's "living memorials" letter in *Scouting*, April 10, 1919, 3; and O. M. Butler, "Forest Good Turns by Scouts the Year Through," *Scouting*, July 1925, 1. On British Boy Scout soldier memorializing, see Proctor, *On My Honour*, 90–93.

29. Hurt, *Community Boy Leadership*, 468. For several of the many examples of Scout pest exterminations, see "Boy Scouts after Flies," *Boys' Life*, July 1911, 31; "Scouts after Caterpillars," *Boys' Life*, July 1912, 22; and "Triple Header Against Mosquitos," *New York Times*, July 5, 1924, X4. Examples of local Scout cooperation with conservation officials in "How the Scout Fish and Game Patrol Works," *Scouting*, October 1, 1913, 8; "The Third Law—'A Scout Is Helpful,'" *Boys' Life*, September 1915, 33; and 1925 BSA Annual Report, 25–27. For a tree census, see "With the Boy Scouts Afield," *Boys' Life*, June 1914, 34. Gifford Pinchot, "The Boy and the Forest," *Boys' Life*, September 1912, 7–8. On the Pennsylvania Scout Forest Guides, refer to James E. West, "National Council Official News: Progress in Forest Guide Movement," *Boys' Life*, March 1921, 28. BSA cooperation with U.S. Forest Service officials in "Boy Scouts Guard Feast," *New York Times*, February 10, 1912, 20; and "Boy Scouts and Forest Service to Co-Operate," *Los Angeles Times*, March 21, 1925, A7. For the National Forest Aide badge, see "To Award Forestry Badges," *Boys' Life*, May 1915, 14. For a synopsis of BSA outdoor and conversation programs as well as local practice examples, consult 1930 BSA Annual Report, 19–24.

30. *Conservation* merit badge pamphlet (New York: BSA, 1920), cover. On conserving forests and resources to develop boys' character, see 1925 BSA Annual Report, 46–47; and "Future of Scouting," *Scout Executive*, October 1925, 1.

31. In the Toledo Council report on boy member retention, 40 percent quit because of moving or the troop dying out, while 31.7 percent quit due to ineffective leadership. 1922 ECR, 100–101. Charles T. Johnson, "A Study of the Boy Scout Organization," 61–63, 121–27. Von Allman, "A Study of the San Francisco District Council," 82–86.

32. Gunner Berg, "Dividends of Scouting as Revealed by Established Facts," *Scouting*, July 1929, 231, 243. "Scoutmaster and His Job," Commission report appendix, 1928 ECR, 54–56, 69–72.

33. Huffman, *Saga of Potato Canyon*, 47–48. Kietzman, *Why I Became a Scoutmaster*, 54.

34. Kietzman, *Why I Became a Scoutmaster*, 149–52.

35. 1928 ECR, 575–79.

36. Walsh, *Thirteen Years of Scout Adventure*, 69–70. For hiking and camping adventure stories, see Henderson, *A Thousand Campfires*, 4–5, 38–70; and Hagood, *52 Years of Adventure*.

37. 1928 ECR, 581–84.

38. "Al Herbert Remembers 1927," in John Taylor, *From Market Square to the Banks of Sherman's Creek*, 8. Walcutt interview in Price, *Thirty Years of Scout Camping*, 27–28, 34–35.

Chapter Five

1. Stowe, "The Boy Scouts of the World," quotation on 1095. For the initial BSA Tenderfoot test, see Boy Scouts of America, *Handbook for Scout Masters* (1914), 22–23. The BSA inherited Baden-Powell's stipulation in the first Boy Scout pamphlet, published in 1906, that the program was intended for "boys of all creeds and classes." For Baden-Powell's first pamphlet, "Boy Scouts—a Suggestion," see Oursler, *The Boy Scout Story*, 29; and Reynolds, *The Scout Movement*, 9. On mainstreaming European immigrant groups in the mid-1920s and later, see Guterl, *The Color of Race*; Jacobson, *Whiteness of a Different Color*, 7–14, 39–90; and Syrett, *The Company He Keeps*, 121–33, 165–72.

2. Julia Grant, *The Boy Problem*.

3. First quotation in Judge Ben B. Lindsey letter to William Barbour (Oct. 24, 1914), folder "Oct. 24, 1914 Letter from Juvenile Court Judge to Mr. Barbour concerning B.S.A.," BSANA. Second quotation in Judge Ben Lindsey letter to Miss Julia Lathrop of Hull House (Oct. 24, 1911) and Jane Addams reply to Lindsey (Oct. 28, 1911), Correspondence 1911–1912 Aug., Frames 488 and 501, Reel 6, *The Jane Addams Papers* (Ann Arbor, Mich.: University Microfilms International, 1984). For judges claiming that Scouting prevented delinquency, see "Noted Men Meet to Aid City Boys," *New York Times*, November 23, 1915, 8; "Arnold Advises More Scouts as End to 'Bad Boys,'" *Chicago Daily Tribune*, December 27, 1922, 7; and "No Scouts Criminals," *Los Angeles Times*, April 12, 1928, 2. For judges arguing that Scouting could reform boys already delinquent, refer to "See in Scout Work End of the Bad Boy," *New York Times*, December 8, 1915, 8; and "A Judge's Opinion of Scouting," *Los Angeles Times*, October 7, 1923, X2, X6.

4. On race dynamics, see Parsons, *Race, Resistance, and the Boy Scout Movement*; Proctor, *Scouting for Girls*, 63–69; Proctor, *On My Honour*, 1–5; Rosenthal, *Character Factory*, chap. 9; and Proctor, "'A Separate Path.'" On religion dynamics in world Scouting, see Proctor, *Scouting for Girls*, 1–17, 59–63; Proctor, *On My Honour*, 139–44; and Wilson, *Scouting Round the World*, 66–70. At the Third International Conference of World Scouts in Copenhagen in 1924, delegates passed resolutions that the movement should work toward forbidding any sectarian propaganda at mixed-faith gatherings and that discrimination in membership based on race, creed, or class was against the foundations of world Scouting (the latter resolution was elaborated on at the 1926 International Conference).

5. John L. Alexander's new "Chivalry" chapter for the 1911 BSA handbook explained that good citizenship required that boys recognize their duty to God but that the BSA was nonsectarian, a policy that West adopted as official in 1912. Macleod, "Original Intent," 21–24. For the early BSA's religious tolerance for members of different denominations, see also Mechling, "God and 'Whatever,'" 179–81.

6. Works analyzing class and masculinity have tended to argue that working-class men defined their identity in opposition to middle-class manhood in fin de siècle American culture. Winter, *Making Men, Making Class*; Powers, *Faces along the Bar*; and Gorn, *The Manly Arts.*

7. On labor criticism of British Scouting, see Rosenthal, *Character Factory*, 8–86, 118, 182–85; Springhall, "Boy Scouts, Class and Militarism"; and Gillis, "Conformity and Rebellion," 254–55. For Socialist and labor union criticism of American Scouting, see Wigginton, "The Boy Scouts," 56; Levy, *Building a Popular Movement*, 25–26; Scheidlinger, "A Comparative Study," 742–44; and Deady, "An Historical Study of the Scout Movement." For list of labor unions opposed to Scouting, refer to John Price Jones, "Memorandum for Mr. West" (Oct. 10, 1911), folder 5, "correspondence West 1911 Sep–Dec.," Box 128, DCBP. On the UMWA ban, see "Boy Scouts under Ban," *Washington Post*, January 28, 1912, 5.

8. On Scout and National Guard uniform resemblance, see Shaver, *Notes from a Pioneer's Journal*, 48–49. "Kentucky Youth Injured in a 'Boy Scout' Battle,'" *Chicago Daily Tribune*, December 31, 1910, 2. On the Bronx incident, see "Boy Scout Kills a Lad," *Los Angeles Times*, March 25, 1912, I1. "Boy Slayer in Court," *New York Times*, May 3, 1912, 20.

9. Baden-Powell, *Scouting for Boys*, 1:41, 49–51; 2:133; 4:245, 262; 5:276–78, 319–22; 6:343, 361.

10. Minutes of BSA National Council Annual Meeting (Feb. 14–15, 1911), 88–93. "IM" letter to BSA national office (Apr. 27, 1911), 78–79, "Standardization Scout Oath and Law." James West letter to Samuel Gompers (Dec. 1, 1911), Gompers reply to West (Dec. 15, 1911), and West's letter with both forwarded letters attached to Theodore Roosevelt (Dec. 18, 1911) in Theodore Roosevelt Papers I, Reels 118, 120. For BSA changes to suit labor leaders, consult Macleod, *Building Character*, 177–78, 204–5, 214–24, 302–3; Scott and Murphy, *The Scouting Party*, 168–75, 183; Hurt, *Community Boy Leadership*, 61, 371–78; and James West, "The Boy Scouts: Socialist's Attack on Their Organization Ignored Its Expressed Purposes," *New York Times*, March 12, 1911, 12. For the Law changes, compare Seton and Baden-Powell, *A Handbook of Woodcraft, Scouting, and Lifecraft*, 32, to Baden-Powell, *Scouting for Boys*, 1:49–51. On labor's appreciation of Seton's particular version of Scouting, see "Labor Upholds Seton's Kind of Boy Scouts: Baden-Powell Variety Called Breeder of Militarism," *Chicago Daily Tribune*, October 17, 1917, 5. On British Boy Scout rifles, drill, and strike-breaking, see also Proctor, *On My Honour*, 14, 100.

11. Arthurs, "Boy Scouts Building for Manhood," first quotation on 281–82. Minutes of BSA National Council Annual Meeting, February 14–15, 1911, second quotation on 61–62. On two-way snobbery, see also Curtis, "The Boy Scouts," 504.

On the "overprivileged" rich boy critique, see "Why Your Boy Should Be a Scout," *Year Book 1918 of the Old Colony Council Boy Scouts of America* (Braintree, Mass.: Old Colony Council BSA, 1918), 23; and Hurt, *Community Boy Leadership*, 4. Macleod argued that BSA leaders believed, like many Progressive reformers, that middle-class standards were "classless." Macleod, *Building Character*, 177–78, 214–24. British Girl Guide officials also praised the uniform and the organization as a great class leveler. Proctor, *Scouting for Girls*, 15–16.

12. On the Taft parade resolution, see "The Boy Scouts of America," *Work with Boys*, October 1911, 89–94. 1912 BSA Annual Report, 36–37. AFL head Samuel Gompers's visit to the city during the summer of 1912 may have influenced the union's change of heart. Brittain, *The Spirit of Scouting '76*, 11–13; and "Boy Scouts Will March," *Washington Post*, September 18, 1911, 5. The recipient of Debs's letter was probably Walter Lanfersiek, an influential leader in the Socialist Party. Hurt, *Community Boy Leadership*, 371–78, quotation on 375. On early tensions between Socialist groups and the BSA, see Charles Bonaparte letter to James West (Aug. 21, 1911) and West reply (Aug. 22, 1911), folder 4, "correspondence West 1911 Apr–Aug," Box 128, DCBP; "Socialism and the Boy Scouts," *Boys' Life*, April 1912, 24; and Leslie, "Coming of Age in Urban America," 468–71.

13. James West's introductory statement in Boy Scouts of America, *Scouting and the Jewish Boy* (New York: BSA Jewish Committee on Scouting, 1928), 7–8.

14. On ethnic minorities in Scouting, see Macleod, *Building Character*, 190–98, 214–16; and Brittain, *The Spirit of Scouting '76*, 9–10. Separate Catholic Scout organization idea discussed in "Catholic Boy Scouts," *Literary Digest* 45, no. 17 (October 26, 1912): 724. On Catholic demands for separate troops and Catholic leaders, consult Arthur Carey letter to James West (Feb. 8, 1911), 39–42, "Standardization Scout Oath and Law." For Catholic concern with Scout initiations, see *Scouting*, June 15, 1913, 2. Catholics helped change BSA leaders' mind on renaming the British "Scout Promise" the American "Scout Vow." Scheidlinger, "A Comparative Study," 742.

15. On the charge that Catholics were excluded from BSA leadership, see Robert Peterson, "The Beginnings of a Partnership," *Scouting*, May–June 2004. James West, "No Religious Test," *Boys' Life*, March 1912, quotation on 31. For growing Catholic support for Scouting, see Hurt, *Handbook for Boys*, 591; "Cardinal Farley Approves Boy Scouts of America," *Boys' Life*, June 1912, 31; "Roman Catholics and Boy Scouts," *Outlook* 102 (September 21, 1912): 99–100; and Wills, *Boy Scouts of America*, 44–48. Boy Scouts of America, Transcript of " 'Western Round-Up,' " 69. Macleod argued that BSA officials protested when churches limited troop membership to boys from their congregations. While some local leaders may have objected, BSA headquarters made it a national policy and actively defended this right. Macleod, *Building Character*, 191–92. "Policies and Regulations of the Boy Scouts of America: A Series of Interpretations, no. 6, Restricting Membership in Scout Troops" (1924), folder, "Troops—(Permanent)," BSANA; and "What Is Scope of Troop Management by the Sponsoring Institution?" *Scouting*, September 1923, 6. On the religious committees, see 1929 BSA Annual Report, 154–55; and Sleutelberg, "A Critical History," 14–15.

16. *Scouting*, July 1, 1913, 4. L. R. Martineau, "MIA Scouts," *Improvement Era*, March 1912, 354–61. There were at least thirty-eight thousand Mormon Scouts under LDS leadership by 1938. LDS-BSA Centennial Book Committee, *Century of Honor*, xi, 19–71; and Wills, *Boy Scouts of America*, 44–48. On Mormon recruitment numbers in 1928, see Wyland, "The Knighthood of Youth," 860.

17. Oursler, *The Boy Scout Story* 121; Dean, "Scouting in America," 127; and Sleutelberg, "A Critical History," 8–12, 38–39. On YMHA Scout recruitment and other patterns, see Robert Peterson, "The Beginnings of a Partnership," *Scouting*, May–Jun. 2004. Jewish Americans also participated broadly in other types of summer camps for both boys and girls. Paris, *Children's Nature*, 86–95.

18. Macleod noted, "The Polish national council backed out of a 1914 agreement to merge its Boy Scouts with the BSA, demanding instead special rules and a handbook in Polish." Macleod, *Building Character*, 215. However, the BSA had already announced its agreement to translate the handbook into Polish. The sticking point for the BSA appeared to be the Polish National Alliance's demand for an independent Scout branch with its own rules. "Polish Boys Unite with Boy Scouts of America," *Scouting*, August 1, 1914, 1; "Training Course for Polish Scouts," Minutes of BSA Executive Board (Oct. 5, 1914), 3–4, folder 4, Box 210, DCBP; James West, "The Polish Scouts," *Scouting*, May 15, 1914, 6; "Little Stories about Scouts in Other Lands," *Boys' Life*, August 1914, 19; and "Polish Boys Unite with Boy Scouts of America," *Scouting*, August 1, 1914, 1–2. The PSA was probably merged into the Harcerstwo organization in Poland around 1918. Pienkos, *PNA: A Centennial History*, 147–49, 229–35; and Scheidlinger, "A Comparative Study," 746–48. On the Falcons training, see "Training Course for Polish Leaders Is Successful," *Scouting*, August 1, 1914, 8; and "The Polish Scouts," *Scouting*, May 15, 1914, 6.

19. For an insightful analysis of Syrian minorities adopting Scouting to assert their modern, middle-class status while retaining their traditional cultures against imperialists, see Watenpaugh, "Scouting in the Interwar Arab Middle East."

20. Dan Beard, "Around the Campfire with Dan Beard," *Boys' Life*, November 13, 1919, 36. For BSA sources promoting 100 percent Americanism, see Frank Rigney sketch, *Scouting*, May 15, 1919, 3; 1919 BSA Annual Report, 61; *Scout Executive*, March 1923, 1; and Hurt, *Handbook for Scoutmasters*, 548. Proctor's overview of Girl Scouting and Guiding found that the American Girl Scouts made efforts to assimilate white immigrants in the mid-1910s to the mid-1920s. Proctor, *Scouting for Girls*, 64–66.

21. Figure 5.1 in 1915 BSA Annual Report, 113.

22. James Wilder, *The Grail: A Story of the Boy Scouts*, 4–26, quotations on 11, 12, Scene 183–184, Scene 200, folder 24, "Script for movie, The Grail," Box 1, James Wilder Papers, Hawaii State Archives. Wilder played the role of the Scoutmaster in the 1917 Edison Company release of his script, renamed *The Knights of the Square Table*. BSA headquarters and publications heartily endorsed the film. See Harty, "*The Knights of the Square Table*," 313–23; "*Knights of the Square Table*: A Great Film by Scout Commissioner James A. Wilder," *Scouting*, July 15, 1917, 11; and the movie ad in *Boys' Life*, September 1917, 31.

23. BSA Press Release, "Says Labor Men Realize Boy Scouts of America Are Not Military in Aim" (no date), folder, "World War—Publicity—News Releases and Scouting," BSANA. On the Boston incident, see "Scout Heads on Defensive; to Go Before Labor Union Committee to Answer Charge of Hostility," *New York Times*, November 5, 1916, E9; "Boy Scouts Repudiate Alleged Slur on labor," *Scouting*, November 15, 1916, 1; and "Labor Investigating Committee Endorses Boy Scout Movement," *Scouting*, December 1, 1916, 1. UMWA retraction in John P. White, Frank J. Hayes, and William Green letter "To the Officers and Members, United Mine Workers of America" (May 28, 1917), reproduced in *Scouting*, August 15, 1917, 4. For quotations, see "Labor Investigating Committee Endorses Boy Scout Movement," *Beaverton (PA) Daily Times*, December 16, 1916, 3. For not engaging in strike matters, see *Scouting*, June 19, 1919, 5; and Hurt, *Handbook for Scoutmasters*, 540.

24. On Catholics not wanting to stand out in World War I, see Lorne Barclay speech in Boy Scouts of America, " 'Western Round-Up,' " 68–69. The pope's approval of "distinctly Catholic units" in the United States in J. Card. Gasparri letter to Michael J. Slattery of the National Catholic War Council (Oct. 7, 1919), folder 7, Box 211, DCBP. See also Boy Scouts of America, *First National Training School*, 1258–59; and Oursler, *The Boy Scout Story*, 228–29.

25. *Scouting*, April 3, 1919, quotation on 8–9. "Col. Roosevelt Urges Army Men to Aid Scouts," *News Bulletin* (undated, probably April 1919), folder "World War—Publicity," BSANA. See also "Extracting the Hyphen," *Scouting*, July 1922, 4. A few local BSA officials took it upon themselves to make systematic efforts to recruit European immigrants. James E. West, "Scouting on the East Side," *Boys' Life*, December 1919, 42.

26. Quotation in "Other Americanization Work," 1920 BSA Annual Report, 32. For helping the Commissioner of Naturalization, see James West, "Bureau of Naturalization Praises Work of Scouts," *Boys' Life*, April 1921, 26; and "Scouts and Americanization," *New York Times*, August 28, 1921, 69. For melting pot imagery and local skits, refer to 1936 ECR, 846–47; Hurt, *Community Boy Leadership*, 415; and Frank Rigney sketch, *New York Times*, August 12, 1926, X6.

27. On the National Council's resolution to do something for immigrant boys, see Minutes of BSA National Council Annual Meeting (Mar. 29–30, 1922), 273; and minutes of BSA Executive Board (Apr.–May 1922), 4, folder 7, "correspondence West 1922," Box 131, DCBP. Report of the Commission on the Underprivileged Boy, 1922 ECR, quotations on 365–70.

28. The proper role of labor union leaders on BSA Local Councils was also discussed at the training conference. 1922 ECR, 210–15. See also Macleod, *Building Character*, 204–5.

29. On a new uniform, see Rowan, *To Do My Best*, 105. Uniform debate discussed in Hurt, *Handbook for Scoutmasters*, 361–67; 1922 BSA Annual Report, 15; and *Scout Executive Bulletin*, September 24, 1923. James West, "National Council Official News," *Boys' Life*, October 1923, quotation on 30. For 1927 study on a cheaper uniform, consult Mark Jones, "Report on a Survey," 190–91. For increasing

pressure to buy a full, standard uniform as late as 1930, see Murray, *The History of the Boy Scouts*, 164–66.

30. "Scouting Idealism," *Scout Executive*, October 1922, first quotation on 5. National conference protest note in "Knights of the Ku Klux Klan to National Offices of the Boy Scouts of America." Quotation in James West letter to George L. Nye (Oct. 16, 1924). Both documents in folder "correspondence West 1924," Box 131, DCBP. Figure 5.2, "'Cosmopolitan' Boy Scout Troops" in *San Francisco Chronicle*, January 29, 1922, 7. See also picture and article about the "International Batallion" in *New York Times*, November 22, 1925, B7; and *Civics* merit badge pamphlet (New York City: BSA, 1930).

31. Boy Scouts of America, *Scouting and the Jewish Boy*, 7–12, 18, 21–23, 29.

32. For discussions of translating information pamphlets on Scouting into foreign languages and other ideas for immigrant outreach, see Boy Scouts of America, "'Western Round-Up,'" 130–31; 1924 ECR, 542–43; "Foreign Born Boys," 1927 BSA Annual Report, 91; 1929 BSA Annual Report, 109–10; and 1936 ECR, 746–48.

Chapter Six

1. E. Russell Patterson, *A Strenuous Afternoon: A Short Scout Play That Any Troop Can Enact*, and Figure 6.1, Normal Rockwell sketches in *Boys' Life*, October 1915, 19–21, 23.

2. On the decline of the yeoman's stature in American society by the turn of the twentieth century, see Hilkey, *Character Is Capital*; and Burns, *Success in America*.

3. These early rural patterns of BSA policies resembled those of the American Girl Scouts organization, whose leaders also found difficulty matching their program and methods to the rural context and country girls' interests. Girl Scout camp leaders often stressed an idealized version of local indigenous folklore; however, they advised girl members to keep their distance from actual country folk who lived near the camps. Miller, *Growing Girls*, 105–18.

4. 1925 BSA Annual Report, 162–65.

5. Charles Hewlett, "A Detailed Analysis of the Difficulties," *Scouting*, February 1, 1916, 4–5.

6. On Boyce and development of Lone Scouting, see Petterchak, *Lone Scout*, 93–99, 111–12, 137–38, 149–51. West told Executives at their 1924 national conference that Boyce had tried to convince the BSA National Council at one of its meetings that the organization should do something for rural boys along the lines of the British Lone Scout program, but "he did not make much of an impression" (1924 ECR, 406–7). On LSA membership stats, see 1923 BSA Annual Report, 16–17.

7. Ashby, "'Straight from Youthful Hearts,'" 775–93; Hackensmith, "Scout Memorabilia," 31–33; and Dean, "Scouting in America," 59, 66–67.

8. On the BSA's plan to use the name Lone Scouts, see "'Lone Scouts' Are Provided for by Boy Scouts of America," *Boys' Life*, April 1916, 26. On the BSA's

Pioneer Branch, see "Plans for New Pioneer Scout Rank Completed," *Scouting*, August 1, 1916, quotation on 1–2; 1916 BSA Annual Report, 46; and 1919 BSA Annual Report, 128. Another BSA effort to attract rural boys was the Lonesome Corner column, which correlated correspondence between isolated boys via *Boys' Life* in the early 1910s. The Lonesome Corner, *Boys' Life*, December 1912, 39; and "Our Lonesome Corner," *Boys' Life*, July 1914, 28.

9. On the Regional Deputies, see Keith Monroe, "The BSA's Legendary Road Men," *Scouting*, November–December 1997, 10–11. The BSA rolled the railroad troops into the Department of Rural Scouting in 1926. On Railroad Scouting, consult Keith Monroe, "The Railroad Scouters," *Scouting*, September 1995, 16, 68–69; and 1929 BSA Annual Report, 129–31.

10. The BSA estimated that active LSA membership was between forty-five and sixty-five thousand in 1923, but this figure probably underestimated the number of Lone Scout devotees. On LSA statistics, see 1923 BSA Annual Report, 16–17; and Petterchak, *Lone Scout*, 106, 114, 136. On BSA Pioneer statistics, see 1926 BSA Annual Report, 142–46.

11. Citing a 1916 letter, Janice Petterchak argued in her biography of Boyce that James West never liked the idea of the independent Lone Scouts organization. Federal charter motivation discussed in Petterchak, *Lone Scout*, 105, 110–11. Boy Scouts of America, " 'Western Round-Up,' " 127–28. On the early stages of the actual LSA takeover process, see 1923 BSA Annual Report, 16–17; 1924 ECR, 406–7; and James E. West, "Memorandum about Lone Scouts of America" (Oct. 24, 1923), folder 10 "Vitalius, E.H.," Box 124, DCBP.

12. For list of companies the BSA convinced to give up use of the word "Scout" or pay a royalty, see "Exhibit A" attached to West letter to Jane Deeter Rippin (Apr. 16, 1924), folder "correspondence West 1924," Box 132, DCBP. For income figures, see 1924 BSA Annual Report, 37.

13. For BSA lawyers' advice on the issue, see Ellis S. Middleton letter to BSA, Attention Mr. F. N. Cooke Jr. (Mar. 18, 1924); Paul Sleman to Colin H. Livingstone (Mar. 19, 1924); and Clarence D. Kerr to West (Mar. 20, 1924), folder "controversy with Boy Scouts over use of name, 1917–1926," Box 10, "Clubs and Organizations," Lou Henry Hoover Collection, Herbert Hoover Presidential Library. West, "Memorandum about Lone Scouts of America."

14. The BSA agreed to pay $8,000 for the remaining LSA merchandise stock, which facilitated the merger. Rowan, *To Do My Best*, 106–8. Perry's speech in 1924 ECR, 409–17, longer quotations on 409, 411. Perry cited Ralph Biggerstaff letter (Aug. 21, 1924). For an analysis of the trademark conflict from the perspective of the Girl Scouts, which also emphasized the BSA's financial royalty interests as a key motivation, see Miller, "Trademark: Scout."

15. Dr. Charles J. Galpin, "Rural Boys" speech, 1924 ECR, 207–13.

16. On Benson's role, see Murray, *History of the Boy Scouts*, 368–69. Robert Peterson, "The Industrial Troops," *Scouting*, October 1987, 12, 68. Cooperation with local school officials in "Rural Schools Asked to Cooperate in Extending Boy Scout Movement," *Weekly News Bulletin of Boy Scout Activities*, December 24, 1927. Benson also identified a group of boys who joined Lone Scouting because they had "highly

individualistic tendencies, who are not of the gang type." O. H. Benson, "Survey of Lone Scouts," 1926 BSA Annual Report, quotations on 147. A 1927 *Scout Executive* article by Field Officer Malcolm C. Douglass and a 1928 BSA Rural Department survey of recent Lone Scouts echoed Benson's findings. Malcolm C. Douglass, "Scouting for the Other Boy," *Scout Executive*, July 1927, 5; and 1928 BSA Annual Report, 171. A 1925 estimate reported that 40 percent of LSA members lived in cities with over twenty-five hundred residents. 1925 BSA Annual Report, 162. The BSA's Rural Department estimated in 1927 that 30 percent of Lone Scouts were under the age of twelve and had been dropped until their coming of age. 1927 BSA Annual Report, 173.

17. *Scout Executive*, June 1927, 1–2. A 1927 administrative study of the BSA by consultant Mark M. Jones also found that the organization could not meet the needs of either rural or busy working-class boys, and that the whole program therefore needed to be reconsidered and revised. Mark Jones, "Report on a Survey," 43–49. For the farm merit badges and numbers earned, see 1927 BSA Annual Report, 169; and 1929 BSA Annual Report, 197. Early BSA farm merit badges discussed in "To Study Scoutcraft," *Washington Post*, May 21, 1911, ES2; and Murray, Pratt, and Jameson, *Official Handbook for Boys*, 24–43. Number of each BSA merit badge earned each year from 1911 to 1981 tabulated in Duersch, *Merit Badge Field Guide*.

18. For two of the many examples of insisting on adult supervision of Lone Scouting, see "Your Lone Scout Friend," *Lone Scout*, May 1928, 1; and 1929 BSA Annual Report, 196–98. BSA's general changes to Lone Scouting detailed in "Functions of Department of Rural Scouting," *Scout Executive*, March 1927, 2–3; John P. Wallace, "Rural Scouting Department," 1928 BSA Annual Report, 169; James West, "Lone Scout Policies: Problems Relating to the Merger" (undated policy bulletin for Local Council Executives—probably 1925), 7; *Scout Executive*, June 1927, 1–2; and "Why Lone Scout Membership Has Dropped," 1928 ECR, 410–13. On changing the tests, see "How Lone Scouts Advance," *Lone Scout*, March 1929, 9. On older Lone Scouts, see "Your Questions Answered," *Lone Scout*, December 1927, 7. The BSA prodded Lone Scouts to join Local Tribes (small rural troops), Farm Journal Tribes, or Mail Tribes (also known as "Corrie Scouts"). 1926 BSA Annual Report, 146; and "Tribe Meetings," *Lone Scout*, October 1928, 6. On the BSA Constitution amendments regarding Farm and Home Patrols, see Constitution Article XI, Section 1, Clause 8 (as amended January 7, 1929, p. 42) in folder, "constitutions and By-Laws," BSANA.

19. Emphasis in original. West, "Lone Scout Policies," 7. For Lone Scouts' self-government, see *Scout Executive Bulletin*, May 9, 1925, 3; and January 14, 1926, 2–23, quotation from Perry at 17. For other changes to Lone Scouting and reinforcement of these policies to boy members, see BSA, *Official Handbook of the Lone Scouts*, 38–41; and *Lone Scout*, March 1927; April 1927; November 1927, 2–4; December 1927; February 1928, 3; March 1928, 3; August 1928, 3; and August 1929, 3.

20. For Lone Scout and BSA farm boy statistics, see 1926 BSA Annual Report, 142–46; 1927 BSA Annual Report, 173; and 1928 BSA Annual Report, 172, 176. In 1928, 276 Local Councils reported 4,728 Lone Scouts and 9,689 farm boys belong-

ing to some form of Boy Scout troop. On removing "deadwood" and the adjustment period, see "Why Lone Scout Membership Has Dropped," 1928 ECR, 410–13.

21. "Scouting in the Home Circle," *Lone Scout*, February 1930, quotation on 1. See also *Along the Lone Scout Trail: A Handbook for Members of the Progressive Farm Tribe* (New York: BSA, n.d.), 4. For a report that "urbanizing" and "grouping" rural boys through regular troop Scouting would encourage farm boys to come to the city and would result in the decimation of farm life and productivity, see 1927 BSA Annual Report, 170.

Chapter Seven

1. Figure 7.1 sketch in *Boys' Life*, August 1921, 7. See also R. A. Cameran sketch with Clarence Elmer poem, "De Bigges' Pile," *Boys' Life*, September 1919, 4.

2. One noticeable difference was that white-run schools and mission troops sponsored most troops for African Scouts, whereas African American churches and organizations sponsored many early African American troops. Parsons, *Race, Resistance*; Parsons, "The Limits of Sisterhood: The Evolution of the Girl Guide Movement in Colonial Kenya"; and Proctor, "'A Separate Path,'" 605–31. Watenpaugh, "Scouting in the Interwar Arab Middle East."

3. Before turning the organization over to YMCA leaders in mid-1910, founder William D. Boyce insisted that the BSA continue to accept all boys, regardless of race, faith, or other factors. Sullivan argued that Boyce required this, despite being an avid believer in the superiority of white men. Sullivan, *Boyce of Ottawa*, 9–11; and Conley, "William Dickson Boyce," 18. For examples of continued rhetoric on the organization's inclusiveness, see Hurt, *Community Boy Leadership*, 367; and Hurt, *Handbook for Boys*, 12.

4. BSA blackface and stereotypes resembled the passive depictions of African Americans in early twentieth-century mainstream white popular culture and scientific theories of racial hierarchy, but they did not emphasize the aggressive critiques of African American men as being inherently violent or rapists. On Baden-Powell's Zulu hero, see *Scouting for Boys* 1:48.

5. 1920 ECR, quotations on 83, 21. See also opening for the 1922 conference in Atlanta by the President of the Atlanta BSA Council in 1922 ECR, 3.

6. "Pickaninny" sketch in *Boys' Life*, November 13, 1919, 26; and 1919 BSA Annual Report, 61. For African American women, see T. S. Christopher sketch, *Boys' Life*, May 1923, 55. On African American schooling in this era, see Tyack, *One Best System*, 217–29.

7. For the story of Smokey, see Stephen Chalmers, "The Mascot of 'Troop 1,'" *Boys' Life*, December 1917, 36–37, 46–47, 64–66, quotation on 37. For examples of primitive Africans in BSA safari fiction and skits, see Thomas S. Miller, "The Shape-Thing of the African Jungle," *Boys' Life*, October 1918, 5–7; and "The Dagger," *Scouting*, May 1927, 14.

8. For Scout minstrel shows, see *Boys' Life*, October 1913, 18; "A Minstrel Show, Then—Fire!" *Boys' Life*, April 1914, 10–11; *Boys' Life*, August 1914, 23;

Boys' Life, October 1915, 33; "African American Faces Make Green Backs," *Boys' Life*, July 15, 1916, 23; "A Minstrel Show for Soldiers," *Scouting*, August 1, 1918, 14; Hurt, *Community Boy Leadership*, 409; H. H. Smaw, " 'Putting On' a Minstrel Show," *Boys' Life*, March 1923, 37, 41; and *Troop Stunts* (New York: BSA, 1931), 25–26. A favorite BSA skit was "Skindirty, the Great African Freak." See In the Scout Cave, *Boys' Life*, December 1917, 60. For minstrel songs, consult *Boy Scout Song Book* (Boston: C. C. Birchard and Co. for the BSA, 1920), 48, 56–57, 62, 69, 117–18; and *Songs Scouts Sing* (New York: BSA, 1930), quotations on 74–76.

9. The Executive Board minutes did not record specific discussion, so it is unclear why the issue surfaced or why the decision was reached. Minutes of Executive Board of the Boy Scouts of America (Nov. 22, 1910), folder 1, "Boy Scouts of America," Box 211, DCBP. For one of the defenses of this policy as Local Council "self-determination," see 1920 ECR, 101. The standard BSA troop charter application in the 1910s did not ask for the race or color of the boys. It did ask for the color and nationality of the Scoutmaster, so most exclusions were probably based on his background or the presumed racial composition of the troop-sponsoring institution. The early American Girl Scouts organization also was officially open to African Americans but allowed Local Councils to exclude or segregate them. Proctor, *Scouting for Girls*, 64–66.

10. Several years prior, the BSA Executive Board had quietly started a study on the African American Scouting issue led by Bolton Smith. Quotation in Smith letter to Ruml (Jan. 15, 1925), folder 969, "Boy Scouts of America—Negro 1925–1926," Box 96, Subseries 8, Interracial Relations, LSRMC. See also 1927 BSA Annual Report, 88–90; and "African American Scouting," typescript to Dan Hoskins (Oct. 31, 1977), 2 (an excerpt from Keith Monroe's manuscript, "Other Men's Sons"), in folder, "Religious Community Negro 1979," BSANA. It is difficult to pinpoint whether white Inter-Racial Service leaders consciously adopted such rhetoric to improve their chances of funding support and for convincing white audiences to allow African American boys to Scout.

11. Memo of Harris interview with Leonard Outhwaite (Feb. 19, 1925). Quotation in Smith letter to Ruml (Mar. 4, 1925). See also John D. Traywick letter to Harris (Mar. 10, 1925). For Outhwaite's consultations, see Leonard Outhwaite letter to Dr. James H. Dillard, Will W. Alexander, and Dr. Thomas Jesse Jones of Phelps-Stokes Fund (Feb. 19, 1926); memo of Dr. James H. Dillard phone call with Leonard Outhwaite (Feb. 26, 1926); Harris letter to Outhwaite (Feb. 26, 1926); Alexander letter to Outhwaite (March 5, 1926); and Outhwaite letter to Alexander (Mar. 8, 1926). For Laura Spelman Rockefeller Memorial's support for the Inter-Racial Service, see 1926 BSA Annual Report, 87–88; 1929 BSA Annual Report, 104–5; and Ruml letter to West re LSRM resolution 666 (Mar. 12, 1926). All documents except BSA Annual Reports in folder 969, "Boy Scouts of America—Negro 1925–1926," Box 96, Subseries 8, Interracial Relations, LSRMC. The LSRM and other elite philanthropists provided the funding for the Inter-Racial Service's first six years. The Rosenwald Foundation, the New York Foundation, and Henry Doehs also contributed in 1929 and 1930.

12. Harris letter to Outhwaite (Dec. 16, 1925), folder 969, "Boy Scouts of America—Negro 1925–1926, LSRMC."

13. Stanley Harris report on Louisville visit on March 12–14, 1925 (submitted March 26, 1925), and "The Louisville Plan of Organization of Scouting for Negro Boys" in folder 969, "Boy Scouts of America—Negro 1925–1926, LSRMC." See also "The Louisville Plan for Colored Boys," *Scout Executive*, October 1924, 5.

14. Harris report to Inter-Racial Committee (Feb. 25, 1927), first quotation on 3–4. Harris interview with Leonard Outhwaite (Sep. 30, 1927). Both in folder 970, "Boy Scouts of America—Negro 1927." Inter-Racial Service 1927 annual report, second quotation on 4–5, folder 971, "Boy Scouts of America—Negro 1928–1931, LSRMC." 1928 BSA Annual Report, third quotation on 77.

15. For the necessity of training African American Scoutmasters, see 1929 BSA Annual Report, 106–7; 1930 BSA Annual Report, 99–100; and 1936 ECR, 532. For one of the claims that it was hard to find enough quality minority troop leaders, see R. M. Wheat, "Colored Department of the Louisville, KY, Council," *Scout Executive*, February 1924, 4. Quotation in Bolton Smith letter to Leonard Outhwaite (Sept. 6, 1928), folder 971, "Boy Scouts of America—Negro 1928–1931, LSRMC."

16. Figure 7.2 in *Scout Executive*, September 1927, 6. On the early African American Scoutmaster training sessions, see *Scout Executive*, September 1927, 6; *Scout Executive*, July 1928, 5; and Stanley A. Harris, "Scouting Celebrates Its Silver Jubilee," *Southern Workman* 64, no. 4 (April 1935): 105–7. On African American colleges hosting Scoutmaster training, see "A Training Innovation," *Scout Executive*, September 1927, 6; 1927 Annual Report, 90; and 1928 Annual Report, 76–77. On General Education Board support, see minutes of Inter-Racial Relations Committee (Feb. 28, 1927); Stanley Harris letter to George Fisher (May 21, 1927); and "Report of Stanley A. Harris on Hampton School" (undated), folder 970, "Boy Scouts of America—Negro 1927, LSRMC." On African American administrators, see "Highlights of the Interracial Service" (BSA, undated; probably late 1970s), 74, folder, "Religious Community Negro 1979, LSRMC."

17. Quotations in Stanley Harris report on Louisville visit on March 12–14, 1925.

18. On African American troop names, see Bowers, *"On My Honor,"* 35. Parsons argued that even segregated and subordinated Boy Scouting and Girl Guiding offered Africans hope for political and cultural status in the early 1900s. Parsons, "The Limits of Sisterhood."

19. For white boys' resistance to African Americans, see Macleod, *Building Character*, 217; and transcript of 1917 Scoutmasters' training conference, Columbia University, February 2, 1917, 74–79, 193–94. On Louisville Eagles, see Stanley Harris report on Louisville visit on March 12–14, 1925. Mississippi uniforms and white Scouts teaching African Americans discussed in A. J. Taylor, "Man with Man in Scouting," 109–10; and "Four very interesting incidents happened in November" (anonymous, probably Stanley Harris or Bolton Smith; undated, probably around Feb. 9, 1929), folder 969, "Boy Scouts of America—Negro 1925–1926, LSRMC." Miami and Atlanta white Scouts' help in 1928 BSA Annual Report, 77.

20. Quotation in Stanley Harris letter to Leonard Outhwaite (Jan. 6, 1927), folder 970, "Boy Scouts of America—Negro 1927, LSRMC." On Klan protests of

Scouting, see Peterson, *The Boy Scouts*, 98–100; Huffman, *Sam Houston Scouts*, 33; and "Knights of the Ku Klux Klan to National Offices of the Boy Scouts of America" protest note and James West letter to George L. Nye (Oct. 16, 1924), folder "correspondence West 1924," Box 131, DCBP.

21. It was apparently typical for southern councils to front half or more of the registration fees when starting African American troops in the second half of the 1920s. This still left the larger costs of the uniform and camping fees, but many southern councils did not allow African Americans access to these things. On subsidizing African American fees and on recognizing that pool discrimination made African American Scout advancement difficult, see R. M. Wheat, "Colored Department of the Louisville, KY, Council," *Scout Executive*, February 1924, 4; and "The Louisville Plan of Organization of Scouting for Negro Boys." On Richmond pool discrimination and the council's gradual development of African American Scouting units and facilities, see Dillon, *On My Honor*, 87–96. Other types of American summer camps run by different youth organizations or as private ventures frequently segregated or excluded nonwhite youth through the 1940s. Paris, *Children's Nature*, 58–59, 72–73, 186.

22. Stanley Harris report on Louisville visit on March 12–14, 1925. The Richmond, Virginia, council eventually allowed African American boys to wear uniforms, but appointed a separate outfitter to make and sell them. For the 1920s African American uniform restrictions, see Peterson, *The Boy Scouts*, 99; and "The Establishment of Interracial Work in the Boy Scouts of America: Based on an Interview with Stanley Harris at Boone, North Carolina, on May 11, 1966," folder "1928 Committee on Inter-Racial," BSANA."

23. For relative Inter-Racial Service success by state, see "Report of Stanley A. Harris, National Director, Inter-Racial Activities to the Committee on Inter-Racial Relations, Boy Scouts of America, Held at the National Office, New York, February 25, 1927," folder 970, "Boy Scouts of America—Negro 1927, LSRMC."

24. On upholding Local Council discrimination in 1931, see E. H. Vitalius (West's secretary) letter to G. Barrett Rich (Mar. 18, 1932), folder 11, "Vitalius, E.H.," and James West letter to Hubert Martin (Nov. 28, 1931) and Vitalius letter to Beard (Mar. 31, 1932), folder 12, "Vitalius, E.H.," both in Box 124, DCBP. For 1940s African American Scouting statistics and developments, see Peterson, *The Boy Scouts*, 141–44, 172–74. On Richmond segregation into the late 1960s, see Dillon, *On My Honor*, 91, 100. On desegregation's effects, see Keith Monroe, abstract from unpublished manuscript, "Other Men's Sons," sent to Dan Hoskins (Oct. 31, 1977), folder "Religious Community—Negro 1979, BSANA."

Epilogue

1. On the Depression's effects on the BSA, see Rowan, *To Do My Best*, 137–43; Dean, "Scouting in America," 126–29; and Keith Monroe, "Depressed but Not Down," *Scouting*, November–December 1985, 8–9. On Scout council deficit spending in the 1920s, see Brittain, *Spirit of Scouting*, 45. Membership statistics in Boy Scouts of America, "Fact Sheet: Historical Highlights," 2001.

2. Good Turn efforts in the 1930s outlined in Wigginton, "The Boy Scouts," 72–83; Murray, *History of the Boy Scouts*, 174–200; Macleod, *Building Character*, 301–2; and "Aid in Relief of Unemployment," 1930 BSA Annual Report, 31–33. San Diego effort in "City Plans Aid for Jobless," *Los Angeles Times*, January 11, 1931, A7. On the National Jamboree and Philmont Scout Ranch, see Oursler, *The Boy Scout Story*, 104, 137–44; and Keith Monroe, "The Jamboree That Wasn't," *Scouting*, October 1988, 12–13.

3. "Report of the Committee on Interracial Activities," 1929 BSA Annual Report, 104–9; 1930 BSA Annual Report, 100–101, 130; "Plan Extension of Boy Scout Program to All Indian Boys," *Weekly News Bulletin of Boy Scout Activities*, June 20, 1931; and 1932 BSA Annual Report, 141.

4. 1936 ECR, 125, 518–32, 954. The published conference proceedings did not list a report by the subcommittee on Indians, Mexicans, Chinese, and Japanese.

5. 1936 ECR, 532–33, 560–63, 577–79.

6. 1936 ECR, 80, 746–48, 840–46, 861–62, 877–81.

7. On some troops eliminating uniform and weekly dues requirement, see Huffman, *Sam Houston Scouts*, 42. Racially integrating Scouting to save money described in 1933 BSA Annual Report, 175. On the increasing number of reform school, handicapped, and Boys' Clubs troops, see 1936 ECR, 741–43. Bank deposit debate discussed in Keith Monroe, "75 Years in the Life of a Magazine," *Scouting*, March–April 1987. Scouting with "less chance" boys in 1939 ECR, 52–66, 355–56, 802–11.

8. Casperson, *A Northern Boyhood*, 247–64, quotations on 247–48, 257–58.

9. For Mayor Reyburn's support of Philadelphia Scouting and the local council's offices, see Philadelphia Council BSA, *Seventy Years of Scouting*, 5, 9–11.

10. Ian Urbina, "Court Advances Boy Scouts Suit against the City," *Philadelphia Daily News*, September 27, 2008; Nathan Gorenstein, "Trial over Local Boy Scout Headquarters Begins," *Philadelphia Inquirer*, August 5, 2010; and Nathan Gorenstein, "Federal Jury Decides in Favor of Scouts," *Philadelphia Inquirer*, June 23, 2010.

Selected Bibliography

Primary Sources

Archival Sources

Daniel Carter Beard Papers. Library of Congress, Washington D.C. (DCBP)
Boy Scouts of America National Archive. Irving, Texas. (BSANA)
Laura Spelman Rockefeller Memorial Collection, Rockefeller Archive Center.
    Sleepy Hollow, New York. (LSRMC)

Newspapers

Chicago Daily Tribune
Los Angeles Times
New York Times
Washington Post

Magazines

Boys' Life
Lone Scout
Scout Executive
Scouting
Weekly News Bulletin of Boy Scout Activities

Published Primary Source Materials, Books, and Pamphlets

Adams, Willard. *My Thirty Years in Scouting*. Rigby, Idaho: Privately printed for
    Willard Adams, ca. 1952.
Alexander, John L. *Boy Scouts* pamphlet. Orange, Mass.: Minute Tapioca Co. for
    the BSA, 1911.
Arthurs, Frank B. "Boy Scouts Building for Manhood." *Outing Magazine* 57
    (December 1910): 276–84.
Baden-Powell, Robert. *Aids to Scouting for N.-C.O.s and Men*. London: Gale &
    Polden, 1899.
———. *Scouting for Boys: A Handbook for Instruction in Good Citizenship*. 6 parts.
    London: Horace Cox, 1908.
———. *Sea Scouting for Boys*. Glasgow: James Brown & Son, 1911.
Beard, Daniel Carter. *The Boy Pioneers: Sons of Daniel Boone*. New York: Charles
    Scribner's Sons, 1911.

———. *The Buckskin Book of the Boy Pioneers of America.* New York: Pictorial Review, 1911.

———. *Hardly a Man Is Now Alive: The Autobiography of Dan Beard.* New York: Doubleday, Doran, 1939.

Boy Scouts of America. Annual Reports (1910–1930).

———. *The Boy Scout Handbook.* Irving, Tex.: BSA, 1998.

———. *Boy Scout Song Book.* Boston: C. C. Birchard, 1920.

———. *Community Boy Leadership: A Manual for Scout Executives.* New York: BSA, 1926.

———. *First National Training School.* New York: BSA, 1925.

———. *The Good Turn Test.* New York: BSA, 1928.

———. *Handbook for Boys,* 2nd ed. New York: BSA, May 1919, May 1927.

———. *Handbook for Scout Masters.* New York: BSA, 1914.

———. *Handbook for Scout Masters.* New York: BSA, 1919.

———. *Handbook for Scoutmasters: A Manual of Leadership.* New York: BSA, 1922.

———. Merit Badge pamphlets, selected.

———. National Training Executives Conference Report (ECR) (1920, 1922, 1924, 1926, 1928, 1936, 1939).

———. *Official Handbook of the Lone Scouts of America.* New York: BSA, undated.

———. *Programs for Scout Masters of Boy Scouts of America: Proof Copy.* Garden City, N.Y.: Doubleday, Page, 1912.

———. *Scouting and the Jewish Boy.* New York: BSA, 1928.

———. *The Sea Scout Manual.* New York: BSA, 1929.

———. Service Library pamphlets, selected.

———. *Songs Scouts Sing.* New York: BSA, 1930.

———. *Standard Capitalization and Terminology of the Boy Scouts of America: Suggestions for Correspondence, Preparing Manuscripts and Proof Readers' Marks.* New York: BSA, 1920s.

———. *The Troop Committee: An Active Committee Insures Progress.* New York: BSA, 1928.

———. *Troop Stunts.* New York: BSA, 1931.

———. " 'Western Round-Up' of Scout Executives." January 21–24, 1920. Transcript. Berkeley, Calif.

Bureau of Municipal Research. *Report on the Boy Scouts of America.* New York: Bureau of Municipal Research, 1914.

Carey, Arthur A. *The Scout Law in Practice.* Boston: Little, Brown, 1915.

Casperson, Ralph A. *A Northern Boyhood.* Niles and Decatur, Mich.: Johnson Graphics for Ralph A. Casperson Books, 1993.

Cheley, F. H. *The Practice of the Oath and Law.* New York: BSA, 1928.

Chesley, Albert M., ed. *Social Activities for Men and Boys.* New York: Young Men's Christian Association Press, 1910.

Curtis, Henry S. "The Boy Scouts." *Educational Review* 50 (December 1915): 495–508.

Denslow, Cornelius. *Making Nature Collections.* New York: BSA Service Library, 1929.

Eastman, Charles A. *Indian Scout Craft and Lore*. 1914; reprint, New York: Dover, 1974.

Edwards, Arvid. *Slices from My Life*. Platte City, Mo.: Printed for A. H. Edwards, 1995.

Eliot, Charles W. *The Training of Boy Scouts*. New York: BSA, 1914.

Fairchild, Henry P. *Conduct Habits of Boy Scouts*. New York: BSA, 1931.

Fetridge, William Harrison. *With Warm Regards: A Reminiscence*. Chicago: Dartnell, 1976.

Fisher, George J. "Health and Endurance." In Murray, Pratt, and Jameson, *Official Handbook for Boys*, 219–33.

Forbush, William. *The Boy Problem*. Boston: Pilgrim Press, 1907.

Geiss, Newton. *Reminiscences of a Berks County Rural Boy*. Kutztown, Pa.: Kutztown Publishing, 1970.

———. *Youth—the Hope of the World*. Kutztown, Pa.: Kutztown Publishing, 1972.

Gladden, George. "Some Practical Aspects of Scouting." *Century*, February 1920, 573–75.

Hagood, J. Hurley. *52 Years of Adventure: Boy Scouting*. Quincy, Ill.: JK Creative Printers, 1996.

Hall, G. Stanley. *Adolescence: Its Psychology and Its Relations to Physiology, Anthropology, Sociology, Sex, Crime, Religion and Education*. 1904; reprint, New York: D. Appleton, 1922.

Henderson, James T. *A Thousand Campfires: A Scouter's Story*. San Angelo, Tex.: Ambush Publishing, 1991.

Hillcourt, William. *Handbook for Patrol Leaders*. New York: BSA, 1929.

Hornaday, William T. *Our Vanishing Wildlife: Its Extermination and Preservation*. New York: Charles Scribner's Sons, 1913.

Hurt, H. William, ed. *Community Boy Leadership: A Manual for Scout Executives*, 2nd ed. New York: BSA, 1922.

———, ed. *Handbook for Boys*, 3rd ed. New York: BSA, 1928.

———, ed. *Handbook for Scoutmasters: A Manual of Leadership*, 2nd ed. New York: BSA, 1929.

Jones, Helen. "The Boy Scouts of America." *Playground*, January 1926, 562–63.

Jones, Mark M. "Report on a Survey of the Boy Scouts of America, 1927." BSANA.

Kenney, Dave. *Honor Bright: A Century of Scouting in Northern Star Council*. St. Paul and Minneapolis: Northern Star Council BSA, 2009.

Kietzman, August F. *Why I Became a Scoutmaster: Forty-Eight Years of Youth Work*. New York: Comet Press Books, 1958.

Lamb, Merritt. *My Scout and Other Poems*. Muskegon, Mich.: W. C. Foote Printing, 1916.

Moffat, S. A. "Volunteer Citizens: The Young Peace Army of America as Developed through the Boy Scouts." *Craftsman*, June 1914, 317–19.

Murray, William D., George D. Pratt, and A. A. Jameson, eds. *The Official Handbook for Boys*. Garden City, N.Y.: Doubleday, Page, 1911.

Price, Luther E. *Thirty Years of Scout Camping: History of Glen Gray and other Scout Camps in Northern New Jersey*. Montclair, N.J.: Montclair Arts and Crafts Press, 1941.

Reimer, Edward. *Matching Mountains with the Boy Scout Uniform*. New York: E. P. Dutton, 1929.

Richardson, Norman, and Ormond Loomis. *The Boy Scout Movement Applied by the Church*. New York: Charles Scribner's Sons, 1915.

Ripley, Sherman. *Games for Boys*. New York: H. Holt and Company, 1920.

Seton, Ernest Thompson. *The Birch-Bark Roll of the Outdoor Life*. New York: Doubleday, Page, 1908.

——. *The Birch-Bark Roll of the Woodcraft Indians*. New York: Doubleday, Page, 1906.

Seton, Ernest Thompson, and Robert Baden-Powell. *A Handbook of Woodcraft, Scouting, and Lifecraft*. New York: Doubleday, Page, 1910.

Shaver, Waldo. *Notes from a Pioneer's Journal of Scouting Stories*. Denver: Privately published, 1977.

Sherman, Waldo H. "The Boy Scouts 300,000 Strong." *World's Work*, September 1911, 14859–72.

Stowe, Lyman Beecher. "The Boy Scouts of the World." *Columbian*, September 1911, 1102–4.

Taylor, A. J. "Man with Man in Scouting: Work with Colored Boys." *Southern Workman* 64, no. 4 (April 1935): 109–10.

Taylor, John. *From Market Square to the Banks of Sherman's Creek . . . 85 Years of Scouting in the Keystone Area Council and 75 Years of Camping at Hidden Valley Scout Reservation*. Privately published, 2002.

Tillery, Floyd. "Little Babbitts." *Forum* 84, no. 6 (December 1930): 338–42.

Von Allman, E. P. "A Study of the San Francisco District Council of the Boy Scouts of America." San Francisco: Council of Social and Health Agencies, October 1924.

Walsh, Stuart. *Thirteen Years of Scout Adventure*. Seattle: Lowman & Hanford, 1923.

Watkins, Prince L. *Yakni: History of the Boy Scout Movement in Northeast Mississippi*. Tupelo, Miss.: Yokona Area Council BSA, 1978.

West, James. *Bulletin to All Scout Officials*. New York: BSA, 1923–1929.

——. *The Lone Scout of the Sky: The Story of Charles A. Lindbergh*. Chicago and Philadelphia: John C. Winston, 1928.

Wilder, James. *Pine Tree Patrol*. New York: BSA, 1918.

Wyland, Ray O. "The Knighthood of Youth." *Improvement Era*, August 1928, 857.

——. *Principles of Scoutmastership*. New York: BSA, 1930.

——. *Scouting in the Schools: A Study of the Relationships between the Schools and the Boy Scouts of America*. New York: Columbia University, 1934.

Yater, Paul A. *A History of Troop 1 (201) Longview, Texas, 1917–2002*. Privately published, 2002.

Secondary Sources

Alexander, Kristine. "Similarity and Difference at Girl Guide Camps in England, Canada, and India." In Block and Proctor, *Scouting Frontiers*, 106–20.

Anderson, H. Allen. *Ernest Thompson Seton and the Changing West*. College Station: Texas A & M University Press, 1986.

Armitage, Kevin. "Bird Day for Kids: Progressive Conservation in Theory and Practice." *Environmental History* 12 (July 2007): 528–51.

———. *The Nature Study Movement: The Forgotten Popularizer of America's Conservation Ethic*. Lawrence: University Press of Kansas, 2009.

Ashby, LeRoy. " 'Straight from Youthful Hearts': *Lone Scout* and the Discovery of the Child, 1915–1924." *Journal of Popular Culture* 9, no. 4 (1976): 775–93.

Banner, Lois. Review of books on men and masculinity. *Signs* 14, no. 3 (Spring 1989): 703–8.

Barker-Benfield, Ben. "The Spermatic Economy: A Nineteenth Century View of Sexuality." *Feminist Studies* 1.1 (Summer 1972): 45–74.

Bar-Yosef, Eitan. "Fighting Pioneer Youth: Zionist Scouting in Israel and Baden-Powell's Legacy." In Block and Proctor, *Scouting Frontiers*, 42–55.

Bederman, Gail. *Manliness and Civilization: A Cultural History of Gender and Race in the United States, 1880–1917*. Chicago: University of Chicago Press, 1995.

Biegert, Melissa. "Woman Scout: The Empowerment of Juliette Gordon Low, 1860–1927." Ph.D. dissertation, University of Texas, 1998.

Blassingame, Wyatt. *Story of the Boy Scouts*. Champaign, Ill.: Garrard, 1968.

Block, Nelson R., and Tammy M. Proctor, eds. *Scouting Frontiers: Youth and the Scout Movement's First Century*. Newcastle upon Tyne, U.K.: Cambridge Scholars, 2009.

Bogan, Samuel. "No Larger Fields: The History of a Boy Scout Council, 1910–1963." Hamden, Conn.: Quinnipiac Council BSA, 1966.

Bolland, Thomas. "Magazine Coverage of the Boy Scouts and Scouting Events and Activities from 1910 to 1991." Master's thesis, Ohio University, 1993.

Bowers, Greg. *"On My Honor": 70 Years of Scouting in York & Adams Counties*. York, Pa.: York Council BSA, 1983.

Boy Scouts International Bureau. *Facts on World Scouting*, 2nd ed. Ottawa, Ontario: Boy Scouts International Bureau, 1961.

Bragg, Ross. "The Boy Scout Movement in Canada: Defining Constructs of Masculinity for the Twentieth Century." Master's thesis, Dalhousie University, 1995.

Braude, Anne. "Making Men by Making Indians: 'Red Men,' Boy Scouts and the YMCA." Edited by Susan Ware. *New Viewpoints in Women's History: Working Papers from the Schlesinger Library 50th Anniversary Conference, March 4–5, 1994*. Cambridge, Mass.: The Arthur and Elizabeth Schlesinger Library, 1994.

Brittain, William J. *The Spirit of Scouting '76: Sixty-five Years of Challenge and Triumph in the St. Louis Area Council, Boy Scouts of America*. St. Louis: St. Louis Area Council BSA, 1976.

Burns, Rex. *Success in America: The Yeoman Dream and the Industrial Revolution.* Amherst: University of Massachusetts Press, 1976.

Camp Fire Girls and Boys. *Wo-He-Lo: The Camp Fire History.* Kansas City: Camp Fire Girls and Boys, 1995.

Carnes, Mark C., and Clyde Griffen, eds. *Meanings for Manhood: Constructions of Masculinity in Victorian America.* New Haven: Yale University Press, 1989.

Cavallo, Dominick. *Muscles and Morals: Organized Playgrounds and Urban Reform, 1880–1920.* Philadelphia: University of Pennsylvania Press, 1981.

Cawelti, John G. *Apostles of the Self-Made Man.* Chicago: University of Chicago Press, 1965.

Choate, Anne Hyde, and Helen Ferris, eds. *Juliette Low and the Girl Scouts: The Story of an American Woman, 1860–1927.* 1928; reprint, New York: Girl Scouts of the U.S.A., 1949.

Conley, Walter F. "William Dickson Boyce: Pioneer Publisher, Individualist and Good Scout." *The Elbeetian Book of Memories.* Vol. 2. Hudson Heights, N.J.: Elbeetian Legion, 1963.

Creighton, Wilbur F., Jr., and Leland R. Johnson. *Boys Will Be Men: Middle Tennessee Scouting since 1910.* Nashville: Middle Tennessee Council BSA, 1983.

Cronin, Brendan Daniel. "Ninety-Two Years of Service: The Boy Scouts of America." Undergraduate thesis, University of Dallas History Department, 2002.

Crotty, Martin. *Making the Australian Male: Middle-Class Masculinity, 1870–1920.* Melbourne, Australia: Melbourne University Press, 2001.

———. "Scouts Down Under: Scouting, Militarism and 'Manliness' in Australia, 1908–1920." In Block and Proctor, *Scouting Frontiers,* 74–88.

Davis, Winston R. *Men of Schiff: A History of the Professional Scouters Who Built the Boy Scouts of America.* Privately published, 2013.

Deady, Rev. Carroll F. "An Historical Study of the Scout Movement in the United States and England." Master's thesis, Catholic University of America, 1928.

Dean, John I. "Scouting in America: 1910–1990." Ph.D. diss., University of South Carolina, 1992.

Deloria, Philip. *Playing Indian.* New Haven: Yale University Press, 1998.

———. "Playing Indian: Otherness and Authenticity in the Assumption of American Indian Identity." Ph.D. diss., Yale University, 1994.

Demos, John, and Virginia Demos. "Adolescence in Historical Perspective." *Journal of Marriage and the Family* 31, no. 4 (November 1969): 632–38.

Dillon, Elizabeth Leeming. *On My Honor: 75 Years of Scouting in Central Virginia.* Richmond, Va.: Robert E. Lee Council BSA, 1991.

Ditz, Toby. "The New Men's History and the Peculiar Absence of Gender Power: Some Remedies from Early American Gender History." *Gender and History* 16, no. 1 (April 2004): 2–19.

Doughty, Robin. *Feather Fashions and Bird Preservation.* Berkeley: University of California Press, 1975.

Dubbert, Joe L. *A Man's Place: Masculinity in Transition.* Englewood Cliffs, N.J.: Prentice-Hall, 1979.

Duersch, Fred, Jr. *Merit Badge Field Guide.* Logan, Utah: Downs Printing, Fred Duersch, 2003.

Dunlap, Thomas. *Saving America's Wildlife: Ecology and the American Mind, 1850–1990.* Princeton: Princeton University Press, 1988.

Elliot, Willis V. *Men of Paul Bunyan Stature: A History of Region Ten.* St. Paul, Minn.: BSA Region Ten, 1968.

Fass, Paula S. *The Damned and the Beautiful: American Youth in the 1920s.* New York: Oxford University Press, 1977.

Filene, Peter G. *Him/Her/Self: Gender Identities in Modern America,* 3rd ed. Baltimore: Johns Hopkins University Press, 1998.

Galt-Brown, James. "Baden-Powell and His Boy Scouts: The Reasons for Their Creation, Growth and Success in Great Britain, 1906–1920." Ph.D. diss., Mississippi State University, 2002.

Gilbert, James. "Controlling Boys." *Reviews in American History* 12, no. 4 (December 1984): 529–32.

Gillis, John R. "Conformity and Rebellion: Contrasting Styles of English and German Youth, 1900–33." *History of Education Quarterly,* Fall 1973, 254–55.

Gorman, Edward J. "A Comparative Study of the Scout and the Non-Scout." Master's thesis, Catholic University, 1929.

Gorn, Elliott. *The Manly Arts: Bare-Knuckle Prize Fighting in America.* Ithaca: Cornell University Press, 1986.

Grant, Julia. *The Boy Problem: Educating Boys in Urban America, 1870–1970.* Baltimore: Johns Hopkins University Press, 2014.

Green, Amy Susan. "Savage Childhood: The Scientific Construction of Girlhood and Boyhood in the Progressive Era." Ph.D. diss., Yale University, 1995.

Greene, Theodore. *America's Heroes: The Changing Models of Success in American Magazines.* New York: Oxford University Press, 1970.

Griffen, Clyde. "Reconstructing Masculinity from the Evangelical Revival to the Waning of Progressivism: A Speculative Synthesis." In *Meanings for Manhood: Constructions of Masculinity in Victorian America,* edited by Mark C. Carnes and Clyde Griffen, 183–204. New Haven: Yale University Press, 1989.

Grinder, Robert. "The Concept of Adolescence in the Genetic Psychology of G. Stanley Hall." *Child Development* 40, no. 2 (June 1969): 355–69.

Griswold, Robert. *Fatherhood in America: A History.* New York: Basic Books, 1993.

———. Review of *Manhood in America: A Cultural History,* by Michael Kimmel. *Journal of Social History* 30, no. 4 (Summer 1997): 999–1001.

Groth, Susan. "Scouts' Own: Creativity, Tradition and Empowerment in Girl Scout Ceremonies." Ph.D. diss., University of Pennsylvania, 1999.

Guterl, Matthew Pratt. *The Color of Race in America, 1900–1940.* Cambridge, Mass.: Harvard University Press, 2002.

Haber, Samuel. *Efficiency and Uplift: Scientific Management in the Progressive Era, 1890–1920.* Chicago: University of Chicago Press, 1964.

Hackensmith, C. W. "Scout Memorabilia: William D. Boyce and the Scouting Movement in America." *Pennsylvania Journal of Health, Physical Education and Recreation*, March 1972, 31–33.

Hall, William E. *100 Years and Millions of Boys: The Dynamic Story of the Boys' Clubs of America*. New York: Farrar, Strauss, Cudahy, 1961.

Hantover, Jeffrey P. "The Boy Scouts and the Validation of Masculinity." *Journal of Social Issues* 34, no. 1 (1978): 184–95.

———. "Sex Role, Sexuality, and Social Status: The Early Years of the Boy Scouts of America." Ph.D. diss., University of Chicago, 1976.

Harty, Kevin. "*The Knights of the Square Table:* The Boy Scouts and Thomas Edison Make an Arthurian Film." *Arthuriana* 4, no. 4 (Winter 1994): 313–23.

Higham, John, ed. "The Reorientation of American Culture in the 1890's." *Writing American History: Essays on Modern Scholarship*. Bloomington: Indiana University Press, 1970.

Hilkey, Judy. *Character Is Capital: Success Manuals and Manhood in Gilded Age America*. Chapel Hill: University of North Carolina Press, 1997.

Hill, Janice. "Building a Nation of Nation-Builders: Youth Movements, Imperialism, and English Canadian Nationalism, 1900–1920." Ph.D. thesis, York University, 2004.

Huffman, Minor S. *Saga of Potato Canyon: A History of the Conquistador Council, Boy Scouts of America*. Roswell, N.Mex.: Conquistador Council BSA, 1984.

———. *Sam Houston Scouts: Seventy-Five Years of History in the Sam Houston Area Council*. Houston: Sam Houston Area Council BSA, 1985.

Huhndorf, Shari. *Going Native: Indians in the American Cultural Imagination*. Ithaca: Cornell University Press, 2001.

Jacobson, Matthew Frye. *Whiteness of a Different Color: European Immigrants and the Alchemy of Race*. Cambridge: Harvard University Press, 1998.

Jacoby, Karl. *Crimes against Nature: Squatters, Poachers, Thieves, and the Hidden History of American Conservation*. Berkeley and Los Angeles: University of California Press, 2001.

Jeal, Tim. *Baden-Powell: Founder of the Boy Scouts*. New Haven: Yale University Press, 2001.

Johnson, Charles T. "A Study of the Boy Scout Organization." Master's thesis, Colorado State Teachers College, 1930.

Johnson, Michael Bruce. "A Diamond in the Rough." *Columbia: The Magazine of Northwest History*, Fall 1995, 13.

Jordan, Ben. " 'Conservation of Boyhood': Boy Scouting's Modest Manliness and Natural Resource Conservation, 1910–1930." *Environmental History*, October 2010, 612–42.

———. "Savages and the 'SHE PERIOD': The Boy Scouts of America's Younger and Older Boy Problems." In Block and Proctor, *Scouting Frontiers*, 158–74.

Kahler, William. "An Historical Analysis of the Professional Career of Daniel Carter Beard, 1850–1941." Ph.D. diss., Texas A & M University, 1975.

Kansas City Area Council BSA. *Trail to Eagle: Six Decades of Scouting in Kansas City, 1910–1970*. Kansas City: Kansas City Area Council BSA, 1972.

Kasson, John F. *Houdini, Tarzan, and the Perfect Man: The White Male Body and the Challenge of Modernity in America*. New York: Hill and Wang, 2001.

Keller, Betty. *Black Wolf: The Life of Ernest Thompson Seton*. Vancouver and Toronto: Douglas & McIntyre, 1984.

Kerr, Rose. *The Story of the Girl Guides*. Rev. ed. Rochester: Stanhope Press, 1936.

Kett, Joseph F. *Rites of Passage: Adolescence in America, 1790 to the Present*. New York: Basic Books, 1977.

Kimmel, Michael. *Manhood in America: A Cultural History*. New York: Free Press, 1996.

———. "Men's Responses to Feminism at the Turn of the Century." *Gender and Society* 1, no. 3 (September 1987): 261–83.

Kolchin, Peter. "Whiteness Studies: The New History of Race in America." *Journal of American History* 89 (June 2002): 154–73.

LDS-BSA Centennial Book Committee. *Century of Honor: 100 Years of Scouting in the Church of Jesus Christ of Latter-Day Saints*. Salt Lake City: LDS-BSA Relationships Office, 2013.

Leslie, W. Bruce. "Coming of Age in Urban America: The Socialist Alternative, 1901–1920." *Educational Studies* 85, no. 3 (Spring 1984): 468–71.

Levy, Harold P. *Building a Popular Movement: A Case Study of the Public Relations of the Boy Scouts of America*. New York: Russell Sage Foundation, 1944.

Lewchuk, Wayne A. "Men and Monotony: Fraternalism as a Managerial Strategy at the Ford Motor Company." *Journal of Economic History* 53, no. 4 (December 1993): 824–56.

Lewis, Paul W. *Scouting in Iowa—the Values Endure: The Story of the Mid-Iowa Council*. Iowa: Mid-Iowa Council BSA, 1999.

Lutts, Ralph. *The Nature Fakers: Wildlife, Science and Sentiment*. Golden, Colo.: Fulcrum Publishing, 1990.

MacDonald, Robert. "Reproducing the Middle-Class Boy: From Purity to Patriotism in the Boys' Magazines, 1892–1914." *Journal of Contemporary History* 24, no. 3 (July 1989): 519–39.

———. *Sons of the Empire: The Frontier and the Boy Scout Movement, 1890–1918*. Toronto: University of Toronto Press, 1993.

Macleod, David. "Act Your Age: Boyhood, Adolescence, and the Rise of the Boy Scouts of America." *Journal of Social History* 16, no. 2 (1982): 3–20.

———. *The Age of the Child: Children in America, 1890–1920*. New York: Twayne Publishers, 1998.

———. *Building Character in the American Boy: The Boy Scouts, YMCA, and Their Forerunners, 1870–1920*. Madison: University of Wisconsin Press, 1983.

———. "Original Intent: Establishing the Creed and Control of Boy Scouting in the United States." In Block and Proctor, *Scouting Frontiers*, 13–27.

Mangan, J. A., and James Walvin, eds. *Manliness and Morality: Middle-Class Masculinity in Britain and America, 1800–1940*. New York: St. Martin's Press, 1987.

McGovern, James R. "David Graham Phillips and the Virility Impulse of Progressives." *New England Quarterly* 39, no. 3 (September 1966): 334–55.

Mechling, Jay. "God and 'Whatever' in the Boy Scouts of America." In Block and Proctor, *Scouting Frontiers*, 175–89.

Mighetto, Lisa. *Wild Animals and American Environmental Ethics*. Tucson: University of Arizona Press, 1991.

Miller, Susan. *Growing Girls: The Natural Origins of Girls' Organizations in America*. New Brunswick, N.J.: Rutgers University Press, 2007.

———. "Trademark: Scout." In Block and Proctor, *Scouting Frontiers*, 28–41.

Mills, Sarah. "'An Instruction in Good Citizenship': Scouting and the Historical Geographies of Citizenship Education." *Transactions of the Institute of British Geographers* 38, no. 1 (January 2013): 120–34.

Mintz, Stephen. *Huck's Raft: A History of American Childhood*. Cambridge: Belknap Press of Harvard University Press, 2004.

Mintz, Stephen, and Susan Kellogg. *Domestic Revolutions: A Social History of American Family Life*. New York: Free Press, 1988.

Morris, Brian. "Ernest Thompson Seton and the Origins of the Woodcraft Movement." *Journal of Contemporary History* 5, no. 2 (1970): 183–94.

Murray, William D. *The History of the Boy Scouts of America*. New York: BSA, 1937.

Nagy, Lazlo. *250 Million Scouts*. Chicago: Dartnell Press, 1985.

Narragansett Council BSA. *Scout Trail, 1910–1962: History of the Boy Scout Movement in Rhode Island*. Providence, R.I: Narragansett Council BSA, 1964.

———. *25 Years of Scouting in Rhode Island*. Providence, R.I.: privately printed, 1935.

Nasaw, David. *Children of the City: At Work and at Play*. New York: Oxford University Press, 1985.

Nash, Roderick. "The American Cult of the Primitive." *American Quarterly* 18, no. 3 (Autumn 1966): 517–37.

Nicholl, David Shelley. *The Golden Wheel: The Story of Rotary 1905 to the Present*. Estover, Plymouth, UK: Macdonald and Evans, 1984.

Oursler, Will. *The Boy Scout Story*. Garden City, N.Y.: Doubleday & Company, 1955.

Paris, Leslie. *Children's Nature: The Rise of the American Summer Camp*. New York: New York University Press, 2008.

Parsons, Timothy H. "The Limits of Sisterhood: The Evolution of the Girl Guide Movement in Colonial Kenya." In Block and Proctor, *Scouting Frontiers*, 143–56.

———. *Race, Resistance, and the Boy Scout Movement in British Colonial Africa*. Athens: Ohio University Press, 2004.

Pendergast, Tom. *Creating the Modern Man: American Magazines and Consumer Culture*. Columbia: University of Missouri Press, 2000.

Peterson, Robert. *The Boy Scouts: An American Adventure*. New York: American Heritage, 1984.

———. "Evolution of the Eagle Scout Award." *Scouting* (November–December, 2002): 18–19, 44.

Petterchak, Janice A. *Lone Scout: W. D. Boyce and American Boy Scouting*. Rochester, Ill.: Legacy Press, 2003.

Philadelphia Council BSA. *Seventy Years of Scouting in the Boy Scouts of America Philadelphia Council, 1910–1980*. Philadelphia: Philadelphia Council BSA, 1980.

Pienkos, Donald E. *PNA: A Centennial History of the Polish National Alliance of the United States of North America*. Boulder, Colo.: East European Monographs, 1984.

Pleck, Elizabeth H., and Joseph H. Pleck, eds. *The American Man*. Englewood Cliffs, N.J.: Prentice-Hall, 1980.

Pote, Harold F. *Fifty Years of Scouting in America and the Pioneers*. Privately printed, 1962.

Powers, Madelon. *Faces along the Bar: Lore and Order in the Workingman's Saloon, 1870–1920*. Chicago: University of Chicago Press, 1998.

Price, Jennifer. *Flight Maps: Adventures with Nature in Modern America*. New York: Basic Books, 2000.

Proctor, Tammy. "Gender, Generation, and the Politics of Guiding and Scouting in Interwar Britain." Ph.D. diss., Rutgers University, 1995.

———. *On My Honour: Guides and Scouts in Interwar Britain*. Philadelphia: American Philosophical Society, 2002.

———. *Scouting for Girls: A Century of Girl Guides and Girl Scouts*. Santa Barbara, Calif.: Praeger, 2009.

———. "'A Separate Path': Scouting and Guiding in Interwar South Africa." *Comparative Studies in Society and History* 42, no. 3 (July 2000): 605–31.

———. "(Uni)Forming Youth: Girl Guides and Boy Scouts in Britain, 1908–39." *History Workshop Journal* 45 (Spring 1998): 103–34.

Pryke, Sam. "The Popularity of Nationalism in the Early British Boy Scout Movement." *Social History* (Autumn 1998): 309–24.

Putney, Clifford. *Muscular Christianity: Manhood and Sports in Protestant America, 1880–1920*. Cambridge: Harvard University Press, 2001.

Reis, Mitchell. *History of the Lone Scouts through Memorabilia*. Windsor, Conn.: Mitchell Reis, 1996.

Reynolds, E. E. *The Scout Movement*. London: Oxford University Press, 1950.

Roberts, Gerald F. "The Strenuous Life: The Cult of Manliness in the Era of Theodore Roosevelt." Ph.D. diss., Michigan State University, 1970.

Rodgers, Daniel T. *The Work Ethic in Industrial America, 1850–1920*. Chicago: University of Chicago Press, 1978.

Rosenthal, Michael. *The Character Factory: Baden-Powell and the Origins of the Boy Scouts*. New York: Pantheon Books, 1989.

———. "Knights and Retainers: The Earliest Version of Baden-Powell's Boy Scout Scheme." *Journal of Contemporary History* 15, no. 4 (October 1980): 603–17.

Ross, Dorothy. *G. Stanley Hall, Psychologist as Prophet*. Chicago: University of Chicago Press, 1972.

Rothschild, Mary Aickin. "To Scout or To Guide? The Girl Scout–Boy Scout Controversy, 1912–1941." *Frontiers: A Journal of Women Studies* 6, no. 3 (Autumn 1981): 115–21.

Rotundo, E. Anthony. *American Manhood: Transformations in Masculinity from the Revolution to the Modern Era*. New York: Basic Books, 1993.

Rowan, Edward L. *To Do My Best: James E. West and the History of the Boy Scouts of America*. Las Vegas: Las Vegas International Scouting Museum, 2005.

San Francisco Area Council BSA. *Twenty Years of Progress*. San Francisco: San Francisco Area Council BSA, 1937.

Scheidlinger, Saul. "A Comparative Study of the Boy Scout Movement in Different National and Social Groups." *American Sociological Review* 13, no. 6 (December 1948): 742–44.

Schlossman, Steven. "G. Stanley Hall and the Boys' Club: Conservative Applications of Recapitulation Theory." *Journal of the History of the Behavioral Sciences* 9, no. 2 (April 1973): 140–47.

Schudson, Michael. *The Good Citizen: A History of American Civic Life*. New York: Free Press, 1998.

Scott, David C., and Brendan Murphy. *The Scouting Party: Pioneering and Preservation, Progressivism and Preparedness in the Making of the Boy Scouts of America*. Dallas: Red Honor Press, 2010.

Sleutelberg, Arnold M. "A Critical History of Organized Jewish Involvement in the Boy Scouts of America, 1926–1987." Rabbinic thesis, Hebrew Union College–Jewish Institute of Religion, New York, 1988.

Spring, Joel. *American School, 1642–1985: Varieties of Historical Interpretation of the Foundations and Development of American Education*. New York: Longman, 1986.

Springhall, J. O. "Baden-Powell and the Scout Movement before 1920: Citizen Training or Soldiers of the Future?" *English Historical Review* 102, no. 405 (October 1987): 934–42.

———. "The Boy Scouts, Class and Militarism in Relation to British Youth Movements, 1908–1930." *International Review of Social History* 16, no. 2 (August 1971): 125–58.

Stearns, Peter N. *Be a Man! Males in Modern Society*, 2nd ed. New York: Holmes & Meier, 1990.

Sterne, Wendy. "The Formation of the Scouting Movement and the Gendering of Citizenship." Ph.D. diss., University of Wisconsin, 1993.

Stocking, George W., Jr. "Lamarckianism in American Social Science: 1890–1915." *Journal of the History of Ideas* 23, no. 2 (April–June, 1962): 239–56.

Sullivan, John F. *Boyce of Ottawa: "Items on Grand Account,"* 2nd ed. Marseilles, Ill.: North Central Graphics, 1985.

Summers, Anne. "Scouts, Guides and VADs: A Note in Reply to Allen Warren." *English Historical Review* 102, no. 405 (October 1987): 943–47.

Summers, Martin. *Manliness and Its Discontents: The Black Middle Class and the Transformation of Masculinity, 1900–1930*. Chapel Hill: University of North Carolina Press, 2004.

Syrett, Nicholas. *The Company He Keeps: A History of White College Fraternities*. Chapel Hill: University of North Carolina Press, 2009.

Tate, Willis. "A Study of Domination and Persuasion as Means of Social Control in a Boy Scout Organization in a Southwestern City of Two Hundred and Thirty Thousand Population." Master's thesis, Southern Methodist University, 1935.

Testi, Arnaldo. "Theodore Roosevelt and the Culture of Masculinity." *Journal of American History*, March 1995, 1509–33.

Thorson, P. V. *History of the Great Southwest Council, 1910–1981.* Albuquerque: printed by author, 1982.

Traister, Bryce. "Academic Viagra: The Rise of American Masculinity Studies." *American Quarterly* 52, no. 2 (2000): 284–99.

Troen, Selwyn K. "The Discovery of the Adolescent by American Educational Reformers, 1900–1920: An Economic Perspective." In *Schooling and Society: Studies in the History of Education,* edited by Lawrence Stone, 239–51. Baltimore: Johns Hopkins University Press, 1976.

Turner, James Morton. "From Woodcraft to Leave No Trace." *Environmental History* 7, no. 3 (July 2002): 462–84.

Tyack, David B. *The One Best System: A History of American Urban Education.* Cambridge, Mass.: Harvard University Press, 1974.

Vallory, Eduard. "Status Quo Keeper or Social Change Promoter: The Double Side of World Scouting's Citizenship Education." In Block and Proctor, *Scouting Frontiers,* 207–22.

Van Slyck, Abigail. *A Manufactured Wilderness: Summer Camps and the Shaping of American Youth, 1890–1960.* Minneapolis: University of Minnesota Press, 2006.

Wade, Eileen K. *The World Chief Guide: Olave Lady Baden-Powell, G.B.E.* London: Hutchinson, 1957.

Wadland, John Henry. "Ernest Thompson Seton: Man in Nature and the Progressive Era, 1880–1915." Ph.D. diss., York University, 1976.

Wagner, Carolyn D. "The Boy Scouts of America: A Model and a Mirror of American Society." Ph.D. diss., Johns Hopkins University, 1979.

Warren, Allen. "Baden-Powell: A Final Comment." *English Historical Review* 102, no. 405 (October 1987): 948–50.

———. "Sir Robert Baden-Powell, the Scout Movement and Citizen Training in Great Britain, 1900–1920." *English Historical Review* 101, no. 399 (April 1986): 376–98.

Watenpaugh, Keith David. "Scouting in the Interwar Arab Middle East: Youth, Colonialism, and the Problems of Middle Class Modernity." In Block and Proctor, *Scouting Frontiers,* 89–105.

Watt, Carey. " 'No Showy Muscles': The Boy Scouts and the Global Dimensions of Physical Culture and Bodily Health in Britain and Colonial India." In Block and Proctor, *Scouting Frontiers,* 121–42.

Watts, Sarah. *Rough Rider in the White House: Theodore Roosevelt and the Politics of Desire.* Chicago: University of Chicago Press, 2003.

Whitmore, Allan. "Beard, Boys and Buckskins: Daniel Carter Beard and the Preservation of the American Pioneer Tradition." Ph.D. diss., Northwestern University, 1970.

Wickberg, Daniel. "Heterosexual White Male: Some Recent Inversions in American Cultural History." *Journal of American History* 92, no. 1 (June 2005): 136–57.

Wigginton, Melinda. "The Boy Scouts of America: Founded in Progressivism and Still Progressing." Master's thesis, University of California Santa Barbara, 1984.

Wilkinson, Paul. "English Youth Movements, 1908–1930." *Journal of Contemporary History* 4, no. 2 (April 1969): 3–23.

Wills, Chuck. *Boy Scouts of America: A Centennial History*. New York: DK Publishing, 2009.

Wilson, J. S. *Scouting Round the World*. London: Blandford Press, 1959.

Winter, Thomas. *Making Men, Making Class: The YMCA and Workingmen, 1877–1920*. Chicago: University of Chicago Press, 2002.

Wyllie, Irvin G. *The Self-Made Man in America: The Myth of Rags to Riches*. New Brunswick, N.J.: Rutgers University Press, 1954.

Zelizer, Viviana. *Pricing the Priceless Child: The Changing Social Value of Children*. Princeton, N.J.: Princeton University Press, 1994.

Index

Active engagement, 87–92

Adams, Willard, 119

Addams, Jane, 156

Adolescence, 76, 84–85; boy problem of, 7–9; Boy Scouts of America's influence on, 221–22; character development during, 41, 43, 46, 121–22; civic training for, 21, 86; constructive leisure of, 55; Good Turn influencing, 93–94; hiking activities in, 129–31, 147; Lone Scouts and, 189–90; military training for, 100–101; Nature Study and, 125; racial recapitulation and, 60–62; role model for, 23; Scout training's influence on, 91–92, 96–98; theories of, 245 (n. 5); work ethic in, 53

Adolescence: Its Psychology and Its Relations to Physiology, Anthropology, Sociology, Sex, Crime, Religion and Education (Hall), 8

African American Boy Scouts, 197, 209–10, 212–13

"African American Faces Make Green Backs," 200

African Americans: in *Boy's Life*, 194, 199; civic leadership and, 195, 208, 213; Girl Scouts and exclusion of, 258 (n. 9); manhood, 198; modern manhood and, 194, 196, 208–13; Scout foils casting of, 197–200; Scout Laws and, 204–5; Scout songs about, 200; Scoutmaster training course of, 206; Scout troops, 200–208; Scout uniforms worn by, 202, 210–11, 260 (n. 22); Second Class Scouting for, 208–13; self-reliance and, 198–99, 204, 210;

stereotypes of, 257 (n. 4); West upholding exclusion of, 212; work ethic, 200, 205

Aids to Scouting (Baden-Powell), 21

Alexander, John, 23

Ambition, channeling, 67–68

American Boy Scouts (Hearst's organization), 24, 162, 227 (n. 12)

American Boy's Handy Book, 21

American Federation of Labor (AFL), 159–61

Americanization, 72, 163, 167–71

American National Guard, 159

Anglo-Saxon Protestants, 13, 42, 45–46, 155, 163, 165, 169, 173–76, 180, 182

Animal conservation, 142–44

Anspach, Charles, 113

Apprenticeship, 5, 8, 43–46, 69, 81, 86–87, 95–96, 146, 184

Arizona legislature, 110

Astor, John Jacob, 72

Attucks, Crispus, 208

Australian Boy Scouting, 241 (n. 21)

Ax-Men, 1–3

Baden-Powell, Robert, 45, 83, 107; *Aids to Scouting* by, 21; banquet honoring, 186; as British Boy Scout founder, 17–18, 20–22; British Oath of, 59–60; career training pushed by, 61; civic teachings of, 84, 239 (n. 4); class hierarchy and, 161; Fourth Law comment of, 71; Girl Guides developed by, 25–26; manhood quotations of, 226 (n. 4); militarism teachings of, 20, 23, 47–48; religious beliefs view by, 74,

157; reverence Law and, 238 (n. 44); Scout handbook from, 22, 24–25, 47–48, 102, 141–42, 197, 242 (n. 23), 246 (n. 8); Scout uniforms created by, 100–101; self-reliance development and, 21–22; West's Big Office criticism by, 13; working-class men comments of, 160, 162

Bailey, Liberty Hyde, 193

Beard, Dan, 12, 61, 83; balanced masculine model and, 2; Boy Scouts of America leadership joined by, 20; manhood quotations of, 226 (n. 4); Melting Pot comments of, 167–68; as National Scout Commissioner, 123; native bird extinction and, 143; natural resource conservation of, 123–24; pioneer-lore enthusiasm of, 24; Professional Scouters and, 27; as public figurehead, 226 (n. 3); self-reliant primitivism of, 19; Seton locking horns with, 24; Sixth Law comment of, 142; Sons of Daniel Boone formed by, 17–18, 21, 72–73; unselfish democratic service and, 3

Benson, O. H., 189

Be Prepared, 199

Big Brother Movement, 9, 161, 172–73

Bird study, 126–28

Blackface, 194, 198, 200, 257 (n. 4)

Boas, Franz, 203

Bomus, Peter, 24, 102

Boston Boy Scouts, 170

Boyce, William D., 185; Boy Scouts of America incorporated by, 23; Boy Scouts of America's boy acceptance of, 257 (n. 3); financial support disappeared from, 24; Lone Scouts of America organization of, 182–91; rural boys recruitment of, 192, 254 (n. 6); welfare capitalism from, 23

Boy problem, 7–9

Boy's Brigade, 21, 47, 226 (n. 7)

Boys Club Federation, 172

Boy Scout handbook, 54, 58, 62–63, 67, 88, 127; hiking activities in, 134–35; largest order of, 223 (n. 3); leadership in, 92–93; nature conservation in, 144; Roosevelt, T., essay for, 85–86, 106–7

Boy Scout Laws. *See* Scout Laws; *specific Laws*

Boy Scout Movement Applied by the Church, The (Richardson and Loomis), 51

Boy Scout National Museum, 113

Boy Scouts: African Americans second class, 208–13; for country boys, 182–86; forest fire fought by, 95; international members in, 226 (n. 7); membership of, 231 (n. 30), 248 (n. 31); militarism stance of, 100–107. *See also specific Boy Scouts organization*

Boy Scouts of America (BSA): adolescence influenced by, 221–22; Beard joining leadership of, 20; Boyce incorporating, 23; Boyce's acceptance criteria to, 257 (n. 3); Catholic Scouting rights defended by, 174–76, 208, 238 (n. 44); central authority and local control in, 33–40; character development progress grid of, 67; civic teachings of, 84–120; competing programs triumph of, 19–27; Congressional charter granted to, 4, 24–25, 28, 100, 109–10; Department of Rural Scouting of, 192; environmental teachings of, 121–52; Equal Access Act, 221; Executive Training Conference of, 92, 146, 174–75, 218; expenditures of, 32–33, 230 (n. 21); expert management and laws of, 47; expert management practiced in, 28–29; First Aid drills of, 48, 51; Girl Scouts elimination sought by, 25–26, 188; government cooperation with, 4, 24, 28, 38, 94, 96, 100, 105–12,

118–20, 127, 145–46, 211, 214–16, 219–22; immigrants welcomed by, 155–67, 197, 221–22; income of, 24, 32–33, 187–88; independent Scout troops and, 24–25; labor unions attracted by, 157–58, 170; leaders' latitude eroding of, 158; Lone Scouts of America absorption failure of, 186–93; membership growth of, 40–43, 228 (n. 15); militarism issue in, 100–7; National Council of, 30–32, 39, 102, 142, 161–62, 165–66, 172, 229 (n. 19); nonsectarian policy of, 89–90, 250 (n.5); officials during World War One, 170–71; organizational structure of, 27–40; Pioneer Scouts of, 185–86; politics influences by, 97–99; Progressive Era membership growth of, 3; public support of, 53, 215; Roosevelt, T., cooperation with, 106–7; Roosevelt, T., endorsing citizenship training of, 84; Roosevelt, T., handbook essay for, 85–86, 106–7; Roosevelt, T., honorary vice president of, 18; Scouting associations merging in to, 25; Seton criticizing executive power in, 27; Seton expelled by, 3, 129; trade movement involvement with, 158–63; versions of, 23; as way of life, 75–83; West as Executive Secretary of, 18–19, 84; West's national policy of, 31–32; West's standardization of, 3; work ethic value in, 11, 50–55, 68–69, 83–84, 194; World War One and officials of, 158, 170–71

Boy Scout Week, 106

Boy's Life (magazine), 54, 62, 70–71, 121, *122*, 131; African American boy in, 194, 199; camping rules in, 138; carefree tramp in, *132*

Bravery Law, 63, 69, 72–73, 78, 204, 209, 237 (n. 40)

Briley, Beverly, 119

British Boy Scout Oath, 45–46, 59–60

British Boy Scouts, 43; Baden-Powell as founder of, 17–18, 20–21; corporate-industrial work and, 29; handbook of, 22–25, 47–48, 102, 141–42, 197, 242 (n. 23), 246 (n. 8); laws, 160; militarism in, 102; Patrol Method in, 21

British Girl Guides, 43

Bureaucratization, 17, 29, 32, 178

Burgess, Thornton W., 62

Burroughs, John, 127

Business success, 63–64

Campcraft, 58, 60, 132

Camp Fire Girls, 26, 193

Camping, 171–72, 208; African American Boy Scout excluded from, 210, 212–13; Be Prepared for, 199; *Boy's Life* with rules on, 138; class rank tests on, 60–61; costs of, 260 (n. 21); credit system tracking, 67; equipment, 99, 110; facilities, 39; Girl Scouts and, 247 (n. 17); Good Turn and, 214–15; Ku Klux Klan intervening in, 210; nature and, 123–24; outdoor life and, 146–51; Pine Tree Patrol, *139*, *140*, 169; practical citizenship from, 135–40; rank and badge progress from, 151–52, 178; relationships built from, 81–82; rural boys and, 183; Scout Oath and, 151; self-reliance from, 57–58; Woodcraft Indians emphasizing, 123; work ethic and sessions in, 150–51

"Camping in America" speech, 136

Canadian Boy Scouts, 12

Capital-labor conflict, 158–59, 162

Carefree tramp, *132*

Carey, Arthur Astor, 2, 47–48, 57, 71–72, 142

Carnegie, Andrew, 102

Carstang, Joseph, 133

Casperson, Ralph, 218–19

Catholic immigrants, 157

Catholic leaders, 164, 170–71

Catholic Scouting, 157, 163–68; Boy
Scouts of America defending rights
of, 174–76, 208, 238 (n. 44); National
Catholic War Council and, 170–71

Central authority, 33–40

Chain of command, 37

Character development, 76, 91, 101;
during adolescence, 41, 43, 46,
121–22; Boy Scouts of America
progress grid on, 67; Boy Scouts of
America's civic training and, 37, 45;
from competition, 56–57; juvenile
courts and, 156; leadership opportunities and, 218; for practical citizenship, 151–52; programs for, 9–10;
rank and badge process in, 239
(n. 4); self-reliance and, 75, 78; service leadership and, 117; work ethic
and, 50–55, 68–69, 194

Cheerfulness Law, 50–51, 55, 78, 131,
150

Child labor laws, 8, 86, 125, 181

Children, 52–53, 86, 97, 239 (n. 2)

Child study movement/experts, 8–10

Citizencraft, 87–92, 239 (n. 4)

Citizenship/civic training: for adolescents, 21, 86; of Baden-Powell, 84,
239 (n. 4); of Boy Scouts of America, 112–20; Boy Scouts of America's
character development and, 37, 45;
civic leadership in, 85; cooperation
in modern, 106; full-orbed, 92–100;
Good Turn for, 88–89; hiking
activities and, 129–35; labor unions
and, 92; militarism and, 19–20;
nature-based milieus used for, 10;
nonpartisan, 87–92, 168; objectives
of, 112–13; Roosevelt, T., endorsing,
84; unselfish service in, 88–89

Civic leadership, 58, 159, 214; adult
leadership in, 9–10; African Americans and, 195, 208, 213; in American melting pot, 167–68; animal

conservation and, 142; gender and
civic norms taught in, 37–38; good
citizenship from, 85; Good Turn
and, 95, 115–16; hiking activities
influencing, 133–34; industrialization and, 5; merit badges from, 91;
militarism criticisms and, 102–3;
nature and, 123; public service and,
93; schoolboy feminization and, 7–8

Civic service, 90, 101, 120, 168

Civilian drills, 103

Class conflict, 161–63

Class hierarchy, 161

Class prejudice, 72

Class rank tests, 60–61

Cleanliness Law, 58–60, 69, 72–74, 78,
94–95, 204, 232 (n. 1)

Clergy Scoutmasters, 228 (n. 15)

Collier, John, 216

Committee on Public Information
(CPI), 106

Competition, 35, 51, 78, 140; character development from, 56–57;
cooperation and, 46, 64–69, 81–82;
hypermasculine values and, 11–12;
Scoutmasters setting up, 66–67;
self-control in, 46

Compulsory schooling, 8, 44, 86, 125,
156, 181

Congressional charter, 220; Boy Scouts
of America granted, 4, 24–25,
28, 100, 109–10; legal monopoly
granted in, 187

Conklin, Robert S., 145

Connecticut Yankee in King Arthur's
Court, A (Twain), 24

Conservation merit badge pamphlet,
146

Constructive leisure, 55

Coolidge, Calvin, 65, 90, 98, 108, 109,
125, 176

Cooperation, 12, 81–82, 212; Boy
Scouts of America and government,
4, 24, 28, 38, 94, 96, 100, 105–12,
118–20, 127, 145–46, 211, 214–16,

Lone Scouts of America (LSA), 181; adolescence and, 189–90; Boyce starting, 182–91; Boy Scouts of America's failed absorption of, 186–93; distinctive programs of, 193; Indian lore emphasized by, 184; membership of, 231 (n. 30), 255 (n. 10), 255 (n. 16), 256 (n. 20); publications of, 184–85; West and merger of, 191, 255 (n. 11)

Loomis, Ormond, 51

Louisville Plan, 203–4

Low, Juliette, 25–26

Loyalty Law, 10, 37, 41, 46, 48–50, 53, 59–60, 68, 77, 83, 103, 116, 138, 158, 160, *168*, 169–71, 176–77

Loyalty ladder, *49, 50*

Macleod, David, 42, 102, 226 (n. 4), 233 (n. 10), 234 (n. 19), 239 (n. 5)

"Making Men of Them," 62

Manesau, Horace, 81

Marr, Weaver, 216

Martial training, 3, 7, 100, 162

"Massa's in the Cold, Cold, Ground," 200

McDonald, L. L., 136

McFarland, J. Horace, 84

McKenzie, Robert, 221

McLean Bill, 143

Mehlhop, Hohn, 148

Melting Pot, 37, 167–72

Membership growth, 40–43, 228 (n. 15)

Men's poverty, 160

Merit badges and pamphlets, 28, 46, 56, 61, 63–64, 81, 91, 143

Middle Tennessee Scout Council, 117

Migratory Bird Act, 143

Militarism, 7, 78; adolescent training in, 100–101; Australian Boy Scouting and, 241 (n. 21); Baden-Powell teachings of, 20, 23, 47–48; in Boy Scouts of America, 101; Boy Scouts' stance on, 100–107; in British

Scouting, 102; civic leadership and criticisms of, 102–3; civic responsibilities instead of, 89, 116; home and child duties replacing, 25; labor unions' criticisms of, 101, 159, 162; Middle Tennessee Scout Council and, 117; modern manhood and citizenship, 19–20; preparedness debate in, 100–107; Scout uniforms and, 103–4, 117, 159–60; Seton's criticism of, 161; skills and values compared to, 12

Military service, 106–7

Modernizing society, 27, 33–34, 172–77, 182

Modern manhood, 27, 37–38, 69; African American boys and, 194, 196, 198, 208–13; balanced authority and, 20–21; Boy Scouts of America's teaching methods for, 43, 152; British Boy Scout Oath and, 45–46; civic leadership and, 39; full-orbed, 4–14, 92–100; Good Turn and, 94; hiking activities and, 129–35; immigrant gangs and, 169–70; militarism and, 19–20; nature and, 123; practical citizenship and, 3–4, 10, 13, 217–18; quotations on, 226 (n. 4); rural conflict with, 178–82, 186–88, 191–92; rural boys and, 182–86; Scout foils and, 197–200; Scout Laws of society and, 69–75; Seton's agreement with, 56; uniform cost and, 217–18; universal vision of, 162–63; urbanizing, industrializing society and, 155; Victorian elements in, 11–12, 40, 44–45, 65, 87; work ethic balanced with, 162–63

Moffett, Samuel, 90

Morgan, Frank Allan, 184, 190, 192

Morgenstern, Julian, 176

Mormon Scouting, 41, 163, 165, 167, 238 (n. 44), 252 (n. 16)

Motivation, 147

Muir, John, 125

Primitive virility, 18, 20, 23
Production, methods and speed of, 53
Professionalization, 27–33, 137
Progressive Era/reform, 6, 34, 38, 84,
239 (n. 5); Boy Scouts of America's
membership growth during, 3;
citizencraft during, 87–92
Protestants, 13, 45–46, 50, 55, 59, 155,
163
Puberty, 8–9
Public schools, 155–56

Racial recapitulation, 8, 55, 60–62, 93
Racial segregation, 6, 103, 209, 222
Rank and badge progress, 67–68, 80,
151–52, 178
Recreation Magazine, 21
Red Cross, 99
"Report of Commission on Turnover,"
146
Resourcefulness, 45, 60–61, 102, 136
Restriction law, 203
Reverence Law and policy, 74–75,
157–58, 238 (n. 44)
Richardson, Norman, 51
Ridder, Victor, 164
Rigney, Frank, *64*, 121, *122, 130*
Riis, Jacob, 4, 17, 57
Robinson, Edgar M., 23, 234 (n. 21)
Rockefeller, John D., Jr., 17, 52–53,
62, 207
Rockefeller Foundation, 14
Rockwell, Norman, 178, *179*
Roosevelt, Franklin D., 215
Roosevelt, Theodore, 4, 24, 156; Boy
Scout citizenship training endorsed
by, 84; Boy Scouts of America co-
operation of, 106–7; Boy Scouts of
America handbook essay of, 85–86,
106–7; as Boy Scouts of America
honorary vice president, 18; Square
Deal of, 236 (n. 27)
Roosevelt, Theodore, Jr., 171
Rotary Club, 89–90, 140
Ruml, Beardsley, 202

Rural boys: Boyce recruiting, 192,
254 (n. 6); camping and hiking not
appealing to, 183; modern manhood
and, 182–86; self-reliance learned
by, 181–82
Rural manhood, 178, *179*, 182, 186–88,
191–92
Rural policies, 254 (n. 3)
Rural Scouting, 185–92
Russell, Dean James, 91, 176
Russell Sage Foundation, 31, 98

San Diego Boy Scouts, 215
San Francisco Boy Scouts, 75
Schiff, Mortimer, 165, 176, 230 (n.25)
Schoolboys, 7–8
Scientific expertise, 7, 120, 245 (n. 3)
Scientific management, 30
Scout foils, 197–200
Scouting and the Jewish Boy (West), 163,
176
Scouting associations, other, 24–25
Scout Laws: African American boys
and, 204–5; American, 46; Anglo-
Saxon men's principals in, 45–46;
business success and, 64–65; Good
Turn and, 115–17; Hall's suggestions
for, 60; Jewish traditions compared
to, 176–77; modern manhood and,
75; modern virtues and, 131–32;
nature values in, 123–24, 147–48;
social distinctions and, 105; social
relations pertaining to, 83; in
society, 69–75; state governments
supporting, 110–11; values reflected
in, 63–64, 77–78; work ethic and,
46–50. *See also specific Laws*
Scoutmasters: African Americans
training course of, *206*; Boy Scouts
of America's use of, 184; clergy as,
228 (n. 15); competitions set up
by, 66–67; handbook, 48, 51,
68, 89, 93, 109–10, 132–33, 135, 242
(n. 23); leadership of, 80; loyalty
and, 169–70; military service and,

106–7; motivation from, 147; rank and badge advancement by, 52, 67–68; time efficiency from, 54–55; training, 29–30, 66, 74, 167, 205–8, *206*; volunteers, 3, 30–31; West's reply about authority of, 96; Wilson urging volunteers as, 28

Scout Oath, 69, 114–17, 147, 233 (n. 10); camping and, 151; good citizenship and, 88–89; hiking activities and, 149–50; labor unions' suggestions about, 170; learning, 218–19; living up to, 76–77, 80; original version of, 234 (n. 21); outdoor life and, 121–22; state governments and, 110–12; well-rounded body and, 55–59; work ethic learned from, 45–46

Scout's Pace, 57, 133–34

"Scout Troop Boasts Many Nationalities," 175

Scout troops: African American, 200–208; full-orbed manhood from, 4–14; immigrants influenced by, 171–72; independent, 24–25; leadership diversity in, 174–76, *175*; local committees of, 33–34; West and experience of, 183–84; World War One conservation work of, 144–45; Young Men's Christian Association supporting, 22–23

Scout uniforms, 22, 78, 116, 242 (n. 25); African American boys wearing, 202, 210–11, 260 (n. 22); Baden-Powell creating, 100–101; cost of, 104, 183, 210, 217–18, 260 (n. 21); debates about, 104–5; Girl, 103–4; immigrants and, 211; militarism and, 103–4, 117, 159–60; purpose of, 103; West enforcing standardizing, 174

Sea Scouting, 66, 169, 231 (n. 31)

Self-control, 46, 58–60

Self-determination, 201

Self-made man, 5, 11, 44, 50, 59–65, 85, 87

Self-reliance, 71; African Americans and, 198–99, 204, 210; Baden-Powell and development of, 21–22; Boy Scouts of America's emphasis on, 63; Boy Scouts of America Laws and, 45–46; British Boy Scout Oath and, 60; from camping, 57–58; character development and, 75, 78; expert management and democratic, 43; First Aid preparing for, 131; hiking and, 57–59, 135–36, 149; individualism and, 83; masculine qualities in, 63, 68, 186; other-directed balance with, 62; outdoor life learning, 60–61, 226 (n. 4); overprivilege interfering with, 162; peace Scouting and, 102; rural boys learning, 181–82; rural recruitment rates and, 185; self-made man and, 50, 61; social cooperation and, 158–59; Sons of Daniel Boone learning, 9–10; volunteers, 19–20; Woodcraft Indians learning, 9–10

Self-support, 59–65

Service leadership, 92–100, 114–18, 120

Seton, Ernest Thompson: Beard locking horns with, 24; becoming disgruntled, 18–19; Boy Scout handbook of, 127; Boy Scouts of America Executive power criticized by, 27; Boy Scouts of America expelling, 3, 129; competing organization of, 20–21; ideal manhood agreement with, 56; Indian role model of, 12, 58; manhood quotations of, 226 (n. 4); militarism criticism of, 161; Native American theme of, 23; as pioneer-lore advocate, 2; self-reliance advocated by, 19; Woodcraft Indians of, 17, 21–22, 84, 123, 184

Sexuality, 58–59, 234 (n. 19)

Shaver, Waldo, 79

Shields, Albert, 91–92

ence essential to, 183–84; Scout-master authority reply of, 96; Scout uniform enforcement of, 174

Wheat, R. M., 207

White Nationality groups, 172–77, 214, 217

Whitman, Charles, 111

Wilder, James "Kimo," 66, 138, *139*, 140, 169

Wilson, Woodrow, 28, 100, 106, 108, 110

Winchester Arms Company, 187–88

Women, 6–7, 25–26, 69, 133, 141–43, 152

Woodcraft Indians, 19–20, 37; camping and nature emphasized in, 123; council decisions obedience of, 238 (n. 1); membership of, 226 (n. 7); as outdoor program, 17–18; programs narrow scope, 21; self-reliance learned by, 9–10; Seton's, 17, 21–22, 84, 123, 184

Woods, Arthur, 107

Work ethic, 13, 75; in adolescence, 53; African American, 200, 205; Boy Scouts of America character values and, 11, 50–55, 68–69, 83–84, 194; camp sessions developing, 150–51; Eighth and Ninth British Laws on, 50; immigrant male, 168; manhood balanced with, 162–63; Protestant, 50, 55, 59; rank and badge advancement for, 80; Scout Laws and, 46–50; Scout Oath helping with, 45–46; thrift in, 52–53; unstruc-tured leisure time ruining, 53; Victorian virtue of, 2; well-rounded body central to, 56

Working-class immigrants, 8–9, 13, 19, 73, 152, 157–58

Working-class men, 160, 162

Working-class street toughs, 73, 169–70

World War One, 12, 26, 101, 105, 107, 109, 111; America as melting pot during, 167–68; Boy Scouts of America leaders' latitude eroded during, 158; Boy Scouts of America officials during, 170–71; Catholic officials during, 170–71; physical exams during, 57; Pioneer Division during, 185–86; Scout membership decline during, 117; Scout's conservation work during, 144–45

Wyland, Ray O., 223 (n. 3)

Yeoman farmer, 181, 186

Young Men's Christian Association (YMCA), 9, 19; Brooklyn's, 188; Fisher working for, 58, 92; Scout troops supported by, 22–23; workers, 113

Young Men's Hebrew Association, 166

Young Men's Mutual Improvement Association (YMMIA), 165

Youth culture, 7, 73, 75, 86

Youth-the Hope of the World (Geiss), 79

Zelizer, Viviana, 86

www.ingramcontent.com/pod-product-compliance
Lightning Source LLC
Chambersburg PA
CBHW020338270326
41926CB00007B/230